Longitudinal Structural Equation Modeling

Methodology in the Social Sciences

David A. Kenny, Founding Editor
Todd D. Little, Series Editor
www.guilford.com/MSS

This series provides applied researchers and students with analysis and research design books that emphasize the use of methods to answer research questions. Rather than emphasizing statistical theory, each volume in the series illustrates when a technique should (and should not) be used and how the output from available software programs should (and should not) be interpreted. Common pitfalls as well as areas of further development are clearly articulated.

RECENT VOLUMES

Longitudinal Structural Equation Modeling

Todd D. Little

Foreword by Noel A. Card

THE GUILFORD PRESS
New York London

Text © 2013 The Guilford Press
A Division of Guilford Publications, Inc.
72 Spring Street, New York, NY 10012
www.guilford.com

Figures © 2013 Todd D. Little

Printed in the United States of America

This book is printed on acid-free paper.

Last digit is print number: 9   8   7   6   5   4

Library of Congress Cataloging-in-Publication Data

Little, Todd D.
  Longitudinal structural equation modeling / Todd D. Little.
      pages cm. — (Methodology in the social sciences)
    Includes bibliographical references and index.
    ISBN 978-1-4625-1016-0 (hardcover : alk. paper)
    1. Social sciences—Statistical methods. 2. Longitudinal method.
  I. Title.
  HA29.L83175 2013
  001.4′33—dc23
                                                            2013002924

Foreword

Our understanding of a phenomenon can advance only as far as our methodological tools for studying it will allow. Fortunately, we are in a time when methods for understanding human behavior and development are advancing at an extraordinary pace. One side effect of this rapid advancement is that applied researchers are often limited more by their ability to understand the existing methodological tools than by an absence of such tools.

Over the past two decades, few have done as much to advance developmental methodology, and scientists' understanding of these methods, as Todd D. Little. In a number of previous books, through regular workshops on data analytic methods (see *statscamp.org*), and through active lines of both developmental and quantitative research, Todd has pushed the envelope of methodology. In this book, Todd offers a powerful and flexible set of tools in longitudinal structural equation modeling. The focus is on bringing together two of the most important advanced analytic tools available. Structural equation modeling is a powerful and versatile approach that offers many advantages over traditional manifest variable analysis, including closer attention to measurement, more accurate effect size estimates, and the ability to test questions that simply cannot be tested using traditional methods. This structural equation modeling approach is applied to longitudinal models, which are arguably the most important models for understanding the natural unfolding of processes over time.

This book offers readers an understanding of longitudinal structural equation modeling that is simultaneously accessible, broad, and deep. The 10 chapters of the book guide readers from a basic understanding of latent variable modeling (such as that obtained by reading Brown, 2006, or Kline, 2011) through state-of-the-science longitudinal models. Whether you are a beginner or seasoned researcher, this book will expand your data analytic skill set.

The first four chapters provide a foundation for subsequent longitudinal modeling. Chapter 1 offers a review of latent variable modeling, and Chapter 2 offers an introduction to design considerations for longitudinal studies. Chapters 3 and 4 further review foundational latent variable principles. Although the material described in these chapters overlaps with that of more general structural equation modeling texts, there are many unique gems of knowledge within these chapters. For instance, Chapter 1 includes a careful consideration of parceling, Chapter 2 offers an insightful discussion of timing of measurement in longitudinal studies, Chapter 3 attends to the oft-neglected topic of scaling latent variables, and Chapter 4 provokes deeper conceptual thinking about model fit than is typically offered. I anticipate that all readers will learn a considerable amount even in these foundational chapters.

The remaining six chapters of this book describe the key analytic models for longitudinal data. Rather than just presenting one favorite model, as do many books, this book offers a balanced approach to describing *different* types of models, in Chapters 5 (longitudinal CFA), 6 (panel models), Chapter 7 (P-technique for time series), and 8 (growth curve models). Along the way, Todd thoroughly covers issues of multigroup analysis, moderation, mediation, and more complex models (e.g., multitrait multimethod, bifactor). The coverage within these chapters strikes a remarkable balance between big-picture ideas and details, between conceptual understanding and data analysis examples, and between accessibility and necessary technical aspects of longitudinal modeling.

Todd gives a balanced presentation of the advantages and challenges of each of these models. This will allow you to choose the model that best answers your research question, rather than adapting your research question to one model and force-fitting it into one analytic framework. A general theme throughout this book is to help you make informed choices regarding your analyses. Todd teaches you how to choose the most useful of a wide range of data analytic tools, and then to use them well.

I am confident that you will find this book a pleasure to read—an extremely rare "page turner" in the quantitative field. Reading this book feels more like taking part in a friendly conversation than listening to a lecture. So, get comfortable, relax, and prepare for the most enjoyable experience that can come from reading a book on advanced data analytic methods. Be sure to have a notepad close by, because the analytic tools described in this book are sure to prompt dozens of research questions that you will soon be able to rigorously test.

NOEL A. CARD
University of Arizona

Prologue

A PERSONAL INTRODUCTION AND WHAT TO EXPECT

How Statistics Came into My Life

For years, folks have encouraged me to write a book on structural equation modeling (SEM). I'd reply that there are lots of books already out there, especially when it comes to the basics of SEM. Ah, they'd answer back, but there aren't any that cover it quite the way you do, especially in the context of longitudinal SEM. Mind you, "covering it quite the way I do" does not mean my way is more erudite than those of others, but it is unique and, I hope, somewhat informative and entertaining. I was an English literature major as an undergraduate at the University of California, Riverside. I came to the challenge of learning statistics with trepidation. When I realized that statistics is where logic and common sense intersect, I learned what Bill Bukowski later described as the point at which the poetry of mathematics becomes the elegant prose of statistical reasoning. I discovered that statistics isn't math but a system of principles to guide my research.

Although I was an English literature major, I was also interested in psychology, and in my senior year I thought I would give the intro to statistics course a try. Larry Herringer, the teaching assistant for the course, was patient and worked very hard to explain the concepts in basic terms. He spoke to me. I learned the material well enough to be invited to help Larry with his dissertation research. A few months later, Larry introduced me to a young assistant professor who was interested in recruiting a graduate student to work with him. I spent a few hours talking with Keith Widaman and Larry about what a PhD program in developmental psychology under the mentorship of Keith would be like. I know that I didn't think it all through, because I was enchanted. What was it, serendipity or a fool's errand? The deadline to apply for the PhD training program was the next day. I applied.

After a few weeks I heard from the graduate admission committee that I could not be accepted to the graduate training program because I had not taken the Graduate Record Examinations (GREs), which were not necessary for the master's program in English for which I had been accepted at a nearby state college. The admission committee at UC Riverside gave me a conditional acceptance if I would take the GREs and post a combined score that was above their minimum threshold. A session of the exam was scheduled for 3 weeks after I heard this news. I thought OK, what the heck. I felt comfortable with the verbal portion of the GREs. I was petrified of the quantitative portion. I had avoided math courses through my entire undergraduate training (in fact, because of various transfers I made, I somehow got more credit than I should have for the one intro to algebra course that I did take). My roommate at the time (now an accomplished neurologist, Bret D. Lindsay, MD) volunteered considerable amounts of his time to tutor me in math in order to somehow help me make up for a lifetime of math avoidance.

I took the GREs and waited for the snail mail report on whether I had achieved the requisite combined score and would be in the PhD program at UC Riverside or would attend nearby California State University to get a master's degree in English. On May 31st I had to notify Cal State of my decision. I had not received my GRE scores. Again, I acted irrationally. I declined the Cal State offer and waited further. On June 1st the mail arrived with official word: I was above threshold and, much to my surprise, my quantitative score was actually better than my verbal score. I immediately went to Larry's office. We celebrated by splitting a bottle of beer that Larry had stowed away for a special event. I then informed Keith.

Keith was patient with me for the duration of my graduate training. As I was Keith's graduate student, many of the other students presumed that I knew what I was doing, and I became an unofficial stats consultant. Putting myself in such a position forced me to understand statistics more deeply and to find ways to communicate it better. In 1991, when I was packing my things to take my first academic position as a research scientist at the Max Planck Institute in Berlin, Germany, I found the empty bottle of beer that Larry and I had shared. On it are Larry's initials and the date of June 1st. The beer was a bottle of Berliner Pils—serendipity again? My 7 years at the Max Planck Institute were incomparable learning years (*Herzlichen Dank an meine Kolleginnen und Kollegen*). The empty bottle sits on a shelf in my office as a reminder of the journey.

My Approach to the Book

If you don't like math or were never much for equations, don't panic (and don't forget your towel). Throughout this book I do cover the math, but I don't rely on it. Plus, I make sure to walk through the equations so you can get a clear sense of what the elements of the equations mean (hopefully you'll soon get comfortable with them along the way). I have never enjoyed math for math's sake. As mentioned, things changed when I took my first statistics course and realized that the numbers and the equations meant something important to me. I presume you are reading this book because you have an inherent desire to learn about how to do longitudinal modeling to answer some interesting questions. The numbers that present will mean something to you. If you are still wary of the numbers, you'll find plenty of other ways to understand the concepts. For example, I use a lot of analogies, metaphors, and similes—I'm a veritable metaphor machine. You'll hear about everything from clouds to plants, toothpaste to irrigation systems, and pressure cookers to flocks of birds. Each of these ideas is used to help clarify a core SEM concept. (See my essay on metaphor in science referenced in the Recommended Readings at the end of this prologue.)

I try to channel my lectures in this book (and I advise the authors who contribute volumes to the Methodology in the Social Sciences series that I edit for The Guilford Press to take a similar approach). You should hear my voice as if you were sitting in my class, attending one of my lectures, or experiencing one of our Stats Camp summer programs. The tone is light and informal—I am talking to you. The material, however, is not without substance. I have learned over the years that I can reach all levels of audience if I make sure that I start each topic or main theme at the very beginning. As I work up through the material, I focus very carefully on linking each rung of the ladder as I ascend to the top of where the field has arisen. I cycle through each topic from its foundations to its peak. This way, there's a comfort zone for understanding regardless of your prior experience or background. Of course, I cherish feedback, so please take advantage of the comments section available on the book's support pages on the website *www.guilford.com/little-materials*.

I offer my preferences, recommendations, and opinions based on nearly 25 years of applied experience. My goal is to show you *how* you can think about statistics in general and longitudinal SEM in particular, not *what* to think. I try to avoid presenting things as proscriptive and prescriptive rules but instead emphasize principles, choices, and justifications. My limited warranty is that anything I espouse may not hold up in the future. At least at the time of this writing, smart and knowledgeable scholars have reviewed the material I present. These smart and knowledgeable reviewers have also voiced opinions on some topics that are different from mine. I have tried to indicate when others may have a different view.

Key Features of the Book

One convention that I employ is an equation box. Each equation is set apart from the text, and each element of the equation is defined in the note to the equation. This convention allows me to focus the text on telling you the meaning of things without bogging down the flow with the distracting "where" clause. I also include a glossary of key terms and ideas introduced in each chapter. The glossary definitions are meant as a refresher of the ideas for those who are already familiar with much of this material, as well as reinforcement for those who are just learning this material for the first time. I recommend that you scan through the glossary terms and definitions before you read the content of each chapter. At the end of each chapter, I also highlight a few key readings with a short annotation. There is a separate list at the end of the book for all the references that are cited, as well as key references that may not have been cited but are important works that have either shaped my thinking or have had an impact on practices in the field.

During the writing of this book I directed the Center for Research Methods and Data Analysis at the University of Kansas. In 2013, I took a new position directing an institute dedicated to methodological innovation and rigor at Texas Tech University. The new Institute for Measurement, Methodology, Analysis, and Policy (*immap.educ.ttu.edu*) provides support on advanced methods and statistics, as well as conducting original research on methodological topics. It will maintain an extensive set of support pages including online resources for this book and scripts for every example that I present. (Go to *www.guilford.com/little-materials* for up to date directions on where to find these resources.) These scripts are written in various software packages, including LISREL, Mplus, and R (lavaan package). Other scripts, examples, and resources are also available at *www.guilford.com/little-materials*. On these pages I also post updates, errata, and other relevant materials. You'll find guides to LISREL, Mplus, and R (lavaan), what to report, how to read the output, and so on. If you find that a guide is not clear, contact the authors of the guide and request clarification—an update with clarification included will then be posted. I will also be adding new material to augment the existing material presented in this volume.

In addition to my role at Texas Tech, since 2002 I have taught at Summer Stats Camps. Each year (typically starting the first Monday after Memorial Day) we offer a broad selection of courses related to advanced quantitative methods. Traditionally, I coteach the SEM foundations course with Noel Card during the first week of Stats Camp, and then I teach longitudinal SEM during the second week. To see where the program is now, visit *statscamp.org*.

Each of the figures that I created for this book is also available in its original form on the support pages. I used Adobe Illustrator to create the figures. Note that I hold the copyright on the figures (mainly so that I can easily use them in other material). I don't mind if you use or modify them, but please acknowledge the original source.

Overview of the Book

When I teach SEM, I use the metaphor of a knowledge tree to introduce how I organize and present the material. The tree's trunk contains all the parts that are essential to build an effective SEM model. After the trunk is well established, it is relatively easy for me to present different techniques as branches off of the core trunk. Therefore, and as you can see from the Table of Contents, I spend a considerable amount of time focusing on many of the foundational issues related to longitudinal SEM.

The design and measurement issues that I describe in Chapters 1 and 2, for example, provide some insights that I have gained as a developmental researcher—the proverbial "I wish I had known then what I know now" kinds of insights. These chapters also cover essential preparatory steps that must be done well in order to fit a good SEM model.

In Chapters 3 and 4, I detail the foundational material associated with SEM in general. As I mention in those chapters, I present that material because I think it is very important that persons reading this book are on the same page when it comes to how I describe the foundational elements of SEM. Plus, I can emphasize brand new developments in many of these foundational elements (e.g., effects coded method of identification), as well as my intuitions on some topics where definitive guidance is still lacking.

Chapter 5 brings the foundations material to its full "tree" height. The longitudinal CFA model that I describe in this chapter is the measurement model for any quality longitudinal SEM model. I then turn to the basics of a longitudinal panel model in Chapter 6 and extend the panel model to the multiple-group case in Chapter 7. I also introduce dynamic P-technique data and how to fit a multiple-group panel model to such data.

In Chapter 8, I discuss various multilevel models that are applied to longitudinal data. The growth curve model is discussed in this chapter, along with the more recent advances in multilevel SEM and how it can be applied to longitudinal data. Chapter 9 covers all the ins and outs of mediation and moderation in longitudinal panel data. I round out the book with Chapter 10, which details a jambalaya of models that can be fit to longitudinal data.

DATASETS AND MEASURES USED

The primary examples that I use in the various chapters are summarized here. I'm extremely grateful to my colleagues and friends for providing me access to their data and allowing me to put this material on the support pages for this book at *www.guilford.com/little-materials*. For all the datasets, missing data were handled using some form of imputation. The internal consistencies of all measures were around .80, so I don't report their specific values here. A few examples come from published papers and are cited when I present them, and so I don't detail them here.

My Dataset with the Inventory of Felt Emotion and Energy in Life (I FEEL) Measure

Participants were 1,146 sixth- through ninth-grade students (50% boys, 50% girls) from an urban school district in the northeastern United States. The sixth-grade students attended nine different elementary schools, seventh- and eighth-grade students attended a single middle school, and ninth-grade students were enrolled in high school. At the first two measurements (fall 1999 and spring 2000), all students were enrolled in the sixth ($n = 382$), seventh ($n = 378$), or eighth grade ($n = 386$). The third measurement occurred in fall 2000. Approximately 70% of the sample was European American, 15% African American, 6% Hispanic American, and 9% from another ethnic background. Socioeconomic status (SES) ranged from lower to upper middle class.

Students who had written parental consent to participate and who provided their own assent (overall around 80% of eligible students) were administered a series of questionnaires over several sessions within their classrooms by trained research assistants. Teachers remained in the classrooms but worked at their desks. Students were assured that school staff would not see individual students' responses to the questionnaires. The broader data collection effort included self-report and peer-report measures of aggression, victimization, and aspects of self-regulation; the survey order was counterbalanced.

The I FEEL

The I FEEL (Little, Wanner, & Ryan, 1997) measures 14 dimensions of internalizing symptoms (i.e., positive emotion, negative emotion, positive energy, negative energy, connectedness, loneliness, positive self-evaluation, negative self-evaluation, calmness, anxious arousal, fearful arousal, hostile arousal, somatic symptoms, physiological symptoms) and asks respondents to report about their own experiences during the prior 2 weeks. The negatively valenced subscales (e.g., negative mood, loneliness) were based on existing depression, loneliness, and anxiety instruments after categorizing the existing scales (e.g., Children's Depression Inventory, Positive and Negative Affect Schedule) into subfacets (e.g., self-evaluation, social difficulties). To provide a balanced measure of mood, positively valenced dimensions (e.g., positive self-evaluation, connectedness) were created to complement each negatively valenced subscale (except for the somatic and physiological symptoms dimensions). Each subscale contains 6 items (total of 84 items), and each item is measured on a 4-point scale (*not at all true*, *somewhat true*, *mostly true*, *completely true*). Higher scores on each subscale correspond to the name of the subscale (e.g., on the Negative Emotion subscale, higher scores indicate greater levels of negative emotion).

Gallagher and Johnson's MIDUS Example

The Midlife in the United States (MIDUS) national survey was initiated in 1994 by the MacArthur Midlife Research Network in order to explore the behavioral, psychological, and social factors associated with healthy aging. The initial MIDUS sample consisted of a nationally representative sample of 7,108 individuals who were recruited using random digit dialing procedures and who completed a phone interview. Of this initial sample, 6,329 individuals (89%) completed an additional battery of self-report questionnaires, including measures of negative affect and neuroticism. The MIDUS2 survey was initiated in 2004 as a longitudinal follow-up to the MIDUS1 sample. For this example, they selected all participants who had at least partially completed the Negative Affect and Neuroticism scales for both MIDUS1 and MIDUS2 and who had reported an age in MIDUS1. These inclusion criteria left 3,871 individuals (2,143 females, 1,728 males). The age of these individuals ranged from 25 to 74 (mean = 47.32, standard deviation = 12.40) at Time 1 and from 35 to 84 (mean = 56.25, standard deviation = 12.34) at Time 2.

Neuroticism

Neuroticism was measured using a four-item scale in both the MIDUS1 and MIDUS2 surveys. This scale asked participants the extent to which four adjectives (*moody*, *worrying*, *nervous*, and *calm*) described them on a 4-point Likert scale with response options ranging from *not at all* to *a lot*. A mean score was computed across the four items after reverse-scoring the items so that higher scores on the scale indicated higher levels of neuroticism.

Negative Affect

Negative affect was measured using six items in both the MIDUS1 and MIDUS2 surveys. This scale asked participants "During the past 30 days, how much of the time did you feel . . . ?" and participants responded using a 5-point Likert scale with response options ranging from *all of the time* to *none of the time*. Example items include "hopeless" and "so sad nothing could cheer you up." A mean score was computed across the six items after reverse-coding items so that higher scores indicated higher levels of negative affect.

Dorothy Espelage's Bullying and Victimization Examples

Participants included 1,132 students in fifth through seventh grades from four public middle schools in a Midwestern state. Ages ranged from 11 to 15 years, with a mean of 12.6 years, in the first wave of data collection. Students included 49.1% (*n* = 556) female and 50.9% (*n* = 576) male, with a racial distribution of 56.5% (*n* = 640) African American, 26.1% (*n* = 295) European American, 11% (*n* = 124) other or biracial, 3.8% (*n* = 43) Hispanic, 1.5% (*n* = 17) Asian, and 1.1% (*n* = 13) American Indian or Alaskan Native. Data were collected over five waves (spring 2008, fall 2008, spring 2009, fall 2009, and spring 2010) and included three cohorts.

Peer Victimization

Victimization by peers was assessed using the University of Illinois Victimization Scale (UIVS; Espelage & Holt, 2001). Students were asked how often the following things had happened to them in the past 30 days: "Other students called me names"; "Other students made fun of me"; "Other students picked on me"; and "I got hit and pushed by other students." Response options were *never, 1–2 times, 3–4 times, 5–6 times*, and *7 or more times*. Higher scores indicate more self-reported victimization.

Substance Use

Alcohol and drug use was assessed with an eight-item scale (Farrell, Kung, White, & Valois, 2000) that asked students to report how many times in the past year they had used alcohol and/or drugs. The scale consisted of items such as "smoked cigarettes," "drank liquor," and "used inhalants." Responses were recorded on a 5-point Likert scale with options ranging from 1 (*never*) to 5 (*10 or more times*).

Family Conflict

The Family Conflict and Hostility Scale (Thornberry, Krohn, Lizotte, Smith, & Tobin, 2003) was used to measure the level of perceived conflict and hostility in the family environment. The scale contained three items from a larger survey designed for the Rochester Youth Development Study. Respondents indicated on a 4-point Likert scale how often hostile situations had occurred in their families in the past 30 days. Responses range from 1 (*often*) through 4 (*never*). In addition, a Sibling Aggression Perpetration Scale was created and included five items that assessed the aggression between siblings. Items were created to be parallel to items from the University of Illinois Bully Scale (UIBS).

Family Closeness

The Parental Supervision subscale from the Seattle Social Development Project (Arthur, Hawkins, Pollard, Catalano, & Baglioni, 2002) was used to measure respondents' perceptions of established familial rules and perceived parental awareness regarding schoolwork and attendance, peer relationships, alcohol or drug use, and weapon possession. The subscale included eight items measured on a 4-point Likert scale ranging from 1 (*never*) to 4 (*always*). Example items included "My family has clear rules about alcohol and drug use" and "My parents ask if I've gotten my homework done."

Bullying

Bullying was measured using the eight-item UIBS (Espelage & Holt, 2001), which includes teasing, social exclusion, name-calling, and rumor spreading. This scale was developed based on student interviews, a review of the literature on bullying measures, and extensive factor analytic procedures (Espelage, Bosworth, & Simon,

2000; Espelage et al., 2003). Students indicated how often in the past 30 days they had engaged in each behavior (e.g., "I teased other students"; "I upset other students for the fun of it"). Response options were *never, 1 or 2 times, 3 or 4 times, 5 or 6 times,* and *7 or more times.*

Homophobic Teasing

Homophobic teasing was measured using the Homophobic Content Agent–Target scale (HCAT; Poteat & Espelage, 2005). The HCAT scale was used to assess homophobic name-calling perpetration. This perpetration scale contains five items and measures how many times in the past 30 days a child has called other students homophobic epithets. Students read the following sentence: "Some kids call each other names: *homo, gay, lesbo, fag,* or *dyke. How many times in the last 30 days did YOU say these words to. . . .* " Students then rated how often they said these words to five different types of people, such as a friend, someone they did not like, or someone they thought was gay. Response options were *never, 1 or 2 times, 3 or 4 times, 5 or 6 times,* or *7 or more times.* Higher scores indicate higher homophobic name-calling perpetration.

OVERDUE GRATITUDE

In any endeavor as large and as long in the making as this book, the number of persons to whom one is indebted is huge. My graduate mentor and friend, Keith Widaman, is responsible for all the good ideas I write about herein. The bad ideas are my mistakes. He taught me everything I know about statistics and SEM (but not everything he knows). My friend and colleague Noel Card has been instrumental in helping me hone many of these ideas over the years. Noel has been a coinstructor in the annual Summer Stats Camps that we conduct every June (see *statscamp.org* for more information), and he has been a long-standing collaborator. Noel also served as a reader and reviewer of the current material and stepped in to write the Foreword. My friend and colleague Kris Preacher has also patiently rectified my thinking on some the topics, and maybe I have influenced his thinking on a few; but either way, the discussions, comments, and assistance that Kris provided are invaluable to me (he's just plain good folk!). My first KU graduate student, and now colleague and friend, James Selig, has been an instrumental part of this journey, and he returns yearly to teach in Stats Camp. James also provided invaluable feedback on the entire contents. My wife and colleague, Pat Hawley, continues to inspire me with her scholarship and commitment to science. My colleagues in CRMDA at KU have all kindly provided feedback and support along the way: Pascal Deboeck, Chantelle Dowsett, Sadaaki Fukui, David Johnson, Paul Johnson, Jaehoon (Jason) Lee, Alex Schoemann, Carol Woods, and Wei Wu. Lightening my administrative burden, Shalynn

Howard, Jeff Friedrich, and Jo Eis Barton have allowed me those few precious extra minutes in a day to write and work on this. The many students in our quant program, in the undergraduate minor, and in the CRMDA are too many to name, but their contributions have been immeasurable and essential.

The Guilford Press, under the wise and generative leadership of Seymour Weingarten and Bob Matloff, has been supportive and patient in the process. Elaine Kehoe did a spectacular job copyediting and Martin Coleman's effort to bring the pieces together is much appreciated. Most notable in this whole process, however, is the incomparable C. Deborah Laughton, editor extraordinaire, whose kind cajoling and helpful advice kept me on task and brought this to fruition.

I'd like to thank Tony Thatcher for sharing the image of the Flathead River used on the cover. Tony and his company (DTM Consulting, Inc.) used inundation modeling in association with complex floodplain modeling and GIS tools to create this impressive view of the meandering pathway of the Flathead. (You can learn more about this image and other musing by Tony at *mountainwhimsy.com*.) For me this image has two meanings. First, I use the metaphor of a meandering river to describe how change can be modeled using the simplex panel model. Second, I grew up fly fishing the Flathead River near my home town of Kalispell, Montana, and the Big Hole River near Melrose, Montana. I still fish them as much as possible every year— one benefit of being a fourth-generation Montanan.

As mentioned, I have taught this material to thousands of students over the years. Their input, questions, and comments have helped us all understand the material better. To those thousands of students who have taken SEM and related courses from me or consulted with me on matters statistical: thanks for pushing me to find clearer, simpler, and varied ways of communicating the ideas that underlie SEM. Many folks have read and commented on various drafts of the chapters. I have tried to keep a tally of them all, but I have lost track. This list is in a random order, and it is, unfortunately, incomplete: Katy Roche, Jenn Nelson, Alex Schoemann, Mrinal Rao, Kris Preacher, Noel Card, Ed Fox, John Nesselroade, Steve West, Sharon Ghazarian, James Selig, John Geldhof, Waylon Howard, and _____ (fill in your name here if I have forgotten you).

To my family and friends, few of whom will understand what's herein but support me none the less.

PROPHYLACTIC APOLOGIES

With apologies to Rex Kline, I do often anthropomorphize my tables and figures, and to Brett Laursen, I also anthropomorphize variables. My tables show, my figures display, and my variables have relationships—but they don't sing or dance or anything like that. If they did, I'd be losing my mind.

With apologies to Kris Preacher, I want to be informal in my communication. I'm a fourth-generation Montanan. Using terms like "folks" is unavoidable.

With apologies to the Smart Innovators in our field, I have tried to be as up-to-date as possible. And I have read a number of papers that may challenge some of my recommendations and conclusions. Where I maintain my view, I do not do so lightly; rather, I'm still not convinced that the basis for my recommendations or conclusions has been sufficiently challenged. I remain open to feedback, and I will gladly share the basis for any errata on the web pages for this book (*www.guilford.com/ little-materials*).

With apologies to all the persons I did not name in my acknowledgments, whose input made this book a better book than it would have been otherwise.

With apologies to my golf game—I added 10 strokes to my handicap during the production of this book. I don't know that we'll get back the game we once had, but we'll try.

KEY TERMS AND IDEAS INTRODUCED IN THIS CHAPTER

Serendipity. The idea of making a fortunate discovery or finding oneself in a fortunate circumstance when the discovery or circumstance found was not what one was looking for or striving for.

Statistics. Statistics is the point at which common sense meets logic, and numbers are used to convey the ideas and the logic. More formally, statistics involves collecting (measuring), organizing (database management), analyzing (descriptively or inferentially), and interpreting (making decisions from) numerical data. Or, as Bill Bukowski (personal communication, 2008) has described it, "If math is God's poetry, then statistics is God's elegantly reasoned prose."

RECOMMENDED READINGS

Little, T. D. (2011). Conveying complex statistical concepts as metaphors. *The Score, 33*(1), 6–8.

> This is an essay that I wrote a few years ago at the request of Dan Bernstein for KU's *Reflections from the Classroom* publication. It was reprinted in 2011 in *The Score*, the newsletter for Division 5 (Measurement, Evaluation, and Statistics) of the American Psychological Association. It conveys why I think metaphors work so well and can be invaluable as a tool for teaching advanced statistics.

Terrell, S. R. (2012). *Statistics translated: A step-by-step guide to analyzing and interpreting data*. New York: Guilford Press.

> I recently reviewed this introductory statistics textbook for Guilford. It's the textbook I would have written: it's relaxed, it speaks to you, it informs you, and, if you're like me, you'll have a few LOL (laugh out loud) moments.

Adams, D. (1979). *The hitchhiker's guide to the galaxy*. London: Pan Books.

Here you'll learn to not panic and why forgetting your towel is a no-no.

Card, N. A. (2011). *Applied meta-analysis for social science research*. New York: Guilford Press.

I learned all that I know about meta-analysis from Noel. He's never meta-analysis he didn't like. I like them. too. Even though my book is not about meta-analysis, I do make recommendations on reporting that would help us in our meta-analytic endeavors.

Bickel, R., & Selig, J. P. (forthcoming). *Multilevel analysis for applied research* (2nd ed.). New York: Guilford Press.

James Selig has come on board to assist in updating and expanding this excellent introduction to multilevel analysis. I have a chapter in this book dedicated to the longitudinal case of multilevel modeling. When the revised Bickel and Selig comes out, it'll be a great resource.

Contents

The companion website *www.guilford.com/little-materials*
provides downloadable data and syntax files for
the book's examples as well as other support materials.

1

Overview and Foundations of Structural Equation Modeling

Longitudinal modeling is a very broad area of statistics and methodology. This book focuses on a relatively circumscribed piece of this broad area; namely, structural equation modeling (SEM) approaches to longitudinal data. By SEM, I mean the general latent-variable modeling perspective on analyzing data—measuring multiple *indicators* to represent underlying *constructs*. I do not cover cross-lagged regression models, for example, but I do cover cross-lagged latent-variable models. I do not cover time-series analysis, but I do cover dynamic P-technique SEM. In other words, this book focuses on the foundations of the SEM latent-variable models that can be applied to any repeated-measures study of change processes (life-course development, response to intervention, learning curves, business trends, economic changes, and so on).

Before I can launch into longitudinal SEM, I feel it is essential for me to paint a larger picture of what I am covering. As I mentioned in the prologue, my goal is to present a full knowledge tree. The trunk of the tree will cover all the necessary first steps before a longitudinal change process can be modeled. In fact, the first five chapters cover the trunk of the tree: from measurement (Chapter 1), design (Chapter 2), specification (Chapter 3), and model evaluation (Chapter 4) issues to establishing a baseline measurement model (Chapter 5). Beginning in Chapter 6, I branch out from there and discuss various latent-variable models that can be fit to longitudinal (repeated-measures) data. When I address each topic, I cover the basics but carry the discourse all the way to the advanced and the emerging levels of thinking. My iterative approach is intended to reinforce the ideas. I risk some redundancy in conveying the ideas in this way, but I see the redundancies as planned refreshers and reminders, particularly for those who are new to much of this material.

In this opening chapter, I discuss a number of core/background issues that underlie SEM in general. Much of this material is meant for the beginning scholar of SEM and is designed to give a broad overview of the world that is SEM. In the material that follows, I foreshadow many key ideas that I explain in greater detail in later chapters. Most of the discussion to follow fits under the general rubric of measurement issues, but not exclusively. I close this chapter with two sections that also are foundational to SEM but aren't related to measurement. In the second-to-last section, I offer advice on how to program SEM models, and, in the final section, I delve into the philosophical issues that permeate the decisions we make and the advice that we receive and give.

AN OVERVIEW OF THE CONCEPTUAL FOUNDATIONS OF SEM

SEM is an analytical approach that allows a researcher to build an elegant and parsimonious model of the processes that give rise to observed data. Whereas classical analysis procedures such as multiple regression, analysis of variance (ANOVA), and the like possess many assumptions about the data and the variables in an analysis, well-executed SEM applications allow the modeler to specify, estimate, and evaluate the nature and veridicality of most assumptions. No statistical procedure is without assumptions, but among the various procedures available, SEM, generally speaking, makes the fewest and allows you to test the most assumptions. SEM is primarily a latent-variable approach in that a number of measured indicators are used to represent and estimate the scores on an underlying construct (i.e., latent variable).

Concepts, Constructs, and Indicators

I prefer to talk of indicators and constructs as opposed to variables and factors. Indicators are variables in the sense that the scores will vary across the measured entities. But indicators imply more. They connote a purposive process rather than a blind endeavor—the idea of crafting an exquisite and meaningful construct. Factors and variables are, respectively, mathematical siblings of constructs and indicators. Constructs and indicators have gone to finishing school, whereas factors and variables have not. In Chapter 3, I extol the many virtues of latent variables, the most notable of which are (1) the ability to correct latent variables for the sources of measurement error that affect the reliability of measurement and, when properly utilized, (2) the ability to establish, as part of the model-building process, the content, criterion, and construct validity of the constructs under scrutiny.

Constructs stem from concepts that we as scholars use to categorize, carve, compartmentalize, and otherwise organize the world around us. Constructs are formalized concepts. Whereas concepts have broad definitions that are looked up easily on the intertubes (aka the Internet), constructs have formal theoretical definitions that often say as much about what the construct *is not* as they say about what it *is*. Aggression, for example, is a well-understood concept that has simple and efficient lay definitions that we all can generally agree upon. In the scientific literature, the formal theoretical definitions are more refined and attempt to demarcate, for instance, the different kinds of aggression (e.g., physical aggression, verbal aggression, material aggression, relational aggression) or their functions (e.g., instrumental, retaliatory, and reactive). From these formal theoretical definitions, operational definitions of what can and cannot constitute a measurable expression of the underlying construct are developed. These indicators are the measured proxies of the constructs (e.g., frequency of hitting is a measurable proxy of physical aggression). The operational definitions provide the blueprint or recipe that is used to build the construct of interest. Or, to paraphrase John Nesselroade (2007, p. 252), *indicators are our worldly window into the latent space.* In other words, the nature of a latent construct can be inferred only by the observed nature and behavior of the indicators that are used to represent them. In this regard, constructs are only as good as the indicators that are developed and used in the measurement process; SEM is not a panacea for poor design and weak measurement.

From Concepts to Constructs to Indicators to Good Models

Once the theoretical and operational definitions of the constructs are in place, models are then developed that must first specify the nature of the measurement structure (which indicators correspond with which constructs) and then specify the expected structural relationships among the latent constructs. Models are explicit statements about the processes that give rise to the observed data. Models, however, are necessarily simplifications of reality, and therefore they are necessarily wrong (i.e., the error associated with parsimony). This inevitable characteristic of all models does not mean that the whole enterprise should be abandoned—quite the contrary. SEM models, which rely on strong substantive theory and are grounded in the most advanced statistical theory, bring clarity and light to the otherwise opaque and seemingly chaotic processes that are "what the world is really like" (Box, 1979, p. 1). When the wrongness is trivial, then the model is an efficient and perhaps useful simplification (MacCallum & Austin, 2000)—a point to which I return later. When a model is efficient and useful, it is a reasonable model that can be used to guide decisions, inform policy, and shape applied practices.

Scientific discovery in general and SEM in particular are organic processes, captured by the mnemonic *I DO SEEK*, to develop and test good models that *DEPICT* reality and allow knowledge to *LEAP* forward (this mnemonic can help you remember the italicized acronyms). The "I" in "I do seek" (from Widaman, 2012; see also Table 1.1) is the *intuition* that we all bring to the scientific table. This intuition is informed by personal experiences, professional training, and challenging the given and accepted. This intuition forms the centroid of good theory that depicts reality and allows scientific findings to leap forward. The "D" is the *design* required to give the intuition-derived theory an adequate and rigorous scientific test. Most of this chapter deals with design issues that must be considered and properly implemented. The "O" is the *operationalization* derived from the concrete theoretical definitions of the core constructs under scrutiny. Most of Chapter 2 focuses on the measurement

TABLE 1.1. I DO SEEK to develop and test good models that DEPICT reality and allow knowledge to LEAP forward

I DO SEEK	DEPICT	LEAP
Intuition	**D**escribe	**L**ogical and internally consistent
Design	**E**xplain	**E**mpirically testable (falsifiable)
Operationalization	**P**redict	**A**ccounts for extant findings
	Improve	**P**arsimonious (sufficient
Specification	**C**hange	verisimilitude)
Estimation	**T**est	
Evaluation		
Kommensuration		

Note. The acronym "I DO SEEK" is from Keith Widaman (2012).

issues that are the direct extension of the process of operationalization. The "S" is the *specification* of the model that is tested. This model is molded to reflect the theory, the design, and the operationalization. Chapters 5–10 discuss various models that can be tailored to fit the question at hand. The first "E" refers to the *estimation* process—fitting the model to the observed data. Chapter 3 covers various technical aspects of estimation. The second "E" in "I do seek" is the *evaluation* process. Does the model fit the data? Is the theory supported or not? Are the parameter estimates of the magnitude and in the direction that the theory would predict? Are they significant? Is there an alternative model that would be a better model? This process of evaluation is introduced in Chapter 4 and revisited thereafter. Finally, the "K" is *kommensuration* (Widaman's [2012] spelling). The process of commensuration involves modifying the model based on the evaluation phase, reestimating and reevaluating the model, and ultimately determining a final good model that provides a strong test of the theory.

Beyond being efficient and useful, good models must be able to adequately DEPICT the reality that is the focus of empirical scrutiny. By DEPICT, I mean that good models *describe* the nature of the relationships among the measured variables. They *explain*, to the degree possible, the causal connections among the modeled constructs. They should also involve *prediction* of future outcomes from antecedent conditions. Good models *improve* the human condition by contributing meaningfully to the collective scientific knowledge pool. They provide the basis for practitioners to help us *change* the unwanted and reinforce or promote the desired. Finally, all these features of a good model are constantly *tested*. More ideally, a good model is tested against another good model in order to provide statistical evidence as to which good model is the better good model.

Good models will also provide the basis by which knowledge can LEAP forward. By LEAP, I mean that the models must have *logical* and internally consistent theoretical statements that link each indicator to each construct and each construct to one another and specify the statistical conditions of these linkages that should emerge. Good models must be *empirically* based and falsifiable. They cannot contain circularities or a lack of specificity such that no matter what happens the model is supported—such models are typically "full of sound and fury, signifying nothing" (Shakespeare's *Macbeth*, Act 5). Good models must also *account* for the body of findings already available insofar as the findings are within the scope of the model's nomological net. A nomological net defines the set of constructs that fit within the scope of the theoretical realm under study, and it specifies the expected relationships (the threads linking the knots) among each construct (the knots of the net). Finally, good models are *parsimonious*. Ideally, the universe of possible models forms a hierarchically nested structure from least parsimonious to most parsimonious. In such circumstances, the mission of the scientific enterprise is to find the level of parsimony that best explains the observed data across the most contexts, circumstances, populations, and/or ages while maintaining the ability to depict reality and allowing the accumulated knowledge to leap forward. Like the economics of acquisition I discuss later, the verisimilitude of a good model is weighed against the economics of precision. The utility of a model at a given verisimilitude-to-precision ratio often defines the point at which a model is deemed sufficiently good and optimally useful.

These characteristics of models may seem obvious and self-evident. If you can look past the cheesy acronyms, these elements represent important truisms of good models that many models, in fact, lack. Moreover, good models should guide the design and execution of a study rather than be developed after the data are already collected. Too often a data collection protocol is designed without a clear model of the expected relations. Such haphazard approaches to data collection will almost always be deficient in key elements that are needed to give a test of the model its full due. Such arbitrary approaches can also contain a number of suboptimal pseudo-indicators that may misrepresent the construct of interest. When a well-conceived model is not used to carefully plan the data collection protocol, the information gathered often is piecemeal at best. Sometimes things can be salvaged through sleuthing and thinking such that an interesting model can receive an adequate test. Many of the large-scale datasets that are contained in clearing houses, for example, usually require combing the dataset to find reasonable indicators that can be assembled to build constructs of reasonable merit.

SOURCES OF VARIANCE IN MEASUREMENT

As can be seen in the previous section, the foundation to a good model is the quality of the constructs that can be assembled. To understand the pieces that make up constructs, I think it is useful to revisit some basic ideas related to classical test theorem. The fundamental statistical concept to convey here is that the variation in responses can be decomposed into different sources. Some sources are desirable, whereas other sources are undesirable nuisances.

Classical Test Theorem

Classical test theorem (and its modernized variants) remains a convenient way to think about measurement. It explicitly states that the score for an indicator (or variable) is comprised of different influences (i.e., sources of variance). Modernized test theory builds upon this idea to explicate some of these different sources that can threaten the validity or generalizability of a measure or construct. Equation 1.1 presents variants of the classical test theorem idea. I've listed three different variants of the theorem. Variant 1.1a states that the score for each individual on a variable, x, is composed of at least three sources of information: a true score (T_i), a variable-specific score (S_i), and a truly random (noise) component (e_i). Variant 1.1b is the sample-aggregate version of this information. It states that the scores on a variable x for a given sample comprise at least three sources of variation: the true-score variance (T), the variable-specific score variance (S), and the random-error variance (e). Variant 1.1c makes it perfectly explicit that more than one variable may be available to represent a construct's true-score variance (the subscripted 1 designates this as one of many possible indicators). Variant 1.1c also makes it explicit that both the S and the e components of variance are each unique to the given variable that is being used as an indicator of a given construct. In Figure 1.1, I show an example that uses three different indicators of a construct, which are labeled x_1, x_2, and x_3.

With x_1, x_2, and x_3 as three different indicators of the same underlying construct, I have drawn two variations of the SEM latent variable in an effort to "visualize"

Equation 1.1. Classical test theorem variants

a) $x_i = T_i + S_i + e_i$
b) $x = T + S + e$
c) $x_1 = T + S_1 + e_1$

- x_i is the score for individual i.
- i is the index that refers to each individual or entity.
- x without a subscript refers to the set of scores across all individuals or entities.
- x_1 is the set of scores for indicator 1 of a latent construct.
- T is the "true-score" variance.
- S is the item- or variable-specific variance.
- e is the truly random variance (noise).

A) Specification of a Construct
(before estimation)

B) Key Estimates for a Construct

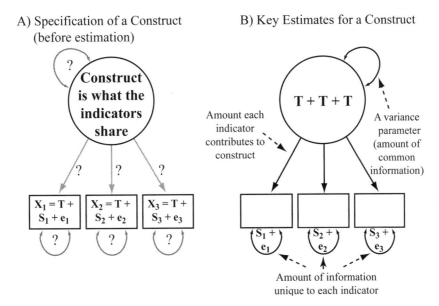

FIGURE 1.1. Schematic of how a latent construct is defined (estimated). Circles (or ovals) represent the unobserved/latent constructs. Boxes (or rectangles) represent the measured/manifest indicators (e.g., items, parcels, or scales). Curved double-headed lines are variance estimates. Straight single-headed lines are loadings or the amount of information in a given indicator that contributes to the definition of the construct.

how SEM captures and creates a construct. Figure 1.1 uses the basic drawing conventions of SEM (see Chapter 3 for more detailed information). Here, boxes are used to represent the measured variables x_1, x_2, and x_3. In Figure 1.1A, I have put the classic test theorem composition of each indicator in each of the boxes. The circle captures the information that is shared among the indicators of the construct (the true-score variance of each indicator).

In Figure 1.1A, the specification phase includes a loading, which is the amount of information that a given indicator contributes to the definition of the construct. This information is the amount of variance that is shared across all the indicators of the construct. Each indicator (box) also has two sources of information that are unique to that indicator. The S component is unique to each indicator and the e (random error) component is also unique. S and e are by definition uncorrelated with each other. S is reliable variance that is associated uniquely with the item or variable; as such, this information is uncorrelated with the T component. Because e is truly random noise, it cannot be correlated with either S or T.

In classical test theorem, the three sources of information are, by definition, independent of one another. An important assumption of classical test theorem is that the S and e components of a given indicator of a construct will be uncorrelated with the S and e of another indicator. Again, because e is truly random noise, it will be independent across all indicators. The S component, on the other hand, is a reliable source of information that *will likely* share some overlap with an S component associated with another, similar indicator of the construct. When this overlap is trivial, it simply is one source of the population misfit that is true of all constructs. When the S components of two indicators overlap sufficiently, however, the model fit will suffer if the association is not estimated. When the S components are allowed to correlate, these estimates are referred to as correlated residuals. A residual is the S-plus-e component of an indicator after the T component is estimated. The S-plus-e component is also called the uniqueness of an indicator or variable.

Expanding Classical Test Theorem

Taking the last idea from Variant 1.1c and wedding it with some ideas from generalizability theory, we get the set of equations that I have listed in Equation 1.2. In this set of equations, I show in an even more explicit manner that multiple indicators of a construct have various sources of variance that contribute to the observed scores. In Equation 1.2, I have replaced T with three sources of common variance, C, M, and O. In these equations, the first source of variance is the most important; namely, the "pure" true score (what I now call C for *construct*); that is, C reflects the pure construct that the indicators are intended to represent. The second source comes from the ideas of Campbell and Fiske (1959). They argued that every measure

Equation 1.2. Classical test theorem meets generalizability theory

a) $I_1 = C + M + O + S_1 + e_1$
b) $I_2 = C + M + O + S_2 + e_2$
c) $I_3 = C + M + O + S_3 + e_3$

- I_n is the set of scores for the indicator n.
- C is the construct variance.
- M is the common method variance.
- O is the common occasion of measurement variance, which is transient.
- S_n is the item- or variable-specific variance for indicator n.
- e_n is the truly random variance (noise) for indicator n.
- Within an indicator, C, M, O, S, and e are independent (uncorrelated).
- Between indicators, only S and e are independent.
- Each source of variance is assumed to be normally distributed.
- Only C, M, and O can have a nonzero mean; S and e have a mean of zero.

is fundamentally and inherently a trait–method combination; thus, each indicator comprises a source that is method-related, M. The third element of Equation 1.2 is an explicit acknowledgment that the occasion (O) of measurement has an impact on the scores of a set of indicators. In Chapter 2, I describe many ways to consider time in longitudinal studies. For now, occasion of measurement can mean the time of measurement, the age of the participants, or the historical moment in time (or all three simultaneously). In longitudinal studies, these dimensions of time are the key source of information that we desire to understand. Sometimes it is information that is controlled for so that the true information about C can be examined. Sometimes it is information that is explicitly estimated and compared to see, for example, whether age differences exist or whether retest effects are evident. Longitudinal studies attempt to measure changes in C that are uncontaminated with the influence of O and, when possible, that are uncontaminated with M.

When a construct contains C, M, and O, the nature of the true construct information is biased downward (similar to how unreliability will attenuate a true association). That is, the component C, which is the desired element to know, is contaminated by both the common method variance (M) and the common variance associated with the occasion of measurement (O). When two constructs share the same method of measurement, the association between the constructs becomes inflated; for instance, constructs that rely on self-reports will share the common method variance associated with self-report and will therefore have inflated correlations. When the two constructs are contaminated with method variance that is different for each construct, the true association among the constructs is attenuated or deflated. A construct assessed using peer reports will have a deflated correlation when it is compared with a construct that is assessed using parent reports, for example. Unfortunately, the amount of contamination of a construct is difficult to ascertain in most circumstances; therefore, the degree of inflation or deflation of the associations among the constructs cannot be determined. If the amount of contamination is uniform across the constructs, then the relative strengths of associations are very meaningful and interpretable, even though the absolute levels are biased. For example, a relative difference in a correlation of .707 versus .5 is meaningful even if the constructs in question are all contaminated by self-report method variance. That is, they differ by about 25%. If the true/uncontaminated correlations were .6 versus .333, there would still be an approximate 25% overlap difference. In other words the relative difference of 25% is the same, but the absolute values in the contaminated case are higher than in the true case.

CHARACTERISTICS OF INDICATORS AND CONSTRUCTS

In addition to the C, M, and O complexity of indicators and constructs, both indicators and constructs can vary along a number of other dimensions that will influence the quality of the measurement process. The characteristics of these dimensions will, therefore, also influence how good the eventual SEM model will be and what can be said about the indicators and the constructs.

Types of Indicators and Constructs

The types of constructs that are found in the social and behavioral sciences vary from highly circumscribed and unidimensional to quite vague and multidimensional. In addition, constructs can vary in the degree to which they are cleanly measured or contain unwanted sources of variance (i.e., the degree to which they are dirty or contaminated). Indicators vary along these dimensions as well. As mentioned, constructs are defined by the amount of information that is shared among the indicators of the construct. The relations that define a construct are linear regressions whereby the construct captures the common variance among the indicators. I cover the mathematics of this process in detail in Chapter 3. For now, I want to emphasize some conceptual issues related to how constructs are defined and represented in an SEM framework.

More specifically, indicators can be categorized according to a couple of different features. One feature is its degree of dimensionality, and the other is its degree of explicitness. Dimensionality refers to the complexity of the indicator's true-score information. Unidimensional indicators have a single source of true-score information. An indicator of simple addition skills is an example of a unidimensional indicator. It contains only the information related to the execution of simple arithmetic. Multidimensional indicators, on the other hand, have two or more discrete sources of true-score information. A math question that is given in the form of a sentence contains at least two sources of true-score information. For example, the question "Arne has three oranges and Kirsten has two apples; how many pieces of fruit do they have together?" requires verbal skill, problem-solving skill, and simple addition skill to solve.

The explicitness of an indicator refers to the specificity of the operational definition(s) employed when creating an indicator of a construct. Some concepts have theoretical definitions that are vaguer than those of others, and the lack of precision in the theoretical definition leaves room for a lack of explicitness in the operational characteristics of the indicators. For example, personal agency beliefs from the action control literature are precisely defined theoretically; as a result, they have explicit operational characteristics that state what can and cannot be used as a measured indicator of the construct. Self-efficacy beliefs, on the other hand, are less precisely defined than agency beliefs (even though they are highly overlapping concepts), and the kinds of items that researchers generate to reflect self-efficacy vary considerably across studies and investigators. Such differences in the linkage between concept, construct, and indicator are not often discussed, but their implications for science are profound. Inconsistent results, for example, may well be traced to the vagueness of the operational procedures that were used and not just to sampling variability or other features of the study design.

Constructs can also vary along these characteristics of dimensionality and explicitness. If all indicators are vaguely defined with multidimensional content, then the construct will be a direct reflection of the vague quality of the operational characteristics, along with the multidimensional features of the indicators. Constructs can also vary in the degree to which they are contaminated or "confounded" by other sources of shared variance among the indicators. Common method variances among indicators (see Figure 1.2 and Equation 1.2), for example, will be carried to the level of the latent construct. As mentioned, when two constructs share the same source of method variance, the strength of the relationship between the two constructs will be overestimated (i.e., inflated). When two constructs have different sources of method variance (e.g., one is self-reported and the other is peer reported), the strength of the relationship between the two constructs will be underestimated (i.e., attenuated). In this case it is not necessarily better to have constructs measured by different methods because of the attenuating nature of the method variance. In this regard, an optimal measurement system would be a multitrait–multimethod (MTMM) approach that would disentangle the method variance from the construct variance (Campbell & Fiske, 1959). If an MTMM approach is not feasible, then the estimated associations among the constructs simply need to be interpreted in light of the inflating or attenuating influence of the method variance involved.

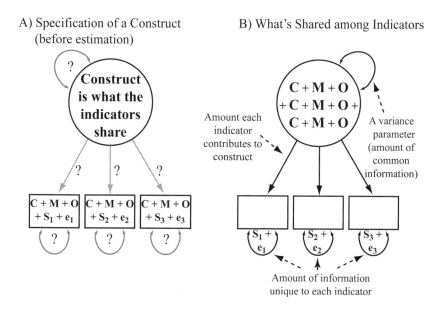

FIGURE 1.2. When indicators share more than the "true" construct variance. C is the "true" construct variance that is shared among the indicators. M is a common method of measurement that is shared among the indicators. O is a common occasion of measurement that is shared among the indicators.

A fundamental feature of indicators of constructs is that they need to be correlated with one another to a sufficiently high degree in order for a researcher to be encouraged that something real underlies the measures that are collected. In my experience, a level of correlation around .4 among parcel-level indictors and .3 for item-level indicators are at the lower end of encouragement when it comes to modeling meaningful latent constructs. Low loadings are not necessarily bad, but the loadings need to be high enough to provide evidence that something is shared among the indicators. Generally speaking, and assuming that the construct's indicators are valid, the higher this correlation goes, the stronger is the empirical evidence that the indicators are, in fact, a reflection of a meaningful construct (see the discussion of good vs. bad indicators). Perhaps more important than the within-construct correlations among the indicators is the idea that the indicators of a construct should, generally speaking, be more highly correlated with one another than they are with indicators of a different construct. Convergent validity of a construct's indicators is found when the indicators correlate highly with each other. Divergent validity of a construct's indicators is found when the indicators correlate less highly with indicators of other constructs.

Categorical versus Metrical Indicators and Constructs

In Table 1.2, I've outlined a conceptual framework for thinking about indicators and constructs in terms of whether they reflect distinct categories or are a reflection of an underlying continuum. I use the term *metrical* to refer to the idea that ordinal, interval, and ratio scaling methods reflect an underlying continuum. Some methodologists will argue that ordinal should not be included in this group, but in my experience, ordinal scaled indicators work pretty well for many research purposes, and, with robust estimation procedures, I expect to find that they will continue to work quite well for most applications of SEM. In the cells of the table are the types

TABLE 1.2. Nature of constructs and indicators and their corresponding analytical approaches

		Nature of the latent variable	
		Categorical	Metrical
Nature of the measured, manifest variable	Categorical	Latent transition analysis	Latent trait analysis; IRT
	Metrical	Latent class; Mixture modeling	Latent variable analysis; CFA

Note. Categorical refers to variables that reflect nominal or polytomous categories. *Metrical* refers to variables that reflect ordinal-, interval-, or ratio-level properties. Many models for longitudinal data can contain more than one of these kinds of variables. *IRT* refers to item response theory and *CFA* refers to confirmatory factor analysis.

of analysis procedures that could be used depending on the nature of indicators and the constructs. In this book, I have chosen to focus almost exclusively on the latent variable analysis of metrical indicators. I do talk some about how categorical indicators can be used in such models (see the next section, for example).

Types of Correlation Coefficients That Can Be Modeled

The types of correlation coefficients that you would calculate when the measured variables are categorical or metrical are presented in Table 1.3. The key feature to note is whether the categorical indicators are naturally categorical or whether they are artificially categorical. In Table 1.3, I use the words *dichotomized* and *polytomized* versus *dichotomous* and *polytomous* to distinguish between variables that are artificially converted to categorical variables (*-tomized*; e.g., high vs. low socioeconomic status) versus naturally occurring categories (*-tomous*; e.g., gender). If you take an otherwise continuous variable and do a median split (dichotomization) or break it up into thirds (polytomization), you are creating artificial categories and losing significant information. MacCallum and colleagues (2002) have shown the potential perils of such a practice. Their bottom line is: Don't dichotomize or polytomize a variable. Instead, conduct your analysis with the variable in its continuous form. The power and precision will be greater than it is when a variable is dichotomized or polytomized. I often recommend to others that the statistical analysis be conducted on the continuous variable, but the presentation of the effect can then be done using the dichotomized or polytomized version of the variable if the effect is more clearly "seen" graphically in this form.

TABLE 1.3. Correlation coefficients to model depending on the nature of the variables

Type of coefficient	Variable 1	Variable 2
Pearson *r*	Continuous	Continuous
Point biserial	Continuous	Dichotomous
Point polyserial	Continuous	Polytomous
Phi	Dichotomous	Dichotomous
Rho or tau	Polytomous	Polytomous
Biserial	Continuous	Dichotomized
Polyserial	Continuous	Polytomized
Tetrachoric	Dichotomized	Dichotomized
Polychoric	Polytomized	Polytomized

Note. Coefficients above the demarcation line are special cases of Pearson's *r* and do not require any special processing to model in SEM. The coefficients below the demarcation line need to be calculated in PRELIS or handled specially in packages such as Mplus.

Using two or more variables to create groups based on cutoff values on the variables, on the other hand, does have advantages that aren't easily accommodated in a continuous-variable metric. Here, the continuous variables are used to approximate a categorical latent variable. For example, liked-most and liked-least nominations are used to identify subgroups of individuals that correspond to theoretically expected sociometric status (see Coie & Dodge, 1983). Or the degree to which individuals use both prosocial and coercive control strategies is used to identify subgroups of individuals that correspond to theoretically expected resource-control types (see Hawley, Johnson, Mize, & McNamara, 2007).

In terms of analysis of -tomized versus -tomous variables, how they are handled analytically varies. If you are using a program such as Mplus, you can easily tell the program which variables are categorical and which are metrical, and it will use an appropriate estimation algorithm. If you are using other software packages, such as LISREL, you will need to run the PRELIS program to calculate the correct measure of association prior to estimating the SEM model. The coefficients below the demarcation line in Table 1.3 are theoretical adjustments to the expected amount of information loss assuming that the underlying variable is both continuous and normally distributed. If either of these assumptions is not tenable, you may want to suffer the information loss and analyze the Pearson correlation, because the correction sometimes will lead to unreasonable estimates of association.

I now discuss a number of additional characteristics of variables and indicators that can be selected and used in an analysis. The first topic is indicators that are selected and used as covariates in SEM models. The second topic is general scaling issues, and the final topic in this section is a discussion of parceling. The first two topics are broad but, I think, useful to the novice modeler, particularly for contexts like longitudinal SEM. The third topic is a brief but useful overview of parcels and parceling techniques.

A SIMPLE TAXONOMY OF INDICATORS AND THEIR ROLES

Table 1.4 presents a simple taxonomy of the types of indicators and their potential role in an analysis. I created this table primarily to help researchers who might be trained in different disciplines, where the terms used are different from the ones that I prefer to use. I also have not been "ultra-precise" in my mappings, but I think these are close enough to work as a guide through the morass of terms. You will also notice that terms like *moderator* and *mediator* are listed in multiple columns. The role played by these variables depends on theory and the nature of their special status. A moderator, for example, can be seen as a potential covariate relationship and as a predictor (see Chapter 9). Similarly, a mediator is simultaneously an outcome variable and a predictor variable.

In the classical statistical world, the roles of independent and dependent variables

TABLE 1.4. A simple taxonomy of the types of variables and their role in an analysis

Covariates	Predictors	Outcomes
Control variables	Independent variables	Dependent variables
Nuisance variables	Exogenous variables	Endogenous variables
Instrumental variables	Predictor variables	Outcome variables
Conditioning variables	Antecedent variables	Consequent variables
Confounding variables	Process variables	Response variables
Suppressor variables	"Causal" variables	Criterion variables
Moderator variables	Regressor variables	Mediator variables
	Mediator variables	Intervening variables
	Intervening variables	
	Moderator variables	
	Treatment variables	
These variables are used as statistical controls to account for their influence on other variables so that the influence among the other focal variables can be seen clearly. These variables are often seen as potential confounding influences that may create or mask a hypothesized relationship.	These variables are treated as the focal variables that are the primary determining influence on an outcome variable. They reflect the hypothesized process or mechanism that gives rise to the outcome variables.	These variables are also focal variables but reflect the outcome of interest. They are the end result of the predicted relationships that one tests after controlling for potential confounds.

Note. These categorizations are simplified, and the precise technical meaning varies across disciplines and individual researchers.

are well defined. When we move into the world of complex models involving many variables, the roles that the variables can play become a bit more complicated. For the most part, however, a variable will play one of three roles: an outcome of interest, a focal predictor of interest, or a potential confound that lingers in the periphery. These potential confounds, covariates, or control variables are underutilized in most SEM models. Perhaps the reason for this paucity of use is that many researchers don't understand how to include them in SEM models, nor do they fully appreciate what covariates can accomplish.

Covariates, control variables, nuisance variables, and conditioning variables are all similar kinds of variables in terms of how to think of them and the role they play in inferences about a particular set of relations. I use the word *covariate* to refer to this general class of control variables. In classical regression parlance, researchers typically divide variables into independent and dependent variables. In SEM, we sometimes call these exogenous and endogenous variables. A covariate is any variable that is used as a statistical control to allow one to examine the (partial or semipartial) influence of an independent variable on a dependent variable. In classical approaches, covariates are entered first into a regression equation before the independent variable(s) is entered. The idea here is to explain away the variance in the dependent variable that is associated with the covariate(s) so that the influence of the independent variable(s) on the dependent variable can be gauged accurately. This process of gauging the unique impact of an independent variable after first entering the covariate into the equation is referred to as a semipartial relationship.

In predictive regression models, the semipartial control is generally pretty accurate because the correlation of the covariate with the other independent variables is accounted for when the unique regression effects are calculated. In longitudinal SEM models with just two time points and where the Time 2 variables are the "outcomes" whereas the Time 1 variables are the predictors, this approach to including covariates would also be reasonable.

A second approach to using covariates is to remove the influence of (i.e., variance due to) the covariate from both the independent and dependent variables. This process results in a full partial regression relationship. This approach is most useful when one is interested in nondirectional relationships between two or more variables or in datasets associated with more complex longitudinal models where multiple waves of directed regression relationships are being estimated. When there are more than two time points in an SEM-modeled longitudinal study, I generally recommend a full partial approach, which I address in Chapter 6.

Finally, in SEM models, and longitudinal models in particular, a third approach is to enter the covariate variables into a model as truly exogenous variables that predict the first wave of endogenous variables, which, in turn, predict the second wave of endogenous variables. This approach assumes that once the influence of the covariate is accounted for at the first measurement occasion, its influence is accounted for "downstream" by indirect influences of the covariates at later measurement occasions. This assumption of how the covariate operates is, in fact, a testable assumption because one can examine the direct influences of the covariates on later waves of variables to see whether there are additional influences that are not accounted for by the indirect pathways. If there are significant "downstream" effects of the covariates, then a full partial approach is most warranted. For example, an initial effect of age differences in measures of ability is likely to be sufficiently controlled for at the first measurement occasion because the age differences in ability are already established and won't change with later measurements. On the other hand, gender differences in beliefs about school performance are likely to change at future measurement occasions because of the malleability of beliefs. The context of gender-specific feedback can continue to be a potential confounding factor. Gender is not a time-varying covariate, but the gender-specific feedback, for which gender is a proxy, may vary with time.

At this point, I've described how static variables can be used as covariates. By static, I mean variables like gender, cohort, and ethnicity that do not change across measurement occasions. Sometimes these variables are predictors of longitudinally changing variables. In this case, the variables would be time-invariant predictors. Age, for example, is often a predictor of changes (and it would not be used as a covariate in this instance). When covariates can vary with each measurement occasion, these covariates are referred to as time-varying covariates. When time-varying covariates are involved, their influence would be controlled for at the measurement occasion on which they are measured and at further measurement occasions.

Examples of potential time-varying covariates include amount of exposure to intervention, length of time spent studying, or number of friends. The idea here is that time-varying covariates are potential confounding variables that can change (vary) at each measurement occasion.

If you are undecided or aren't sure which way to go in terms of how to control for covariates, I suggest you use the full partial approach. It is the fullest of the control methods and does not depend on the type of model that you are trying to specify. That being said, the most common question I get on the use of covariates is "When should I include them?" The answer to this question is "It depends." If the covariates are known confounds of the relationships you are examining, I recommend including them in each model at each step of the model-building process. If the covariates are secondary concerns, I think you can wait to include the covariate influences at later stages of the model-building process. At this stage, you just want to be sure the potential covariates don't have an impact on the primary results. You should also be careful not to throw too many covariates into a model. Covariates should still be selected because they have a theoretically meaningful potential influence on the modeled relationships. When a large number of covariates are thrown into a model, the estimation can be cumbersome, the patterns of effects are difficult to interpret, and the modeled relationships are overcontrolled. By overcontrolled I am referring to what can happen due to effect of random variation. By chance alone, a covariate might happen to be associated with the focal constructs; when this source of random information is removed from the focal construct, overcontrol has occurred. Given that SEM is a theory-driven enterprise, throwing a bunch of covariates into a model as an atheoretical afterthought simply does not make sense.

RESCALING VARIABLES

As a general measurement issue, it is sometimes necessary to rescale variables before including them in an SEM model. One of the most important assumptions of SEM is that the variables used are multivariate normal. When the individual variables are all univariate normal, the likelihood of their being multivariate normal is pretty good. When some of the variables are skewed or kurtotic, the likelihood of their being multivariate normal is not so good. Maximum likelihood estimation is robust enough to tolerate moderate violations of the multivariate normal assumption, and the so-called robust estimation methods can also handle non-normal data. Some scholars suggest performing a transformation on the variables that violate univariate normal assumptions to help in the process of stabilizing your model and its estimates (Tabachnick & Fidell, 2007). Here, square-root, log, or inverse transformations are sometimes recommended to make the variables more univariate normal. In my experience, however, such transformations have little influence on the overall conclusions that are drawn from the results of the models. Granted, some point estimates differ, some standard errors are different, the model fit information is slightly different, but the big-picture conclusions and generalizations are not substantially different. A bigger concern is that the metric of the measured variables is dramatically changed and that the interpretation of the scores on the latent variables, as well as their associations, becomes quite muddied. Moreover, as robust estimation procedures are readily available, the need to transform the raw data has become mostly a moot issue. My recommendation, therefore, is to resist the temptation to use transformations that attempt to make the distribution more normal (bell-shaped). Instead, apply a robust estimation approach, such as bootstrap estimation.

Another type of rescaling is simply to change the metric of the variables to be on comparable scales. This type of transformation does not change the shape of the distribution but instead rescales the scores to a different metric from the original one. I use such transformations when I have variables that are on very different metrics (e.g., age in years vs. millisecond reaction times). I do this type of transformation primarily because some SEM software packages seem to have a harder time converging on estimates when the metrics are quite different and an easier time when the metrics are roughly similar. A secondary reason is that I have a better feel for the magnitudes of the associations among variables when they are on a similar metric. Most modelers are able to see the patterns of associations in a correlation matrix pretty easily. When the covariance metric is similar across variables, you can see the same kinds of relative patterns that you can see in a correlation matrix, which helps with model evaluation and in troubleshooting estimation problems.

As mentioned, most SEM software will have estimation difficulties when the variables used in a model are on very different metrics. The reason for this estimation problem is that the covariances that are calculated and the parameters used to recreate the covariances (i.e., the model-implied covariance matrix) differ by orders of magnitude. For example, a covariance between two variables coded on a 0–1 metric might have meaningful differences in its estimates in the second decimal place, whereas a covariance between two variables coded on a 0–100 scale would have meaningful differences in the units place. If all the variables are put on a roughly similar metric, the meaningful information is in the same place, and the programs will find a solution to the specified model more expeditiously.

Dividing or multiplying the variables by a constant value is a common procedure to put them on a roughly common metric. Such transformations are monotonic in that they don't affect the individual-differences standings or the associations among the variables; monotonic transformations only influence the metric and the resulting meaning of the metric of a variable. Typically, you don't want to do a full z-score standardization of each variable, because then you lose the covariance metric that is needed for the SEM procedures, and you lose any information about mean-level changes over time. With longitudinal data, keeping the integrity of relative mean-level changes over time is crucial, and you want to use a metric that would still satisfy the need to estimate models on covariances and not correlations.

The percentage or proportion of maximum scoring (or POMS) transformation is one that I typically recommend. In Table 1.5, I give two versions of POMS: 1.5A is the proportion of maximum scoring using the theoretical maximum score, and 1.5B is the percentage of maximum scoring using the observed maximum score (in these examples I use an arbitrarily chosen 5-point Likert scale for illustration purposes). The theoretical versus observed maximum score can be swapped between formulas 1.5A and 1.5B; you can multiply by 100, which would make the score a percentage, or not multiply by 100, which would keep the score a proportion. For longitudinal models it is important to remember that the max score used for the transformation must be the same values used to transform each time of measurement. This common value is needed in order to see any longitudinal changes on the construct. If the max score is different for each time point, the meaning of the change information is lost.

Another situation where rescaling is useful is when variables are recorded on different Likert-type scales; for example, a measure may be given to respondents on a 5-point Likert scale at one age group but given at another age group on a 7-point scale. In a situation like this, a transformation is needed. That is, to compare any growth or change on the instrument, the scores on the measures must be put on a comparable metric across the two age groups. There are some possible rescaling approaches that you can employ: convert all of the measures to a 0–1 scale, convert all of the measures to a percentage or proportion of maximum scale, or convert the narrower scale (e.g., 1–5 in the preceding example) to the metric of the wider scale (e.g., 1–7; see Table 1.5C).

Another transformation that can be done is to standardize all the variables in an analysis across time to be on a similar metric. Here, you would need to calculate the grand mean over time and the grand standard deviation over time and use that mean and standard deviation to transform the scores within each time point (i.e.,

TABLE 1.5. Several alternative rescaling formulae to put all variables on similar metrics

A) $R1 = (O - 1) / S_{max}$	B) $R100 = ((O - 1) / O_{max}) \cdot 100$	C) $R7 = (((O5 - 1) / 4) \cdot 6) + 1$
• $R1$ is the rescaled variable, which we want to become a 0 to 1 scale.	• $R100$ is the rescaled variable as a percent of the maximum score.	• $R7$ is the rescaled variable, which we want to become a 1 to 7 scale.
• O is the original scale; in this example assume a 5-point scale from 1 to 5.	• O is the original scale, in this example assume a 5-point scale from 1 to 5.	• $O5$ is the original scale; in this case it is on a 5-point scale from 1 to 5.
• 1st: subtract 1 to make the scale go from 0 to 4. If the scale already starts at 0, don't subtract 1.	• 1st: subtract 1 to make the scale go from 0 to 4. If the scale already starts at 0, don't subtract 1.	• 1st: subtract 1 to make the scale go from 0 to 4. If the scale is already on a 0 to 4 scale, you don't need to subtract 1.
• S_{max} is the new scale maximum.	• O_{max} is the maximum scale value that was observed in the data after subtracting 1 or the max if it already started at 0.	• 2nd: dividing by 4 makes the scale go from 0 to 1.
• 2nd: dividing by S_{max} makes the scale from 0 to 1 or less than 1 if the scale maximum is not observed.	• 2nd: dividing by O_{max} makes the scale go from 0 to 1.	• 3rd: multiplying by 6 makes the scale go from 0 to 6.
• This rescoring method is a proportion of maximum scoring (you can convert to a percent if you multiply by 100).	• 3rd: multiplying by 100 makes it a percent, which ranges from 0 to 100.	• 4th: adding 1 makes the scale go from 1 to 7.

Note. These transformations do not change the distribution of the variables. They are monotonic transformations, like a *z*-score transformation. The original scale is put on a metric that is relatively more interpretable, or at least similar, across some or all of the variables in the analysis.

don't use the mean and standard deviation within a given time point, because you lose any information about change in means and variances). If you have multiple groups and longitudinal data, you would calculate the grand mean across time and groups, as well as the grand standard deviation across time and groups. With this method you can leave the scores in a grand z-score metric (again, however, the mean and standard deviation used must be the overall mean and standard deviation so you don't lose change information). You can also add a grand constant and multiply by a selected value to put the indicators on a so-called t-score metric (e.g., mean of 100 and a standard deviation of 15, or a mean of 10 and a standard deviation of 2, or a mean of 50 and a standard deviation of 10—there is no official definition of the mean and standard deviation of a t-score as far as I know). The choice of the rescaling method here does not "normalize" the data, nor does it change the shape of the distribution or the strength of an association between any of the variables. Rescaling simply provides a metric that makes the estimated values more interpretable (and can help with convergence problems). Of course, rescaling variables when they are already in meaningful and interpretable metrics may not be desired unless you are experiencing convergence problems.

The final recoding issue is reverse-coding of variables. I generally recommend that all indicators be coded so that a high score on each indicator has the same interpretation (e.g., more X or less Y). For example, if I have one indicator of anxiety that is worded as something like "I don't get nervous" with a Likert scale of *disagree* to *agree*, a high score would mean less anxious. If the other indicators are worded such that a high score means more anxious ("I am easily aroused"), I would reverse-code the "I don't get nervous" item. If the Likert scale is a 1–7 scale, I can simply create a new variable that is 8 minus the values of the original variable ($8 - 7 = 1$ and $8 - 1 = 7$). It is also a good habit to name the latent construct by what the higher values mean. For example, if all my indicators are coded such that a high score means less anxiety, I would call the construct "lack of anxiety" or "nonanxiousness." If the indicators are coded such that a high score means more anxiety, I would label the construct "anxiety" or "anxiousness." In a similar vein, when creating dummy codes to represent gender or ethnic categories, I recommend labeling the variable with the meaning of a high score. For example, if gender is coded 0 = female and 1 = male, then I recommend calling the variable "male." Then you don't have to ask "Which gender is coded as 1?"

PARCELING

Parceling refers to taking two or more items and packaging them together (i.e., averaging them), much like a parcel you would take to the post office. The parcel (instead of the original items) is then used as the manifest indicator of the latent construct. Parceling is a premodeling step that is done before the data are fed into the SEM software. When packaging items to form a parcel (or a scale score for that matter), I strongly recommend averaging the items as opposed to summing them. If you take sums and the number of items going into a parcel differs, the parcels will have different metrics, giving materially different means and variances. If you average the items, the parcels will have roughly similar metrics with similar (and comparable) means and variances. Moreover, the scores on the parcels will reflect the actual scale that was used to record the item-level information. The original scale is usually meaningful, and it provides a point of reference for interpreting the mean levels and variances.

Parcels have a number of statistical and analytical advantages over item-level analyses. Parcels also pose some challenges; the whole idea still engenders some debate in the methodology community. The debate can generally be traced to two opposing philosophical camps. The con arguments stem from the strict empiricist traditions of classical statistics. As my colleagues and I put it (Little, Cunningham, Shahar, & Widaman, 2002), the strict empiricist viewpoint suggests:

> Parceling is akin to cheating because modeled data should be as close to the response of the individual as possible in order to avoid the potential imposition, or arbitrary manufacturing of a false structure. (p. 152)

We went on to describe the alternative, more pragmatic viewpoint:

> Given that measurement is a strict, rule-bound system that is defined, followed, and reported by the investigator, the level of aggregation used to represent the measurement process is a matter of choice and justification on the part of the investigator. (pp. 152–153)

If your philosophical view is aligned with the former, you can skip to the next section. If you are undecided on the issue, I recommend you read Little et al. (2002) and Little, Rhemtulla, Gibson, and Schoemann (in press). Both of these papers describe the con arguments and provide reasoned arguments as to when the con arguments are not applicable. My most important admonition here is to be thoughtful when you create parcels. If you are thoughtful in parcel creation, parcels have many advantages and avoid the potential pitfalls that the con arguments highlight.

The motivation to create and use parcels is that they possess a number of advantages. These advantages can be summarized into two classes: their fundamental psychometric characteristics and their behavior when estimating a model. These advantages are summarized in Table 1.6.

In terms of the psychometric advantages of parcels over items, the first three that are listed in Table 1.6 (higher reliability, greater communality, higher ratio of common-to-unique factor variance) are saying essentially the same thing. Per the principles of aggregation, parcels will have greater reliability than the items that are used to create them. As a result of having greater reliability, parcels will have more true-score variance than items, which will also make the factor loadings stronger

TABLE 1.6. Key advantages of parcels versus items

Psychometric characteristics

Parcels (as opposed to the items) have . . .
- Higher reliability
- Greater communality
- Higher ratio of common-to-unique factor variance
- Lower likelihood of distributional violations
- More, tighter, and more-equal intervals

Model estimation and fit characteristics

Models with parcels (as opposed to the items) have . . .
- Fewer parameter estimates
- Lower indicator-to-subject ratio
- Lower likelihood of correlated residuals
  and dual factor loadings
- Reduced sources of sampling error

Note. These advantages pertain to the smaller set of parcels that are made up of a larger set of items. The advantages accrue based on the principles of aggregation and the law of large numbers.

(increased communality) and the unique factors smaller. As a result, the ratio of common-to-unique factor variance will be higher. All three of these related features of parcels are a good thing when it comes to fitting an SEM model. Regarding the advantages of the distributional properties, parcels are more likely to be normally distributed than are items.

When quantitative specialists discuss the conditions under which parcels can be used, many would agree that parcels are not problematic when the indicators are at least congeneric in nature (i.e., are truly indicators of the construct) and the construct is unidimensional "in the population." *In the population* means that if we had access to the whole population we would be able to tell which indicators go with which constructs and what each construct is truly made of—the kind of thing only an omniscient being or higher deity would know. We, as mere mortals, never know what exactly things are like *in the population*; we can, however, infer things about the population from the sample. Unfortunately, sampling variability comes into play and can muddy the waters a bit. Sampling variability is the inherent variability around the true population values for a given parameter estimate of any statistical model that is produced when you draw repeated samples from the population (or, more precisely, any given sample may deviate from the population values to some degree). On average, any given randomly drawn sample will provide estimates of the population parameters that are equal to the true population values, but there will be variability in these estimates from sample to sample. The larger the sample size, the lower the sampling variability; the more homogeneous the population, the lower the sampling variability.

In Figure 1.3, I have presented a geometric representation of how parcels can work. In the circle denoted A, I have a "universe" of possible indicators for a construct. The construct's true center is depicted by the large dot in the center of the circle. The small dots are possible indicators that can be selected to represent the construct. Moving to circle B, I have selected six possible indicators. Numbering clockwise starting in the upper left of the area, I have assigned indicator 1 (I_1) and Indicator 2 (I_2) to be in parcel 1 (P_1). I have assigned I_3 and I_4 to be in P_2. I_5 and I_6 are assigned to P_3. In this geometric representation, dots that are closer to the centroid will have much larger loadings on the construct than will dots that are farther away. Any dots that are closer to each other will have higher correlations with each other than they will with other dots that are farther away. Given these simple geometric properties, we can see that I_2 and I_3 would be more highly correlated with each other than they would be with the actual construct they are supposed to measure. In fact, an analysis of the item-level data would result in a correlated residual between I_2 and I_3. In addition, because I_1 is quite far away from the centroid of the construct, it is likely to have a secondary loading on another construct.

If you take the average of the indicators that were assigned to each parcel, you would create a new parcel-level indicator that is at the midpoint of the line connecting the two indicators. The location of the larger dots labeled P_1, P_2, and P_3 in circle B are the locations of the parcel-level indicators that would result from averaging the corresponding item-level indicators. In circle C of Figure 1.3, I have connected the three parcels with lines to depict the triangulation on the centroid that the three

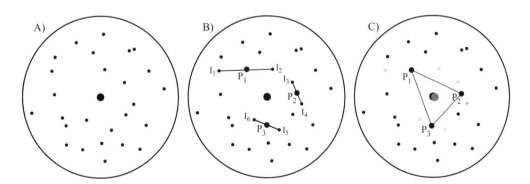

FIGURE 1.3. A geometric representation of how parceling works. Each circle represents the domain of possible indicators of a construct. The construct's "true" centroid is the larger dot in the center of each circle. The average of any two variables would be the midpoint of a straight line, as depicted in B; the average of three or more indicators would be the geometric center of the area that they encompass. The latent construct that would be indicated by the parcels is the center dot, in gray, that nearly overlaps the true centroid, as in C.

parcels would now measure. Here, the geometric midpoint of the triangle created by the three parcels is the estimated factor centroid, which, as can be seen, is close to the "true" centroid.

The parceling example that I have depicted in Figure 1.3 is not necessarily the optimal set of parcels that could have been created from the chosen indicators. Because we don't know the true location of a construct's centroid, we can only try to approximate an optimal solution given the items that were selected to represent the construct in the first place. I generally have found good results using a balancing approach whereby I assign the item with the highest item–scale correlation to be paired with the item that has the lowest item–scale correlation. I then select the next highest and next lowest items to be in the second parcel and repeatedly assign items in this manner until all items have been assigned to a parcel. In longitudinal models the selection of items to parcels needs to be the same at each time point. Here, I have used the average loading across the time points to create the rankings of the items. I generally do not recommend random parceling. Random parceling would be OK under conditions where there are lots of items and the items are all equally good (i.e., the assumption of tau-equivalent or parallel indicators), but usually we have indicators that are only congeneric (i.e., some items are better than other items).

Indicators of a construct are congeneric when they are truly indicators of the construct (in the population) but can vary in terms of the size of their loadings and intercepts. Most factor models and SEM models assume that indicators are congeneric, which is the least restrictive of assumptions about indicators. In my experience, most indicators in the social and behavioral sciences are only congeneric. As mentioned, the assumption of tau-equivalent or parallel indicators is more restrictive. Indicators of a construct are tau equivalent when their loadings are all at about the same level (again, in the population), but they can vary in terms of their intercepts. The strictest assumption about a set of indicators is that they are parallel in the population. Here, the loadings and the intercepts are all essentially equal. Indicators in the ability-testing domain can sometimes achieve this level of precision across items.

One key assumption in all this is that the statistical model being fit to the sample is the correct model for the data. In other words, we assume that the model would be true *in the population*. As MacCallum and Austin (2000; see also Box, 1979) point out, however, "all models are wrong to some degree, even in the population, and the best one can hope for is to identify a parsimonious, substantively meaningful model that fits observed data adequately well" (p. 218). So there is always some variability due to the fact that my model is going to be wrong to some degree, anyway (hopefully not too much . . .).

Parceling reduces both the sampling variability of the selected sample and the amount of incorrectness of my model in the population. The benefits of reducing the likelihood of correlated residuals and dual-factor loadings are both aspects of how parcels reduce sampling variability (a dual loading or correlated residual could be just a sampling fluctuation) or population misfit (a dual loading or correlated residual could be true of the item-level data in the population, but it is no longer true of the parcel-level data in the population). In other words, there is a true model in the population for item-level data that probably has some "true" correlated residuals and dual loading that we might be tempted to not estimate because the misfit is mistakenly attributed to sampling variability. A true model also exists in the population for the parcel-level data, but this model is less likely to have those "true" correlated residuals and dual-factor loadings. The principle of aggregating the true-score variances of items while reducing their uniquenesses is the reason that parcels have this quality.

I have found parcels to be extremely useful and effective in nearly all circumstances, even when the construct I'm working with is multidimensional (see Little et al., in press). There are times that I won't parcel items, such as when my empirical question is about the behavior of the items across two or more samples or two or more time points. On the other hand, when the substantive questions are about the constructs and the possible differences in those constructs (e.g., differences across time or across groups), then creating parcels to use as indicators of the constructs is justified. Transparency and ethical behavior are important when using parcels. In terms of transparency, a researcher needs to be clear and honest about what he or she did when creating the parcels and why the parcels were used. The ethical part comes in when one plays around with problematic items until a particular parceling scheme works out such that a preferred outcome materializes that would not have otherwise. I trust that you are not the unscrupulous researcher that ethicists worry so much about.

WHAT CHANGES AND HOW?

Many if not most developmental change trends, if measured across the lifespan, will have a nonlinear function. Most developmental studies, however, are unable to cover the entire lifespan. When such studies cover only a limited amount of the lifespan, the resulting estimate of the trend line will often be closely approximated as a linear trend. In Figure 1.4, I have depicted two stylized and hypothetical examples of lifespan trends (these could also be other trends of change, such as trends in response to therapy or trends in hormones in response to a stressor). In panel A, the true nonlinear trend is depicted. In panel B, the observed trend lines from three different studies covering three different segments of the lifespan are pieced together. Each individual study was able to detect and therefore depict the trend line only as a linear trend. When pieced together, however, the trend lines do a rather good job of tracing the true nonlinear trajectory. The fact that nonlinear trends can be represented reasonably well with segmented linear trends should not be considered a damnation of one's theory. To detect a nonlinear trend, the important part to measure is, in fact, at the extremes, well beyond a bend (contrary to some who argue to oversample at

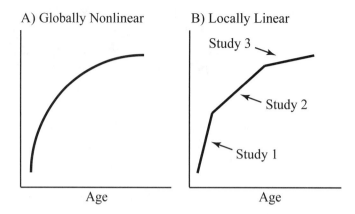

FIGURE 1.4. Globally nonlinear, locally linear.

the bend). The ends need to be very well located to show curvature in between the end points.

Any developmental/longitudinal study must start with an idea about what it is that changes. There are four dimensions of a dataset to consider when thinking of change. The first dimension is the individual-differences standing. Here, there is a distribution of scores at one occasion of measurement and a second distribution of scores at a second measurement occasion. The question of change is "Have the standings in the distribution of individual differences changed?" And is this change reliably predicted by prior information about each person?

The second dimension is the mean level of the group. The mean level is the typical score in the distribution. Has this typical score gone up or down over time? Is there a specific functional form that can characterize the group-level growth trajectory? The mean level may go up or down as a function of an intervention or an experimental manipulation. In such situations, the focus of the study is the statistical significance of any mean-level change.

A third dimension is the degree of dispersion in the distribution. Has the distribution become more dispersed or less dispersed over time? That is, has the variance changed over time? We don't often think of variances when we think of change processes. If the mean can be thought of as the typical score in a distribution, the variance can be thought of as an index of the typical amount of deviation from the mean (particularly when we transform the variance into the standard deviation). Some developmental changes may lead to more homogeneous responses and thereby shrink the typical deviation (shrink the variance). Other developmental changes may lead to more heterogeneous responses and thereby increase the variance of the distribution. In a repeated-measures experiment to influence attitudes, for example, a key outcome of the experimental manipulation may be to make the group of respondents more aligned with the mean. This type of manipulation would not change the mean level of the experimental group, nor would it change the correlation of the individual-differences standings between the pre- and posttreatment scores. It would, however, make the variance significantly less between pre- and posttreatment.

A fourth dimension is the within-person changes over time. This idea is captured by the intraindividual differences in change. Here, we can think of the "score" as the change, either up or down, associated with each individual. This distribution will have a mean and a variance just like a static distribution of scores. I describe this dimension in much greater detail when I discuss multilevel growth curve models in Chapter 8.

Any developmental research question has to become a statistical question about one of these four dimensions of what can change in a quantitative study. In the course of the later chapters, I describe the statistical models that can be used to model the expected developmental changes.

SOME ADVICE FOR SEM PROGRAMMING

On the support pages for the book (*www.guilford.com/little-materials*) you will find all the scripts that produce the model estimates and results that I present herein. These scripts are written in various software packages, including LISREL, Mplus, and R (lavaan). Other scripts, examples, and resources are also available. On these pages, I also post updates, errata, and other relevant materials. Perhaps most useful for researchers are the various KUant guides that are posted and regularly edited by the students in the quantitative training programs at KU and the staff of the CRMDA at KU. You'll find guides to LISREL, Mplus, R (lavaan), what to report, how to read the output, and so on. If you find that a guide is not clear, contact the authors of the guide and request clarification. The guides provide details of writing an SEM script and interpreting its output. In this section, I offer a very general overview of what an SEM script would look like.

Any program script consists of three chapters. The first chapter is the introduction—you introduce the SEM program to your data. Specifically, you give the SEM program all the relevant information about where the data file is located, the number of variables and their labels, the sample size, and so on. This first chapter of a script has nothing to do with SEM per se; it is simply the step needed to allow the SEM package to work with the observed data. The dataset that is read in can be the raw data, or it can be the sufficient statistics (which can be broken down as means, standard deviations, and correlations; as means and covariances; or as an augmented moment matrix).

The second chapter of an SEM script is the specification chapter. Here, you provide the SEM software a complete description (or translation) of the drawing of the SEM model you have in mind. Some software will prompt you to actually draw the diagram and then translate the drawing internally. In Chapter 3 of this book, I introduce you to the drawing conventions of SEM. The drawing and what it represents is, I think, one of the most important features of SEM. Every box and circle that has a line linked to it is a statement of theory. Every box and circle that does not have a line linked to it is also a statement of theory, though often implicitly for many modelers. In this regard, the diagram of the SEM model is a complete and thorough statement of the theoretical expectations. Here, in terms of the chapters of an SEM script, the second chapter is critical, because the diagram must be fully specified for the SEM software to properly estimate the model.

The third and final chapter of an SEM script is the conclusion. Here, the script contains directions to the SEM software about what output should be presented and which special output options are requested. The OUTPUT requests allow you to control what information you would like to see in order to evaluate the adequacy of the model. These three chapters of an SEM script are common to all SEM software. They also contain a complete record of the story that the SEM model represents. It is a valuable and complete documentation of a given step in the SEM model-building process.

All SEM software will give you the ability to annotate your script. Usually a special symbol, such as ! or * or /, signifies the beginning of a written comment. These symbols are handy because you can also use them to deactivate lines of code that you have written by converting the code into an inert comment ("comment out" the line of code).

The history of a project must be carefully documented. Given that a typical SEM project may have dozens or more tests conducted throughout its development, keeping an accurate record of exactly what was specified and a copy of the results is essential. I recommend, therefore, that you use very clear descriptive names of the files you create, annotate the file with a clear description of what the program does, and create a file dictionary that summarizes all the information.

I would like to offer a word of insight regarding graphical user interfaces (GUIs) when generating SEM models. I'm generally not a fan of GUIs because most SEM models that are fit to real data problems exceed the drawing capacity of the interface. GUIs' shortcomings are accentuated with longitudinal models because its visual representation capabilities are quickly outstripped by the complexity of a longitudinal model, especially when trying to represent both the measurement model (the linkages between boxes and circles) and the structural model (the linkages among circles). Moreover, using a GUI makes it too easy to lose track of all the changes made during the modeling process; the ability to annotate the files created along the way is also hampered when a GUI is used. Here, the simplicity of GUIs breeds sloppiness in record keeping and provides only a limited awareness of how things can and do work.

Whether scripting or using a GUI, quite often you will find that your specified model simply won't converge. Of course, this lack of convergence can be a symptom of a misspecified or unidentified model. A model can be misspecified in two ways.

One way occurs when the model you fit to the sample data is not the model that in reality is appropriate for the population. This type of model misspecification usually will not lead to convergence problems; instead, it shows up as a poorly fitting model, and sometimes tests of alternative models can be biased. The type of misspecification that affects convergence occurs simply when your program script has an error in it such that the model you intend to fit to the data is not properly coded in your script. Errors such as excluding a parameter that you intend to estimate or adding a parameter that you did not intend to estimate may cause estimation difficulties.

Sometimes the lack of convergence happens because the program needs better start values in order to find an optimal solution. Providing start values for many SEM programs is sometimes a matter of art and other times a matter of luck. I have learned a few tricks that work. Start loadings at .7, or in the middle of where the loading space can be. Start covariances among constructs at a relatively low level. Be careful when starting a covariance that is close to the boundary of being an out-of-bounds estimate. Even when the actual covariance is very high, start the covariance at a lower level of association than you think should be the case. A similar piece of advice goes for the residuals of the indicators. Here, be careful not to start the residuals at a value that is very close to 0, even if the expectation is that they will be close to 0.

Another trick to assist with convergence is to make sure that all the indicators are on roughly the same metric. If you have some variables like income that have meaningful differences in the hundredths place and other variables like millisecond reaction times that have meaningful differences in the hundredths place, the iterative convergence algorithms will have trouble finding the right values for the parameter estimates. The POMS scoring that I introduced earlier in this chapter (Table 1.5) is a very efficient and meaningful way to recode all the variables to be on a roughly similar metric.

PHILOSOPHICAL ISSUES AND HOW I APPROACH RESEARCH

This section is critical because I need to explain where I am coming from philosophically and how I approach research. All statisticians have a philosophical bent, either implicitly or explicitly. I am making mine explicit because it will establish a common understanding of the ideas that are at the foundation of longitudinal SEM. Another reason I am making my views explicit is that too often these ideas are implicit, and it is very difficult to understand why different researchers will have different views on common issues. We saw this already to some degree in my discussion of parcels. These philosophical issues, however, pervade many of the decisions that we all will make. I think it is important to recognize the philosophical metatheory that shapes how we all approach research.

I am a pragmatic developmentalist as opposed to a hard-core empiricist. This philosophical bent permeates my recommendations throughout this book; however, when I offer a recommendation, I provide the background or reasoning for it so you can judge for yourself if my positions are tenable or not. My pragmatism stems from the fact that I am a developmental researcher who works with real data in an effort to shed a ray of light on some theoretically interesting or meaningful idea (following Box [1979], I try to find out "what the world is really like"; see the subsequent quote). Most hard-core (and often dogmatic) empiricists rarely soil their hands with real, quasi-experimental data. If they were inclined to play with such data, they would not likely let theory get in the way of well-behaved data or well-controlled analyses. Mind you, I am not arguing for the opposite perspective, that is, never let data get in the way of good theory (sometimes data have something important to tell us and will change our theory).

I absolutely want to do the very best analysis job possible and to use strong empirical justification to answer the theoretical question at hand. To do so, however, sometimes means that assumptions are violated or tests may not possess ideal power or precise error rates. In such situations, I won't throw up my hands and say "it can't be done"; instead, I acknowledge the less-than-optimal qualities of real-world data and try to find a way to reveal what they contain with justifiable use of a strong and reasonably appropriate analytic method. No single study stands alone on its own merits; instead, it simply contributes to the larger pool of scientific knowledge, where suboptimal answers are typically weighted less. Such work will still make a contribution to the body of knowledge. Given the eventual self-correcting tendency of an open community of scholars, even suboptimal answers can keep our evolving knowledge base on track.

Box (1979) conveys some of this view rather eloquently:

> We cannot expect to get good results unless we are really prepared to engage in the hazardous under-taking of finding out *what the world is really like*. It requires us, as statisticians, to have some knowledge of reality. . . . The wise investigator expends his effort not in one grand design (necessarily conceived at a time when he knows least about unfolding reality), but in a series of smaller designs, analyzing, modifying, and getting new ideas as he goes . . . the rules that ought to apply to the statistics of most real scientific investigations are different, broader, and vaguer than those that might apply to a single decision or to a single test of a hypothesis. (pp. 1–2)

As I mentioned in the prologue, my goal is to walk you through *how* to think about SEM as applied to longitudinal data rather than *what* to think about it. I have this as my goal because statistics in general and SEM in particular are about making a series of reasoned decisions in an ongoing manner. These decisions must optimally balance between (1) the error of inferring that something exists when it does not (e.g., inferring that a model is supported when it is not) and (2) the error of not finding what you expect to find (e.g., rejecting a model as poor fitting). These errors must be balanced not only against each other but also against the gravity of the question being asked. Answers to some questions have higher stakes or reflect a more mature area of inquiry; others have less dire consequences if an answer is inaccurate, particularly when the inquiry is more exploratory in nature. The economics of scientific inquiry also need to be factored in. Is the return on statistical precision worth the expense of more data acquisition? Is the violation of an assumption, for example, sufficient grounds to invalidate a result? Given that validity is a matter of degree, modest validity still has merit—just less so than does a study of greater validity.

At its core, SEM is a theory-guided enterprise, and, as such, theory should be in the driver's seat. The analysis plan must be shaped and tailored to fit the theoretical questions and expectations at hand rather than forcing the question into a rigid, rule-bound, conforming-to-consensus expectation about how to do science (e.g., Procrustean application of ANOVA procedures). When theory takes a back seat, decision errors will compound. Although SEM is ideally suited to address theoretically motivated quasi-experimental research questions, even traditional experimental designs that tout objective rigor and precise control when conducting the experiment will benefit from the application of SEM as the analytic method of choice (see Chapter 5 for an example and details of the benefits). The fact that SEM makes fewer assumptions and that many of the assumptions are empirically testable compared with traditional ways of testing experimental outcomes is a primary reason that SEM would be a preferred analytical approach. For quasi-experimental applications, the ability of SEM to be molded and shaped to fit the question is one of its greatest assets. Nearly all statistical models can be specified in an SEM framework (see Wu & Little, 2011; also see Chapter 9, Figure 9.1, this volume, for a list), and the SEM framework can be adapted to optimally address a given research question, even the atypical question.

The idea that somehow science is an objective enterprise with a *right* way to do things is, unfortunately, a misguided fiction propagated from rigid empiricist ideals. In a similar vein, conducting a "conservative" test of a given hypothesis is also an erroneous attempt to reify the results from using the scientific method—hypostatizing the idea that somehow a conservative test is more correct or truer than the alternative. Results, findings, outcomes, and good-fitting models are never *Truth* or *Fact*. The best we can hope for is a certain verisimilitude (truth-like value) between our conclusions and the reality of the unseeable world. The best test, therefore, is neither a conservative test nor a liberal test; the optimal test is one that is analytically tailored to the question and that thoughtfully balances the errors of inference, the gravity of the question, and the economics of both data acquisition and statistical precision.

Science should not be a purely subjective and unregulated enterprise, either. The various disciplines have developed generally agreed-upon rigor and processes that logically and reasonably allow the community of scientists to agree on the verisimilitude of a study's conclusions. Moreover, science is a publicly discussed and scrutinized activity that relies on the equilibrium among knowledgeable peer reviewers, reasonable and wise editors, and the self-correcting and self-monitoring community of properly trained scholars. Granted, some methods require less formal training to become properly proficient in their acceptable application. A large measure of the rigor and procedures associated with SEM is grounded in advanced statistical theory. Because the methodological maturity of different disciplines varies, many disciplines are populated by researchers who are keenly aware of and familiar with the tenets and conclusions of advanced statistical theory, whereas some disciplines lag behind the leading edge of social science statistical theory. A goal of this book is to make approachable the advanced statistical theory and its applications across the entire social, educational, and behavioral sciences. I would also like to see this material spread into areas of research that conveniently assume that these advanced methods and techniques have little relevance in the conduct of "hard" science. The methodological hubris found in such disciplines can limit novel and perhaps para-digm-shifting research. As a flexible and almost limitless tool, SEM affords novel application and nuanced discovery.

At the beginning of this section, I quoted Box as saying "the rules that ought to apply to the statistics of most real scientific investigations are different, broader, and vaguer than those that might apply to a single decision or to a single test of a hypothesis." The classical school of statistics primarily involves the single-hypothe-sis-testing mentality. In the modeling school, for which SEM is the analytical tech-nique of choice, the rules of engagement are different, broader, and vaguer than those applied from a classical perspective. These differences sometimes are at odds when a reviewer trained from a classical perspective, for example, comments on an analysis conducted from a modeling perspective. Because few SEM models are alike and models must necessarily be molded to fit the question, the rules for doing so must be flexible and must leave room for interpretation. The shades of gray that stem from the ambiguity in the rules are to be embraced. When SEM models are codified with black and white, right and wrong, steps and procedures, the greatest strength of SEM, its flexibility, becomes undermined. Reviewers who state emphatically a right way or a wrong way to conduct an SEM model should be admonished—the rules are different from those of the classical world; they are broader and necessarily vaguer.

SUMMARY

In this chapter I have laid the groundwork of how I approach SEM in general and given students who are unfamiliar with SEM in particular some general ways to think about SEM, indicators, and latent variables. The topics I covered here are mostly foundational ideas related to measurement and statistics. Because SEM is very explicit about the measurement relations of the model and tests most of the core assumptions of measurement, I think it is important to keep these measurement issues in mind as you proceed in planning or conducting the full SEM model. In

Chapter 3, I go into more precise details about how (mathematically) constructs are created from measured indicators.

Addressing these core measurement issues as carefully and thoughtfully as possible is a core element of a good SEM model. A second core element is the design that is used to collect the data. In Chapter 2, I turn to many of the core design issues of longitudinal SEM.

KEY TERMS AND CONCEPTS INTRODUCED IN THIS CHAPTER

Aka. Also known as.

Congeneric indicators. Indicators of a construct are congeneric when they are truly indicators of the construct (in the population) but can vary in terms of the size of their loadings and intercepts. Most factorial and SEM models assume that indicators are congeneric, which is the least restrictive of the assumptions about indicators.

Constructs. Constructs are the core concepts that researchers attempt to measure and draw conclusions about. Constructs cannot be measured directly. Their characteristics can only be inferred from the behavior of the indicators that are measured to represent them. Constructs are the knots of a theory's nomological net.

Empiricism/empiricist. Although these terms have various meanings across philosophical settings, when considered in the context of the philosophy of science, empiricism emphasizes the experimental method, adherence to the rules of inquiry, and a belief in existence of the null hypothesis as the means of acquiring scientific knowledge. Blind objectivity and "dust bowl" empiricism (i.e., pure induction, free of any theoretical basis) are at the extreme of this approach to scientific inquiry. Research from this perspective in its extreme form is typically handcuffed by the method of inquiry.

Indicators. Indicators are measured variables that one has selected to use as an indirect proxy or gauge of a latent variable. Like all variables in statistics, the scores on an indicator vary across individuals or measured entities. Unlike a variable, an indicator is carefully constructed and chosen by the researcher to be as close a reflection of the latent variable (or construct) as possible.

Interindividual differences. The deviations or dispersions between individual entities (usually persons in behavioral science research) from a measure of central tendency (usually the mean of the distribution). Interindividual differences, therefore, are commonly represented as a distribution of scores with a mean (m) and a variance (s^2). A person's standing in the distribution is his or her individual-differences score.

Interindividual differences in intraindividual differences. The deviations or dispersions between entities in their within-entity intraindividual differences scores (within-entity variability) over time or situations.

Intraindividual differences. With intraindividual differences, the focus is now on the deviations or dispersions of an individual entity's scores over time or situations (within-entity variability). Such scores are typically represented as an overall level score (e.g., an intercept) plus a consistent change score (e.g., a linear slope) plus unexplained variability.

Parallel indicators. The strictest assumption about a set of indicators is that they are parallel in the population. Here, the loadings and the intercepts are all essentially equal.

Parcels and parceling. Parceling is the name of the technique by which aggregates of items or smaller units of measurement are used to form larger units as indicators of the underlying latent constructs. The term *parcel* refers to the aggregate score of items (or smaller unit of measurement, such as the score on a given trial) that is used as the measured indicator of constructs in an SEM model.

Pragmatism/pragmatist. A pragmatic view of scientific inquiry is decidedly flexible, self-correcting, intuitive, and openly subjective—yet within the context of SEM, these features are empirically testable and often will provide critical tests of theoretical suppositions. That is, empirical methods are essential to test the intuitions of the researcher, but the manner and procedures are tools that a researcher can shape to fit a given research question.

Sampling variability/error. Sampling variability is the inherent variability (random) around the true population values (parameters) of a given statistical model that is produced when you draw a given sample from the population. It is the variability that would occur if repeated samples (of the same size) were taken from the population. On average, any given randomly drawn sample will provide estimates of the population parameters that are equal to the population, but there will be variability in this behavior from sample to sample. All things being equal: (1) the larger the sample, the lower the sampling variability; (2) the more homogeneous the population, the lower the sampling variability; (3) the greater the reliability of a measure, the lower the sampling variability.

Standard error. The standard deviation of the distribution for a given parameter estimate. The standard error is often theoretically calculated based on assumptions about the likely distribution of a given parameter estimate. The significance of a parameter estimate is often determined by dividing the observed estimate by the standard error. This statistic is called a Wald test and is distributed as a z-score (e.g., a z-score of 1.96 is the .05 p-level, and 2.58 is the .01 p-level). A bootstrap estimate is a way to estimate the standard error as an empirically derived value. The significance of a parameter can also be determined by comparing two nested models, one in which the parameter of interest is freely estimated and the second in which the parameter of interest is constrained to 0 (or to some other theoretically meaningful value). The significance of the difference in model fit determines the significance level of the tested parameter.

Statistical big three. The mean and the variance of each variable, as well as the (linear) associations among variables. These are the sufficient statistics that allow statistical inference about the population given the sample. The actual observations of the individuals are not necessary to draw inferences if one has the sufficient statistics. In SEM models with the mean structures, the statistical model contains parameter estimates that characterize each element of the statistical big three: variances, covariances, and means.

Tau-equivalent indicators. Indicators of a construct are tau equivalent when their loadings are all at about the same level (again, in the population) but can vary in terms of their intercepts.

Verisimilitude and veridicality. Both of these terms capture the essence of the truth-like value of findings and theories—that is, the degree to which something, such as a finding or a theory, is an accurate reflection of reality. All findings are probabilistic inferences, and all theories are false to some degree. Therefore, the best that we can hope for is a veridical finding that sheds light on the verisimilitude of a particular theory. *Truthiness* is another word floating around that is used to mean something like verisimilitude and veridicality.

RECOMMENDED READINGS

Books I Have Edited That Have Shaped My Worldview

Card, N. A., Selig, J. P., & Little, T. D. (Eds.). (2008). *Modeling dyadic and interdependent data in developmental research.* Mahwah, NJ: Erlbaum.

Laursen, B., Little, T. D., & Card, N. A. (Eds.). (2012). *Handbook of developmental research methods.* New York: Guilford Press.

Little, T. D. (Ed.). (2012). *The Oxford handbook of quantitative research methods.* New York: Oxford University Press.

Little, T. D., Bovaird, J. A., & Card, N. A. (Eds.). (2007). *Modeling contextual effects in longitudinal studies.* Mahwah, NJ: Erlbaum.

Little, T. D., Schnabel, K. U., & Baumert, J. (Eds.). (2000). *Modeling longitudinal and multilevel data: Practical issues, applied approaches, and specific examples.* Mahwah, NJ: Erlbaum.

> These edited volumes are key sources for many of the ideas that I cover throughout the entire book. If I have failed to properly cite the source for some idea that I present herein, it probably has come from one of these wonderful chapters and I "remember" it as my own. I apologize in advance if that is the case and prophylactically cite all the authors who contributed works to the preceding volumes.

General Issues with SEM and Theory Construction

Jaccard, J., & Jacoby, J. (2010). *Theory construction and model-building skills: A practical guide for social scientists.* New York: Guilford Press.

> As I emphasize, the tie between theory and model is inseparable. Jaccard and Jacoby offer seasoned and sage advice on the process of theory construction and how theory links to models—good models.

MacCallum, R., & Austin, J. (2000). Applications of structural equation modeling in psychological research. *Annual Review of Psychology, 51*(1), 201–226.

> These authors give a very readable overview of SEM and its applications in psychology and related social science fields.

On the Practice of Parceling and Selecting Indicators

Little, T. D., Lindenberger, U., & Nesselroade, J. R. (1999). On selecting indicators for multivariate measurement and modeling with latent variables: When "good" indicators
are bad and "bad" indicators are good. *Psychological Methods, 4*, 192–211.

> Although parcels aren't addressed directly in this simulation study, the study does
> provide some important guidelines for making appropriate selections of indicators
> for constructs. It also gives more on the geometry involved so that Figure 1.4 in this
> chapter might become more understandable.

Little, T. D., Cunningham, W. A., Shahar, G., & Widaman, K. F. (2002). To parcel or not
to parcel: Exploring the question, weighing the merits. *Structural Equation Modeling,
9*, 151–173.

Little, T. D., Rhemtulla, M., Gibson, K., & Schoemann, A. M. (in press). Why the items
versus parcels controversy needn't be one. *Psychological Methods*.

> I think we (Little et al., 2002) did a pretty good job of describing the issues (both
> pro and con). We clarified when and why using parcels isn't cheating and the con-
> ditions in which you can use them, as well as the conditions in which they should
> not be used. That being said, the debate continues; therefore, Little et al. (in press)
> provides counterarguments to the more recent criticisms, as well as giving detailed
> algebraic proofs of how parcels work.

2

Design Issues in Longitudinal Studies

This chapter focuses on important issues related to the foundations of longitudinal SEM (i.e., the tree trunk idea I outlined in Chapter 1)—namely, timing of measurements, conceptualizing time, and planned missingness (with a discussion of imputation). These topics are loosely design related, and a full appreciation of these issues likely requires some conceptual understanding of SEM, which I tried to provide in the previous chapter. The chapter order for the presentation of these issues is not a traditional one, and I could easily present them in a later chapter. I'm discussing them here, however, because I want novice SEM users to appreciate these ideas before the other topics are presented, and I make reference to them along the way. Given that these issues would and should be considered up front at the design phase of a study—well before a model is actually fit to data—discussing the ideas here seems logical to me. On the other hand, I could make this chapter the closing chapter because you would then have the context of the various models to use as a frame of reference and would be able to hang these ideas on the scaffold that has already been created. My recommendation is to read it now as Chapter 2 and read it again after going through the remaining chapters.

TIMING OF MEASUREMENTS AND CONCEPTUALIZING TIME

In the social and behavioral sciences, longitudinal studies usually index time as age in years or as the occasions of measurement, which quite often are the same (e.g., 10-year-olds measured at Time 1 are 11 a year later at Time 2 and 12 at Time 3, and so on). In this section, I discuss and highlight some alternative ways to consider time that will assist you in thinking about the design of a longitudinal study. If done with a bit of forethought, a properly designed longitudinal study will improve your ability to capture the change process that you desire to model. For a very rich but challenging discussion of the issues that I touch on here, you can try to find a copy of Wohlwill's (1973) classic book, *The Study of Behavioral Development*. More recent (and more approachable) discussions of the importance of mapping theory to methods and methods to theory have emerged (see, e.g., Collins, 2006; Lerner, Schwartz, & Phelps, 2009; Ram & Grimm, 2007).

Most developmentalists have been schooled that "behavior is a function of age": $B = f(\text{age})$. This way of thinking about developmental change processes is somewhat limited, however. First, age is not a causal variable and is really only a proxy of the multitude of effects that covary with age and experience (Wohlwill, 1973). Second, as Wohlwill notes with regard to age functions, "the particular form of this functional relationship is rarely taken seriously, let alone given explicit expression" (p. 49). In other words, a reliance on chronological age as the de facto index of change engenders a limited view of developmental change processes. A more flexible way to consider development is that "change is a function of time": $\Delta = f(\text{time})$. This alternative formulation encourages a broader consideration of the primary time dimension of a longitudinal model and moves away from the equal-interval age divisions that typically index developmental change (Lerner et al., 2009). Identifying and modeling change using the right time dimension will maximize the likelihood that a study will represent accurately the developmental/change processes of interest.

Before I get too far in this discussion, I need to briefly outline the five basic types of developmental designs that are commonly used. In Figure 2.1, I have laid out a table with a hypothetical set of age cohorts along the left edge (y axis) and potential times of measurement along the horizontal dimension (x axis). The implied ages that

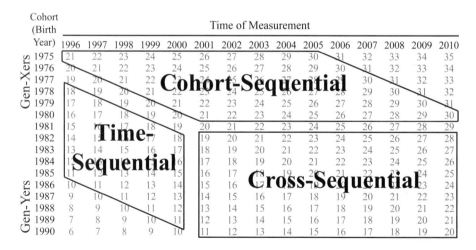

FIGURE 2.1. Traditional sequential designs. Ages are entered in gray in the body of the table. Any given row would be an example of a longitudinal design, and any given column would be an example of a cross-sectional study. A cohort-sequential design would consist of starting a new cohort at a certain age and then following longitudinally. A cross-sequential design starts with a traditional cross-sectional study and then follows all participants longitudinally. A time-sequential design is a repeated cross-sectional design, with some participants followed longitudinally.

would be assessed are in the body of the table grids. Each of the five designs can be found in this figure. In addition to the three sequential designs that are labeled in the body of the figure, the cross-sectional design and the single-cohort longitudinal design can be found. A single-cohort longitudinal study would be depicted by any given row of Figure 2.1, and a cross-sectional study would be depicted by any given column in the table.

Cross-Sectional Design

Of the five developmental designs, only the cross-sectional design does not include a repeated assessment as part of the data collection protocol. The cross-sectional design makes age comparisons by selecting different samples of persons from different age cohorts. The cross-sectional design is quite limited in its ability to describe developmental processes. It can hint at developmental differences, but this hinting is always confounded with age cohort differences and strongly influenced by between-group sampling variability. Cross-sectional designs are, therefore, most useful for yielding preliminary data to determine whether the measures used are appropriate for the age cohorts that would be studied in a longitudinal manner. The cross-sectional design is also useful to determine whether the internal validity relationships among the constructs are as expected and whether the age cohort differences are in the direction of the expected age differences. If the answer to these questions is generally yes, then pursuing a longitudinal component would be warranted. If any of the answers is no, then some more planning and measurement development would need to be done before a longitudinal study would be launched. In other words, cross-sectional studies are not much more than feasibility studies for longitudinal studies.

Cross-sectional designs are well suited to addressing measurement validity issues across different age cohorts. The factorial invariance of constructs across age cohorts can be assessed and validated before engaging in a longitudinal study. I discuss factorial invariance in detail in Chapter 5; but, briefly, factorial invariance is testing whether or not the indicators of a construct measure the construct in the same way, either across age cohorts in a cross-sectional study or across time in a longitudinal study. Assuming that factorial invariance is supported, then a number of characteristics of the constructs can be examined. Within each cohort, factorial invariance establishes the content validity of the constructs' respective indicators. When multiple constructs are measured, the concurrent criterion-related validities among the constructs can be examined. In terms of differences across the age cohorts, the differences in the mean levels of the constructs, the variances of the constructs, and the strength of the criterion associations among the constructs can each be examined. Because of the inherent confound of age, cohort, and time of measurement, however, any interpretation of the group differences as somehow reflecting age differences would not be valid.

Single-Cohort Longitudinal Design

The single-cohort longitudinal design (any given row of Figure 2.1) and the sequential designs depicted graphically in the body of Figure 2.1 each have a repeated-measures component. As such, they can be analyzed using a traditional panel model or the more dynamic growth curve model. The key difference between these two statistical models is how variability is modeled.

The traditional panel design focuses on slices of variability that are temporally static and focuses on the individual-differences relationships in a series of sequential "snapshots." In such a snapshot, various features among the constructs are examined: namely, the content validity of the indicators, concurrent criterion validity among the constructs measured at each time point, and predictive criterion validity relations among the constructs over the interval(s) specified. In addition, changes in construct means and variances can be tested across each successive measurement occasion. The growth curve models, on the other hand, focus on the more "fluid" variability over time, with particular focus on the variability in individual trends (interindividual differences in intraindividual change). The panel model is one in which a series of vertical slices are made in a flowing developmental process, whereas the growth curve model attempts to cut a slice horizontally across the time frame encompassed by a given study.

The single-cohort longitudinal study does allow you to examine change relationships. This design is limited because age is perfectly confounded with both age cohort and time of measurement. That is, in a single-cohort longitudinal study, any observed changes may be related to age, but they are also related to any time-of-measurement effects (i.e., events that co-occur with the measurement occasion). In addition, the observed effects may not generalize to other cohorts because of possible cohort effects related to the age sample that was originally chosen (e.g., baby boomers vs. Generation Xers). More concretely, let's say I selected a group of 18-year-olds to follow every year for 10 years. At the time of this writing (2012), my sample of 18-year-olds would all be from the 1994 age cohort. My population of generalization, then, is youths born in 1994. The youths born in 1994 have experienced a number of events that future 18-year-olds born today likely will not experience (e.g., the 9/11 terrorist attacks, Hurricane Katrina). Tragic events such as these are likely to influence a number of attitudes, beliefs, behaviors, and cognitions of a given sample of youths. In this regard, any "age" differences may be due more to the cohort from which the sample is drawn than to true age differences.

In addition to the age cohort confound, time of measurement confounds any age differences. If data were collected in 2008, for example, the sample of participants would have experienced major events that would have co-occurred with the measurement occasion: a major economic downturn and the ability to vote in a pretty historic presidential election. At this measurement occasion, the specter of limited job or educational opportunities would have likely had an influence on many youths in the sample. Similarly, the "hope of change" that was at the core of Barack Obama's 2008 presidential campaign would have inspired or influenced many of the sampled youths at the time. Any estimates of the constructs' means, variances, or correlations in the sample at this measurement occasion might be a reflection of being a certain age, they might be a reflection of the events co-occurring with this measurement occasion, or they might be a reflection of the past events that the cohort has experienced. To address these confounds, methodologists have thought about ways to study age changes that are not so inextricably confounded. The three so-called "sequential" designs each attempt to remedy some of this inherent confounding.

In Figure 2.1, I have superimposed outlines of an example of the three "sequential" designs over the ages listed in the figure. Each sequential design attempts to minimize the confounding among age, cohort, or time of measurement that is inherent in any longitudinal study. To minimize this confound, developmentalists such as K. Warner Schaie (Schaie & Hertzog, 1982) and Paul Baltes (1968) discussed alternative sequencing designs that would allow one to disentangle some of these confounded effects. From these discussions, three primary designs emerged: the cross-sequential, the cohort-sequential, and the time-sequential.

Cross-Sequential Design

The cross-sequential design starts with a cross-sectional design and then follows all the participants over time. Many people confuse this design with the *cohort*-sequential design. It is *cross*-sequential because it starts with a cross-sectional design and then adds a longitudinal sequence to each cohort of the original cross-sectional sampling. In the cross-sequential design, cohort and time of measurement are the two time dimensions that are "manipulated" and controlled by the experimenter. The cross-sequential design is perhaps the most popular longitudinal design used today, even though it is the least powerful design to use if one aims to examine a developmental function as a reflection of age. The reason for this weakness is the fact that any age differences are confounded with the interaction between cohort and time of measurement. Specifically, age differences at a younger versus older age are confounded because older cohorts (e.g., the Generation Xers or Gen Xers) would provide "age" estimates that occurred before influential time-of-measurement effects, whereas younger cohorts (e.g., the Generation Yers or Gen Yers) would provide these estimates after the time-of-measurement effects. More concretely, youths assessed at the same age but who are from two different cohorts would have confounded estimates of true age differences. For example, the older cohort, Gen Xers, would have been measured pre-9/11, and the younger cohort, Gen Yers, would be measured post-9/11. On the other hand, this design is very well suited to examining change processes over time, controlling for potential differences in cohorts.

Cohort-Sequential Design

The cohort-sequential design is like starting a longitudinal study at the same age over and over again. That is, each year, a new sample of participants of a certain age are selected and enrolled in a longitudinal study. Here, each new "cohort" is enrolled in a longitudinal sequence that covers the same age span. This design is particularly well suited to identifying age differences while controlling for cohort differences. An important limitation of the cohort-sequential design, however, is the assumption that time-of-measurement effects are trivial, because any time-of-measurement effects are confounded with the interaction of age and cohort. Potentially powerful time-of-measurement effects such as 9/11 can have influences across all cohorts, yet the effects would show up as a cohort-by-age interaction with this design. The problem here is that the analysis cannot disentangle whether the effect was a time-of-measurement effect or a true age-by-cohort interaction. In other words, pre- versus post-9/11 effects would be confounded with Gen Xers measured at older ages versus Gen Yers measured at younger ages.

Time-Sequential Design

The time-sequential design is probably the least used of the sequential designs, but it is particularly useful for identifying time-of-measurement effects and age effects. The age range is kept the same and repeatedly assessed (with only some participants being repeatedly measured). With this design, the age window is critical, and repeated testing of new and continuing cohorts at different times of measurement would identify the age-related changes that are not confounded with time-of-measurement differences. That is, time-of-measurement effects can be estimated and thereby controlled when looking at age differences. In this design, the cohort effects are the fully confounded factor. That is, any cohort effect would appear as an age-by-time interaction, which would not allow one to conclude whether the effect was a cohort effect or a true age-by-time interaction. Here, an effect of Gen Xers versus Gen Yers would be confounded with younger participants measured pre-9/11 versus older participants measured post-9/11.

As to which design to use, the questions to ask relate to what type of change function is important to examine: Which one of the three constituents (age, cohort, time of measurement) of a longitudinal design will be critically important in understanding the change phenomenon to be studied? Has other work identified which of these factors is likely to be trivial? In such situations, the choice of design becomes straightforward. If, on the other hand, you can't say which factor is worth "ignoring," then you can consider some alternatives. Some hybrid designs have also been introduced that attempt to remove the confounding among all three of the age, cohort, and time-of-measurement effects. Schaie and Hertzog (1982), for example, offered an "optimal" design that involves different random sampling schemes that effectively use aspects of both cohort-sequential and time-sequential designs to disentangle age effects, as well as cohort versus time-of-measurement differences. Similarly, the accelerated longitudinal design (discussed later in the chapter) can be used to estimate age effects controlling for some cohort and time-of-measurement effects.

Cohort and time-of-measurement effects are not always confounds that must be controlled by the nature of the design. Another way to think of these effects is as potential context effects that are measurable. If you include measures of these effects or measures that adequately gauge how a person responds to particular events, then you can either control for them statistically or use them to predict the amount of variance that is due to the cohort or time-of-measurement effects.

A key point of the preceding discussion is that you need to consider the overall longitudinal design that is most appropriate for the change process being modeled. As I continue to emphasize throughout this book, strong theory will guide your thinking through most of these design/statistical conundrums.

Other Validity Concerns

In addition to the cohort and time-of-measurement effects that I just described, a number of other potential validity threats are found in longitudinal studies (see Campbell, Stanley, & Gage, 1963; Schaie & Hertzog, 1982). The "classic" threats include regression to the mean, retest effects, selection effects, selective attrition, and instrumentation effects (e.g., factorial noninvariance).

Regression toward the mean is the tendency for extreme scores to move closer to the mean of the distribution at subsequent measurements. Regression to the mean is purely a phenomenon of unreliability in repeated-measures situations. The random variation is the reason that extreme scores at the first time point will tend toward the mean at the second time point. Because regression to the mean is only a function of unreliability, it is easily remedied by the use of latent-variable SEM. When multiple indicators of constructs are used, the variance of the construct is thereby measured without error. The random variation that is responsible for regression to the mean is removed from the measurement process by virtue of the multiple indicators. The effect of regression to the mean appears only in the manifest variables, which contain the measurement error, and not the latent variables, which are composed of 100% reliable variance.

In contrast to regression effects, retest effects are more nefarious and difficult to remedy. Retest effects occur when a measure is sensitive to repeated exposure, whether it is practice that leads to improved performance or reactivity that leads to changes in responses due to the act of being assessed. Most measures are sensitive to repeated exposures, but the impact may vary depending on the measure. Some measures will increase in mean levels, whereas some will decrease as a function of repeated exposure to the instrument. Repeated exposure can also have a homogenizing effect in that the extremes of a scale may be responded to less and less over time, thereby shrinking the variance of the variable over time. One of the best ways to estimate and correct for retest effects is to randomly assign participants to receive or not receive a given measurement occasion. Such designs can be treated as intentionally missing data designs (see upcoming section).

Selection effects are fundamental to any study in which a sampling plan fails to provide a representative sample of the population to which one wishes to generalize. Avoiding the lure of convenience samples and pseudo-random selection will go a long way toward increasing the quality of behavioral and social science research in general and longitudinal studies in particular. A related problem of longitudinal studies is selective attrition. Selective attrition occurs when dropout from a study (attrition) is not a random process but is related to some characteristic(s) of the sample. As you'll see shortly, selective attrition is relatively easy to address using modern missing data estimation procedures if one plans ahead and measures known predictors of dropout. Note that oversampling selected groups is not the same as selective sampling. Oversampling can be converted to representative analyses by using population weights to adjust parameter estimates accordingly.

Instrumentation effects can influence longitudinal studies in a couple of ways. First, the measurement properties of the phenomenon of interest can change over time. When the measurement properties of an instrument change with age, then the measurement properties of the construct are not factorially invariant, and conclusions about changes in the constructs would not be valid. Fortunately, this type of instrumentation effect is a testable issue (for more details, see Chapters 5 and 6).

Second, instrumentation effects can influence conclusions from a longitudinal study when the measurement tool is not sensitive to change. Most measures developed in the social and behavioral sciences have been developed with so much focus on reliability that they are no longer sensitive to change. Because test–retest correlations have been maximized, for example, such measures no longer contain the items or the item content that might have been sensitive to change. In fact, the test–retest model for reliability has likely resulted in long-term damage to the work of researchers who desire instruments that are reliably sensitive to change. The test–retest correlations capture only stability information, and the effort to maximize this stability in the development phase of a measure undermines the usefulness of the measure for identifying and modeling change processes. Developmentalists should consider this problematic aspect of measures when designing a study and selecting measures. I would encourage all developmental researchers to modify, adapt, or develop measures so that they are sensitive to change. We also need further work in the area of change measurement. Research on measurement can take advantage of advances in computerized testing. For example, one useful way to measure change (perhaps) would be a measure that populates itself with the responses from the first measurement occasion and then asks the respondent to indicate how much his or her current response (e.g., attitude, belief, mood, cognition, etc.) has changed from the prior occasion of measurement.

Related to this instrumentation issue is the heterotypic versus homotypic expression of an underlying construct with age. An example of a homotypic expression would be happiness. The facial expressions of the emotion of happiness stay pretty much the same throughout the lifespan. The facial indicators of a happy expression (i.e., the various changes to the mouth, eyes, forehead) remain consistent indicators of the happy expression across all ages (i.e., the indicators are factorially invariant). An example of a heterotypic expression is aggression, particularly as it changes from toddlerhood to adolescence. Screaming and grabbing give way to name calling and punching. During early childhood, aggression is expressed with the cognitive and physical tools available to toddlers. During adolescence, aggression is expressed with the more advanced cognitive and physical tools of the adolescent. A measure of aggression that has items assessing toy taking, screaming, and kicking would probably work quite well for assessing the frequency of aggressive behavior in toddlers but would not capture the aggressive means of adolescents.

If a study contains constructs that are heterotypic or uses "age appropriate" measures for different phases of the study, then careful consideration must be given to how the construct is measured over time. When a measurement tool must change during the course of a study, the scores across the different measures must be comparable in order to talk about the same construct changing over time. With age-appropriate measures, for example, too often the younger age-appropriate measure is swapped out completely for the one that is now appropriate for the older ages. When this kind of wholesale change takes place, all ability to map or model the changes in the construct over time are lost. There is no way to know how a score on the old measure relates to a score on the new measure. This problem can be remedied by transitioning between measures. If at least one measurement occasion exists where both the old instrument and the new instrument are given to the same group of individuals, the degree to which they measure the same thing can be tested and the measures can be calibrated. That is, how do the scores on the two instruments relate to one another? With longitudinal SEM, this process of calibration is relatively straightforward.

Figure 2.2 shows a couple of ways in which measures across time can be calibrated and linked if there is at least one occasion of measurement at which both measures are administered. In Panel A of Figure 2.2, the indicators of the two different measures load on the same construct at the overlapping time point (Time 2 in this hypothetical example). The loadings and intercepts of the indicators for Measure A are specified to be factorially invariant over time (see Chapter 5 for details on factorial invariance). The loadings and intercepts of the indicators for Measure B are also factorially invariant. If this model fits the data, then the scores on the two measures have the same latent construct meaning (i.e., the factors' scores have the same meaning), and changes in the construct over time would be accurate and comparable over time. In Panel B of Figure 2.2, I have shown a variation of this type of model but have allowed for a "bias" factor. Assuming that Measure A has some systematic

A) Establishing comparability of different measures of the same construct over time: No bias

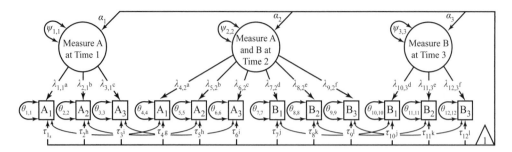

B) Establishing comparability of different measures of the same construct over time: Bias corrected

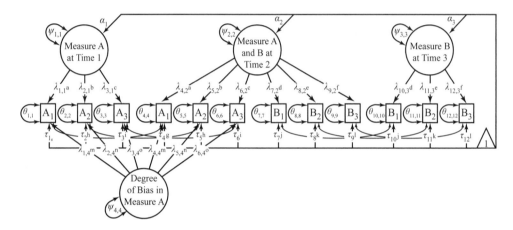

FIGURE 2.2. Two models for establishing comparability of different measures of the same construct over time, with and without a "bias correction" factor. The corresponding loadings and intercepts that are equated across time are designated by a superscripted letter (a–o). The residual variances among the corresponding indicators are allowed to associate over time.

bias to it (e.g., parent reports are used for Measure A while classroom observations are used for Measure B), the bias construct corrects the scores on the construct for differences due to the systematic bias. The model in Panel B makes the presumption that one measure is biased while the other is not. A model with a bias factor for both measures would not be identified unless some limiting constraints are placed on the model parameters.

Even if you took a random subsample of participants to give both measures to, this subsample could provide the linking functions between the two instruments that could be applied to the whole sample. For that matter, you could derive the linking functions on an independent sample and apply them to the longitudinal study. Of course, this latter approach makes a number of assumptions about the comparability of the two samples that may not be tenable and would require using a tricky multiple-group model to provide the linking functions (I'm getting off track here . . .).

Temporal Design

Temporal design refers to the timing of the measures that you want to employ. It is an overlooked aspect of longitudinal research design, even though Gollob and Reichardt (1987) outlined three basic principles of temporal design nearly two decades ago. First, they stated that causes take time to exert their effects. We can modify this statement to assert that effects of change take time to unfold. Whichever way you want to assert it (i.e., as causal effects or change effects), we need some appropriate quantity of time between measurements to see it. The second principle is that the ability to detect effects (either causal or change) depends on the time interval between measurements. With the rare exception of an on–off mechanism of change, this principle is a pretty accurate reflection of most developmental change processes. Some effects are cumulative and reach an eventual asymptote, which may or may not reset. Other effects rapidly reach a peak and diminish quickly or slowly over time. Figure 2.3 depicts a number of potential patterns of unfolding (causal or change) effects. Each pattern varies in the strength of its expression over time. I think it is helpful to consider the pattern of change that you might expect when you design your study so you can adequately capture the change process.

The implications of these two principles of temporal design are twofold. The

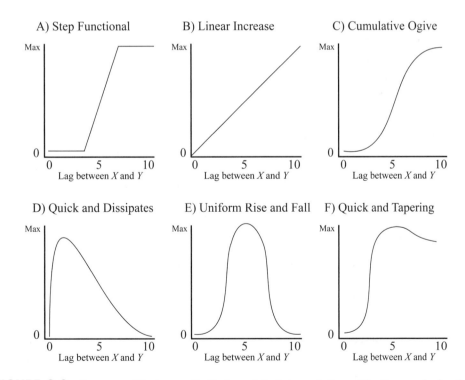

FIGURE 2.3. Some possible types of effects and their lag relations. The time scale for the lag between X and Y can be on any scale, from milliseconds to years. The size of the effect can also vary from small to medium to large.

first implication, which Gollob and Reichardt (1987) stated as a third principle, is that because different lags would show different magnitudes of effects, to understand the effect, assessments must occur at different lags. Measuring multiple lags would allow you to model the temporal unfolding of the effect of interest. The second implication, which can also be stated as a principle, is that because effects have an optimal temporal lag (when the effect is at maximum influence), we should design studies to measure at intervals that correspond to this optimal lag. When an optimal design approach is considered, however, it assumes that the shape of the effect is the same for all individuals, which can be a tenuous assumption. This problem is an instance of the ergodicity assumption (Molenaar, 2004). This assumption means that effects or patterns of change in a group of individuals would generalize to each individual. For many change processes, such an assumption may not be reasonable.

If the focus of the study is on the effect itself, Gollob and Reichardt's (1987) third principle dictates that a study must measure multiple lags in order to model the unfolding of the effect. On the other hand, if you are interested in the system-of-change effects that lead to some outcome, you'd want to measure at intervals that capture the optimal lag of the effects of interest. If you measure one variable at its optimal lag and another variable at a suboptimal lag, the optimally measured variable will likely appear to be a more important change predictor than the suboptimally measured variable. This problem is similar to the unreliability problem in that a variable that is measured less reliably than another variable will often not appear to have as important an effect as the more reliably measured variable. Latent-variable modeling overcomes this problem of unreliability by correcting for it when we use multiple indicators of a construct. For the optimal effect problem, a poorly timed measurement interval is more difficult to "correct for." A measurement strategy that varies lag would allow calculating the functional form of the effect over a span of occasions to identify the point of maximum effect.

In addition to ensuring the correct temporal ordering of variables, the timing of measurements has to be as fast as or faster than the change process that you want to capture. That is, the amount of time between measurement occasions needs to be short enough to keep pace with the underlying process that is changing (see Chapter 1, the section titled "What Changes and How?"). Too often, occasions of measurement are determined by the convenience of the calendar (e.g., yearly intervals in the spring or biyearly in the fall and spring). If one is studying the change and development of relatively stable or trait-like constructs such as personality or intelligence, then yearly intervals of measurement are probably sufficient. If malleable constructs such as mood or self-esteem are the focus of study, the intervals of measurement must be closer together. Unfortunately, even a casual inspection of the literature indicates that the most common intervals for longitudinal studies are 1 year or longer. Such intervals can detect only slow-change trends and provide little information on the true processes that underlie the observed changes.

Lags within the Interval of Measurement

Often, a study will be executed such that a measurement occasion spans some specified period of time. For example, in a fall assessment of school-age youths, I might start collecting data in late September and finish by the end of October. Here, the occasion of measurement is actually a 6-week span. In a school-based study, this 6-week difference, from the beginning to the end of the assessment occasion, can have an impact on the measures that are collected. The potential influences include the fact that students at the end of the window will have had 6 more weeks of social interactions and educational instruction and, generally, will have undergone more developmental change. In addition, spillover becomes more likely as students are assessed in the later parts of the window. These students likely hear about the kinds of questions that are being asked and may begin to form ideas of what the study is about (for a detailed discussion of data collection lag effects in longitudinal studies, see Selig, Preacher, & Little, 2012). Any of these factors could influence the strength of an observed effect.

Usually, if we think about this "window" at all, we think it won't have much of an impact. I have been guilty of this thinking in my own *past* work. For the "stable" constructs in my protocol, these short-term processes probably have not had much of an impact. But for the more malleable constructs (e.g., affect, esteem), these processes may have had an influence. In my older datasets, I won't know whether they did, because I did not code for the date of administration of a given protocol. Had I known then what I know now, I would have coded when a student received the protocol, and I could have created an index of time that reflects the protocol administration time. This variable could easily be included as a covariate or moderator in the models that I discuss in later chapters (see Selig, Preacher, & Little, 2012, for details of using lag as a moderator variable).

The more I work with researchers and study developmental changes, the more I realize how critical it is to get the timing of the measurements right. For the most part, measurements in developmental studies are selected too often on the basis of convenience than on the basis of a clear theoretical rationale. The power of an appropriately designed longitudinal study is simply underutilized in practice. It's kind of a sad state of affairs. I hope to see lots more future research that really focuses on the timing of measurements.

Episodic and Experiential Time

Aside from the traditional ways of conceptualizing time and this overlooked issue of the time lag within measurement occasions, time can be indexed to model change in a couple of other ways: episodic time and experiential time. In both of these ways of representing change as a function of time, the actual chronological age of the participants can still be included in these models as either covariates, moderators, or predictors.

Episodic time refers to the length of time during which a person experiences a particular state or context. Time before the episode and time after the episode reflect different potential change processes. Here, the index of time that we want to model is not necessarily the chronological age of the participant but where the participant is in relation to the key developmental episode that we are interested in capturing. Puberty is a classic example of a normative event that has distinct developmental repercussions regarding its timing and the change processes that occur prior to and after the pubertal event. The idea here is to organize your data so that you remap the occasions of measurement now to correspond with the "time" prior to the event and the "time" after the event. Table 2.1 provides a schematic representation of how to reorganize a longitudinal design into an episodic time design. Wohlwill (1973) provides an example of such a design using the maximum velocity of growth as the centering "event" and then modeling the growth function as time before and time after maximum velocity. The idea here is to "group individual functions into families in terms of some parameter of the developmental function such as rate or asymptotic level, in order to arrive at meaningful relationships to other situational or behavioral variables" (p. 142). Such a reorganization of the data allows one to examine nomothetic features of the change process separately from chronological age. As mentioned, chronological age and/or cohort can still be included in such

TABLE 2.1. Transforming a longitudinal design into episodic time

	Data collection wave crossed with episode occurrence					
Pattern	Wave 1	Wave 2	Wave 3	Wave 4	Wave 5	Wave 6
Pattern 1	P	P + 1	P + 2	P + 3	P + 4	P + 5
Pattern 2	P - 1	P	P + 1	P + 2	P + 3	P + 4
Pattern 3	P - 2	P - 1	P	P + 1	P + 2	P + 3
Pattern 4	P - 3	P - 2	P - 1	P	P + 1	P + 2
Pattern 5	P - 4	P - 3	P - 2	P - 1	P	P + 1
Pattern 6	P - 5	P - 4	P - 3	P - 2	P - 1	P

	Episodic occurrence crossed with data collection wave										
	P - 5	P - 4	P - 3	P - 2	P - 1	P	P + 1	P + 2	P + 3	P + 4	P + 5
Pattern 1						W1	W2	W3	W4	W5	W6
Pattern 2					W1	W2	W3	W4	W5	W6	
Pattern 3				W1	W2	W3	W4	W5	W6		
Pattern 4			W1	W2	W3	W4	W5	W6			
Pattern 5		W1	W2	W3	W4	W5	W6				
Pattern 6	W1	W2	W3	W4	W5	W6					

Note. Multiple cohorts could also be transformed in such a manner. A dummy code to represent age cohort would be included within each pattern to account for potential cohort differences. The missing data are treated as missing at random and imputed.

models to examine its impact on the growth functions that are modeled around the episodic centering point.

In Table 2.1, I have created a hypothetical longitudinal study of a group of adolescents and used puberty as the event. The table shows different patterns or subgroups of adolescents based on the point during the study at which they experienced the onset of puberty. If I were conducting a cohort-sequential or a cross-sequential study, I would identify the patterns in each age cohort and assign them to the new index of time, centered on the pubertal event. Even if I had censored data (i.e., kids who were past puberty prior to the study or kids who did not reach puberty during the course of the study), I can still reorganize the data according to the scheme depicted in Table 2.1. In this case I would add a P − 6 and a P + 6 time point to the episodic time sequence in the bottom half of Table 2.1. I would then identify the Pattern 0 and Pattern 7 youths who either already had reached puberty (Pattern 0) sometime before the start of the study or did not reach it (Pattern 7) during the course of the study. The impact of censoring on the trends when including the P − 6 and P + 6 groups can be accommodated by including a dummy-coded variable for each of these latter two patterns (Pattern 0 and Pattern 7) and estimating their effects as covariates on the parameters of the episodic time model. Similarly, if I used a cohort-sequential or a cross-sequential design and transformed it into an episodic time sequence, I could include dummy codes for cohort and chronological age as covariates in the estimated models.

By way of another example, let's say I have measured a group of 15-year-olds at 12 measurement occasions separated by 1 month. The research question is how the members in this group of youths change in their social relationships prior to their 16th birthdays versus how they change after their 16th birthdays. At the first measurement occasion, approximately 1/12 of the sample experiences his or her 16th birthday. For this subgroup, the first measurement occasion corresponds to the window in which the birthday event has occurred, and each subsequent measurement corresponds to an occasion of measurement after the event. For another 1/12 of the sample, the birthday event does not occur until the 12th measurement occasion. For this subgroup, all the measurement occasions fall prior to the event. If I added a time-sequential design or cohort-sequential design on top of these monthly measurements, I could also disentangle potential time-of-measurement effects or cohort effects.

A related index of time is experiential time. Grade in school is a classic example of this index of time. With this type of index of time, age within grade level can also be included to examine differences that may be related to being younger versus older within a given grade level. Another example of experiential time might be the length of time in an intimate relationship. Although episodic time and experiential time are related, the primary difference is the focus. Experiential time is focused on how long participants have experienced a state or process and would use chronological age as a covariate or moderator of the change relationships being modeled. Episodic time, on the other hand, focuses on an event or episode as a potential turning point in a larger developmental process. As with experiential time, chronological age can be included and used as a covariate or moderator of the modeled change process.

MISSING DATA IMPUTATION AND PLANNED MISSING DESIGNS

The prior discussion of time lags and restructuring data is essentially describing a missing data design. Table 2.1, for example, shows how transforming to episodic time introduces missing data cells (e.g., Pattern 1 has the first five measurements missing, and Pattern 6 has the last five measurements missing). Modern missing data approaches easily handle and address both planned and unplanned missing data. To illustrate the usefulness of planned missing data designs, however, I need to first discuss missing data imputation in the context of unplanned missing data.

Modern approaches to handling missing data are not cheating, nor is there a dubious quality to the procedures. Modern approaches to imputation include the full-information maximum likelihood (FIML) estimation method and the multiply imputed, data-based expectation maximization (EM) and Markov Chain Monte Carlo (MCMC) algorithms (see Enders, 2010, for a detailed and really clear explication of these algorithms). These approaches are applied in two different ways. The first way is what I refer to as a model-based approach. With a model-based approach the parameters of a statistical model are estimated in the presence of missing data, and all information is used to inform the parameters' values and standard errors (FIML). The second way to address missing data is to use a data-based approach. With a data-based approach, missing data points are filled in multiple times and then used to allow unbiased estimation of the parameters and standard errors of a statistical model. As long as the model-based or data-based approach uses one of the modern algorithms, the results will be essentially identical, and the parameter estimates will be as accurate as possible, given that you have missing data in the first place.

Any of these modern missing data approaches are acceptable (I'll talk more on this later; you can get a full account of all the approaches and their pros and cons in Enders, 2010). These modern approaches to handling missing data entered the scene in the late 1970s and emerged in a more widespread manner in the late 1990s, particularly when computing power made using the techniques feasible. In some disciplines, the modern approaches have become standard practice, whereas in many other disciplines they are still viewed with unfounded skepticism. In fact, in the I hope not too distant future, I can see myself saying in front of a class of my students, "Believe it or not, but up to about 2010, scientists across the social, behavioral, developmental, and educational sciences thought that modern missing data imputation was like cheating and a very dubious procedure?!" . . . (classroom erupts in laughter). As a reviewer, I've even had authors object to my recommendation to impute missing data on "moral" grounds. My reply was that if science is about accuracy of generalization (and if we treat science as a religion), the morally unconscionable position is to *not* impute. This skepticism stems from a lack of understanding of the mechanisms of missing data and how modern approaches work. This skepticism also impedes researchers' willingness to use planned missing designs. To help ease you into the whole idea of embracing missing data as a design element, I first need to discuss the three mechanisms that give rise to missingness.

Missing Data Mechanisms

Missing data can arise from three basic mechanisms: a truly random process, a measured/predictable process, and an unmeasured/unpredictable (but not random) process. In the missing data literature, these three processes or mechanisms are respectively labeled *missing completely at random* (MCAR), *missing at random* (MAR, which is one of the biggest misnomers of a statistical concept out there), and *missing not at random* (MNAR, which is another notable misnomer). I, like most methodologists, use these acronyms to discuss the mechanisms that give rise to missing data, so you'll probably want to commit these to memory. Figure 2.4 provides a graphical

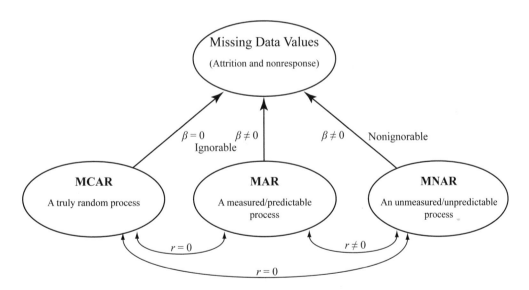

FIGURE 2.4. The three missing data mechanisms and their association with the missing values. A graphical representation of the three missing data mechanisms. MCAR = missing completely at random (i.e., due to a truly random process); MAR = missing at random (i.e., due to a measured process); and MNAR = missing not at random (i.e., due to an unmeasured process). An MCAR process, by definition, is uncorrelated with MAR and MNAR. MAR and MNAR, on the other hand, can have a nonzero overlap. All three mechanisms will typically be involved in producing missing data. MAR is a predictable and therefore recoverable process; MNAR is not, because the process is not measured.

representation of these missing data mechanisms and their associations with the missing data information.

In longitudinal research, missing data are often classified as related to attrition or to nonresponse. These classifications are not the mechanisms that give rise to missingness; they are more descriptive of where the data are missing than of why the data are missing. Attrition refers to data that are missing for a whole case at one or more subsequent times of measurement. For example, participants who move away and cannot be contacted would have missing data due to attrition. The data would be classified as missing due to attrition if a person simply refuses to participate in subsequent follow-up measurements. On the other hand, missing data due to nonresponse are typically described as the within-occasions missing data. In this situation, missing data stem from only a part of the protocol not being completed. In cross-sectional studies, missing data are classified only as reflecting nonresponse. In my view, missing data due to attrition are more likely related to the MAR process, whereas nonresponse is more likely related to the MCAR process. Whether my hunch about the underlying process or mechanism is correct or not, both of these two classifications for missing data are easily handled by modern missing data procedures.

As mentioned, modern missing data imputation techniques fall into two categories: model-based approaches and data-based approaches. The model-based FIML approach is applied one time, whereas the data-based EM or MCMC method is applied a number of times (multiple imputation, MI), depending on how much information is missing. MI involves running your analysis on multiple versions or replicates of the imputation approach. Because the amount of missing data in longitudinal research is usually on the large side, a large number of multiple imputations will often be required (e.g., 100). The number of multiples that are needed will depend on the percentage of the data that is missing and, more accurately, on the "fraction" of the information that is recoverable. Generally speaking, the greater the correlations among the variables, the better the fraction missing will be (I discuss the idea of fraction missing in more detail later). Either of the modern approaches attempt to correct for the bias that occurs from data that are selectively missing (the classical approaches do not attempt to correct for bias), and the modern approaches gain back much of the loss in power that occurs when data are missing, regardless of the mechanism (the classical approaches do not attempt to regain power). In fact, the classical approaches (listwise or pairwise deletion) are akin to surgery to remove the injured parts of the data. The modern approaches are akin to reconstructive surgery to restore the affected area to its original condition. Importantly, modern imputation is not plastic surgery to change or disguise the look of something—it is a restorative and reconstructive procedure.

If you have high amounts of missing data and a poor fraction of recoverability, you may need to do 100 imputations and run your analysis 100 times, summarizing the results across the 100 replicates. At a minimum you'll probably do this 20 times if you have modest amounts of missing data. Not too long ago the minimum number of multiple imputations was 5; now it is 20—much like Thursday is the new Friday, 20 is the new 5. If you have really small amounts of missing data (around 5% or less), you *may* be OK with imputing just one time. With modern computers and advances in software, the ability to run an analysis 100 times and summarize the results is a relatively easy process. Later, in Chapter 8, I'll provide an example of an analysis that uses multiple imputation and summarizes the results across 100 imputed datasets.

Model-based approaches started out with multiple-group estimation and later developed into FIML estimation. Both of these approaches have been instrumental in helping skeptical scholars get comfortable with the idea that we can "use all the data available" and that we don't need to analyze complete cases only (listwise deletion) or resort to pairwise deletion.

In most studies, all three mechanisms of missing data will be involved, even though we can't verify the degree to which any one of the mechanisms is actually involved. For the data points that are MCAR (missing truly at random), the missing data imputation procedures easily provide accurate estimates that recover the missing data with no bias (and increased power). Unfortunately, MCAR is probably the least common of the missing data mechanisms, particularly for longitudinal data. For the data points that are MAR (missing for a potentially knowable and therefore predictable reason), the missing data imputation procedures often do a very good job. The degree to which modern approaches are able to recover the missing data process depends on (1) whether correlates of the missing data mechanism are measured and included on your dataset and (2) the strength of the relationship of this known process and the missing data. In longitudinal research, for example, attrition is associated with such variables as SES, gender, and parental involvement. If these variables are measured on the dataset and are used in the imputation process, some degree of the missing data process related to these variables will be recovered.

The phrase "recover the missing data process" is a nonstandard way of thinking about how imputation works, but I think it is helpful. I mean, more precisely, that the estimates of your model will more closely resemble the estimates you would have gotten had there not been any missing data. When your estimates are close to the "true" values, a greater amount of recovery of the missing data process has occurred, and your model estimates are less biased than they would be if you did not attempt to recover the information loss.

The amount of the recovered information depends on the strength of the associations that variables in your dataset (such as SES, gender, and parental involvement) have with the missing data mechanism. If the fraction missing is small (e.g., a multiple R^2 predicting missingness of .10), then a small amount of the missingness is being systematically recovered, but the imputed data still resemble the population more so than do the unimputed data. In this case, the recovery process is not perfect, but it is always in the direction of better generalizations. If we assume that the data are missing because of a combination of MCAR and MAR processes, and if we take care to measure known predictors of missingness, the quality of generalizations from a study will be superior to any of the classical approaches to handling missing data. As mentioned, fraction missing is the proportion of the information that is missing due to these missing data mechanisms. It ranges from 0 to 1, where 0 = no missing information to 1 = all information missing (i.e., lower values are better). It is often calculated based on between-imputation variability, but recently Savalei and Rhemtulla (2012) show how to calculate fraction missing using FIML. They also have a nice section on interpreting the fraction of information missing in terms of confidence interval width inflation, effective N, and the like.

For the data points that are MNAR (missing for an unknown reason that is not random), the missing data imputation procedures may or may not recover any of the missing data mechanism. Here, the key to any potential recovery is what the unknown reason is and whether the dataset contains proxies or distal covariates of the unknown reasons. For example, if SES is the process leading to missing data and I do not have a measure of SES on my dataset, the missing data process would be classified as MNAR—the missingness is occurring for a reason, but unfortunately, I don't have a measure of it. I might have other variables on my dataset that are correlated with SES, such as being in a single-parent household and receiving free or reduced-cost lunch. If I have measured these latter two variables on my dataset, they would predict missingness to some degree because they are correlated with SES—the true reason for missingness. In this case, even the MNAR missing data mechanism is partly recoverable.

Table 2.2 provides an overview of the missing data mechanisms and the potential recoverability and bias of the missing data process compared with the classical approaches (e.g., listwise or pairwise deletion). In the table, I make the distinction between analyzed and unanalyzed variables. If you recall, FIML estimation is a model-based method of recovering the information lost from the missing data

TABLE 2.2. Types of missing data mechanisms and their potential recoverability/bias using modern methods compared to the classical approaches to handling missing data

	No association with any observed variable(s)	An association with analyzed variables	An association with variable(s) in dataset
No association with unobserved/unmeasured variables	MCAR • Fully recoverable • Unbiased	MAR • Mostly recoverable • Unbiased	MAR • Mostly recoverable • Unbiased
An association with unobserved/unmeasured variables	MNAR • Not recoverable • As biased as not imputing	MNAR + MAR • Partly recoverable • Less biased than not imputing	MNAR + MAR • Partly recoverable • Less biased than not imputing

Note. "Recoverable" refers to recovering the missing data processes, and "bias" refers to the accuracy of conclusions relative to analyzing complete case data only. In all instances, power will be maximized by estimating missing data. The "association" here refers to the reliable relation between the measured or unmeasured variables and the missing data process. In most cases, this association is assumed to be linear. The distinction between analyzed and unanalyzed variables refers to the variables selected for a given analysis versus the variables on the dataset that are not selected for a given analysis.

processes. It relies on the assumption that the data are a combination of MCAR and MAR and that the variables associated with the MAR process are included in the model being estimated. If the variables associated with MAR are not included in the model, the information that they could have conveyed about the missing data is not available, and the FIML estimation would inappropriately treat all the missing data as if they were MCAR (truly random) when some of them are, in fact, MAR (missing for a knowable reason but it is not included in the model).

In this unfortunate situation of misanalyzing missing data, the resulting model estimates would not be corrected for the missing data process, and the generalizations would be weakened. Now, through using FIML estimation, you can (and should) include the variables that you think are associated with missingness at least as auxiliary variables in order to inform the estimation of the key (focal) parameters of the model. Some drawbacks to this approach, in my view, are (1) the extra estimation demands that are incurred by increasing the number of variables and parameters to be estimated and (2) the fact that model fit information is not based on the variables that are the focus of the analysis but instead includes the additional auxiliary variables (although some ways of including auxiliary variables have no impact on fit).

When using auxiliary variables and FIML estimation, one needs to be selective of the variables that are included in order to minimize these potential problems. Given that longitudinal models are already inherently large, adding auxiliary variables can get cumbersome when you try to work with them (and if they also contain missing values, the number of missing value patterns will be too large for the system to converge). In short, using this model-based approach with auxiliary variables, particularly with longitudinal data, is not one that I would normally prefer over MI.

On the other hand, if I use a data-based approach (e.g., using NORM, Amelia II, mice, or Proc MI) and if I include all available variables on my dataset in the imputation process, my imputed data would have as much of the missing data mechanism represented as possible (under the standard assumption that the relations are linear). Then, when I select a subset of variables to include in a model, the missing data process would still be recovered and represented in the data that I am analyzing; this recovered information in the data would maximize the generalizability of my analyses (given the variables that I have included in my protocol). In addition, theoretically meaningful nonlinear predictors of missingness are easily included with a data-based approach. For example, if missingness is nonlinearly related to SES—such as an accelerating rate of missingness as SES decreases—I can include a variable to capture that missingness (e.g., the powered polynomial of SES—SES^2).

Recommendations and Caveats

In my own work, I have found other advantages of data-based approaches to imputation. For example, I can impute at different levels of analysis, such as imputing item-level missingness, and then create parcels of the items to be used as indicators in my SEM model. In addition, with large datasets, imputing all the items simultaneously can be very difficult if the patterns of missing data vary from one another. Often the modern approaches will not converge if there are too many missing data patterns (model-based FIML approaches in particular). I have recommended a couple of approaches that can handle the imputation problems associated with very large datasets, but they rely on a data-based approach to imputation. You can retrieve a guide to imputing with very large datasets from *www.guilford.com/little-materials*; at this website, we introduce an approach for analyzing multiple-imputed datasets that does not require intensive analysis and recombining of results.

Both model-based and data-based approaches are effective and provide the same degree of recoverability and the same degree of (un)bias when the same variables are used. However, I generally recommend a data-based approach to handling missing data. I think it is easier and more straightforward to include a broader and more comprehensive array of potential auxiliary variables than when a model-based approach is used.

In longitudinal datasets, the amount of missing data often approaches levels that make even quantitatively minded scholars nervous. Experienced statisticians know, however, that the modern approaches to missing data imputation are quite effective and that even in the worst-case scenario the quality of generalization is not compromised or biased (relative to not imputing); that is, the quality of generalization is no worse than with pairwise deletion, which is almost always better than listwise (whole-case) deletion.

The nature of the data in longitudinal studies poses a couple of unique quandaries for imputation. I'm often asked, for example, about reimputing the Time 1 missingness once Time 2 data have been collected and merged with the overall dataset. My recommendation is yes, reimpute if possible. A common concern that investigators have voiced is that results from analysis of the Time 1 data may have already been published. Reimputing the Time 1 data can lead to slightly different results associated with the Time 1 variables when the follow-up paper is submitted for review. In my view, this concern is a nonissue. The paper submitted at Time 1 reflects the best test of the hypotheses at the time that the analyses are conducted. The longitudinal extension is addressing a different question—a question of change. I recommend reimputing with the later waves included because the change process itself may be predictive of the Time 1 missingness. We know more as a field about modern missing data procedures. One would expect, therefore, that estimates and their standard errors at Time 1 will change when new waves of data are collected (i.e., when more information is made available). The initial estimates based solely on the data that had been collected at Time 1 are not wrong—they are the best available at Time 1. More importantly, they are much better estimates than what complete-case, pairwise, or listwise deletion methods would yield!

The next most common question is "How much missing data can I really impute?" The answer to this question depends on a number of issues that haven't been fully worked out in the missing data literature. The amount that can be confidently imputed is much higher than most people would think, particularly if the dataset contains variables that represent the MAR process and if there is trustworthy coverage of the linking associations. What I mean by "trustworthy coverage of the linking associations" is a vague notion, but it can be thought of in terms of sampling generalizability. A sample of 100 participants with 60% missing means that generalizability of the observed associations is based on the 40% of data points from the 100 observations that are present—this amount of information that links the variables together is relatively small ($n = 40$) and probably not very trustworthy. On the other hand, 1,000 participants with 60% missing means that inferences are based on a much larger sample of observed data points ($n = 400$). Here, the amount of information that links the variables together is relatively large and probably trustworthy (at least more trustworthy than 40). In either scenario, modern approaches to missing data imputation will lead to the best possible inferences, given the data at hand. If the choice is to either (1) throw out the data because too much is missing or (2) try to glean the available information from the dataset, I would likely choose using a modern method of imputation.

A number of factors can be used to your advantage to ensure high-quality estimation in the presence of missing data. First, try to avoid unplanned missingness. Designing efficient protocols that do not burden participants, providing adequate incentives for participation, taking proactive steps to maintain contact with participants, and making them feel like valued members in the study—each will minimize attrition and nonresponse. Second, be sure to measure variables that are likely to be associated with attrition and dropout. Carefully crafting a protocol to capture any missing data mechanisms will significantly enhance your ability to generalize back to the original population from which your sample was drawn.

Keep in mind that missing data imputation is an agnostic affair when it comes to designating some variables as independent and others as dependent, for example. The goal of modern approaches is to estimate a covariance matrix and mean vector that resemble the population from which the original sample was drawn. In this regard, the misconception that one can't impute the dependent variable, for example, is ill founded when either FIML or MI is used (other methods can introduce bias). With the data-based MI approach, implied data points are inserted into locations where data are missing. These inserted data points are like pillars that support the bridge across the missing data divide. The bridge allows a full estimation of the variance, covariance, and mean that connect the observed data in the presence of the missing data. With the model-based FIML approach, the parameter estimates are directly adjusted to reflect their values to be what they would have been had no data been missing.

Planned Missing Data Designs in Longitudinal Research

Unplanned missingness can be a bane for research generalizations. Planned missingness, on the other hand, has tremendous (and for the most part unrealized) potential. More specifically, John Graham and colleagues (2003; Graham, Taylor, Olchowski, & Cumsille, 2006) have described the merits of planned missing data designs particularly in longitudinal research (see also Mistler & Enders, 2012). Planned missingness yields incomplete data that are MCAR because the missingness is planned and controlled by the investigator. As such, the data necessarily meet the MCAR assumptions. The various modern missing data approaches easily accommodate and accurately recover the missing data mechanism when it is MCAR. An important consequence of this accurate recovery is that a study can incorporate missing data patterns that are due to the MCAR mechanism and thus recover the information! For basic research purposes in particular, such designs will likely become commonplace.

Although a number of planned missing designs are possible, one of the first to be carefully articulated is the three-form design. As the name implies, three different forms are created, and then participants are randomly assigned one of the three forms to complete. The key to the three-forms design is that each form contains a common set of questions. This common set of questions should be carefully constructed to include those variables that are most likely to be associated with the MAR process to aid in recovering nonplanned missingness. In a longitudinal application of the three-forms design, these common variables would include variables that are likely to be associated with attrition as well as nonresponse. For example, SES, mental health, and marital status are good candidate variables to include in the common set of variables. Table 2.3 provides an overview of a three-forms design. In this example, the variables have been divided into four sets, each containing one-fourth of the total number of variables that one desires to administer. Any given participant receives 75% of the total variables.

In order to improve the fraction missing (i.e., the degree to which missingness is recoverable via strong linear associations among the observed and missing data), you can distribute the items of the scales you are interested in assessing by assigning some of the items to the common set, some to Set A, some to Set B, and some

TABLE 2.3. The general layout of a three-form planned missing data design

Form	Common variables	Variable set A	Variable set B	Variable set C
1	1/4 of variables	1/4 of variables	1/4 of variables	None
2	1/4 of variables	1/4 of variables	None	1/4 of variables
3	1/4 of variables	None	1/4 of variables	1/4 of variables

Note. The distribution and proportions of variables across the different sets do not have to be uniform.

to Set C. For example, if I had a 10-item measure of positive affect, I would assign 3 items to the common block, 2 items to Set A, 2 items to Set B, and 2 items to set C. I might then randomly assign the 10th item to be in any one of the three sets. With this approach the amount of information about positive affect for each participant is quite high. On average each participant has responded to 75% of the items for a given scale.

Another planned missing data design that is particularly germane to longitudinal research is the accelerated longitudinal design. In this design, the data from a cross-sequential design (see Figure 2.1) is transformed to reflect the span of ages that are represented by the whole sample. As mentioned earlier, a cross-sequential design starts with a cross-sectional sampling and subsequently assesses the multiple cohorts of individuals sequentially over time. In the example in Table 2.4, the cross-sequential design has six age groups (ages 11–16 each assessed six times at 4-month intervals). This table depicts the cells that are observed and the cells that are missing. A key issue with such a design is to have enough overlapping data so that the coverage of associations is trustworthy; trustworthiness is a somewhat vague idea. In the context of planned missing designs, each pairwise set of associations must have enough representative observations to generate a covariance estimate that adequately reflects the population covariance.

In Table 2.4, I have shown six measurement occasions with three overlapping ages for each of the age cohorts. This overlap of ages for each of the cohorts provides the information necessary to project the associations among all variables both backward and forward in time. It is also possible to fit models with only one overlapping age or measurement occasion per cohort. Because of the uncertainty of cohort

TABLE 2.4. Transforming a cross-sequential design into an accelerated longitudinal design

Age/Cohort	Age in years;months for each cohort at each assessment					
	0 mo	4 mo	8 mo	12 mo	16 mo	20 mo
Age 11 yr	11;0	11;4	11;8	12;0	12;4	12;8
Age 12 yr	12;0	12;4	12;8	13;0	13;4	13;8
Age 13 yr	13;0	13;4	13;8	14;0	14;4	14;8
Age 14 yr	14;0	14;4	14;8	15;0	15;4	15;8
Age 15 yr	15;0	15;4	15;8	16;0	16;4	16;8
Age 16 yr	16;0	16;4	16;8	17;0	17;4	17;8

	Full span of the ages covered																				
	11;0	11;4	11;8	12;0	12;4	12;8	13;0	13;4	13;8	14;0	14;4	14;8	15;0	15;4	15;8	16;0	16;4	16;8	17;0	17;4	17;8
Age 11 yr	W1	W2	W3	W4	W5	W6															
Age 12 yr				W1	W2	W3	W4	W5	W6												
Age 13 yr							W1	W2	W3	W4	W5	W6									
Age 14 yr										W1	W2	W3	W4	W5	W6						
Age 15 yr													W1	W2	W3	W4	W5	W6			
Age 16 yr																W1	W2	W3	W4	W5	W6

Note. Multiple cohorts could also be transformed in such a manner. A dummy code to represent age cohort would be included within each pattern to account for potential cohort differences. The missing data are treated as missing at random and imputed. "Mo" refers to months, "yr" refers to years, and "W*n*" refers to wave of data collection.

differences in the change process, some methodologists encourage researchers to have at least two measurement occasions in which the ages of the cohorts overlap.

One of the features of the accelerated longitudinal design is that we can begin to estimate age trends while controlling for cohort differences. The differences in the estimates for the age-11 cohort measured at the fourth wave versus the age-12 cohort measured at the first wave is partly due to cohort differences. Differences are also related to time-of-measurement effects. By including a dummy code for cohort and a dummy code for wave of assessment, these influences can be estimated and controlled for. In order to identify all the model estimates, some assumptions are needed about the uniformity of cohort differences across the waves and about the time-of-measurement differences across cohorts.

MODELING DEVELOPMENTAL PROCESSES IN CONTEXT

Nearly every longitudinal study that has been conducted makes some sort of comment about how the modeled process is subject to contextual influences. Usually, these comments occur in the limitations section of the discussion when the authors admit that they have not measured or controlled for the impact of context on the focal developmental process. A few years ago, my colleagues and I edited a book (Little, Bovaird, & Card, 2007) that discusses the merits of and shows the methods for modeling contextual influences on developmental processes. I briefly summarize some of the key points that can be found in that volume.

The context in which a person develops (physically, socially, emotionally, spiritually, etc.) is multidimensional and multilayered. First and foremost, the context of this development encompasses all the circumstances in which development unfolds (i.e., its settings). The context is the set of features that influences the performance or the outcome of a developmental process. The context also defines the conditions that are relevant to an outcome. In the discussion sections of most longitudinal studies, terms such as *circumstances*, *times*, *conditions*, *situations*, and so on are used when trying to convey the layers and levels of influence. The ecology of development is also another way to think of context. Here, the ecology defines the relationship between organisms and their environment. In Figure 2.5, I display a Venn (aka Ballantine) diagram of how these ecologies can vary along a social dimension, a physical dimension, and a personal dimension.

Each ecology exists in a nested manner, and each level has influences that can be measured as variables. These hierarchically nested variables can be used in an analysis model to examine their influence on the developing individual. For example, Bronfenbrenner's (1975, 1977) nested structure of the social ecology is perhaps the most famous and widely used conceptual model of context. The hierarchically nested nature of his model is depicted in Figure 2.6. The social ecology focuses on

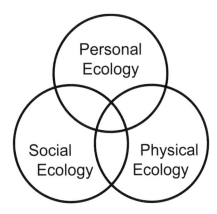

FIGURE 2.5. Ecologies of human development.

the social and cultural interactions and influences that affect the developing individual. The microsystem represents the influence of the immediate family, close friendships, and romantic partners. The mesosystem captures the next most distal level of social influences, such as peer groups, neighborhood communities, clubs, worship, and the like. Larger cultural influences are also represented at the higher levels of the nested data structures.

Keith Widaman developed a similar system of overlapping contextual influences that focuses on the physical ecology of the developing individual and not just the social ecology (Figure 2.7). The local/home ecology of the physical environment can include the in vitro environment or the immediate physical environment. At the

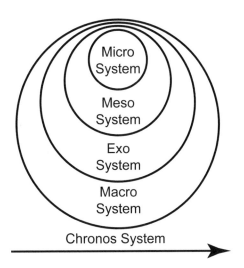

FIGURE 2.6. Bronfenbrenner's hierarchy of the social ecology.

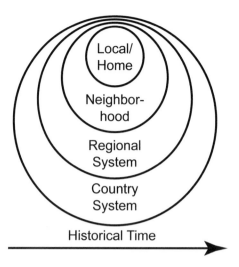

FIGURE 2.7. Widaman's hierarchy of the physical ecology.

next level, physical characteristics of the surroundings, such as neighborhood orderliness, hours of daylight, and the visible signs of community wealth, can affect the development of the individual within those contexts.

Finally, turning to Figure 2.8, I present a possible hierarchy of the personal ecology. Figure 2.8 is not meant to be a strong statement of whether the affective system is nested within the behavioral-cognitive systems or vice versa. Instead, the goal is to highlight that genes and ontogenetic expressions, as well as age-related expressions of the personal ecology, are taking place within the core affective, behavioral, and cognitive systems.

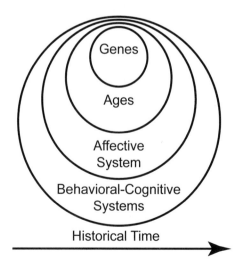

FIGURE 2.8. A possible hierarchy of the personal ecology.

Because contexts exist, they can be measured. The process of measuring the features and characteristics of the different levels of context often requires some innovation and careful consideration. Once a measure of a contextual influence is created or adapted, however, the nature of the contextual variable is represented in a statistical model in a handful of ways.

Contextual variables can be entered as a direct effect that varies at the level of the individual and influences the individual directly. They can be entered as indirect (mediated) effects, whereby a contextual variable varies at the level of the individual and influences the individual through its effect on an intervening variable. An indirect effect is not necessarily a causal statement but rather an acknowledgment that the effect is distal and that its influence is now channeled through one or more proximally measured variables. Contexts can also be entered as mediating effects. Here, the distal context influences the proximal context, which in turn influences the individual. The primary difference between an indirect effect and a mediated effect is the causal hypotheses that underlie how and why the effect permeates from distal to proximal. Often this distinction is simply one of theory and additional empirical evidence supporting a strong causal conclusion. Statistically speaking, an indirect effect and a mediated effect are the same estimated parameter. Contextual variables can be entered as moderating effects, which are interactive influences that change the strength of relationships for any of the preceding effects (see Chapter 9 for a detailed discussion of mediation and moderation).

Reciprocal effects and feedback loops are another way that contextual variables can be conceptualized. Statistically, however, such effects are entered as direct, indirect, mediating, or moderating influences. The key to demonstrating a reciprocal effect or a feedback loop is the timing and spacing of the measurement occasions. When properly designed, such effects are represented as cross-time associations that can be entered statistically as direct, indirect, mediated/mediating, or moderated/moderating influences.

The final type of statistical influence that represents the manner in which context can have an influence is via hierarchically nested effects. Nested data structures occur when the context is a larger sphere of influence that affects to some degree each of the entities contained within it. In the multilevel-modeling literature, the entities contained within the larger units are referred to as Level 1 units, and the hierarchical level units are referred to as Level 2 units. Students (Level 1) contained in classrooms (Level 2) is the classic example. In longitudinal studies, however, the Level 1 unit is often the time of measurement that is nested within the individuals, who would then become the Level 2 units; higher units such as the classrooms would then become Level 3 units (even higher units, such as schools, would be Level 4 units, and so on; see Chapter 8 for a discussion of multilevel nested data structures as contextual variables).

Nested structures are larger units of context that can have direct, indirect, mediating, or moderating effects; or they may be mediated and/or moderated. Some key factors in modeling nested data structures include sampling enough of the larger units so that the hierarchical influence can be estimated as a random variable in the statistical model. Nested data structures can be represented as fixed effects when the number of larger units is relatively small. Here, the higher level "units" can be represented as groups in a multiple-group framework; or, if there is no evidence of moderation across the higher level units, the units can be represented as a set of dummy-coded variables to estimate and thereby control for their influence.

In the second half of this book, I present examples of various models that contain contextual features and how they can be modeled. I also provide more detailed discussions of the steps involved. For now, my main goal is to remind researchers that context does indeed matter and that we have the analytic capacity to model influences.

SUMMARY

In this chapter, I covered a number of foundational issues related to SEM that are closely tied to longitudinal data analyses. Perhaps the most important message to take away from this chapter is: *plan ahead*. Too often folks collect longitudinal data just for the sake of having it. Clearly, well-conceived and well-executed longitudinal studies can provide a wealth of information about change processes, growth functions, and predictors of both; however, poorly designed and haphazardly collected longitudinal data are theoretically dubious at best and empirically crappy at worst.

With careful and proper planning, a good longitudinal study would have a clear beginning, a circumscribed and efficient focus, and a clear ending. Many ongoing longitudinal studies have so many fundamental design and measurement problems that continued data collection on them is difficult to justify and mostly unwarranted. The resources that are being ill spent on haphazardly designed longitudinal studies, regardless of the theoretical merits of the project, should probably be redirected and reprioritized.

KEY TERMS AND CONCEPTS INTRODUCED IN THIS CHAPTER

Accelerated designs. Multiple cohorts of individuals are studied repeatedly, and the cohorts differ in age at the first time of measurement. However, the initial ages of the cohorts (e.g., 10, 12, 14, and 16 years of age) and the points in time at which they are measured (e.g., 2000, 2001, and 2002) are selected to ensure that members of the different cohorts will be of at least one identical age at different time points. The overlap of ages enables change across years to be estimated in less than elapsed calendar time.

Construct validity. An ongoing process of research using a particular construct. Showing that a construct has good characteristics in different contexts of samples, other constructs, age groups, and the like provides ongoing support for the utility of the construct. Any one study is a piece of the construct validity pie.

Content validity. Refers primarily to the internal relationships among the items and the pool of potential items that can be selected to be indicators of a given construct. Content-valid indicators provide coverage of the domain of interest (a nonstatistical judgment) and, in a confirmatory factor analysis (CFA) framework, have strong loadings on the construct of interest and no indication of dual loadings onto other constructs. That is, the indicators converge on the construct of interest and diverge or discriminate from the indicators of other constructs. The size of the loadings and the fit of the CFA model are used to inform content validity.

Context. The circumstances in which an event occurs; a setting. A context is the set of features that influence the performance or the outcome of a process. A context also defines the conditions that are relevant to an outcome. The word *context* stems from *contextus*, a putting together, and from *contexere*, to interweave, braid. Synonyms include *circumstances, times, conditions, situation, ambience, frame of reference, background, framework, relation,* and *connection.*

Criterion validity. This form of validity comes in two flavors, concurrent and predictive. In SEM models, with multiple constructs included in the model, all of the potential relationships among the constructs are potential criterion validity relationships. Traditional descriptions of criterion validity describe it as the association between a new measure and an established measure of the same general construct. This idea is narrow. A criterion is a statement of an expected association or mean difference that is supported by data. In this regard the expectation of a –.5 correlation between two constructs, for example, is a criterion validity finding. A strong statement of all the expected associations among the constructs is a broader and more rigorous definition of criterion validity.

Cross-sectional design. A design in which individuals from two or more age cohorts are assessed at only one time point.

Ecology. The ecology of human development involves examining the relationship between organisms and their environment. These ecologies can vary in a nested manner along a social dimension, a physical dimension, and a personal dimension.

Episodic time. Episodic time relates to identifying a key event or episode, such as puberty, graduation, or retirement. The assessment occasions are reorganized by centering each individual's data on the episode. Chronological age would be included in such models as a covariate or a moderator of the relationship.

Experiential time. The length of time during which individuals experience a state or influence. Chronological age would be included in such models as a covariate or moderator of the relationships.

Intensive designs. A person or group is studied on a large number of occasions. Collins (2006) defines these designs as involving at least 20 relatively closely spaced times of measurement. However, Nesselroade (e.g., Jones & Nesselroade, 1990) indicates that, when a single person is studied, there may be 100 or more times of measurement.

Missing completely at random (MCAR). As the name implies, the MCAR mechanism is a truly random process that underlies the missing data. When data are MCAR, most missing data imputation procedures will do a reasonably good job of recovering the missing information and lead to accurate and unbiased generalizations. Unfortunately, data are only rarely missing completely at random, particularly in longitudinal work, where nonrandom attrition is the norm.

Missing data imputation. The process of estimating population parameters from the sample with missing data. Model-based imputation procedures such as full information maximum likelihood (FIML) estimation provide model parameter estimates in the presence of missing data. Data-based augmentation imputation generates data that are placed in the missing data cells, which allows population estimates to be made. These estimates are not about the individual; instead, they are estimates of the variance–covariance matrix and mean vector that reflect the population, given the sample and the missing data. A model's parameter estimates, when derived from an imputed covariance matrix and mean vector, are fundamentally the same as the parameter estimates derived from model-based imputation procedures, all things being equal.

Missing data mechanism. The reason for the missing data. In the missing data literature, three reasons for missingness are discussed: missing completely at random (MCAR), missing at random (MAR), and missing not at random (MNAR). In longitudinal research, both attrition and nonresponse give rise to missing data. These two kinds of missing data, however, share these three underlying reasons.

Missing not at random (MNAR). This name, too, does *not* imply what the mechanism actually is. Here, the MNAR mechanism is a systematic influence that is the reason for the missing data, but the systematic influence is unmeasured. Because the reason is unmeasured, there is no information on the dataset that allows recovery of the missing data. This mechanism can be converted to an MAR process if you plan your data collection to include variables that are likely to be associated with the reason for missing data. In addition, having proxies and correlates of the MNAR process in your imputation procedure can aid in recovering at least some of the information lost because of this missing data mechanism.

Missing at random (MAR). This label is actually a misnomer; the MAR mechanism is a *non*random, predictable process. The important feature of this mechanism is that the data are missing for a reason that is known, measured, and used in the imputation process. When variables associated with missingness exist in the dataset and are used in the imputation process, the missing data points' influence is accounted for and included in the imputation process. The process of correcting the dataset to account for the known reason renders the data functionally random. Modern missing data imputation procedures assume that the missing data are MAR, which is less restrictive than MCAR.

Panel designs. A cohort (e.g., people born in 1990) is studied at three or more times (e.g., 2000, 2001, and 2002). Collins (2006) defines these designs as involving eight or fewer times of measurement that are separated by at least 6 months.

Sequential designs. Multiple cohorts of individuals are studied repeatedly, typically at three or more times. Attrition and retest control groups are often part of sequential designs.

Single-cohort designs. A group of individuals (members of the same birth cohort; e.g., people born in 1990) is studied repeatedly, that is, at multiple occasions (two or more times, e.g., 2000 and 2001).

RECOMMENDED READINGS

Missing Data Imputation

Enders, C. K. (2010). *Applied missing data analysis.* New York: Guilford Press.

> Comprehensive yet extremely readable coverage of modern missing data theory and estimation procedures. It will become the new "key" justification once it is at arm's reach in your personal library.

Graham, J. W., Cumsille, P. E., & Elek-Fisk, E. (2003). Methods for handling missing data. In I. B. Weiner (Ed.-in-Chief), W. F. Velicer & J. A. Schinka (Vol. Eds.), *Handbook of psychology: Vol. 2. Research methods in psychology* (pp. 87–114). New York: Wiley.

> Like Schafer and Graham (2002), this chapter provides a great overview of missing data procedures.

Graham, J. W., Olchowski, A. E., & Gilreath, T. D. (2007). How many imputations are really needed? Some practical clarifications of multiple imputation theory. *Prevention Science, 8,* 206–213.

> This article gives some guidance on how much missing data you can have and clarifies ideas like the fraction missing versus the percentage missing.

Graham, J. W., Taylor, B. J., Olchowski, A. E., & Cumsille, P. E. (2006). Planned missing data designs in psychological research. *Psychological Methods, 11,* 323–343.

> This article provides the rationale and impetus for planned missing data designs. Read it and then cite it as to the reasons that planned missing data is a powerful research design.

Schafer, J. L., & Graham, J. W. (2002). Missing data: Our view of the state of the art. *Psychological Methods, 7,* 147–177.

> Still a "key" justification for using modern missing data procedures—clearly written and compelling.

Mapping Theory with Model and Model with Theory

Lerner, R. M., Schwartz, S. J., & Phelps, E. (2009). Problematics of time and timing in the longitudinal study of human development: Theoretical and methodological issues. *Human Development, 52,* 44–68.

> A thoughtful discussion and alternative view on many of the issues that I present in this chapter.

McArdle, J. J. (2009). Latent variable modeling of differences and changes with longitudinal data. *Annual Review of Psychology, 60,* 577–605.

> A detailed statistical overview of various statistical models that can be fit to longitudinal data by the incomparable Jack McArdle.

Collins, L. M. (2006). Analysis of longitudinal data: The integration of theoretical model, temporal design, and statistical model. *Annual Review of Psychology, 57,* 505–528.

Ram, N., & Grimm, K. J. (2007). Using simple and complex growth models to articulate developmental change: Matching theory to method. *International Journal of Behavioral Development, 31,* 303–316.

> Both of these recent papers give outstanding rationales for matching theory, method, and model.

Wohlwill, J. F. (1973). *The study of behavioral development.* New York: Academic Press.

> Wohlwill's book is a classic, although it is a dense "read." The ideas are timeless and worth spending the effort to work through.

3

The Measurement Model

Perhaps, like every rose has a thorn, every latent-variable SEM model begins with a confirmatory factor analysis (CFA) model. The CFA model is a crucial first step because it tests the adequacy of the expected relations and constraints between the measured indicators and the underlying latent variables. The CFA model is also called the measurement model. The measurement model provides the basis for evaluating the adequacy of the measurement properties of each construct and the overall fit of the CFA model. This information is used to evaluate the structural model that eventually is specified and fit to the data. The success of the eventual structural model is very often tied to the quality of the underlying measurement model. Properly specifying and then determining the adequacy of the measurement model is where this step can become a bit thorny. In this chapter, I discuss a number of general issues that are part of the measurement model. Even if you are an experienced SEM user, I would encourage you to read through this material so that you'll be familiar with the terminology that I prefer to use. I also present material not typically covered in introductory SEM material. I've tried to make this chapter very up-to-date, and I haven't shied away from offering opinions or recommendations on a number of key issues. If you are new to the study of SEM, this chapter and Chapter 4 cover a lot of ground. I recommend that you also pick up a copy of Tim Brown's (2006) book, *Confirmatory Factor Analysis for Applied Research*, wherein he covers all the nuts and bolts of CFA. Let's first start with the basics: the drawing and labeling conventions of an SEM model.

DRAWING AND LABELING CONVENTIONS

Even a casual observer will notice that path diagrams are a key component of latent-variable modeling because of what they can convey. To familiarize you with the drawing and labeling conventions, I have depicted in Figure 3.1 a simple CFA model with the possible parameter estimates labeled.

Figure 3.1 presents some of the key features of the graphical system used for

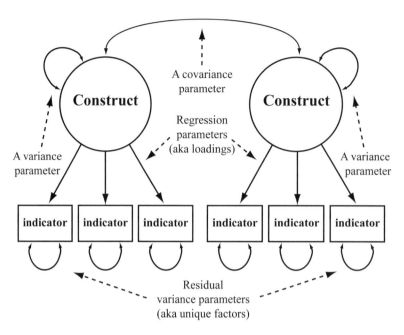

FIGURE 3.1. Drawing conventions for SEM. Circles (or ovals) represent the unobserved/latent constructs. Boxes (or rectangles) represent the measured/manifest indicators (e.g., items, parcels, or scales). Curved double-headed lines are variances if they start and stop on the same circle or same square. Curved double-headed lines are covariances if they start and stop on different circles or squares. Straight single-headed lines are directed regression-like relations. I am depicting the unique factors as simply residual variance parameters; see Figure 3.2.

representing the essential elements of SEM. Circles (or ovals) are used to represent latent constructs. As I discussed in Chapter 1, latent constructs are the unobserved variables that we are attempting to measure. They are things that we presume exist but cannot measure directly (e.g., aggression). We can only infer their existence from measurements that can be directly recorded (e.g., punching someone). Boxes (or rectangles) are used to represent the measured or manifest indicators. Indicators are things that we can directly assess, observe, or record (e.g., frequency of punching someone). Indicators can be items on a questionnaire, observations made in a lab, or responses recorded in an experiment, among other observable and numerically quantifiable things.

In SEM, the scores on the indicators are said to be "caused" by the underlying latent construct. That is, if I am trying to measure a construct such as positive affect, the degree to which a respondent possesses this unobservable construct "causes" his or her response to an item such as "In the past two weeks, I have felt happy." Items such as this are intended to tap into this unobservable mood state. Such indicators are called *reflective* indicators because they are a reflection of the construct. These kinds of indicators are also called *effects* indicators because they correlate with one another due to the effects of the construct (i.e., they are the effects of the construct that is the causal mechanism). In Figure 3.1, this directed relationship is depicted by a straight arrow pointing to the box (i.e., the box is being predicted by the circle). Stated differently, the manifest indicator is regressed onto the latent construct, just as a dependent variable is regressed onto an independent variable in a regression analysis. I write "cause" with quotes because I am not really talking about "cause" in a teleological or literal sense. Instead, the relations between indicators and constructs behave as if they are causally linked, and the direction of the arrows thus has important interpretative meaning.

Some authors use so-called *formative* indicators that have the arrows turned around (and the interpretation is turned upside down). With these kinds of indicators, the construct is formed from the confluence of the selected indicators. These kinds of indicators are also called *causal* indicators because they "cause" the construct rather than the construct "causing" the indicators. Because formative indicators have limited utility (a topic that is beyond the scope of this book), I do not present or discuss them here (see Howell, Breivik, & Wilcox, 2007, for a detailed rationale as to why such indicators should be avoided).

The last drawing convention shown in Figure 3.1 is the double-headed curved arrow. These curved arrows are parameters of the model that represent a variance relationship when they start and end with the same circle or same box. In addition, these types of curved lines are used to represent a covariance relationship when they start and end with different circles or boxes.

To further illustrate some drawing conventions in SEM, I have drawn two forms of the same simple model in Figure 3.2. On the left side, I have explicitly drawn the unique factors (the small circle associated with each indicator). Technically speaking, the representation on the left is more in the spirit of the factor analysis tradition that gave rise to SEM (see *Factor Analysis at 100* by Cudeck & MacCallum, 2007). From this perspective, the variance of an indicator is divided between two unobserved (i.e., latent) variables. The first latent variable is the underlying construct that a set of indicators is expected to reflect. The second latent variable is the unique factor that is associated only with a given indicator (i.e., u_1, u_2, and u_3 in Figure 3.2). The unique factor is actually the sum of two sources of information: (1) the random unreliability of the measurement process and (2) reliable variance that is specific to the indicator (sometimes this second source is described as a "method" factor—the reliable variance associated with the method by which the variable was collected). Although drawing the unique factors is technically a more precise way to depict what is actually being estimated, the shorthand way (on the right in Figure 3.2) is simpler, takes less space, and conveys essentially the same information (Jack McArdle was one of the first to introduce the shorthand way). Because of these advantages, I use this convention throughout the book. In a similar vein, some modelers introduce

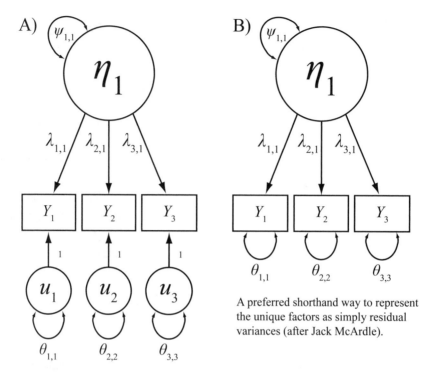

FIGURE 3.2. More drawing conventions for SEM: A) the technically accurate way and B) a simpler shorthand way. Both drawings are identical models mathematically and pretty much conceptually. On the left, residual variance information is treated as a unique factor with some estimated variance. On the right, the residual variance information is represented as "unexplained" variance in the indicator. Unexplained variance in an indicator (see B) is the same thing as a unique factor (see A).

"disturbance" factors to represent unexplained variance in a latent construct when it is predicted by (endogenous to) some other variable in the model. Just as with the residual variances of the indicators, the variance of the disturbance factor can be represented in these diagrams as a residual variance term that connects directly to the circle.

To summarize the drawing conventions, circles are latent constructs, boxes are measured indicators, straight lines are directional regression-like relationships, and curved lines represent nondirectional variances, residual variances, or covariance relationships. These drawing conventions are very powerful organizing tools because they graphically depict lots of information about the model being fit. I find them to be extremely useful ways to think about a research topic in general and as an aid to designing a study from the get-go. My first response to students who visit me is often "show me your drawing" (sometimes I say hello first). When the drawing is complete, it's worth not only a thousand words but also a thousand numbers. Once you learn to draw and read these drawings, they convey volumes of information.

DEFINING THE PARAMETERS OF A CONSTRUCT

Statisticians like to use Greek letters to represent most unobserved statistical ideas such as population parameter estimates and latent variables; hence all the Greek in Figure 3.2. Technically speaking, the parameters of a construct are the parameters of a model for a hypothesized construct. That is, parameters are features of models. The CFA model for a construct is what I first focus on. To aid in the following discussion, therefore, I've provided a Greek cheat sheet in Table 3.1 that defines the most common Greek letters associated with SEM. I don't discuss all of the letters and their associations with SEM, but I have put them in here for completeness (e.g., I don't discuss the x-side of the LISREL model very much, but their Greek letters and

TABLE 3.1. A Greek cheat sheet for SEM geeks

Letter name	Upper case	Lower case	Usual meaning and interpretation in SEM
Lambda	Λ	λ	The estimated loading of an indicator on a construct; the loading is also referred to as a scaling parameter, the indicator's reliability, and a validity coefficient.
Psi	Ψ	ψ	The (residual) variance of a construct or the (residual) covariance between two constructs, when defined as endogenous constructs.
Phi	Φ	φ	The variance of a construct or the covariance between two constructs, when defined as exogenous constructs.
Theta	Θ	θ	The residual variance of an indicator or the residual covariance between two indicators.
Beta	$\mathbf{B}$	β	An estimated regression of one construct onto another (endogenous on endogenous).
Tau	$\mathbf{T}$	τ	The intercept (i.e., mean) of an indicator when the regression line of the indicator on the construct is zero.
Alpha	$\mathbf{A}$	α	The mean of the latent construct as defined by the scaling constraint to identify the means structure (endogenous constructs).
Gamma	Γ	γ	Also an estimated regression of one construct onto another. Here, endogenous variables are predicted by exogenous variables.
Kappa	$\mathbf{K}$	κ	The mean of the latent construct as defined by the scaling constraint to identify the means structure (exogenous constructs).
Sigma	Σ	σ	Σ is the model implied variance-covariance matrix; σ is the standard deviation of an indicator; and σ^2 is the variance. σ can also be a covariance.
Eta		η	An endogenous construct is called an "eta."
Ksi		ξ	An exogenous construct is called a "ksi" or "xi." I prefer "ksi."
Chi		χ	χ^2 is an index of model mis-fit that follows a typical χ^2 distribution.
Delta	Δ		Used to denote the change between any two nested estimates as in $\Delta\chi^2$ or ΔCFI.

Note. **Bold** uppercase Greek letters usually refer to matrices of the parameters, and the *italicized* lowercase versions refer to a particular parameter of the model or element of a matrix. Some parameters are fixed elements, and some are estimated elements.

meanings are included in the table; also not all Greek letters are included as some are rarely used in the context of SEM).

The Greek letter eta, η, is the label used to name or refer to a latent construct. In Figure 3.2, the latent construct, η_1, has a variance that is denoted with the Greek letter psi (ψ). Psi is typically used to represent variances and covariances among latent constructs. The Greek letter theta, θ, represents the residual variances (or covariance associations among the indicators' residual variances; see Figure 3.9 for an example). The regression relationships between the indicators and the latent constructs are designated by the Greek letter lambda, λ. These parameters and their labels stem from the fundamental equation of SEM depicted in Equation 3.1 (technically, this equation is the CFA part of the SEM model). Some of these parameters are fixed for scaling and identification purposes, some are fixed to represent expected theoretical relationships, and the rest are estimated when the model is fit to data.

Equation 3.1 is the matrix algebra representation of the parameters denoted in Figure 3.2. The Greek letter sigma, Σ, is used to refer to the variance–covariance matrix that is calculated based on the fixed and estimated parameters contained in the matrices on the right side of the equation: $\Lambda\Psi\Lambda' + \Theta$. This matrix is also called the model-implied covariance matrix. The matrix lambda, Λ, contains the estimated loadings (i.e., the λ's in Figure 3.2) that link the indicators to their underlying construct (you may have noticed that I use bold capital Greek letters to represent the matrices and italicized lower-case letters to represent individual parameter estimates). The matrix psi, Ψ, contains the estimated variances and covariances

---

Equation 3.1. Fundamental SEM equation

$$\Sigma = \Lambda\Psi\Lambda' + \Theta$$

Conceptual meanings

- Σ is the model-implied variance–covariance matrix.
- Λ is the matrix of loadings or estimates of the relations of the indicators to constructs.
- Ψ is a matrix of variances and covariances among the constructs.
- Θ is the matrix of residual variances or unique factors and residual covariances among the indicators.

Matrix characteristics

- Σ is a square and symmetric matrix with i rows and i columns, where i is the number of indicators in the model.
- Λ is a full matrix with i rows and c columns, where c is the number of latent constructs.
- Ψ is a square and symmetric matrix with c rows and c columns.
- Θ is also a square and symmetric matrix with i rows and i columns.
- Λ' is the transpose of the Λ matrix.

among the latent constructs—for the model depicted in Figure 3.2 there would be only a single element in this matrix, which is the variance of the construct ($\psi_{1,1}$). Some authors use the Greek letter ksi, ξ, to refer to constructs and the letter phi, φ, to represent the variance and covariances of the latent constructs. These Greek letters (ξ and φ) convey the idea that the constructs are *exogenous*ly measured (i.e., that nothing predicts them). I prefer Ψ and η because, conceptually speaking, all constructs are *endogenous*ly measured (i.e., something does or *can* predict them). Particularly in longitudinal research, the point at which measurements begin is often a point in development beyond conception (or the origins of the universe for that matter). In the initial CFA model, when none of the constructs predict one another, the elements of Ψ are variances and covariances. When a construct is predicted by another variable in the model, the elements of Ψ are interpreted as residual variances and residual covariances. Finally, the residual variances of each indicator (which are the same as the variances of the unique factors) and any potential covariances among these unique factors are contained in the matrix theta, Θ. I often refer to these as just "residuals" (when it is the unique factor variance) or "correlated residuals" (when the estimate is a covariance between two different unique factors).

The estimated parameters contained in these matrices are derived from the observed variances and covariances among the indicators. This observed matrix is labeled **S**. (Because **S** contains the calculations of the sample's sufficient statistics, some statisticians use the Roman letter, **S**.) SEM generally involves an iterative estimation process of finding parameters for the specified model that have the highest likelihood of producing the observed data. In fact, one method of estimating these parameters is called maximum likelihood (ML). ML estimation isn't too far removed from the basic linear least-squares equations with which we are familiar from classic regression analysis. The least-squares criterion is a form of ML estimator in the sense that when the sum of the squared deviations of the observed scores from the predicted values is as small as it can get, the regression model parameters have the maximum likelihood of having produced the observed scores. There are many nuances to ML estimation that I don't cover, but you can read about them in Brown's (2006) book. Also, Enders's (2010) book on missing data contains an excellent chapter that discusses the inner workings of the ML estimator. One popular feature of the ML estimator is that it provides an estimate of the degree of misfit between the observed matrix **S** and the model-implied matrix Σ. This information is indexed as a model chi-square, χ^2. This χ^2 value has degrees of freedom equal to the number of unique elements (i.e., observed variances and covariances) in the **S** matrix minus the number of estimated parameters contained in Equation 3.1. I discuss the uses and interpretations of the model χ^2 later when I talk more specifically about model fit in Chapter 4. First, I want to discuss how the model estimates are derived for a simple model that fully explains the observed data (i.e., has 0 degrees of freedom and is commonly referred to as a *saturated* or *just identified* model).

Table 3.2 shows the cell-by-cell equations for the model-implied variance–covariance matrix that Equation 3.1 produces if I fit the simple model depicted in Figure 3.2. As noted in the table, a unique solution for these parameters is not possible because there is no scale set to provide the metric for the estimates (and the model is not identified). I turn to the issues of scale setting and identification in the next sections. First, however, I want to point out that these equations are quite straightforward and that you can derive them by simply tracing the diagram in Figure 3.2. Start by putting your finger on one of the boxes. Move it up the line to the circle, go out and around the variance of the latent construct ($\psi_{1,1}$) and then back down one of the loadings to a box of your choice (seriously, give it a go). As indicated in Table 3.2, each parameter that you trace over is multiplied together. If you chose Y_1 as the starting box and Y_2 as the ending box, you have the implied covariance between Y_1 and Y_2 that the model is reproducing (i.e., $\lambda_{1,1}\,\psi_{1,1}\,\lambda_{2,1}$). If you chose Y_1 as the start and went back to Y_1, you have the amount of reliable variance in Y_1 that is explained by the construct. If you then add the residual variance to this cell, you get the total variance in Y_1. You can review a nice presentation of Wright's rules for "tracing" path diagrams by checking out Loehlin (2004, pp. 12–17). Throughout this book I describe many of the rules as they come up. You can also pick up a guide to the tracing rules at *www.guilford.com/little-materials*. For this simple example, you can derive each equation of the model-implied variances and covariances by tracing from a box up the loading through the variance of the circle and back down another loading. Because the primary estimates in Θ are the unexplained variances (i.e., the unique factors), they are simply added to the diagonal of the model-implied matrix. Any residual covariances in Θ would be added to the off-diagonal cell corresponding to the location of the residual covariance (but this model does not have any residual covariances). That is, theta has the same dimensions (same number of rows and columns) as the product of $\Lambda\Psi\Lambda'$, and the fundamental equation calls for it to be added in on a cell-by-cell-basis. I show an example of this later in the chapter.

TABLE 3.2. Implied variance–covariance matrix, Σ, from the model parameters found in Figure 3.2 and Equation 3.1

	Y_1	Y_2	Y_3
Y_1	$\lambda_{1,1}\,\psi_{1,1}\,\lambda_{1,1} + \theta_{1,1}$	Same information as is listed below	
Y_2	$\lambda_{1,1}\,\psi_{1,1}\,\lambda_{2,1}$	$\lambda_{2,1}\,\psi_{1,1}\,\lambda_{2,1} + \theta_{2,2}$	the diagonal
Y_3	$\lambda_{1,1}\,\psi_{1,1}\,\lambda_{3,1}$	$\lambda_{2,1}\,\psi_{1,1}\,\lambda_{3,1}$	$\lambda_{3,1}\,\psi_{1,1}\,\lambda_{3,1} + \theta_{3,3}$

Note. Y_1–Y_3 are three hypothetical measured variables. A unique solution for these parameters is not possible because the model is not identified and there is no scale set to provide the metric for the estimates. The first subscripted number for the λ parameters refers to the variable number, and the second number refers to the construct number. Covariance matrices are square (same number of rows and columns) and symmetrical (the same information is contained above and below the diagonal).

SCALE SETTING

To understand the concept of scale setting, I like to use the analogy of a cloud. A latent construct is like a nebulous cloud. Because it floats around, I can't measure its dimensionality. Every time I take one measurement, the cloud moves, and my measurements keep changing—never adding up to give me what I need. If, however, I take a tack (designed specifically for use with "clouds") and pin it down somewhere (*doink*), I can then use that pinned-down point as my point of reference for all of my measurements of the information contained in the cloud. This analogy is meant to convey the need both to fix at least one parameter to a scaling value and to highlight the arbitrariness of scale setting. Every latent construct, regardless of the number of indicators or the number of degrees of freedom available, must have at least one element of the estimated parameters pinned down (*doinked*). And it doesn't matter (for the most part) where I pin it down. In most SEM packages, the default for pinning down the estimates is to fix the loading of the first indicator to be 1.0. This fixing allows each of the other estimates to be calculated relative to the fixed (pinned down) loading of 1.0; accordingly, for many applications of SEM, the choice of where to pin down the estimates is an arbitrary one.

I now walk through an example of how the estimates are calculated. Table 3.3 provides the sufficient statistics (i.e., correlations, standard deviations, and means) for three indicators of positive affect: *glad*, *cheerful*, and *happy*. As seen in the top portion of the table, the items correlate moderately positively with each other. In fact, the internal consistency estimate (Cronbach's alpha) for these indicators is .82. As mentioned, I have also listed the standard deviations, variances (the square of the standard deviations), and the means. These are listed in the bottom half of the table, and I return to these in a moment.

Selecting the first indicator to be the "marker" variable has a long history of

TABLE 3.3. Basic descriptive statistics among three indicators of positive affect

	Glad	Cheerful	Happy
Glad	1.0		
Cheerful	.552	1.0	
Happy	.563	.663	1.0
SD	.842	.889	.835
Var (SD²)	.709	.791	.697
Mean	3.07	2.93	3.11

Note. These data are based on 823 children in grades 7 and 8 who responded to the questions framed with "In the past 2 weeks, I have felt . . . " Response options were *Almost Never*, *Seldom*, *Often*, and *Almost Always*.

being *the* method of scale setting (unfortunately, the marker variable method has many undesirable consequences that I elaborate on later). Figure 3.3 shows the maximum likelihood estimates from fitting this simple model to the data in Table 3.3 three different times (that's a lot of 3's!): once selecting the first variable as the marker, once selecting the second, and once selecting the third. For didactic purposes, I report the results from fitting the model to the correlations and not the covariances, because correlations are easier to understand. Also, when dealing with correlations, the square of a loading times the construct's variance estimate (e.g., $\lambda^2_{1,1} \cdot \psi_{1,1}$) plus its residual variance (e.g., $\theta_{1,1}$) will sum to 1.0 for each indicator. When the estimates are based on the proper covariance metric, the equation $\lambda^2 \cdot \psi + \theta$ will reproduce the observed variance of the indicator, which is somewhat different for each indicator (as shown in Table 3.3, but not in Figure 3.3 as I fit the model to the correlations). Table 3.4 provides the cell-by-cell equations derived from selecting the first indicator to be the marker variable (i.e., fixing its loading to 1.0 to set the scale for the estimates).

If you take a few moments to verify, for example, that $\lambda_{1,1} \cdot \psi_{1,1} \cdot \lambda_{1,1} + \theta_{1,1} = 1.0$ for each of the three ways of scale setting, you should start to get a sense that the choice of which indicator to use to make the "scale" setting constraint is arbitrary. Also, notice that the residual variance estimates don't change from one solution to the other. The fact that the residual variances don't change from one solution to the next is a good thing. The residuals represent the amount of variance in each indicator that is unrelated to (unexplained by) the latent construct. This amount of variance should not change by the method of scaling. Another feature to note is that the estimated variance of the latent factor is, in fact, the amount of reliable variance

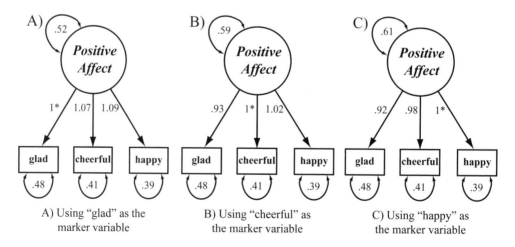

A) Using "glad" as the marker variable

B) Using "cheerful" as the marker variable

C) Using "happy" as the marker variable

FIGURE 3.3. Three different solutions using different marker variables to set the scale of the estimates. 1* is the fixed parameter. Each model reproduces the observed correlations exactly. That is, all three solutions lead to the same identical model-implied matrix, which, in this case, exactly reproduces the observed correlations (Table 3.3).

TABLE 3.4. Implied variance–covariance matrix, Σ, using the first variable as the "marker" variable

	Y_1	Y_2	Y_3
Y_1	$1.0\, \psi_{1,1}\, 1.0 + \theta_{1,1}$	Same information as is listed below	
Y_2	$1.0\, \psi_{1,1}\, \lambda_{2,1}$	$\lambda_{2,1}\, \psi_{1,1}\, \lambda_{2,1} + \theta_{2,2}$ the diagonal	
Y_3	$1.0\, \psi_{1,1}\, \lambda_{3,1}$	$\lambda_{2,1}\, \psi_{1,1}\, \lambda_{3,1}$	$\lambda_{3,1}\, \psi_{1,1}\, \lambda_{3,1} + \theta_{3,3}$

Note. By fixing one parameter of the equations to 1.0, this model is just identified, meaning that there are just as many estimates as there are available unique bits of information in the observed matrix, S. That is, there are 6 estimated parameters: 3 variances plus 3 unique covariances (6 bits of information) in the observed data. Here, $\lambda_{1,1}$ is fixed at 1.0 to set the scale.

captured in the indicator that is chosen as the marker variable. With the marker variable method, the construct takes on the "persona" of the chosen marker variable (i.e., the construct's variance is the reliable variance of the marker variable, and the construct's mean is the mean of the marker variable). The relations among the other indicators are estimated relative to their relations with the marker variable. In this regard, the metric of the latent construct is arbitrary; it is in the metric of the (often haphazardly) chosen marker variable. Generally speaking, I do *not* recommend using the marker variable method of scale setting (as I alluded to before). There are two methods of scale setting that I do recommend, however: the fixed factor method and the effects coding method.

The fixed factor method (also called the reference factor method) is the second most common method of scale setting. This method explicitly recognizes that the metric of the latent variable is arbitrary, so why not just fix its variance? If we fix it to 1.0, the estimated latent factor relations are thereby estimated in a standardized metric (when the variance is 1 it also means the standard deviation = 1; Table 3.5 shows the reproduced matrix using this method of identification). When more than one construct is estimated, this method has the added advantage of providing estimates of the between-construct relations in correlation metric (i.e., the covariance between constructs in Figure 3.1 would be a correlation if the two constructs' variances are

TABLE 3.5. Implied variance–covariance matrix, Σ, using the fixed factor method of scaling

	Y_1	Y_2	Y_3
Y_1	$\lambda_{1,1}\, 1.0\, \lambda_{1,1} + \theta_{1,1}$	Same information as is listed below	
Y_2	$\lambda_{1,1}\, 1.0\, \lambda_{2,1}$	$\lambda_{2,1}\, 1.0\, \lambda_{2,1} + \theta_{2,2}$ the diagonal	
Y_3	$\lambda_{1,1}\, 1.0\, \lambda_{3,1}$	$\lambda_{2,1}\, 1.0\, \lambda_{3,1}$	$\lambda_{3,1}\, 1.0\, \lambda_{3,1} + \theta_{3,3}$

Note. In this method of scaling, $\psi_{1,1}$ is set to 1.0. Only loadings and residuals are estimated relative to the construct variance being set to 1.0, and the 1.0 in the above equations in the table falls out.

fixed to 1.0). Given that correlations are a lot easier to interpret and understand than are covariances, this feature is nice.

Another feature that I like about this method is that relations among the indicators are estimated as relative optimal balances of their information. That is, pinning down the estimates by fixing the variance at the construct level (i.e., at the top) allows the estimated relations to come out as if they were a pendulum. Once the ML estimator determines the optimal balance, equilibrium is achieved, and the relative indicator relations "dangle" in an optimally balanced pattern below the construct. Some may suggest that this feature is a matter of aesthetics and perspective, but later on I return to this analogy to illustrate that it has real implications for estimating the parameters of a model.

As an aside, this idea that where you place the 1.0 to set the scale has implications for estimation and hypothesis testing was discussed nicely by Gonzalez and Griffin (2001). They showed that standard errors and significance tests based on the Wald test (i.e., dividing an estimate by its standard error to get a z-value of the significance from 0) are biased by the method of scale setting. As an additional aside, the value at which you choose to set the scale can be any nonzero positive value. Choosing 1.0 to be the scale value has nice mathematical properties, but technically speaking one could pick any value that is not exactly 0—all estimates would be scaled in the units of the fixed value. Fixing the residual variance of a construct to be the nonzero scaling value is possible but rare. The residual, by definition, is the leftover part after finding an optimal solution for common variance among the indicators. Sometimes a residual will be fixed to a nonzero value, such as when I have only a single indicator for a construct and I know from prior research how much variance is reliable and how much is unreliable (see discussion of identification in the following section). In this case, I would also fix the loading or the variance of the construct to add up to the amount that is reliable and the amount that is unreliable. Such an approach, however, is suboptimal because I must assume that the variable has the same level of reliability in the sample being analyzed. In general, I try to avoid using such *limiting assumptions* to specify and estimate a construct. If I use multiple indicators (minimum of three) for each construct when I design the study in the first place, I avoid this problem of imposing additional identification constraints.

The recently introduced effects coding method of scaling (Little, Slegers, & Card, 2006) is also one that I recommend. This third method of setting the scale is relatively new and is the only scale setting constraint that is nonarbitrary and provides a real scale. The fixed factor method is less arbitrary than the marker variable method and the scale it provides is meaningful, but it loses information about the actual scale that the indicators were measured on. If the scale of the indicators is meaningless in its own right, then the fixed factor method is my preferred method. On the other hand, if the metric of the indicators is meaningful, then I prefer the

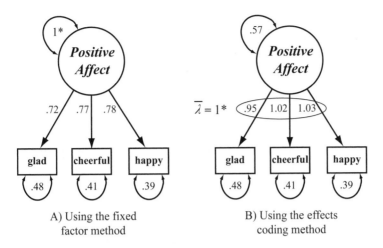

FIGURE 3.4. Two better methods for scaling the estimates of a latent factor. As in Figure 3.3, each model reproduces the observed correlations in Table 3.3 exactly; * indicates the parameter is fixed to set the scale. In B, the loadings must average 1.

effects coding method of scale setting. The results from fitting the simple CFA using these two methods of scale setting are depicted in Figure 3.4.

If you take a close look at the estimates in Figure 3.4, you will see some consistent features among them. First, the residual variances don't change with either of these methods of scale setting, just as they didn't when I walked through the different marker variable models. A second feature is specific to the fixed factor method of scaling. Namely, if you square the loading and add the residual, you get 1.0. Because I estimated these models based on the correlations, 1.0 is the variance of the indicator (correlations are derived from standardized data, where the mean is 0 and the standard deviation is 1). Finally, if you look at the effects coding method, you'll see that the loadings average 1.0. These loadings, however, are all estimated loadings that are now providing an unbiased and optimal balance of the information contained among these three indicators.

In Panel B of Figure 3.4, the estimated latent variance of .57 is the average of the amount of reliable variance that each indicator contributes to the definition of the latent construct. This feature of the interpretation of the latent variance is attractive for a couple of reasons. First, latent-variable estimates of variances, means, and associations provide population estimates of the true values that are devoid of the nuisances of sampling error and unreliability that are inherent in manifest variables. In this regard, the latent-variable estimates of means, variances, and associations are more generalizable than the manifest metric estimates if the sample is generalizable (i.e., a random representative sample); these estimates are both unbiased and consistent across studies that use samples from the same population. By way of contrast, the observed variance of these variables after taking the simple average of the variables produces a variance of .73 (from Table 3.3). The manifest variance estimate will always be larger than the latent variance estimate. The reason that the observed variance is larger than the latent variance is because the unique information associated with each indicator (i.e., its error variance) is removed from the estimated latent variance. The unique/error information is the sum of both the unreliable variance and the item-specific variance. When variables are averaged (or summed) in manifest metric, these sources of information are contained in the average (or sum), which produces an estimate of the variance that is larger than it should be. In latent-variable modeling, these residual parts are separated from the common variance among the indicators.

In terms of the equations that reproduce the observed correlations, the equations I wrote out in Table 3.2 are now all in play because no single estimate is constrained to be 1 (and therefore no parameter falls out of the calculations). In other words, because the scaling of the estimates is accomplished by a constraint that has a unique solution, each of the parameters is involved in the calculations. For example, $\lambda_{1,1}$ is estimated as the value that would solve the constraint $\lambda_{1,1} = 3 - \lambda_{2,1} - \lambda_{3,1}$. By mathematical necessity, $\lambda_{2,1}$ is estimated as the value that would solve the constraint $\lambda_{2,1} = 3 - \lambda_{1,1} - \lambda_{3,1}$, and $\lambda_{3,1}$ is estimated as the value that would solve the constraint $\lambda_{3,1} = 3 - \lambda_{1,1} - \lambda_{2,1}$. It does not matter which parameter is constrained to solve the algebraic constraint; once two of them are estimated, the other is determined. Because of this deterministic quality, only two estimates are being made and the third is a given, and therefore this method of scale setting provides the same model degrees of freedom and the same model fit as the other methods of scale setting. In our running example, the reason that 3 is in these equations is because there are three loadings being estimated (sample syntax in the language of various software packages is located at *www.guilford.com/little-materials*). If the construct had four indicators, one loading would be constrained to be 4 minus the other 3 estimated loadings, for example.

The three methods of scale setting are mathematically equivalent ways to estimate the parameters of a latent construct. The big difference is the meaning of the estimated values because they are interpreted relative to the fixed (pinned down) parameter. As I'll discuss in Chapter 5, the marker variable method poses some additional problems beyond the meaning of the estimates; as a result, I recommend the fixed factor method or the effects coding method. The only time I use the marker variable method is to generate start values for the effects coding method. Most SEM software converges easily with the marker variable method and often requires fewer iterations than do the other two methods. Providing start values that are "in the ballpark" of the eventual estimates helps the software converge more quickly and helps prevent it from veering off course and failing to find the correct solution (this happens more often than you'd think). I discuss more about estimation issues and tricks that I've learned along the way in the final chapter.

IDENTIFICATION

Identification refers to the balance of the known information available with the unknown parameters that are estimated from the data. In SEM, the known information is the number of unique variances and covariances (and means). The estimated parameters of each construct must be identified. When there are more known variances and covariances than parameter estimates a construct is said to be *overidentified*. When the known bits are equal to the unknown parameters, the construct is *just identified*. A construct is *underidentified* when there is not enough information to uniquely inform each of the estimated parameters. Construct identification should not be confused with model identification. Nearly all SEM models will have many more known bits of information than parameter estimates and almost always will be overidentified. The model's degrees of freedom reflect the number of unique variances, covariances, and means that are not used to estimate the parameters of the model. I discuss model identification issues in more detail in Chapter 4; for now, I want to focus on construct identification.

With three or more indicators for a construct, all the parameter estimates needed to define a construct are identified after the scaling constraint is placed on one of the parameters (there are enough degrees of freedom to uniquely estimate the parameters, assuming that no correlated residuals are specified). For example, in Table 3.3, there are six unique pieces of information: three variances and three covariances. Using Figure 3.3A as an example, there are six freely estimated parameters for that construct, making it a *just-identified* model. In other words, with three indicators of a construct, the solution is said to be *just identified*. In this case, there are just as many estimates being made as there are unique observed pieces of information available. With three indicators of a construct, there are three variances and three covariances that provide the unique observed pieces of information to inform the parameter estimates for a given construct.

When a construct has more than three indicators, the parameter estimates are *overidentified*. With four indicators, for example, there are four variances and six unique covariances to inform the estimates for that construct (10 unique bits of information). A construct with four indicators has nine parameters that define it (as shown in Figure 3.5). After the scaling constraint is placed on one of these parameters, only eight parameters need to be estimated. In Figure 3.5, I fixed the variance of the construct at 1.0 to set the scale, which leaves the four loadings and the four residuals as freely estimated parameters of this model. This model has two degrees of freedom remaining after estimating the essential parameters. As I mentioned in Chapter 2, these degrees of freedom are added to the overall model's degrees of freedom. In many situations, these additional within-construct degrees of freedom can arbitrarily influence the overall model fit information. I recommend, to the extent possible, that just-identified constructs be utilized to avoid this arbitrary improvement in model fit.

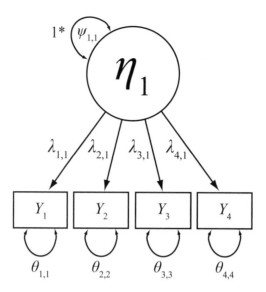

FIGURE 3.5. Parameters for a construct with four indicators. In this example, I fixed $\psi_{1,1}$ to 1.0 to set the scale for the other parameters.

When only one or two indicators of a construct are available, there's not enough unique information to provide support for the estimates, leading to an *underidentified* construct. The issue is degrees of freedom to determine the estimates; degrees of freedom are like money. The unique bits of information are the currency used to pay for a given estimate. When I don't have enough money for a full meal, I have to go to the dollar menu, and like the typical dollar-menu fare, the result is less than satisfying (except for maybe a sausage breakfast burrito). When there is a single-indicator construct in a model, there is only one bit of information—the variance of the indicator. Even after I fix one of the estimates to set the scale, the other two parameters aren't identified. In this situation, I have to add a further restriction. To make this additional restriction, I have to make an assumption about the measurement of the construct. Any assumption that I place is a limiting assumption. That is, I am making a limit on the estimation based on the assumption.

There are instances in which a construct will have only one indicator. A single-measure construct should not be confused with a factor because a factor is a mathematical extraction that accounts for shared variance in two or more indicators (see Brown, 2006). With only a single item to represent a construct (e.g., "I'm satisfied with my life" as an indicator of life satisfaction), there is no way to estimate how much variance is reliable (i.e., the shared variance among two or more indicators is the same thing as the amount of reliable variance). In the case of a single-indicator construct, I can assume that the indicator is measured without error and fix the residual variance of the indicator to be zero. This assumption is a very restrictive assumption in that nearly all measures have some degree of measurement error. If I choose this assumption to provide the needed identification constraint, the resulting construct will have a variance estimate that is larger than it should be (i.e., the reliable variance plus the error variance), and all covariances of this construct with other constructs will be underestimated (because the error variance is not accounted for). On the other hand, I might have a reasonable basis to make an assumption about how much of the variance of the construct is reliable. In this case, I can make the limiting assumption that the residual variance should be the proportion of the indicator's variance that is assumed to be unreliable.

Figure 3.6 shows four different ways that a single-indicator construct can be identified. I chose the "cheerful" item to demonstrate the methods of identification. "Cheerful" has an observed variance of .791 (see Table 3.3). Following the marker variable convention, if I set the scale by fixing the loading to 1 and add the limiting assumption that this indicator is measured without error (i.e., fix the residual to 0), the estimated variance of the construct becomes .791. Following the fixed factor method, I set the scale by fixing the variance to 1 and add the limiting assumption of no error; the loading would carry the total variance of the indicator. The estimated loading would become .889, which is the square root of the indicator's variance. The reason the estimate becomes .889 is that the equation for reproducing the variance of an indicator is $\lambda^2 \cdot \psi + \theta$. If ψ is set at 1 and θ is fixed to 0, then the solution for λ has to be the value that when squared reproduces the variance of the indicator. In this case, the square root of .791 is .889; thus, $.889^2$ is .791.

I can also make the assumption that the indicator has some measurement error,

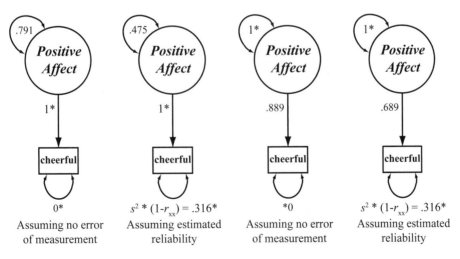

A) Marker variable / Effects coding methods   B) Fixed factor method

FIGURE 3.6. Different identifications for a single-indicator construct. r_{xx} is the estimated reliability of the single indicator. s is the observed standard deviation of the single indicator. s^2 is the variance of the single indicator.

and I can make an informed guess as to how much that error would be. Here, a careful review of the literature to determine a best estimate of the reliability of the scale would probably provide a good estimate. Let's say I did a literature review and found that, across multiple studies of similar samples using the same (or very similar) measures, the average reliability of a three-item scale of positive affect is .82. I now have a baseline to make a conjecture about the reliability of the single item "Cheerful." Using the Spearman–Brown prophecy formula (Equation 3.2), I would calculate the reliability for a scale of positive affect that was one-third the length of the three-item scale. With this estimate in hand, I can then use the constraints outlined in Figure 3.6 to fix the residual to be the proportion of .791 that I have deemed to be unreliable. In this case, the Spearman–Brown formula indicates that the reliability of this single indicator would be .60. Now I can fix the residual to be 40% of the total variance (.791 · .40 = .316). If I want to use the marker variable or effects coding method of scaling, I would fix the loading to be 1, and the estimated variance of the construct would emerge as .475. If I use the fixed factor method, the estimated loading would emerge as .689. Both methods would yield an explained variance estimate of .60, which is the amount that is reliable (take a look at the programs on *www.guilford.com/little-materials* to see for yourself; you'll also find an Excel spreadsheet with the Spearman–Brown formula programmed for tests of different reliability and different numbers of items).

If I have two indicators of a construct, I'm in a little better position, but I only have three unique bits of information to work with: the two variances of the indicators and their covariance with each other. After setting the scale by using any of the three methods of scale setting, I'm down to four estimates. In many applications of SEM, the lack of local identification can be made up for by borrowing information from other parts of the model. Also, in longitudinal research, the loadings of the like indicators are constrained to be equal to one another over time (I discuss this idea,

---

Equation 3.2. Spearman–Brown prophecy formula

$$r_{pp} = L\, r_{xx} / \{1 + (L-1)\, r_{xx}\}$$

where $L = n_p/n_i$

- r_{pp} is the anticipated reliability of a measure that is either longer or shorter than the one in hand.
- r_{xx} is the estimated reliability of the in-hand measure.
- L is the length factor (i.e., the proportional increase or decrease in the "prophesized" length).
- n_p is the projected new length (number of items) of the measure.
- n_i is the current length (number of items) of the measure.
- The accuracy of this formula depends on the idea that all items of the scale are equally good indicators (i.e., they have equal item-level true-score variance, or essential tau-equivalence).

called factorial invariance, in Chapter 5). When the equality of loadings over time is specified, I would now have enough degrees of freedom to inform the estimates. When I have only two indicators of a construct and I don't have longitudinal data, identification can become an issue. A simple limiting assumption I can enforce is that the two indicators are both equivalent reflections of the construct. That is, I can specify an equality constraint on the loadings. The equality constraint produces a single estimate that is placed in the location for both loadings (i.e., the loadings would be the same value). Figure 3.7 shows two alternatives for identifying and scaling a construct with only two indicators. Take a moment to verify that the variances of each indicator are being reproduced by the estimates using $\lambda^2 \cdot \psi + \theta$.

I generally advocate using three indicators per construct to provide a just-identified local solution for the statistical estimation of each construct's parameters. In my view, an overidentified model allows too much room for movement as I go from the optimally fitting measurement model to a restricted structural model. Having a just-identified construct is like having a three-legged stool; it sits firmly even if it's on uneven terrain. An overidentified construct, on the other hand, is like a four-legged chair that can wobble when weight is redistributed from the center to an edge of the seat. When a measurement model is fit, the terrain is even; hence both the stool and the chair would be optimally balanced, and either would produce the same information. In the structural model, however, when constraints are placed on estimated relations among constructs, the weight of the model is moved around, and the overidentified chair can wobble depending on the direction and strength of the weight of the constraint(s). A three-legged just-identified stool, on the other hand, will not wobble. When I collect data, my rule of thumb is to measure indicators in multiples of three. If the construct can be well represented with three items, then three is a sufficient number. If more indicators are needed to stabilize the inferences

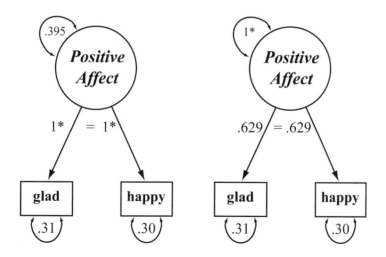

FIGURE 3.7. Identification constraints for two indicators of a construct.

about the construct, then I measure six or nine items and parcel them into three indicators to create a just-identified construct representation (I discussed parcels in Chapter 2; see also Little, Rhemtulla, Gibson, & Schoemann, in press). Having a just-identified measurement model for each construct also means that any degrees of freedom in the model are produced by between-construct relationships because the within-construct relationships are reproduced by the saturated parameter space associated with each construct's measurement elements.

A model's degrees of freedom (*df*) is the difference in the number of known parameters (*b*) and the number of freely estimated parameters (*a*): $df = b - a$. In some models it may be difficult to keep track of the large number of elements; accordingly, the formula $b = p(p + 1)/2 = 10$ could be very helpful (*p* is the number of indicators contained in the input matrix; see Brown, 2006, pp. 67–68).

Before turning to the next topic, take a moment to review the previous material. If there are parts that you didn't quite follow, take the time now to read it again or study the support files on *www.guilford.com/little-materials*.

ADDING MEANS TO THE MODEL: SCALE SETTING AND IDENTIFICATION WITH MEANS

In addition to the covariance structures reproduced in Equation 3.1, SEM models are able to use and model the means of the indicators in order to estimate the means of the latent constructs. Means are very useful bits of information to include in many, if not all, SEM models. Knowing the relative locations of the constructs, particularly if the metric is interpretable, provides rich information; and many times, key hypotheses are about the means of the constructs. To address such questions, some researchers revert back to the scale means to run some form of an ANOVA. This practice should be avoided. Reverting back to manifest variables to test hypotheses about the means should not be done if the data are amenable to a latent-variable CFA approach. In a CFA model, the means are also corrected for attenuation and do not require the assumption of tau-equivalence among the indicators being averaged (as is assumed in scale averages of manifest variables).

The general equation for the mean structures is shown in Equation 3.3. In Figure 3.8, I've added a new figural convention to the standard ones, which is the triangle with the number 1 in the center of it. This symbol represents the column vector constant (intercept) that is used to estimate a mean when a variable is regressed upon it: the column of 1.0's is the intercept of a regression equation. That is, when a variable is regressed onto a vector constant, the vector of 1.0's does not vary; as a result, the estimated value of the scores that do vary becomes the mean of the distribution of those scores when the latent variable is 0.

The mean of each indicator is estimated in the matrix tau, **T**, which is actually a

Equation 3.3. The mean structures equation

$$E(y) = \mu_y = \mathbf{T} + \mathbf{\Lambda A}$$

- y are the scores on the indicators.
- $E()$ is the expectation operator (i.e., the mean of y).
- μ_y is the model-implied vector of means of the indicators, y. It is the mean structures analogue of Σ.
- $\mathbf{\Lambda}$ is the matrix of loadings or estimates of the relations of indicators to constructs.
- $\mathbf{T}$ is the column vector of indicator means.
- $\mathbf{A}$ is a column vector of latent construct means.

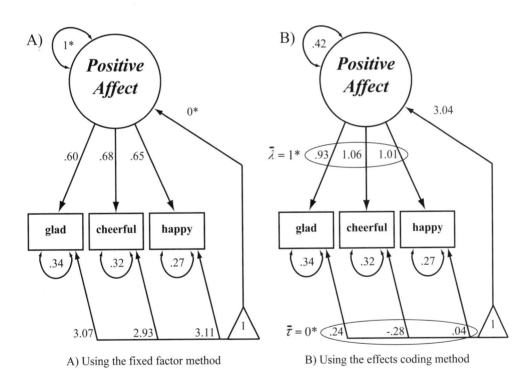

A) Using the fixed factor method B) Using the effects coding method

FIGURE 3.8. Adding the means structures and their scaling constraints. Each model now reproduces the observed correlations, standard deviations, and means in Table 3.3 exactly (if you calculate using tracing rules, they will be within rounding error). In B, the intercepts are constrained to average 0. Keep in mind that correlations can be converted to covariances using the variances of the variables following Equation 3.3.

vector (a single column of means with a row entry for each indicator in a given model). The matrix Λ is the same matrix of loadings that was estimated in Equation 3.1. Because the loadings are included in Equation 3.3, the means structures model is inherently linked to the covariance structures model. Moreover, the strength of a loading of an indicator on a construct works as a weighting factor for determining the estimate of the latent mean. That is, indicators with stronger loadings contribute more of their mean-level information to defining the construct's mean. The Greek letter alpha, $\mathbf{A}$, is used to represent the estimated means of the latent constructs. When I work out the individual equations, the lowercase Greek letter tau, τ, is used to depict the mean of the indicators, and the lowercase Greek letter alpha, α, is used to represent the mean of the latent factor. In my labeling of these parameters, I am following the LISREL model's y-side nomenclature (as an aside to those who know the full LISREL model, I think it is simpler to focus on just the y-side and not make a distinction between x-side and y-side; there is no loss in generality in doing so).

Just as the covariance structures dimension of the SEM model requires a scale setting constraint, so too does the mean structures part. For the means, however, 0 is the fixed scaling point. The reason 0 is used instead of a nonzero value (as was needed in the covariance part of the model) is that means are estimated as distances from 0 (either positive or negative). Pinning down the estimates for the means involves pinning down the location of the 0 such that the distances from that chosen 0 point can be calculated.

In addition to adding the means model to the diagrams presented in Figure 3.8, I'm also estimating the parameters based on the covariance matrix among the indicators instead of the correlation matrix. That is, I used covariances as the information to be analyzed for the covariance structures part of the model. For analysis purposes, correlations can be converted to covariances by taking each element in a correlation matrix and multiplying it by the product of the two standard deviations that are involved, as shown in Equation 3.4a.

In Equation 3.4, c_{ij} is the covariance between variable i and variable j, and r_{ij} is the correlation coefficient between the two variables. The standard deviations of i

---

Equation 3.4. Covariances and correlations

a) $c_{ij} = r_{ij} \cdot (sd_i \cdot sd_j)$

b) $r_{ij} = c_{ij} / (sd_i \cdot sd_j)$

- c_{ij} is the covariance between variable i and variable j.
- r_{ij} is the correlation between variable i and variable j.
- sd_i is the standard deviation of variable i.
- sd_j is the standard deviation of variable j.

and j are denoted as sd_i and sd_j, respectively. When the association is a variable with itself, c_{ij} becomes the variance of the variable because $r_{ij} = 1$ and sd_i is the same as sd_j, which gives the simple square of the standard deviation. I can also reverse this process to get r_{ij} from c_{ij} by dividing the covariance, c_{ij}, by the product of the two standard deviations (as shown in Equation 3.4b).

If I calculate $\lambda^2 \cdot \psi + \theta$ for each indicator, I get the total variance of each indicator in its observed metric (see Table 3.3 for the variances). The estimated variance of the latent construct using the effects coding method is still the weighted average of the amount of reliable variance that each indicator contributes to the definition of the latent construct. This parameter is now being estimated in the metric of the measured indicators. Recall that these indicators were measured on a 1–4 scale.

Regarding the means structures, the mean of the latent factor is fixed at 0 to set the scale if you are using the fixed factor method. Some authors also fix the mean of the latent factor to set the scale of the means structures even when they choose the marker variable method of scaling for the covariance structures. If it were me, I'd be consistent and fix the marker variable intercept to 0. More specifically, I would fix the intercept of the marker variable to 0 if I used a marker variable to set the scale for the covariance structures information. I don't show an example of the marker variable method in Figure 3.8 because I want to discourage its use in general.

Referring back to the estimates in Figure 3.8A, we see that as a result of using the fixed factor scale setting method, the product of a loading and the latent mean will be 0, and the estimated means of the measured indicators are fully reproduced as estimates in **T**. Notice that the magnitudes of the loadings and the estimates of the residuals are now different from the estimates I made for this part of the model using correlations. This change simply reflects the fact that the scale of the variances is no longer in a standardized metric (i.e., where the variances are transformed to be equal to 1); instead, they are estimated in the raw metric of the indicators, where the variances are the observed variances obtained from the raw data (see Table 3.3).

Panel B in Figure 3.8 shows the application of the effects coding constraint for the means structures part of the model, where the loadings are constrained such that they sum to 0. To achieve this constraint, I simply constrain one of the intercepts to equal 0 minus the other two estimates (e.g., $\tau_1 = 0 - \tau_2 - \tau_3$). The effects coding model in Figure 3.8B produces the model-implied covariance matrix and the model-implied row of means that is shown in Table 3.6. For example, the mean of "Glad" that is listed in Table 3.3 would be reproduced by taking the τ_1 value of .24 and add it to the .93 loading times the 3.04 latent mean. Within rounding error, this equation would equal the observed mean of "Glad," which is 3.07. As I have mentioned before, the method of scaling does not affect the fit of a model. It affects only the parameter estimates that emerge. When the equations are worked out, the model-implied information is exactly the same for each method of scale setting.

TABLE 3.6. Implied variance–covariance matrix, Σ, from the model parameters found in Figure 3.8 (Panel B) and the model-implied vector of means

	Y_1	Y_2	Y_3
Y_1	$\lambda_{1,1}\,\psi_{1,1}\,\lambda_{1,1}+\theta_{1,1}$	Same information as is listed below	
Y_2	$\lambda_{1,1}\,\psi_{1,1}\,\lambda_{2,1}$	$\lambda_{2,1}\,\psi_{1,1}\,\lambda_{2,1}+\theta_{2,2}$	the diagonal
Y_3	$\lambda_{1,1}\,\psi_{1,1}\,\lambda_{3,1}$	$\lambda_{2,1}\,\psi_{1,1}\,\lambda_{3,1}$	$\lambda_{3,1}\,\psi_{1,1}\,\lambda_{3,1}+\theta_{3,3}$
μ	$\tau_1+\lambda_{1,1}\,\alpha_1$	$\tau_2+\lambda_{2,1}\,\alpha_1$	$\tau_3+\lambda_{3,1}\,\alpha_1$

Note. Each tau, τ, is the mean of the indicator from the regression of the indicator on the construct. Alpha, α, is the mean of the latent construct. Mu, μ, is the model-implied mean of each indicator. The scale for the estimates of the means depends upon which element is fixed at 0.

ADDING A LONGITUDINAL COMPONENT TO THE CFA MODEL

To illustrate additional features of the longitudinal measurement model, I have drawn the CFA model for the three indicators of the same underlying construct at two time points (Figure 3.9). In a moment, I'll fit this model to the positive affect indicators. For now, take note of the two features of this model. First, I've drawn and labeled the parameters using the generic Greek lettering to indicate the fact that Equation 3.1 and Equation 3.2 are still the central underpinnings of the model. Second, the residual variances of the corresponding indicators are allowed to correlate with each other over time. In this example, Y_1, Y_2, and Y_3 are the same indicators measured at two different time points. In addition to the information that is common to the construct, the corresponding indicators (e.g., Y_1 at Time 1 and Y_1 at Time 2) share specific information that is unique to the indicator.

Because each indicator occurs at more than one time point in the model, the unique parts (the item-specific variance, to be more precise) are expected to correlate with each other. These correlated residuals are specified in longitudinal models a priori. Even if these estimates turn out to be nonsignificant, I recommend that they remain in the model. If these estimates are not exactly 0, some amount of misfit would be produced by not estimating them. This slight amount of misfit would be forced into the other parameter estimates of the model and would introduce some bias (which should be avoided) in the model parameters.

The model-implied covariance matrix reproduced by the longitudinal model in Figure 3.9 is presented in Table 3.7. Each equation is very similar to those I introduced earlier in this chapter. These equations can also be captured using tracing rules. When tracing, I go out of a circle along only one route (i.e., via an arrowhead pointing to the construct). The variance estimate of a construct is a double-headed curved arrow that starts and ends with the same circle. This "roundabout" is a two-way street, so I can enter on either end and exit out the other. But once I've done

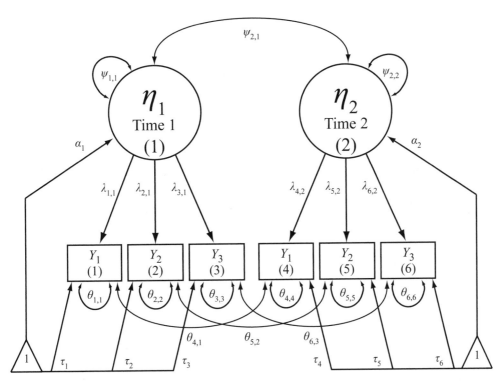

FIGURE 3.9. Diagram of a simple longitudinal model. Because Y_1, Y_2, and Y_3 are the same indicators measured at two different time points, their residuals (unique factors) are allowed to correlate over time. For labeling purposes, boxes are numbered uniquely, beginning with 1 and ending with 6. Circles are also numbered uniquely, beginning with 1 and ending with 2. The parameters are then designated using these uniquely assigned numbers.

TABLE 3.7. Model-implied covariance matrix and means from the longitudinal model depicted in Figure 3.9

	Time 1			Time 2		
	Y_1 (1)	Y_2 (2)	Y_3 (3)	Y_1 (4)	Y_2 (5)	Y_3(6)
Y_1 (1)	$\lambda_{1,1}\,\psi_{1,1}\,\lambda_{1,1}+\theta_{1,1}$					
Y_2 (2)	$\lambda_{1,1}\,\psi_{1,1}\,\lambda_{2,1}$	$\lambda_{2,1}\,\psi_{1,1}\,\lambda_{2,1}+\theta_{2,2}$				
Y_3 (3)	$\lambda_{1,1}\,\psi_{1,1}\,\lambda_{3,1}$	$\lambda_{2,1}\,\psi_{1,1}\,\lambda_{3,1}$	$\lambda_{3,1}\,\psi_{1,1}\,\lambda_{3,1}+\theta_{3,3}$			
Y_1 (4)	$\lambda_{1,1}\,\psi_{2,1}\,\lambda_{4,1}+\theta_{4,1}$	$\lambda_{2,1}\,\psi_{2,1}\,\lambda_{4,1}$	$\lambda_{3,1}\,\psi_{2,1}\,\lambda_{4,1}$	$\lambda_{4,2}\,\psi_{2,2}\,\lambda_{1,1}+\theta_{4,4}$		
Y_2 (5)	$\lambda_{1,1}\,\psi_{2,1}\,\lambda_{5,1}$	$\lambda_{2,1}\,\psi_{2,1}\,\lambda_{6,1}+\theta_{5,2}$	$\lambda_{3,1}\,\psi_{2,1}\,\lambda_{5,1}$	$\lambda_{4,2}\,\psi_{2,2}\,\lambda_{5,2}$	$\lambda_{5,2}\,\psi_{2,2}\,\lambda_{5,2}+\theta_{5,5}$	
Y_3 (6)	$\lambda_{1,1}\,\psi_{2,1}\,\lambda_{6,1}$	$\lambda_{2,1}\,\psi_{2,1}\,\lambda_{6,1}$	$\lambda_{3,1}\,\psi_{2,1}\,\lambda_{6,1}+\theta_{6,2}$	$\lambda_{4,2}\,\psi_{2,2}\,\lambda_{6,2}$	$\lambda_{5,2}\,\psi_{2,2}\,\lambda_{6,2}$	$\lambda_{6,2}\,\psi_{1,1}\,\lambda_{6,2}+\theta_{6,6}$
μ	$\tau_1+\lambda_{1,1}\,\alpha_1$	$\tau_2+\lambda_{2,1}\,\alpha_1$	$\tau_3+\lambda_{3,1}\,\alpha_1$	$\tau_4+\lambda_{4,2}\,\alpha_2$	$\tau_5+\lambda_{5,2}\,\alpha_2$	$\tau_6+\lambda_{6,2}\,\alpha_2$

Note. Y_1, Y_2, and Y_3 are the same indicators measured at two different time points.

this, I have to go back down a line to a box. On the other hand, to trace the association between an indicator of a construct at Time 1 and an indicator of a construct at Time 2, I go through the path labeled $\psi_{2,1}$. In Table 3.7, I have highlighted the lower quadrant that contains the nine estimated covariances among the Time 1 and Time 2 indicators. Notice that the estimated covariance between the two constructs in Figure 3.9, $\psi_{2,1}$, is involved in each of these nine equations.

From a latent-variable perspective, this restricted model is quite reasonable. The model stipulates that the main reason that a variable at Time 1 correlates with another variable at Time 2 has to do with the association of the underlying latent construct between the occasions of measurement. The only exception to this restricted association is that the unique factors (i.e., the residual variances) of the like indicators at each measurement occasion are allowed to correlate. This additional amount of association is estimated in the theta matrix and is added to the three cells that form the subdiagonal (i.e., the diagonal found in the lower quadrant) of the theta matrix. The analogy I like to use here is of an ice cube tray (a square and symmetric tray). The observed matrix is the level of the ice in each cell of the tray. We are trying to reproduce that pattern of ice in the tray by specifying a very restricted flow pattern between the cells of the tray. In this model, the main flow from one side to the other is allowed through only one open path, $\psi_{2,1}$. However, we expect the amount of ice in three of the cells to be a little higher than the main path can accommodate; hence we allow three small channels to fill these cells ($\theta_{4,1}$, $\theta_{5,2}$, and $\theta_{6,3}$).

In Figure 3.10, I have put the parameter estimates from fitting this two-construct model to the indicators of positive affect at two time points (see Table 3.8). In Chapter 4, I discuss estimating and evaluating model fit, and in Chapter 5 I discuss the whole concept of factorial invariance. For now, I only want to discuss a couple of points about this model and then introduce the idea of phantom constructs. The first thing to notice is that the estimated association between these two constructs is a covariance of 0.23. The implied correlation between these two constructs is .55. That is, using Equation 3.4, the covariance can be converted into the correlation by taking the covariance of 0.23 and dividing it by the product of the two standard deviations $[0.23/(0.42^{1/2} \cdot 0.43^{1/2}) = .55]$.

ADDING PHANTOM CONSTRUCTS TO THE CFA MODEL

Phantom constructs aren't normally a part of the standard discourse in the world of SEM. On the other hand, the idea of a phantom construct has been around for some time now. David Rindskopf (1984) introduced the idea of using phantom constructs as estimation devices that allow neat things to be done in SEM models. A construct is a phantom construct when it does not have measured indicators, and it is used to "trick" the SEM program into providing an estimate in a form and metric that it normally would not. In this section, I describe a use of phantom constructs that I

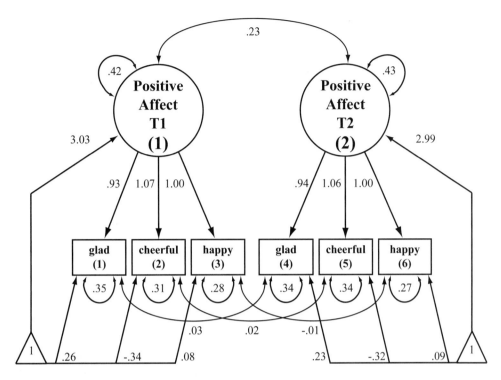

FIGURE 3.10. Estimates for two time points with positive affect. In this model, the loadings and intercepts are not yet equated over time. This model is referred to as the configural invariant model. I discuss factorial invariance in Chapter 5. Model fit: $\chi^2_{(n=832,\ 5)}$ = 18.41; RMSEA = .057$_{(.031;\ .086)}$; CFI = .992; TLI/NNFI = .968. I used the effects coding method of identification.

have found useful in my own modeling activities. It may seem like this topic is a bit out of place here, but I want to show how phantom constructs work mathematically before I show how to use them to make important comparisons across groups or across times.

Because phantom constructs are estimation devices, they are no more than mathematical conveniences that allow me to estimate parameters in different ways (e.g., as a standard deviation estimate as opposed to a variance estimate or as a correlation instead of a covariance). The key feature of phantom constructs is that they provide *estimates* of parameters that emerge in a mathematically more useful form (e.g., a correlation is more useful than a covariance). For example, in many applications of SEM, longitudinal models included, adding phantom constructs provides the mathematical convenience of estimating associations among constructs in a correlation metric while still providing estimates of all parameters based on the covariance information contained in the raw data. Although I can estimate construct relations as correlations by fixing the factor variances to set the scale, this method of estimating correlations fails to work when factorial invariance is tested across time (again,

TABLE 3.8. Sufficient statistics for the three indicators of positive affect at two time points

| | Time 1 | | | Time 2 | | |
	Glad	Cheerful	Happy	Glad	Cheerful	Happy
Glad	1.0					
Cheerful	.552	1.0				
Happy	.563	.603	1.0			
Glad	.319	.358	.278	1.0		
Cheerful	.244	.359	.319	.560	1.0	
Happy	.322	.364	.321	.562	.597	1.0
SD	.842	.889	.835	.841	.909	.840
Var (SD^2)	.709	.791	.697	.707	.826	.705
Mean	3.07	2.93	3.11	3.03	2.86	3.09

Note. Same sample of 823 7th and 8th graders at two time points assessed in the fall of two successive school years.

for details of factorial invariance, see Chapters 5 and 6). In other words, when two or more time points or two or more groups are involved, fixing the variance to 1.0 to set the scale won't solve the problem because factorial invariance will be imposed. In these situations, where I cannot fix the latent variance to 1.0, phantom variables offer a convenient tool to still represent latent associations in a correlational metric.

Figure 3.11 is the same model fit as shown in Figure 3.10, but it now has phantom constructs included. Notice that the model parameters for the loadings, intercepts, residuals, and latent means have not changed from those in the model shown in Figure 3.10. Moreover, the model fit is exactly the same as that for the model without the phantom constructs (see Figure 3.10). The only difference between these two models is the inclusion of the phantom constructs.

These higher order phantom constructs are used to convert the variances of the two constructs into standard deviations and the covariance between them into a correlation. The key to using phantom constructs for this purpose is that the variances of the lower order constructs (i.e., the constructs that are directly predicting the indicators) are fixed at 0. These constraints force all the variance captured by the loadings of the indicators on the lower order construct to get squeezed into the regression parameter that links a lower order construct with its associated phantom construct. The other key is that the phantom construct must have a scale set for it. Setting the scale of a phantom construct by fixing its respective variance to 1.0 makes the variance standardized. As a result, the association between each of the phantom constructs is now in correlation metric. The link between the phantom

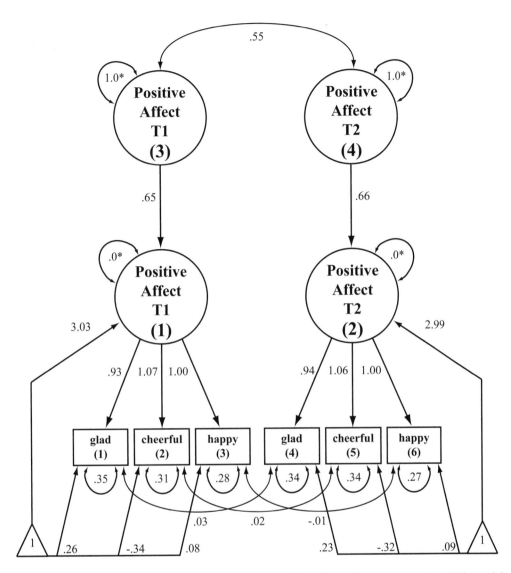

FIGURE 3.11. Estimates for two time points with positive affect, phantom constructs. This model is mathematically the same as that fit in Figure 3.10, except that phantom constructs have been introduced. Model fit: $\chi^2_{(n=823,\ 5)} = 18.41$; RMSEA = $.057_{(.031;\ .086)}$; CFI = .992; TLI/NNFI = .968. *designates parameters that are fixed to the value indicated.

construct and its corresponding lower order construct is a regression coefficient that makes the value of the parameter estimate a standard deviation instead of a variance estimate. In other words, the regression coefficient is the standard deviation of the lower order construct because the regression of the lower order constructs onto the phantom constructs predicts all the variance of the lower order constructs. The original variance of the lower construct is reproduced by tracing up the regression path that links the lower to the phantom construct, going up and around the variance of the phantom construct and then back down the regression. Because the variance of the higher order phantom construct is fixed at 1 to set its scale, the variance of the lower order construct is reproduced as simply the square of the linking regression (this mathematical feature is true only because the lower order construct's variance is restricted to equal 0 so there can't be anything left over).

In Equation 3.4a, the formula for a covariance is the correlation multiplied by the respective standard deviations of the two variables. In Figure 3.11, the original covariance of 0.23 found in Figure 3.10 is reproduced (within rounding error) as 0.65 (the standard deviation at Time 1) times .55 (the estimated correlation) times 0.66 (the standard deviation at Time 2). In other words, I have taken the variance–covariance information that was estimated in Figure 3.10 and reconfigured the model to estimate these values as standard deviations and correlations, as shown in Figure 3.11.

The usefulness of phantom constructs is demonstrated in a hypothetical example depicted in Figure 3.12. In this figure, I have shown the estimates as they often would be estimated; namely, in their variance–covariance metric. In Panel A, I have a hypothetic measurement occasion with an estimated covariance between construct A and construct B of 0.81. In Panel B, a different measurement occasion has an estimated covariance of 0.82 between these two constructs. If I were interested in testing whether the strength of the association between the two constructs is the same at both measurement occasions, I would normally put an equality constraint on the two estimates and evaluate the change in model fit via the χ^2 difference test (see Chapter 4 for details of this test and other issues related to model evaluation and testing). This test would tell me that the 0.81 and the 0.82 are not statistically different from one another, and I would be tempted to conclude that the two constructs have the same magnitude of association in the two groups. I would be wrong. The reason I would be wrong is that the metric of the covariance of 0.81 is derived from the two variance estimates, which are relatively small (1.21 and 1.22), compared with the metric of the 0.82 covariance, which is derived from the 1.59 and 1.47 variance estimates. Because the variances are very different, the meanings of the 0.81 and 0.82 are also very different.

I could evaluate the standardized solution and would see that the implied correlation is .54 versus .67. I would not be able to test, however, whether these implied correlations are different from one another because they are postestimation transformations of the model parameters. The only way to test these correlations for differences is to make these values become estimated parameters in the model. Here's where phantom constructs become beneficial. In other words, to put the two estimates on a comparable metric, it is imperative that phantom constructs be employed—it's the only way to get estimates on a common, and therefore comparable, metric. On the right side of Figure 3.12 is the same hypothetical data fit as phantom constructs. In Panel A the variances of 1.21 and 1.22 become standard deviations of 1.11 and 1.11

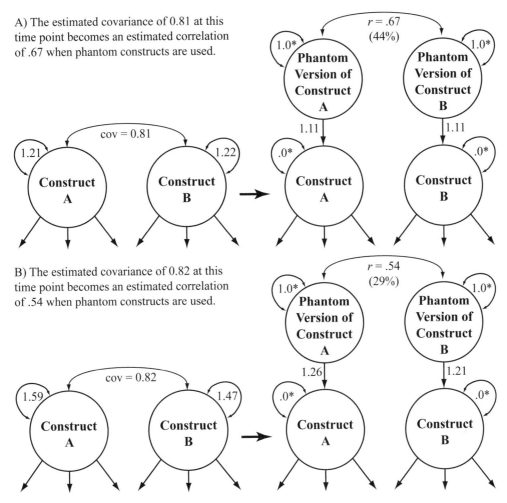

A) The estimated covariance of 0.81 at this time point becomes an estimated correlation of .67 when phantom constructs are used.

B) The estimated covariance of 0.82 at this time point becomes an estimated correlation of .54 when phantom constructs are used.

FIGURE 3.12. Hypothetical example showing why phantom constructs are useful. The models on the left show estimated covariances, and the models on the right demonstrate the phantom construct decompositions of the variances and covariances into standard deviations and correlations. Time 1 is in Panel A (upper panel), and Time 2 is in Panel B (lower panel).

(rounding differences), and the covariance of 0.81 becomes an estimated correlation of .67. In Panel B, the variances of 1.59 and 1.47 become standard deviations of 1.26 and 1.21. The covariance of 0.82 becomes an estimated correlation of .54. Now, because these two correlations are estimated parameters of the model, I can test them for differences by placing an equality constraint on the two parameters and evaluating the change in χ^2 for the model. I would find that these two parameters are significantly different, and I would then be able to conclude that the strength of the associations between these two constructs at these two measurement occasions are different across time.

In later chapters, I work more closely with phantom constructs to show how to perform specific tests of the standardized estimates. The important point now is that statistical tests can be performed only on parameters of a model that are actually estimated. All SEM software can do postestimation transformations of the estimated parameters to show what their standardized value would be. Unfortunately, there is no way to test postestimation values in any statistical way. In other words, performing statistical comparisons across standardized parameters is not possible unless they can be obtained as estimated parameters in a model. Phantom constructs allow me to do just that—estimate parameters in a common standardized metric on which I can then perform tests. I revisit the uses and benefits of phantom constructs in later chapters.

SUMMARY

I covered a lot of ground in this chapter. I strongly urge you to reread this material if any of it was new to you. The issues that I address in this chapter can be thorny for folks who are new to SEM in general, and some of the issues are misunderstood even among seasoned modelers. I recycle through many of these ideas as they come up in later chapters, but these issues are not the focus of future discussions and are more cursorily covered. If you are a bit uncertain about these issues, you'll have difficulty following the other ideas that I convey. Now would also be a good time to test your understanding by taking the quiz associated with this chapter, available on the web at *www.guilford.com/little-materials*.

KEY TERMS AND CONCEPTS INTRODUCED IN THIS CHAPTER

Degrees of freedom (df). The difference between the number of unique variances and covariances and means minus the number of parameter estimates contained in a model. Parameters that are fixed to set the scale do not count as estimated parameters. The number of unique variances and covariances in a covariance matrix is equal to $p \cdot (p + 1)/2$, where p is the number of manifest variables in the observed covariance matrix. The term *degrees of freedom* is also used to refer to the "number of unique variances and covariances (and means)." Degrees of freedom are the unused unique elements. When nothing is estimated, degrees of freedom equal the total unique elements. When a parameter is estimated, a degree of freedom is used up. Thus, degrees of freedom are like dollars. You spend one for every unique parameter estimate in a given model.

Exogenous versus endogenous constructs. Constructs are classified into two general kinds. Exogenous constructs are ones that have their origin outside the system. Endogenous constructs originate inside the system or downstream in the system. In other words, endogenous variables have one or more paths pointing into them from other variable(s), whereas exogenous variables have no paths pointing into them from other variable(s). In a longitudinal study, the constructs measured at Time 1 are sometimes considered exogenous because they reflect the origin of the study. Constructs measured at later time points are considered endogenous. In my view, constructs measured at Time 1 should be classified as endogenous constructs because they are not measured at the origin, when the construct emerged as a measureable entity.

Latent variable, latent factor, construct. These three terms are used interchangeably to refer to the unobservable "thing" or "entity" that gives rise to the observed measurements represented by the manifest indicators.

Measured/manifest variable/indicator. These terms can be intermixed (measured indicator, manifest indicator). Indicators are the things that we can actually record. We use the recorded data as input information to specify, estimate, and evaluate a hypothesized SEM model that attempts to reproduce the recorded information with a set of theoretically meaningful parameter estimates.

Measurement model. The initial confirmatory factor analysis (CFA) model that underlies the structural model. The measurement model tests the adequacy (as indexed by model fit) of the specified relations whereby indicators are linked to their underlying construct.

Model-implied matrix/vector. The matrix or vector that one computes from the set of estimated model parameters. These estimates are compared with the observed matrix and mean vector to determine how well the model reproduces the observed estimates. Usually the model-implied matrix does not reproduce the observed data precisely because we are attempting to estimate a parsimonious model that can effectively reproduce the data with a restricted, theoretically chosen set of constraints.

Over-, under-, and just identified. When the number of unique elements available to inform the parameter estimates of a construct is greater than required, the construct is overidentified (i.e., available degrees of freedom are greater than the number of parameters estimated). When the available degrees of freedom are equal to the number of parameters estimated, the construct is just identified. When more parameters need to be estimated than there are degrees of freedom available to inform the estimates, the construct is underidentified. When the construct is underidentified, additional constraints must be placed. Such constraints are based on assumptions that cannot be tested and therefore are limiting assumptions.

Phantom construct. An estimation tool that allows estimates of model parameters in alternative forms and metrics. A construct is considered a phantom construct when it does not have any measured indicators. The information contained in the phantom construct is derived from information found in other constructs. The example in this chapter used phantom constructs to standardize the relationships among lower order constructs by predicting all the variance in the lower order constructs, which is reproduced as the regression coefficient that links the higher order phantom construct with the lower order indicated construct.

Reflective and effects indicators versus formative and causal indicators. Indicators of latent constructs come in two classes. Reflective or effects indicators are said to reflect the construct; that is, the construct "causes" the indicators. In this regard, the covariances among the indicators are due to the effects of the construct. Therefore, the direction of prediction (the direction of the arrows) is from the construct to the indicator. The other class of indicators is called formative or causal indicators. Here, the indicators are seen as the causal mechanism that gives rise to the construct (hence the arrows go from the indicator to the construct). The number of reasons that formative indicators are problematic is substantial—I stopped counting at 27.

Saturated model. This model has just as many estimates as there are unique elements in the variance–covariance matrix (and mean vector), and the model reproduces the observed data exactly (i.e., with perfect fit).

Structural model. A model in which directed regression relationships are specified among the latent constructs. A longitudinal structural model is presented in Chapter 6.

RECOMMENDED READINGS

General Issues in CFA

Brown, T. A. (2006). *Confirmatory factor analysis for applied research.* New York: Guilford Press.

> As I mentioned at the beginning of this chapter, Tim Brown's (2006) book covers all the nuts and bolts of CFA. It is a full treatment that is very accessible. You'll notice when you read Tim's book that he makes some recommendations that I don't make, and vice versa. I think it is important to understand that there is no one correct way to do SEM. It is always a matter of wise judgment and principled reasoning.

Cudeck, R., & MacCallum, R. C. (2007). *Factor analysis at 100: Historical developments and future directions.* Mahwah, NJ: Erlbaum.

> This book's got lots of great chapters on the origins of SEM.

Little, T. D. (1997). Mean and covariance structures (MACS) analyses of cross-cultural data: Practical and theoretical issues. *Multivariate Behavioral Research, 32,* 53–76.

> I discuss the use of phantom constructs, building upon the ideas that David Rindskopf introduced in 1984. In this paper, I discuss phantom constructs for converting covariances to correlations. I also discuss a number of issues related to factorial invariance and the implications for cross-cultural comparisons.

Loehlin, J. C. (2004). *Latent variable models: An introduction to factor, path, and structural equation analysis* (4th ed.). Mahwah, NJ: Erlbaum.

> Although I cited him in this chapter for his coverage of tracing rules, John Loehlin's book is a great overview of latent-variable models in general.

Issues in Scaling and Construct Identification

Gonzalez, R., & Griffin, D. (2001). Testing parameters in structural equation modeling: Every "one" matters. *Psychological Methods, 6,* 258–269.

This paper discusses why the Wald test (dividing a parameter estimate by its standard error) should not be used as an indication of significance in SEM models, particularly if the test is a critical test.

Little, T. D., Slegers, D. W., & Card, N. A. (2006). A non-arbitrary method of identifying and scaling latent variables in SEM and MACS models. *Structural Equation Modeling, 13,* 59–72.

This is the article that introduces the effects coding method of identification.

4

Model Fit, Sample Size, and Power

"Is my model fit OK?" "Is my sample size big enough?" "Do I have enough power?" These questions are common and fundamental to SEM models. My answer to these questions is, "it depends." In fact, the two most common answers that I give to questions about SEM are, "it depends" and "we don't know." Even here, "we don't know" is a fair answer to these key questions. As I walk through the issues that underlie these questions, keep in mind that this chapter is likely to have the most changes as future editions are released.

Before I begin, I want to point out that SEM analyses attempt to reproduce the *sufficient statistics* that summarize the observed data. Equation 3.1 (i.e., $\mathbf{\Sigma} = \mathbf{\Lambda\Psi\Lambda'} + \mathbf{\Theta}$), for example, attempts to reproduce the matrix $\mathbf{S}$, which is the summary of the observed data in terms of the variances of the variables and the covariances among them. Similarly, when we add the means of the indicators into the model (Equation 3.3; i.e., $\mu_y = \mathbf{T} + \mathbf{\Lambda A}$), the summary of the means of the observed data are being reproduced (not the raw data). In fact, for many purposes, the input data to the SEM programs can simply be these sufficient statistics—although some estimators (e.g., FIML when there is missing data) and some types of SEM models (e.g., multilevel SEM) may require that the raw data be read in.

MODEL FIT AND TYPES OF FIT INDICES

The fit of a model can be gauged by using two different ways of thinking about model fit. The first way is termed the statistical rationale, and it relies solely on the statistical fit of a model provided by the χ^2 statistic. The second way is termed the modeling rationale, and it uses a number of alternative measures of model fit that can be classified into two general types: relative fit indices and absolute fit indices. Relative measures of model fit rely on a null model to gauge model fit. A null model provides a measure of bad model fit (in fact, the worst fitting model). This worst fitting model can be used to index the relative improvement in model fit that a hypothesized model provides. The saturated model is at the other extreme. The saturated model fits the observed data exactly and typically has no degrees of freedom. Absolute fit indices typically compare the hypothesized model to the saturated model, whereas relative fit indices usually compare the hypothesized model to the null model. I have depicted the relations among these models in Figure 4.1 as a continuum from least restricted (perfect fitting, saturated) to most restricted (worst fitting, null).

The hypothesized or tested models that are fit to data will generally (hopefully) fall toward the good side of this continuum. The levels of fit go by various terms. I've listed a few in the figure to show their relative relationships. The precise values for switching from one category of fit to the next are generally fuzzy, and I give some guidance on these as I move through the measures of model fit.

Statistical Rationale

As I mentioned, the first approach to evaluating model fit is the statistical approach (see Little, 1997). Here, the model χ^2 provides a statistically precise measure of the difference between the implied model estimates and the observed data. The model χ^2 value has certain degrees of freedom (the difference between the number of unique sufficient statistics analyzed and the number of estimated parameters in the model). The χ^2 test is a test of exact fit using the central χ^2 distribution as the reference for determining probabilities. A problem with the χ^2 test is that it is highly sensitive to sample size, a problem that is compounded when many degrees of freedom are involved. In most typical applications of SEM, the χ^2 test will be significant, indicating that the reproduced matrices (covariance matrix and mean vector) are not statistically equal to the observed matrices. Even if I adjusted the p-value for such a test in an attempt to balance Type I and Type II error, given the power of the test, the statistical hypothesis testing rationale for such a test is not easily defensible. Moreover, the "preferred" outcome of the χ^2 test of model fit is to accept the null hypothesis of no difference between the observed matrix ($\mathbf{S}$) and estimated (model-implied)

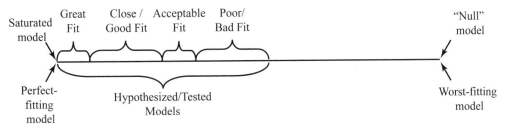

FIGURE 4.1. Continuum of conceptual relations among models. This continuum goes from the worst fitting, "null" model on the right to the perfect-fitting, saturated model on the left, with the hypothesized model and the different categories of fit in between. These category labels are loose terms, and the precise division between categories varies.

matrix (Σ). As any Stat 101 student learns, we do not "accept" the null; we can reject it or fail to reject it. Using the χ^2 test of model fit for testing our preferred hypothesis of no differences ($\mathbf{S} = \mathbf{\Sigma}$) in this way is trying to turn hypothesis testing on its ear (i.e., the preferred outcome is the null hypothesis of no difference), which is neither advisable nor preferred.

As MacCallum and Austin (2000) note, models are just approximation tools that we use to guide our thinking and to try to make some sense of the world. At the same time, they also caution us that model fit should not be used to provide unjustified enthusiasm over the implied accuracy of a given model:

> With respect to model fit, researchers do not seem adequately sensitive to the funda-mental reality that there is no true model . . . , that all models are wrong to some degree, even in the population, and that the best one can hope for is to identify a parsimoni-ous, substantively meaningful model that fits observed data adequately well. At the same time, one must recognize that there may well be other models that fit the data to approximately the same degree. . . . It is clear that a finding of good fit does not imply that a model is correct or true, but only plausible. (MacCallum & Austin, 2000, p. 218)

Because of the fact that (1) the χ^2 test is overly sensitive to trivial influences when sample size is moderately large and (2) it is a test of exact fit, which is not a feasible criterion (and the goal is to "accept" the null), quantitative specialists have developed a number of alternative measures of model fit. All of these alternative measures of model fit are consistent with the idea that all models are imperfect mod-els, even in the population.

Modeling Rationale

A modeling rationale for evaluating model fit recognizes this fundamental real-ity that models are gross approximations of the actual processes that generate the underlying data. In this regard, model fit is judged by the relative degree to which a given model approximates the data. As I mentioned, the various alternative fit mea-sures fall into one of two categories, absolute and relative fit measures.

Steiger and Lind (1980) provided what is now a very popular formalization of this approximation idea when they introduced the root mean square error of approxi-mation (RMSEA; see Equation 4.1; it is usually pronounced R-M-S-E-A; practice saying this until it comes trippingly off the tongue, lest you sound uninitiated). The RMSEA is classified in the absolute fit category because it uses the saturated model as the comparison standard (i.e., only the model's χ^2 information is used). It provides an index of the amount of misfit per degree of freedom in the model. Because the expected value of a χ^2 is equal to the degrees of freedom, the amount of misfit is the value of the χ^2 above and beyond the expected value. This value, which is termed the noncentrality parameter, is divided by sample size minus 1 in order to remove the effect of sample size on the χ^2. The RMSEA has an additional correction factor for

Equation 4.1. The root mean squared error of approximation (RMSEA)

$$RMSEA = \sqrt{\{(x_t^2 - df_t / (N-1)\} / (df_t / g)}$$

- χ^2_t is the tested model's χ^2.
- df_t is the degrees of freedom for the tested model.
- N is the sample size.
- g is the number of groups.
- $\chi^2_t - df_t$ is termed the noncentrality parameter.
- A central χ^2 is equal to the df (i.e., the expected value of a χ^2 is equal to the df).
- Rules of thumb for interpreting the RMSEA:

Poor fit:	> .10*ish*
Mediocre fit:	.10 – .08*ish*
Acceptable fit:	.08 – .05*ish*
Good/Close fit:	.05 – .02*ish*
Great fit:	< .01*ish*

the number of groups (i.e., the g in Equation 4.1; see Steiger, 1998). This sample-size corrected amount of misfit is then divided by the degrees of freedom of the model to obtain the amount of misfit per degree of freedom.

In the details noted for Equation 4.1, I've provided some guidelines for interpreting model fit using the RMSEA. In my experience, many if not most models provide acceptable model fit when they are around .08. Another nice feature of the RMSEA is the ability to calculate a confidence interval around the point estimate. This confidence interval is useful because it provides information about the range in which the true value may fall and highlights the idea that any of the model fit measures should be considered heuristically. Stated differently, we want to avoid reifying any model fit criteria as we have done with the $p < .05$ hypothesis testing criterion.

Because the RMSEA is based on the noncentral χ^2 distribution, the qualities of this distribution can be used to identify the lower and upper confidence intervals for the estimated RMSEA value. Traditionally, the 90% confidence interval is used for the RMSEA estimate. Because the RMSEA has a confidence interval, it can, in fact, be used to provide some statistically based tests of model fit. Two general tests have been suggested. These two kinds of tests redefine both the null hypothesis and the alternative hypothesis that are used to evaluate overall model fit.

The first type of test is the test of not-close fit (or not-acceptable fit), and the second type of test is the test of close fit (or acceptable fit). Keep in mind that in null hypothesis testing, the "thing" that is being tested is what I hope to reject. I hope to reject this prespecified value in favor of an alternative, or I have a situation in which I have failed to reject it. For example, I can choose close fit to be the null and not-close fit to be the alternative, or I can chose not-close fit to be the null and close fit to be the alternative. If I reject the test of not-close fit, then the alternative of close fit is supported. If I reject the test of close fit, then the alternative of not-close fit is supported. As mentioned, the null RMSEA for these tests is commonly specified at .05. When the null RMSEA is specified at .05, I would refer to the tests as tests of close and not-close fit. When the null RMSEA is specified at .08 (which I recommend for most applications), I would refer to the tests as tests of acceptable fit and not-acceptable fit.

In Figure 4.2, I have listed two hypothetical tests of not-acceptable fit in Panels A and B. Here, the null hypothesis is that the population RMSEA is equal to the predetermined value of .08. The alternative hypothesis is that the population RMSEA is lower than this criterion, indicating that I have achieved acceptable model fit. In Panel A, the upper value of the RMSEA confidence interval is below the .08 criterion, and therefore I can reject the null hypothesis of being at the border of acceptable fit in favor of the alternative hypothesis of having acceptable fit. In Panel B, however, the upper value of the confidence interval exceeds the criterion; therefore, I would fail to reject the null and would have to presume one of two things: either I lack power to reject the null (and would need a larger sample size next time), or my model has poor fit not only in my sample but also in the population (this situation would be a good indication that I need to reconsider my model).

The other use of this type of hypothesis testing logic is the test of close/ acceptable fit. Here, the null hypothesis is that the population RMSEA is .05 (close fit) or .08 (acceptable fit), and the alternative is that the population RMSEA is greater than specified null value. Like the χ^2 test of model fit, this formulation of the null

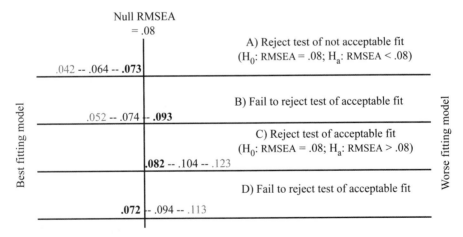

FIGURE 4.2. Rejecting or not rejecting tests of not acceptable fit and tests of acceptable fit. The null hypothesis for each of these tests is that the RMSEA is .08. The hypothetical RMSEA values listed on each line represent the lower 90% confidence value of the RMSEA, the point estimate of the RMSEA, and the upper 90% confidence value of the RMSEA, respectively. The bold confidence value is the one used to determine the significance of the test that is depicted. The gray confidence value would not be involved.

hypothesis is backward in that we want to fail to reject the null (i.e., the preferred outcome is the null outcome, which amounts to "accepting" the null as the preferred outcome). As you can see in Panels C and D of Figure 4.2, the failure to reject the null hypothesis (Panel D) is the preferred outcome because we want our model to have at least acceptable fit!

The logic of the test of not-close fit (or not-acceptable fit) is the more sound way to go, I think. As mentioned, many methodologists place the null hypothesis of close fit at a stringent RMSEA = .05 level. In my figure, I used .08 as the criterion of acceptable fit. I think that you could also use .10 as the "null" criterion of poor fit to see whether your model achieves at least better fit than that. I heartily agree with Browne and Cudeck (1992, 1993), who also were early promoters of the RMSEA, when they state explicitly that models with an RMSEA of about .08 provide acceptable approximations to the data. In my hypothetical tests listed in Figure 4.2, therefore, I am conducting tests of acceptable fit (again, if I put .05 as the null, then I would be testing close fit). You might wonder why the 90% confidence interval of the RMSEA is used for making these tests. The main reason is that these tests of model fit are one-tailed. They are the expectations that are specified a priori, and therefore we want to lump all of the alpha Type I error rate (typically .05) on one side or the other, which is what a 90% confidence interval provides. In Figure 4.2, I have put in bold the critical side of the confidence interval that is involved in the two types of tests and put in gray the side that is not relevant to the test.

Many factors influence model fit and the interpretation of the model fit indices. One factor that is not often discussed in this context is the precedent in the research area in which you are working. If published models have RMSEA values that are routinely in the .05 range for a given area of study and your models are coming in at .08, you might have a difficult time convincing reviewers that you have achieved an acceptable level of model fit. On the other hand, if the precedent in the literature is around .08 and you're in the same ballpark, the level of model fit would not be an issue. Another factor that can influence model fit is the general quality of the indicators that are used to create the constructs. Underdeveloped indicators (i.e., indicators with relatively low reliability and validity) are not as well behaved (because of their poor psychometric characteristics) as well-developed measures and will introduce nuisance information that shows up as mediocre model fit. If the theoretical ideas being tested are new and have merit, the underdeveloped nature of the measures can be excused. Follow-up work can focus on measurement improvements that would increase the quality of the indicators used in a model and thereby improve the general levels of model fit.

Another measure of absolute fit that is becoming more popular is the standardized root mean square residual (SRMR). This measure of model misfit, as the name implies, gets the average of the squared residuals in standardized metric and then takes the square root to get a value that represents the typical amount of misfit. By squaring the residuals, we can get both the positive and negative deviations included in the amount. By standardizing, we eliminate differences in the metrics across different variables and different models. Averaging and square-rooting brings this information together in a meaningful metric. It happens that values of SRMR that are acceptable generally follow the same guidelines for interpreting the RMSEA. SRMR has not been well evaluated for longitudinal models in any systematic way, and so I can't strongly endorse it at this point, but this may change if someone conducts some Monte Carlo work evaluating its performance in the context of longitudinal and multiple-group models.

Now I want to turn attention to the relative fit measures of overall model fit. These measures depend on a null model to gauge the amount of information that a model is able to reproduce. The traditional null model, however, is not appropriate. Hence the need for the longitudinal null model.

The Longitudinal Null Model

Keith Widaman and Jane Thompson (2003) provide a thorough and enlightening discussion of the null model in SEM and why the default null model calculated by most SEM packages is not appropriate.

In longitudinal panel models, as well as with multiple-group models, the default null model is usually wrong. The null model should provide a measure of how much information is contained in the observed data matrix. The *usual* null model, which is appropriate for single-group and single-time-point models, gauges this information by fitting a highly constrained model to the data and seeing how badly it fits. In fact, the null model is the worst fitting model that one can reasonably conceive under a reasonable "null" expectation. For example, a common null expectation about a covariance matrix is that all the covariances are 0. The default null model, in fact, specifies that the indicators have only a variance and that all covariances are fixed at 0. When this model is fit to the data, the estimated χ^2 provides an index of how much information is actually contained in the observed covariances contained in the matrix. If the covariances are generally small, the amount of information will be small, and if the covariances are large, the amount of information will be large. Widaman and Thompson (2003) go on to write about null models for various kinds of tested models. My focus in this book and in this discussion is on panel models in which multiple constructs are measured with multiple indicators and multiple time points and where the indicators' means, variances, and covariances are being modeled.

In longitudinal panel models, most indicators are represented at more than one time point. When the observed matrix contains repeated assessments of the same indicators of the same constructs (i.e., the same things are measured at different measurement occasions), a reasonable "null" expectation is that the variances of the like indicators have not changed. As I show in more detail later, longitudinal panel models attempt to estimate potential changes in the variances of constructs that are repeatedly measured.

As with the variances, the means of the like indicators should have a similar "null" expectation; namely, that the mean levels of indicators measured more than once would not differ across measurement occasions. If multiple groups are also being compared, the null expectation would be that both the variances and means of the corresponding indicators do not differ across each group, as well as across measurement occasions. I show a more detailed example of this null model in Chapter 5, where I also discuss the concept of factorial invariance. Factorial invariance involves making tests of the means of the indicators, and so the null expectation about the means should be included in the null model.

Specifying the appropriate null model, however, does not always lead to better measures of model fit. If the variances and means do not change much in the observed data, or if they are not very different across groups, then these parameters are contributing very little information to the overall null model χ^2. The tested/hypothesized measurement model will not recover much information, and the model fit statistics might be worse than when they are based solely on the covariance structures information. On the other hand, if the data show changes over time or differences between groups, then the model fit statistics likely will improve relative to the traditional independence null model.

The null model should be nested within the tested hypothesized model. A model (C for child) is nested when it can be derived from another model (P for parent) by specifying constraints on the parameters of model P. I explain this idea in more detail later, but by way of illustration: to obtain the independence model, I would constrain all the parameters, except the residual variances, to be 0. That is, the covariances among the constructs would be 0, the variances of the constructs would be 0, and the loadings would be 0. For the longitudinal panel null model, it is nested within the strong factorial invariant model (I discuss the model in detail in Chapter 5). Conceptually, this nested relationship could be achieved by fixing the residual variances to 0 and all the latent parameters to 0 but keeping the cross-time equality constraints on the loadings and intercepts. In practice, this panel null model is estimated differently (see the examples on *www.guilford.com/little-materials*) but achieves the same model misfit and degrees of freedom.

To illustrate a null model for a longitudinal panel model, let's bring a second time of measurement in for the positive affect items. For some context, I selected Time 1 as the fall of a school year; Time 2 is in the fall of the next school year, about 1 year later (I have skipped the spring assessment for now; see the prologue for a description of the sample and measure). Table 3.6 in Chapter 3 contains the sufficient statistics (means, standard deviations, and correlations). The input data matrix contains 27 unique bits of information to model: 15 covariances, 6 variances, and 6 means. The standard independence model specifies that there are no covariances among these variables. The independence model, therefore, constrains all possible covariances among the indicators to be 0. With the traditional independence model, the means and variances are estimated, but no constraints are placed on them. With a longitudinal null model, on the other hand, the means and variances of the three indicators at Time 1 are constrained to be equal to their counterparts at Time 2. The addition of these constraints leads to six fewer estimates (and thereby adds six more degrees of freedom to the specified null model). As the saying goes, degrees of freedom are like money; you have to spend one to estimate a parameter. In this case, we save degrees of freedom by equating the Time 2 parameters to be equal to the Time 1 estimates, for which we've already paid. The χ^2 value generated by each of these null models is shown in Figure 4.3 just below the model and the parameter estimates. The formulae for two of the more common relative fit indices are presented in Equations 4.2 and 4.3.

At this point, I need to digress a bit. The χ^2 value that is produced and reported as the default fit value varies in the different software packages. Two of the most commonly used χ^2 values are the minimum of the fit function χ^2 and the normal

A) Traditional (independence) null model

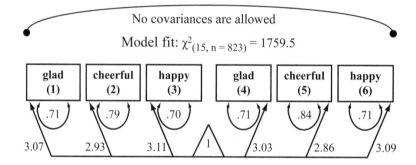

B) Appropriate longitudinal null model

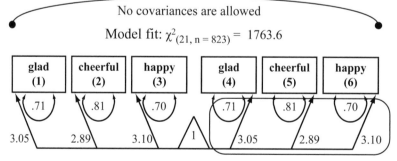

Constrained to be equal to Time 1

FIGURE 4.3. Traditional independence null model (A) versus the appropriate longitudinal null model (B). In both null models, no covariances are allowed in order to gauge the amount of information contained in the observed covariances. In the longitudinal null, the additional expectations that the means and variances do not change over time are added to the null model specification.

Equation 4.2. The comparative fit index (CFI)

$$CFI = 1 - \frac{\max[(x_t^2 - df_t), 0]}{\max[(x_t^2 - df_t), (x_0^2 - df_0), 0]}$$

- χ^2_t is the tested model's χ^2.
- df_t is the degrees of freedom for the tested model.
- χ^2_0 is the null model's χ^2.
- df_0 is the degrees of freedom for the null model.
- The max operator selects the maximum value of the numbers separated by commas.
- Rules of thumb for interpreting the CFI:

  Poor fit: < .85*ish*
  Mediocre fit: .85 – .90*ish*
  Acceptable fit: .90 – .99*ish*
  Very Good fit: .95 – .99*ish*
  Outstanding fit: > .99*ish*

  (These categories are my invention.)

theory weighted least squares χ^2 that was introduced to the LISREL program in version 8. A third commonly used χ^2 value is the Satorra and Bentler (1994) scaled χ^2 (it is a correction to the χ^2 when the data are not multivariate normal). The minimum of the fit function χ^2 value is based, as the name implies, on the actual fit function of the model. The χ^2 value that is used for the null model can also be based on model fit as indexed by the fit function, the weighted least squares (WLS) adjusted value, or

Equation 4.3. The Tucker–Lewis index/non-normed fit index (TLI/NNFI)

$$TLI / NNFI = \frac{(x_0^2 / df_0) - (x_t^2 / df_t)}{(x_0^2 / df_0) - 1}$$

- χ^2_t is the tested model's χ^2.
- df_t is the degrees of freedom for the tested model.
- χ^2_0 is the null model's χ^2.
- df_0 is the degrees of freedom for the null model.
- Rules of thumb for interpreting the TLI/NNFI are the same as for the CFI, which are my invention:

  Poor fit: < .85*ish*
  Mediocre fit: .85 – .90*ish*
  Acceptable fit: .90 – .99*ish*
  Very Good fit: .95 – .99*ish*
  Outstanding fit: > .99*ish*

by the Satorra–Bentler scaled value. I recommend that the minimum fit function χ^2 values be used for calculating the relative fit measures that I describe next.

The comparative fit index (CFI) has emerged as a consistently well-performing measure of model fit. As shown in Equation 4.2, the CFI is basically the ratio of misfit of the tested model (i.e., the noncentral χ^2 of the tested model), or 0 if there is no misfit to the misfit of the null model. It is possible to have a model in which the χ^2 is smaller than the degrees of freedom. In such situations, I may be overfitting the model by allowing unneeded parameter estimates. Usually, however, the numerator will be a noncentral χ^2 value that is positive and the denominator will be the null model's noncentral χ^2 value.

The Tucker–Lewis Index (TLI), or non–normed fit index (NNFI), gets its name because it was developed by two different researcher teams at different times and for slightly different purposes. Tucker and Lewis (1973) developed this measure for exploratory factor analysis applications to help determine whether extracting one more factor would lead to a meaningful change in the amount of information gained. Bentler and Bonett (1980) developed this measure in the context of a set of fit measures that included a normed fit index that cannot exceed 1.0 and the NNFI (this one), which can exceed 1.0. You can call it TLI, NNFI, or TLI/NNFI, depending on your preference. Mplus uses TLI for this measure, whereas LISREL uses NNFI, for example.

Like the CFI, TLI/NNFI is also a ratio, but it is a ratio of ratios. That is, it contains the ratio of the χ^2 per degree of freedom for both the null and the tested models. This ratio for the tested model is subtracted from that of the null model. In the denominator, 1 is subtracted from the null model's ratio. Recall that the expected value of the χ^2 is equal to the degrees of freedom. Thus, the expected ratio of the tested model's fit is subtracted from the ratio of the null model's fit per degree of freedom. When the χ^2 value is less than the degrees of freedom, this index can exceed 1.0. Again, in such situations I may be estimating more parameters than are needed to account for the relationships in the data.

In my experience, models with .90+ values for the CFI and the TLI/NNFI can be quite acceptable models, particularly when the mean structure information is included. Of course, models with good fit can also be poor models for other reasons, such as parameter estimates that are badly fitting, or for theoretical reasons. I do have a fundamental problem with the criteria that are sometimes quoted as the level one needs to achieve for acceptable model fit. The reason I have a problem with the criteria is that most simulations that have evaluated model fit indices have focused on single-occasion and single-group covariance structure models. Moreover, most of these simulations do not include population misfit in the models (i.e., when parameters that are fixed to 0 are not exactly equal to 0 in the population). Instead, the only error that is introduced is random sampling error. This kind of simulation means that the model is perfect in the population and that on average it is perfect in the sample. No model is perfect even in the population. The guidelines for detecting appropriate models with good fit against random error around a perfect model don't match up with the kinds of models that are applied to real data. In real data, some amount of model misspecification (i.e., parsimony error) is always going to be present even if the model were fit to the population. In the spirit of these fit measures, then, the goal is to come up with a parsimonious approximation of reality. In my view, therefore, the recommendations from these simulation studies do not generalize to longitudinal models, to multiple-group models, or to models that aren't perfect in the population.

In Figure 4.4, I have reproduced Figure 3.10 with the estimated parameters. I can now calculate the fit of this model based on the correct longitudinal null model that is presented in Figure 4.3. Using the longitudinal null model, the fit of the tested model (Figure 4.4) is quite good. The data example that I am using is based on high-quality data (normally distributed and highly reliable variables), and many of my examples will consistently have good fit, but I show some warts as well. For this simple example, the corrected CFI and TLI/NNFI are both well above .95, and the point estimate of RMSEA was in the acceptable range, $.057_{(.031; .086)}$, but I would

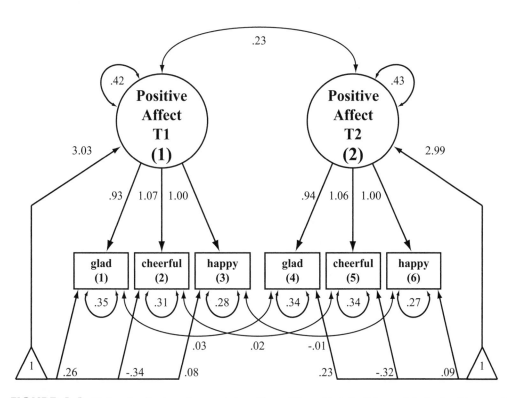

FIGURE 4.4. Estimates for two time points with positive affect. In this model, the loadings and intercepts are not yet equated over time. This model is referred to as the configurally invariant model. I discuss factorial invariance in Chapter 5. Model fit: $\chi^2_{(n=832,5)} = 18.41$; RMSEA $= .057_{(.031; .086)}$; CFI $= .992$; TLI/NNFI $= .968$. I used the effects coding method of identification.

fail to reject a test of acceptable fit because the upper limit is greater than .08. This failure to reject is not uncommon with small models. The CFI and TLI/NNFI based on the default null model were .99 and .98, respectively. In this example, using an appropriate null model had little influence on the CFI, but it did have an effect on the TLI/NNFI.

Most of the SEM models that I have published, however, do not achieve the outstanding or even the good level of fit but are perfectly acceptable and useful models. Even a casual inspection of other models published in various literatures shows that many models don't have levels of fit that are in the very good range, and yet most of these models have great utility and value. Too often, folks fitting a model to typical data get worried when the model is just at the acceptable level. I have labeled these levels of fit "acceptable" because they are just that: "acceptable" (worth accepting, satisfactory, perfectly adequate)! The fit is acceptable at these levels of the fit indices, especially if the model is steeped in theory, the parameter estimates are as expected, and there is no indication that some part of the model is misspecified. When these conditions are met, the baseline CFA model (aka the measurement model) is the best model given the data and the indicators. Later, when I talk about fitting structural models and testing competing models, these are all conducted against the baseline of the best fitting CFA model that makes no constraints on the latent relationships.

Summary and Cautions

These various measures of model fit should be evaluated with caution. First, model fit indices are global measures of how well the model as a whole reproduces the observed data as a whole. Any evidence of local misfit is not apparent in these measures. Two models can achieve the same level of global fit, for example. For one model, the misfit is equally distributed across all parts of the model. For a second model, the misfit may be near 0 for many parts of the model but quite pronounced in other parts. This feature of global fit measures is why evaluating the "tolerance" information is critical. By tolerance information, I mean the fitted residuals, the modification indices, and the standard errors. The fitted residuals are the differences between the estimated values of the reproduced matrix and the observed value for each element of the observed matrix. These residuals should be normally distributed with a mean of 0. Any evidence of skew, platykurtosis (fat tails), or outliers suggests local misfit. Modification indices are usually sensitive to such problems even when the overall model fit is reasonable. Modification indices are estimates of how much improvement in model fit will occur if the parameter associated with the modification index is freely estimated. Nonuniform standard errors across the various model parameters can also be an indication of local misfit. I discuss modification indices, evaluating residuals, and model modifications in detail in Chapter 5.

A second area in which global model fit statistics are inadequate is in identifying person-level misfit. Rensvold and Cheung (1999) suggest using the jackknife to systematically explore the influence of an individual's data to model fit. The jack-knife is a form of resampling whereby one case is removed from the dataset and the model is run on the $N-1$ remaining cases. This process is done systematically for each case in the dataset. Group jackknife is a similar idea in that a set size of two or more cases is chosen and the set size of cases is removed in each run of the model until all combinations of the chosen set size have been removed. Both of these approaches would give information about model fit and how much each case contributes to model misfit. This area of person fit is still being developed, and I expect we'll soon have better methods and better guidance for identifying outliers and how to treat them.

A statistical rationale is not well suited to evaluating model approximations (as I've already said), but it is well suited to test specific hypotheses about a given model or to test differences between two or more models when they are nested (cf. MacCallum, Browne, & Cai, 2006). The difference in χ^2 between two nested models is also distributed as a χ^2 with degrees of freedom equal to the difference in the degrees of freedom of the two nested models (of course, certain regularity conditions should hold, such as that the models are not grossly misspecified). As I mentioned earlier, a model is nested within another model when the only difference between the two models is one or more constraints. Examples of nested constraints include fixing one or more parameters to be 0 (or to a specific, theoretically meaningful value) and constraining two or more parameters to equality (or some form of theoretically meaningful inequality). The model with the constraints is said to be nested within the model that does not have the constraints. Usually the nested model is a theoretically interesting and more parsimonious model than the freely estimated model. Using the model χ^2 in this manner does involve a number of assumptions that may or may not be realistic. Of course, if I am conducting multiple comparisons using the χ^2 difference test, I will adjust the p-value for the number of comparisons. A little later, when I discuss power, I have more to say about adjusting p-values with this method of significance testing.

SAMPLE SIZE

Most SEM estimators, particularly the ML estimator, are based on asymptotic theory. Asymptotic theory basically means that very large samples are required in order to satisfy the needs and assumptions of the estimator. When the assumptions are satisfied, the estimates are unbiased. With ML estimation, as the sample size approaches infinity, the estimator will yield its best linear unbiased estimates. An estimator is said to be robust when it produces relatively unbiased estimates even when the assumptions of the estimator are violated. One of the key assumptions of ML estimation is multivariate normality. Generally speaking, larger samples increase the likelihood that the data will be approximately multivariate normal. In light of these concerns, the sample size issue boils down to how far away from infinity one can get and still have unbiased estimates using ML estimation. Or, as the late Jeff Tanaka (1987) stated, "How big is big enough?"

In this section, I offer guidance based more on experience and my read of the field. Most Monte Carlo studies that evaluate sample size issues don't fully consider all the features that are needed to really address this question, particularly in the context of longitudinal models in which the loadings and intercepts are usually equated over time and the corresponding residuals are allowed to correlate. As a result, we still lack clear guidance to the question. Most of the old heuristics, such as a 5:1 or a 10:1 ratio of observations to parameter estimates (or constructs, or variables), are simply inadequate (and should not be perpetuated any further). The fundamental question is "Do I have an adequate sample to provide a set of sufficient statistics (variances, covariances, and means) that I can trust to be accurate representations of the population?" And an important follow-up question is "Am I trying to make a very fine-grained distinction in my model that might require a little more power and precision to test?" I digress a bit in the following to make my point about sample size in SEM.

Figure 4.5 shows the confidence curves of the mean at sample sizes that range from 40 to 500 (these confidence curves are the plots of the confidence intervals at each successive sample size, which are different from those introduced by Birnbaum, 1961). In the figure, I have displayed three sets of confidence intervals such that the most extreme top and bottom lines form the 99% confidence interval, the next extreme lines form the 95% interval, and the two lines in the adjacent middle

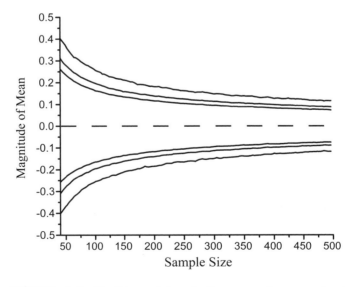

FIGURE 4.5. Confidence intervals for means from sample sizes 40–500. These confidence curves are the 99%, 95%, and 90% confidence intervals around a population mean of 0 from a normal distribution.

reflect the 90% confidence interval. The straight dashed line shows the true population value, which in this case is a mean of 0. As population confidence intervals, these confidence curves represent the sampling error that can occur on any one selection of a sample at a given sample size. I should note that these confidence curves assume that the distribution is normal. (One can construct similar graphs for any distribution. The simulation program that generated these data is available at *www.guilford.com/little-materials*.)

A couple of things are apparent in Figure 4.5. First, the distribution of means is symmetric, meaning that the amount of error above the true population value of 0 is the same amount as below the population value. The second key feature is how quickly the standard errors are reduced as sample size increases from 40 to about 100 or so. Between 100 and 150 the rate of error reduction transitions from rapid to slow. The rate after about 150 is steady but quite slow. The information in this figure can guide one's choice of sample size: At what sample size am I sufficiently confident that the sample mean will be reasonably close to the true population mean that I would be comfortable making inferences about the population? For many questions in the social and behavioral sciences, sample sizes of around 100 would probably provide sufficient confidence; for others, sample sizes closer to 150 would be desired. Another way to consider this sample size issue is in terms of effect sizes. At sample size of 100, the effect size that can be reliably detected would be a Cohen's *d* of about 0.20, while at a sample size of 150 the detectible effect size would be a *d* of about 0.10. Even at sample sizes of 500, the magnitude of a detectable mean difference is close to a *d* of about 0.10.

In Figure 4.6, I've plotted similar confidence curves for the standard deviations versus the variances. In this figure, I simply want you to take note of the fact that the confidence intervals of the standard deviations are symmetrical (like the means), whereas the standard errors of the variances are not symmetrical. Instead, the confidence curves show that the distributions are positively skewed (the upper tail, with the larger numbers, is longer than the lower tail) and on a different scale. Because variances are the squared value of the standard deviations (where standard deviations are defined as the second moment of a distribution), the positive skew and scale differences are expected; however, the influence of the standard errors of the variances will be seen shortly.

Some of the key factors that would influence the quality of the data to produce accurate estimates of the sufficient statistics (means, standard deviations, and correlations) include: (1) the heterogeneity and representativeness of the sample, (2) the precision of the measures in terms of reliability and scaling (e.g., ordinal scales are less precise than interval scales), (3) the convergent and discriminant validity of the indicators *and* the constructs, and (4) model complexity (i.e., complex models typically have highly correlated parameter estimates, which makes estimating them harder with small sample sizes).

A random sample from a homogeneous population would not need to be as large

A) Standard deviations

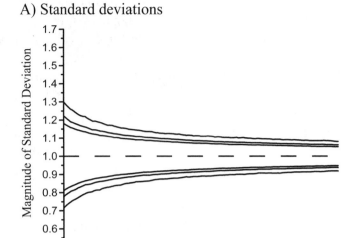

B) Variances

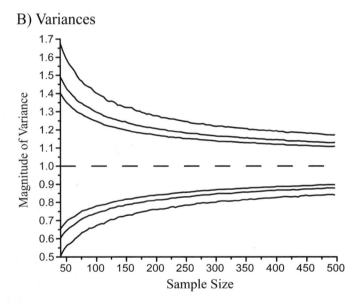

FIGURE 4.6. Confidence intervals for standard deviations and variances from sample sizes 40–500. The confidence curves are the 99%, 95%, and 90% confidence intervals around a population value of 1.0 from a normal distribution.

to represent the population well as would a convenience sample or one from a heterogeneous population. At issue here is the sampling variability that can influence the precision of the estimated covariances and means. If there is more inherent potential for sampling variability, I need to sample more entities to minimize its influence on the sample estimates of the population means, variances, and covariances. Clearly, I want to achieve estimates of these sufficient statistics that are reasonably close to the population values so that I can be confident in my conclusions and generalizations about the population from which my sample was drawn.

The precision of the measures also improves the overall precision of the sufficient statistics. Very reliable indicators with good scale qualities (interval or ratio, normally distributed) will provide reasonably precise estimates of the sufficient statistics and are more likely to satisfy the multivariate normal assumptions of the ML estimator. If I have psychometrically sound measures, the sample size requirements aren't as big as they are when I have modest measures (however, see my discussion of parcels in Chapter 2 as a way to create more psychometrically sound indicators from such measures).

The convergent and discriminant validity relationships are also important to consider when determining sample size needs. Indicators of a construct that form a nice positive manifold (i.e., all the constructs' indicators correlate positively and strongly at greater than about .6 with one another) and that are uniformly much less correlated with indicators of other constructs generally make it easy for the SEM software program to find the correct optimal solution for the parameters of each construct (loadings, intercepts, residuals, construct variance), as well as the relationships among the constructs. Here, for example, tau-equivalent indicators of constructs (indicators that are about equally good) would generally be better than just congeneric indicators (i.e., with some being strong indicators of a construct and some being weak indicators of a construct).

Figure 4.7 displays the confidence curves around a correlation coefficient at different magnitudes of correlation. This figure shows that the stronger the association is between any two variables, the more precise the estimate is at all levels of sample size. This relationship is related to the power to detect a correlation of a given magnitude. For example, at a sample size of 100, I could reasonably detect a correlation of .3 as being significantly different from 0. At a sample size of 100, I also have reasonable power to detect whether a .5 correlation is significantly different from a correlation of .3. At this same sample size, I can detect whether a .7 correlation is different from a .6 correlation and whether a .9 correlation is different from a .85 correlation (or different from 1.0). That is, the stronger the correlation, the narrower is the standard error of its estimation. For covariances, on the other hand, the story is not as simple.

Figure 4.8 shows the sampling confidence curves around covariance estimates at different magnitudes of covariation. Here, the precision of a covariance estimate is not as consistently improved as the magnitude of association increases. These

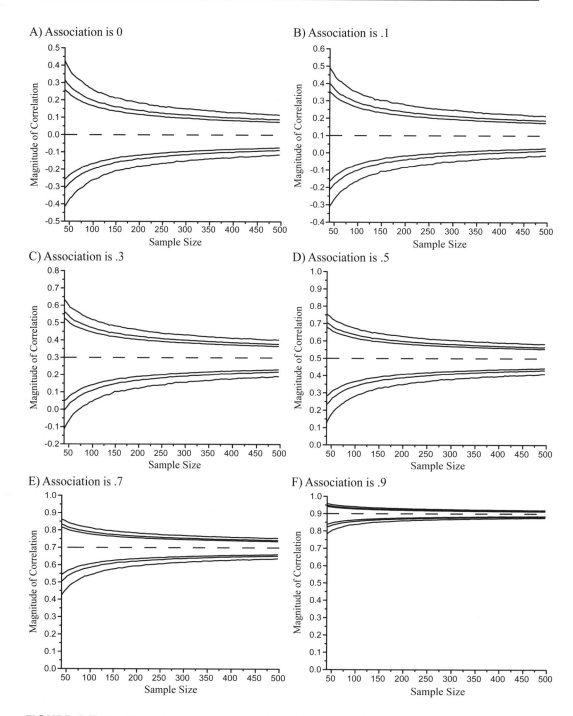

FIGURE 4.7. Confidence intervals for correlations from sample sizes 40–500. These confidence curves represent the 99%, 95%, and 90% confidence intervals for the population values depicted by the dashed straight line.

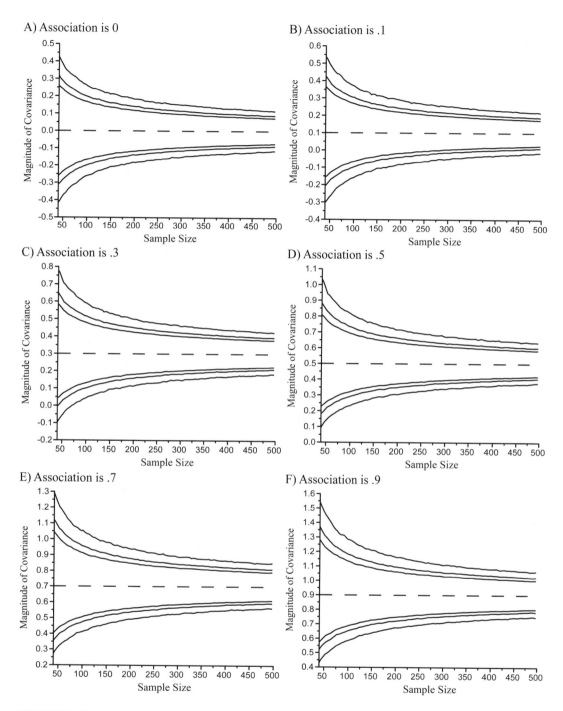

FIGURE 4.8. Confidence intervals for covariances from sample sizes 40–500. These confidence curves represent the 99%, 95%, and 90% confidence intervals for the population values depicted by the dashed straight line.

gradients are based on sampling from a normal distribution with a mean of 0 and a standard deviation of 1. Therefore, the expected value of the covariance is a correlation (i.e., on average the variance should be 1.0). However, on any given draw from such a population, the standard deviation will not necessarily be 1.0, and, when squared as the estimated variance, it produces a more variable estimate of the covariance between any two variables. You will notice that these gradients look pretty much the same at all levels of association. The lines follow a similar pattern in that precision after about 120 participants is slowly improved.

As mentioned, many factors will influence the sample size needs of an SEM model. For most real-world applications of SEM models in which I have been involved, sample sizes that are a bit larger than 100 observations have been adequate for single-group models, and sample sizes around 75 per group have been adequate for multiple-group models. Most of my models, however, are moderately large in terms of degrees of freedom; as you'll see in the next section on power, models with more degrees of freedom generally have more power than models with fewer degrees of freedom. From the perspective that I have outlined here, then, the fundamental issue in sample size determination is whether one has confidence that both the variance–covariance matrix and the vector of indicators' means are sound representations of the population. The confidence gradients that are depicted in Figure 4.8 can be used to gauge the precision of the covariances that you would get for a given sample size. The confidence curves for the means in Figure 4.5 would give you the precision for the means of the indicators.

MacCallum, Widaman, Zhang, and Hong (1999) showed that the traditional rules of thumb for determining sample size in the world of exploratory factor analysis have no basis. SEM, in my view, is no different. Once I have a large enough sample size (~120 or so) to trust that the statistics derived from my sample are reasonable representations of the population, I can go forward and model with impunity. It does not matter how many parameter estimates are being made. When I have three tau-equivalent indicators for each construct, then the key measurement model parameter estimates (loadings, intercepts, residuals) are locally just identified, regardless of the model size, meaning that the estimates of each construct's parameters are well conditioned. The rest of the model's parameter estimates are based on the between-construct relationships. This part of a model is typically overidentified, meaning that I'd have lots of power to identify a misspecified model.

As mentioned, the sampling error gradients in this chapter provide a good basis with which to gauge sample size for a typical longitudinal panel model. The more fine-grained the analyses need to be, the more precise the sufficient statistics need to be. If the research question requires scalpel-like precision, then a very large sample size will be needed. Many research questions are well answered at more modest sample sizes when a good set of indicators for each construct is available and the model for the relationships among the constructs is not too complex. The typical panel model would fall into this category. Other, more complex models, such as continuous time models, longitudinal multitrait–multimethod models, longitudinal models with higher order factor structures, and multilevel longitudinal models, for example, typically make greater demands on the data and, as such, would require larger sample sizes in order to gain greater precision from the data.

POWER

Power in the context of SEM models can be broken down into two separate issues. The first issue is the ability to detect whether a specific parameter is significantly different from 0 or significantly different from another estimated parameter. This issue relates to effect sizes and their standard errors. These kinds of tests are typically conducted as nested model comparisons or as Wald tests (i.e., dividing a parameter estimate by its standard error). The Wald test is still commonly used and reported, but it is fallible as an indicator of significance because it gives a different answer depending on the method of scaling you use for your constructs. Gonzalez and Griffin (2001) showed that the correct test of significance is achieved from using the χ^2 difference test. For the most part, therefore, tests of important parameters are best examined as nested model comparisons using the χ^2 difference (aka likelihood ratio) test. As I discuss later, however, MacCallum and colleagues (2006) have suggested an alternative significance testing approach—the test of small differences.

The second issue related to power is the ability to determine whether the model as a whole is a reasonable model or a ridiculous model—I want enough power to reject a ridiculous model. This type of power test addresses the question of whether my model has adequate fit or not. This question about the model—data fit focuses on whether I can detect that a hypothesized model is consistent with the data and whether an alternative model can be rejected as having poor fit. Tests of parameter significance and model—data fit can be done either post hoc or a priori (Hancock, 2006). I focus solely on the a priori case because one should always perform a power analysis before collecting data. Especially if you are seeking funding for a project, you'll need to be quite thoughtful in your power calculations.

Power estimation for SEM depends on the number of model parameters, the magnitude of any misspecified parameters, the location of the parameters of interest within the model, the reliability of indicators, model complexity, and sample size, among other things (Preacher, Cai, & MacCallum, 2007). The power to detect whether a particular parameter is significantly different from 0 is relatively straightforward. Here, the sample size demands are not necessarily as stringent as those used for the power to evaluate the adequacy of an overall model. To evaluate power for testing parameters, you need to have a good idea of the effect sizes that you expect to find. For example, the correlation in Figure 4.4 of .23 would be classified as a medium–small effect following Cohen's general rules for small, medium, and large effects. The confidence curves presented in this chapter can help inform your needs for sampling precision and the sample size you'd need to detect a correlation of that magnitude.

When making comparisons between two models, the conventional idea is that when the two models are nested, the difference in χ^2 between the two models is also distributed as a χ^2 with degrees of freedom equal to the difference in the degrees of freedom of the two nested models. Recall that a model (say model C for child) is nested within another model (say model P for parent) when the child model, C, is specified simply by placing a constraint on one or more of the parameters in the parent model, P. That is, model P (where, compared with Model C, more parameters are freely estimated or unconstrained) and model C (which contains one or more constrained parameters that were previously freely estimated in model P) are nested; specifically, model C is nested in model P because model C was derived simply by placing one or more constraints on model P. In this case, the fit of model P ($\chi^2_{(p)}$) will always be better than the fit of model C ($\chi^2_{(c)}$). The null expectation for comparing these two models is that the difference is nonsignificant ($\Delta\chi^2_{(p-c)} = \chi^2_{(p)} - \chi^2_{(c)}$ = $\Delta df_{(p-c)}$). Recall that the expected value of the central χ^2 is equal to its degrees of freedom; therefore, the expected value of the difference in χ^2 ($\Delta\chi^2$) is equal to Δdf. When this null expectation is in fact correct (and if all the assumptions of SEM estimation are also met), then this test is accurate and unbiased.

For purposes of power analysis, however, we need to know whether we have enough power to detect a difference between models when a difference actually exists. In this case, the behavior of the χ^2 follows a different distributional expectation. Now, we have to examine the behavior of the noncentral χ^2. The distribution of the noncentral χ^2 is the distribution of the difference in χ^2 minus the expected value (which, again, is the degrees of freedom). In formula form, the noncentral χ^2 is $\Delta\chi^2_{(p-c)} - \Delta df_{(p-c)}$. In traditional hypothesis testing, the null distribution and the alternative distribution are both normal. The amount of the alternative distribution that exists outside the Type I error boundary is the amount of power that a given test has of detecting a bogus null hypothesis. With the χ^2 distributions, the null distribution and the alternative distribution have rather different shapes depending on degrees of freedom. Figure 4.9 shows the overlap of the central and noncentral χ^2 at different degrees of freedom. Regardless of the shapes, the proportion of the alternative distribution that exceeds the Type I error boundary of the null distribution is still the power of a given test to detect that the null is in fact false.

MacCallum et al. (2006), as well as Preacher et al. (2007), describe an alternative test of significance in SEM and detail ways to conduct power calculations in the context of their proposed significance testing approach. Briefly, they propose that instead of conducting a test of exactly no difference (the null hypothesis that is examined with the $\Delta\chi^2_{(p-c)}$ test) one should conduct a test of a small difference. The test of a small difference, in general, relies on the noncentral χ^2 distribution, and it depends on defining how much of a small difference is meaningful.

Because we do not yet have well-established guidelines on what would be

A) 1 Degree of Freedom

B) 10 Degrees of Freedom

C) 20 Degrees of Freedom

D) 40 Degrees of Freedom

E) 100 Degrees of Freedom

F) 1,000 Degrees of Freedom

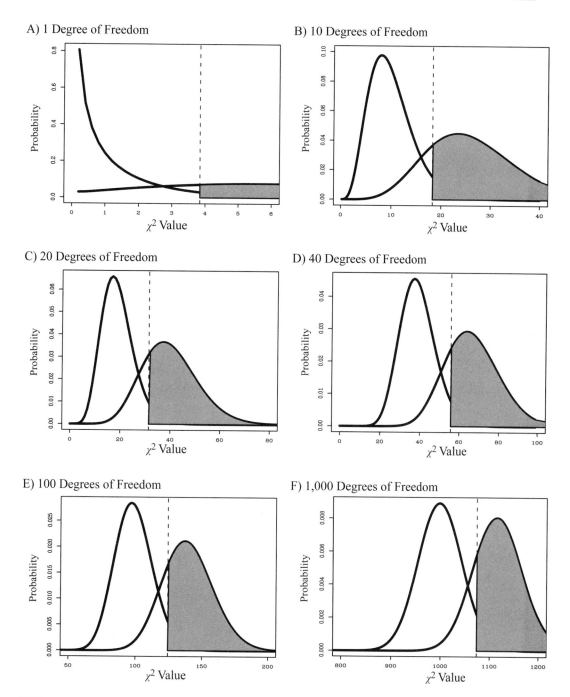

FIGURE 4.9. Central and noncentral χ^2 distributions illustrating the power to reject a null hypothesis with 1, 10, 20, 40, 100, and 1,000 degrees of freedom. The nominal error rate used to generate these graphs was .05.

considered an appropriate standard for a small difference, I still focus on using the traditional $\Delta\chi^2_{(p-c)}$ test. Although this latter test may be overly sensitive to differences, the criteria for using it are well established. I do think, however, that the statistical and theoretical arguments for developing tests of small differences have merit and will likely gain momentum once we have a better grasp of the standards for "small" that we can generally agree upon.

For a test of a single parameter estimate or a circumscribed set of estimates, the power to detect a difference between a null and an alternative estimate is relatively easy if you are using a program like Mplus. Mplus has a Monte Carlo simulation option to determine power in the context of your model. The key at this point, as with any power analysis, is having good guesses about what the actual parameter estimates will be. For the neomodeler, this task may seem daunting. I start with loadings and residuals. My models have loadings in the standardized realm that are in the .7 range (about 50% common variance). The remainder is error. If I am modeling items, I might choose loadings in the .5 range (about 25% common variance, with the remainder being error). After that, I have to make a reasoned guess at the strength of the correlations among the constructs. Past research and theory should be helpful here. Most correlations in the social and behavioral sciences are hard-pressed to exceed .4. The exceptions to this rule are the well-established high relationships (around .7). I generally recommend working with a range of values to estimate power from the low end to the high end given reasonable guesses about the size of the parameter estimates you might observe.

Hancock (2006) provides examples of how to conduct power analyses using any software. The procedures that he outlines require that you obtain the model-implied covariance matrix from the unconstrained model. This model-implied matrix is then used as the input data in a subsequent analysis where the parameter(s) of interest are constrained and the impact of the constraint(s) on model fit is examined.

For SEM, power estimation has generally focused on the RMSEA (Browne & Cudeck, 1993; MacCallum, Browne, & Sugawara, 1996; Steiger & Lind, 1980). This measure of model misfit was originally introduced in a conference paper by Steiger and Lind (1980) and caught the eye and imagination of many methodologists. I already introduced the formula for the RMSEA earlier in this chapter, but I suggest you go back and take a few minutes to study its components again. The RMSEA is a measure of model misfit per degree of freedom when misfit is based on the sample-size-corrected fit function and when the expected value (i.e., the model degrees of freedom) has been subtracted (this value is termed the noncentrality parameter).

To determine the power of a test that a model is appropriate in the population, we begin with the idea that there is a criterion of good model fit (see earlier discussion). This criterion of model fit is at the border of acceptable, such as RMSEA = .05 or RMSEA = .08. As I mentioned, I generally prefer RMSEA of .08 as my border of acceptable fit. The next step is to state what the alternative would be. As depicted in Figure 4.2, the alternative can be that my model fit is better than the acceptable fit line (tests of not-close or not-acceptable fit), or it can be that my model fit is worse than the acceptable fit line (tests of close fit or acceptable fit). For power analysis considerations, in particular, I think the logic of the test of not-acceptable fit is most defensible.

The other critical element of these power calculations is the degrees of freedom of the model you are testing. If you are doing a priori power calculations, you need to clearly determine what the model will look like and count up your degrees of freedom. If I have three indicators per construct, the degrees of freedom of the CFA/measurement model follow a systematic pattern. Two constructs yield a model with 8 degrees of freedom, three constructs yield 24 degrees of freedom, four constructs yield 48 degrees of freedom, five constructs yield 80 degrees of freedom, six constructs yield 120 degrees of freedom, and so on. If you have a longitudinal model, the degrees of freedom of the model won't increase quite this quickly because residuals among the corresponding indicators are allowed to be estimated as correlated residuals across time. The number of these correlated residuals would be equal to three times the number of constructs added up for each wave (when I have three indicators per construct). When I test for and impose factorial invariance, I gain back degrees of freedom (2 *df* per construct, per wave of measurement when I have three indicators per construct—I explain why this is the case in more detail in Chapter 5).

In Figure 4.10, I have depicted in a stylized manner the way in which degrees of freedom will rapidly increase as more constructs are included. In the quite simple example of Figure 4.10, I have depicted three constructs assessed at three times of measurement. Each construct has three indicators, which means that each construct is just identified and all the degrees of freedom of the model come from the parsimony of how the constructs relate to one another (at least for the configurally invariant model). Thus, in the boxes that overlay the matrix elements, I have listed the key latent construct parameter that is primarily informed by the information contained in the 3-by-3 box of nine potential associations among the indicators. This parameter is always the latent construct's correlation with another latent construct. The only exception to this rule is the "subdiagonals" of the matrix, where the correlated residuals that are calculated for each cross-time association among the corresponding/like indicators are allowed to correlate (I discuss the reasons for this in more detail in Chapter 5).

To illustrate power in the context of SEM models and the ability to detect whether my model is reasonable or not, I have depicted a set of power gradients for the RMSEA test of close fit and the tests of not-close fit (left side of Figure 4.11) and tests of acceptable fit and not-acceptable fit (right side of Figure 4.11). For these power gradients, I have fixed sample size at 100 (Panel A), 200 (Panel B), and 300 (Panel C) but varied the degrees of freedom of a given model from 1 to 800. In each panel, I depict the null RMSEA as .05 (the straight line in the graph on the left side of each panel) or .08 (the straight line in the graph on the right side of each panel).

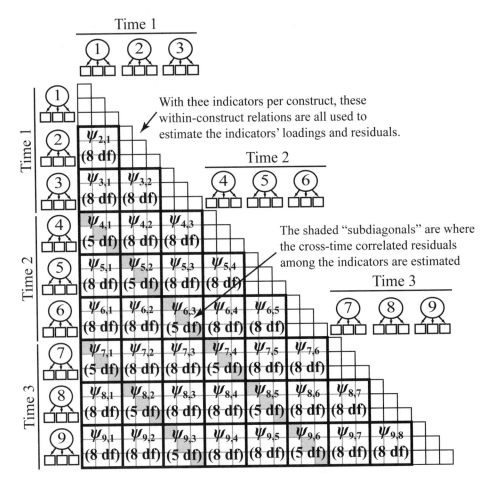

FIGURE 4.10. A stylized model-implied matrix denoting where degrees of freedom quickly compound as more constructs are added. In this stylization, I have three indicators for each construct, which makes the open triangles along the diagonal fully saturated by estimates of each indicator's loading and residual. The shaded subdiagonals contain the estimated cross-time correlated residuals, and thus only 5 degrees of freedom are contributed by those blocks of relationships. For the remaining blocks of relationships, only the latent correlation is uniquely derived from the block, giving 8 degrees of freedom per block. This simple model of three constructs at three time points would have a total of 261 degrees of freedom.

The power gradients are for 0.7, 0.8, and 0.9 power, respectively. The lines closest to the null line are easier to reject and thus are the ones with the lowest power. The outside lines are the hardest to reject and reflect the 0.9 power gradient. The power gradients below the null hypothesis line are the values of RMSEA needed to achieve the desired level of power when you are using the test of not-close or not-acceptable fit. The power gradients above the null hypothesis line are the values of RMSEA needed for the tests of close fit or acceptable fit.

More specifically, the alternative RMSEA for the test of not-close fit requires

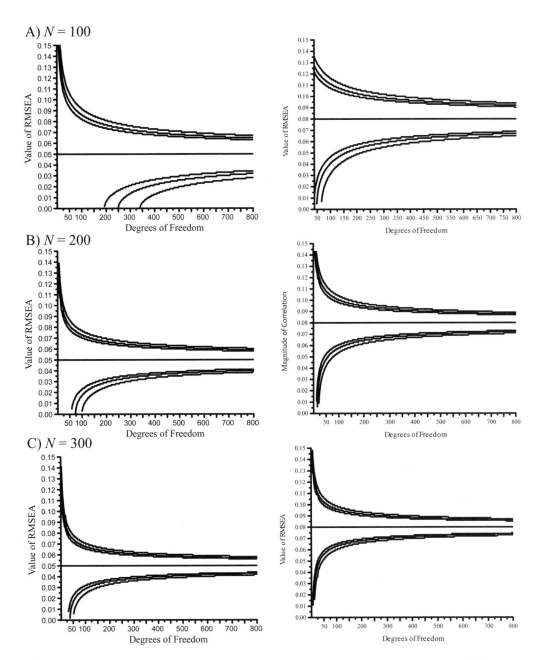

FIGURE 4.11. RMSEA power curves for tests of close fit and not-close fit and for tests of adequate fit and not-adequate fit. These power curves are for 0.7, 0.8, and 0.9 power. For the panels on the left, the tests of not-close fit are above the .05 null value, and tests of close fit are below. For the panels on the right, the tests of not-adequate fit are above the .08 null value and tests of adequate fit are below.

perfect fit at $N = 100$ until you get to about 190 degrees of freedom. Then you see that one can reject the null in favor of an alternative with 0.7 power (the first power gradient) but would need an RMSEA of nearly 0 to do so until you get to about 220 degrees of freedom. To reject the null and accept the alternative with 0.9 power at $N = 100$, the model would require about 350 degrees of freedom.

For sample sizes of 300, on the other hand, the power gradients start to show an ability to reject the null of .05 in favor of the alternative at rather small models (e.g., degrees of freedom around 25). For the null RMSEA of .08, on the other hand, the alternative value of RMSEA of .01 is detectable at even 1 degree of freedom. These power gradients provide a lot of useful information for determining the power of your model. The stylized model in Figure 4.10, for example, has 261 degrees of freedom. If I were to estimate this model using a sample size of 100, I could reject the null of .08 in favor of the alternative if my model RMSEA were about .06 with 0.7 power and an RMSEA of about .055 with 0.8 power.

SUMMARY

As I mentioned at the beginning of this chapter, there are lots of developments that are likely to take place in the context of model fit, sample size, power, and the like. More simulation work that includes population misfit is being conducted to give better guidance of model fit criteria, and many tools are being developed that will allow for Monte Carlo simulations (e.g., see simsem and semTools as part of the R package). In this chapter, I have presented a number of ideas that I see as guiding principles rather than rules or absolutes. Most of the figures in this chapter provide broad views on issues such as sampling variability (e.g., Figure 4.7 vs. Figure 4.8) and power (e.g., Figure 4.9 and Figure 4.11). This chapter, coupled with Chapter 3, covers nearly all of the tree trunk topics that form the foundations of SEM. The last major foundation topic that I cover before delving into the various longitudinal models is the concept of factorial invariance. As with the material I covered in Chapter 3, the material in this chapter needs to be well understood before you proceed to the next chapters.

KEY TERMS AND CONCEPTS INTRODUCED IN THIS CHAPTER

Absolute fit indices. Indices that compare the hypothesized model to the saturated model and therefore assess the degree of decrement from a perfectly fitting model.

In the population. This phrase is meant to capture the hypothetical idea of what something should be for the whole population. For example, "all models are wrong even in the population" means that if we had access to the entire population of individuals (or any entity to which we want to generalize), the model that we are fitting to the data would still not quite capture all the processes and relations that give rise to the observed data. Usually, we consider these population misspecifications as generally small and trivial. Therefore, a model that is fit to the sample is going to have these small and trivial population-level misspecifications, as well as the sampling variability that is going to contribute to model misfit.

Longitudinal panel null model. An extension of the independence null model in that it also includes the constraint that the variances of repeatedly measured variables do not change over time. When the mean structures are also modeled, the longitudinal null model also adds the constraint that the means of the repeatedly measured indicators do not change over time. These constraints on the variances and the means of like-measured indicators are also imposed across groups when multiple groups are included in the analysis.

Null model. A model that attempts to gauge the amount of information in a sample of data. The null model is the worst fitting model that can be specified while being theoretically defensible. The default null model is often termed the independence model. The independence model specifies no covariances among the observed indicators but does estimate the observed variances and means of the indicators.

Power analysis. In the context of SEM, power analysis involves evaluating the probability that you can detect true differences between models, as well as whether your baseline model is viable in the population. The basic logic is the same as the "1 − Type II error rate" that we use in traditional hypothesis testing, but the calculation of power in SEM for model evaluation and model comparisons is a bit more involved. Power analysis is also useful for detecting whether a parameter is significantly different from 0 in the population. Such power calculations can be made for tests of no differences and for tests of small differences.

Relative fit indices. Relative measures of model fit rely on a null model to gauge model fit. Because the null model provides a measure of bad model fit (in fact, the worst fitting model), it can be used to index the relative improvement in model fit that a hypothesized model provides.

Saturated model. A model in which there are just as many estimates as there are observed bits of information (and all parameters are locally identified). That is, such a model would have no degrees of freedom and would perfectly reproduce the matrix S and the observed means.

Standard error. The standard error of an estimate is an index of the uncertainty in a parameter estimate. This uncertainty is typically gauged by calculating the standard deviation of the distribution for a given estimate based on a specific sample size (i.e., a theoretical standard error). Under the assumption that this distribution is normal, the standard error can be used to test for the significance of an estimate. The larger the sample size, the smaller the potential error. The standard error can also be used to create confidence intervals or confidence bounds to assess whether the true population value is contained within the interval. When the distribution is not normal, bootstrap estimation can be used to calculate the empirical confidence intervals of an estimate, which allows significance testing when the distribution is any form that it may be.

Sufficient statistics. The fundamental equations of SEM attempt to reproduce the observed variance–covariance matrix S and the means of the indicators. These summary statistics (means, variances, and covariances) are termed the sufficient statistics of a set of observed data in that they are sufficient to be the input data to an SEM analysis. That is, they are sufficient to represent the meaningful information in the raw data such that the raw data can, in fact, be discarded.

RECOMMENDED READINGS

The Longitudinal Null Model

Widaman, K. F., & Thompson, J. S. (2003). On specifying the null model for incremental fit indices in structural equation modeling. *Psychological Methods, 8*, 16–37.

> In addition to providing the logic for a longitudinal null model, the authors discuss a number of appropriate null models for different SEM analyses. The traditional independence null model actually has limited applicability.

Understanding Power

Hancock, G. R. (2006). Power analysis in covariance structure analysis. In G. R. Hancock & R. O. Mueller (Eds.), *Structural equation modeling: A second course* (pp. 69–115). Greenwich, CT: Information Age.

> This chapter is a very thorough and comprehensive treatment of power analysis for SEM models.

Person Fit

Rensvold, R. B., & Cheung, G. W. (1999). Identification of influential cases in structural equation models using the jackknife method. *Organizational Research Methods, 2*, 293–308.

> A good resource and procedure for thinking about and identifying person fit and influential cases in SEM.

Alternative Significance Testing Procedures

MacCallum, R. C., Browne, M. W., & Cai, L. (2006). Testing differences between nested covariance structure models: Power analysis and null hypotheses. *Psychological Methods, 11*, 19–35.

> These folks offer an alternative way to consider significance testing in SEM.

5

The Longitudinal CFA Model

Now that I have covered a number of the basics of measurement, developmental designs, and the foundations of SEM, I can turn the focus toward applying these ideas to longitudinal data. As with any SEM model, I begin with the CFA, or measurement model. The longitudinal CFA model addresses a number of important questions about the model, the data, and the sample. These questions include: (1) Are the measurements of each construct factorially invariant across measurement occasions?, (2) how stable are the cross-time relations of the constructs?, (3) how stable are the within-time relations among the constructs?, (4) have the constructs' variances changed over time?, and (5) have the constructs' mean levels changed over time? In this chapter, I describe how to assess each of these questions.

FACTORIAL INVARIANCE

Any comparison of the same constructs across time or across groups assumes that the measurements are factorially invariant. One of the key strengths of SEM is that we can test this assumption. Factorial invariance is probably the most important empirical question to address in any analysis that involves more than one group and/or more than one time point. Factorial invariance is also one of the most misunderstood concepts. In some senses, understanding what factorial invariance means is pretty simple, and in other ways it can feel convoluted. Let me start with a metaphor before I jump into Equation 5.1 and Table 5.1.

Two botanists see two plants. One plant is on the south side of a hill; it is tall, has broad leaves, and a slender stem. The other is on the north side of a hill; it is short, thin leaved, and has a thick stem. Although these outward characteristics and differences are easily observed, they wonder whether the two plants are the same species or not. If the plants are the same species, they argue, then the different growth patterns have been shaped by the context of being on the north or south side of a

137

hill. Otherwise, the differences occur because they are different species of plant. To test their conjectures, they carefully dig down to the roots of the plants. If each plant is the same species, it should have a signature root system. In this case, they see that the first plant has three roots, which follow a particular pattern of length and thickness: the first is medium long and medium thick, the second is longest and thickest, and the third is shortest and thinnest. They carefully dig up the other plant and see that it, too, has three roots that follow the same pattern of relative length and thickness, except that, for this plant, they see that, like the plant itself, all the roots are longer and thinner by about the same proportions. Because both plants have the same number of roots that follow the same pattern of length (loadings) and thickness (intercepts), they conclude that the plants (constructs) are fundamentally the same species (factorially invariant) and that the observed differences (cross-time differences or group differences) are due to the context. They also notice that the amounts of dirt and spindly bits still on the roots appear to be about the same, but they ignore this information because it's just dirt and spindly bits (residuals).

Indicators are like the roots of a construct. Any observed differences at the level of the construct can be attributed to the construct only if the relative root structure of the construct can be shown to be the same across constructs. That is, the lengths (loadings) and thicknesses (intercepts) of each corresponding root structure (indicator) must be proportionally about the same in order to conclude that the construct is fundamentally the same and that the apparent differences are true construct-level differences. This plant metaphor works well in thinking about between-group differences. A longitudinal metaphor that I have used to convey the same idea is to imagine a small constellation of birds. Are they a flock of birds traveling as a connected unit, or are we witnessing a temporary confluence? If the birds (indicators) are a flock (a construct), then they travel across the vista maintaining their relative relationship to one another (longitudinal factorial invariance), even as the flock as a whole rises and falls (the construct can change over time). If, on the other hand, one or more of the birds veer away from the others, the flock (construct) is no longer a flock (it lacks factorial invariance). In longitudinal SEM we can see clearly when the flock is no longer a flock because our tests for longitudinal factorial invariance show us when an indicator no longer has the same relationships with the other indicators. In other analytical techniques (e.g., repeated-measures ANOVA), we can only assume that the flock remained a flock, which can be a dubious assumption in longitudinal research. Yet another metaphor that some prefer is to think of factorial invariance as like a paternal certainty test. Construct certainty is assured when the "*DNA*" is shown to be the same.

Meredith (1964, 1993) provides the most definitive mathematical argument concerning when and how factorial invariance will hold. The fundamental idea here is that if the influences that change the constructs are expressed as influences on only the indicators' true scores, factorial invariance will hold. When only the true scores of the indicators are affected, then the influences have changed only the construct information and not the item-specific information of a given indicator. On the other hand, if the indicators' unique factors are affected in a meaningful way, the indicators will not maintain their relative relationships to one another, and factorial invariance will not be supported.

Meredith termed the various potential influences *selection influences.* In his original discussions, the focus was on selecting two groups of individuals and attempting to determine whether factorial invariance holds. With longitudinal data, the selection mechanism is time and its associated influences. Such influences are found both within (e.g., maturation) and outside (e.g., contextual experiences) the individual. Regardless of whether the focus is across groups or across time, Meredith's proofs demonstrate that even under extreme selection influences, factorial invariance will hold if the various influences affect only the indicators' true-score variance and not their indicator-specific variances. Stated another way, the influences can affect only the common-factor variance of an indicator and not its unique indicator-specific variance. In longitudinal research, age, experience, context, and personal choices are all factors that can influence changes in the measures over time. The key question here is whether these influences have affected the indicators' true scores and not their unique factors (or at least not by very much). More precisely, we acknowledge that selection can influence the unique factors, but if the amount of this influence is trivial, we can still draw valid conclusions about the nature of the longitudinal changes in the common variance among a set of indicators for a given construct.

As mentioned, the proposition that primarily common-factor information is affected by selection influences is easily tested in the SEM framework. When I do not use SEM but instead use a classical technique such as repeated-measures ANOVA, this proposition cannot be tested. Instead, factorial invariance becomes an assumption of the analysis that may or may not be accurate. In keeping with the spirit of Meredith (1964, p. 185, last paragraph, last sentence), if the assumption is not accurate, any conclusions about changes in the construct of interest are at best dubious, at worst invalid, etc.

OK, now I can turn to Equation 5.1 and Table 5.1. In Equation 5.1, I've listed the full set of SEM equations for both the mean and covariance structures. These were presented in Chapter 3, so I won't go through them again in detail except to note that now I have combined the covariance and mean information into Equation 5.1a, and I have put a subscript "*o*" by each of the key elements of these equations. The subscript *o* refers to the occasion of measurement. When a matrix is subscripted with *o*, it represents the idea that the parameter estimates are unique to (freely estimated in) a given occasion of measurement (i.e., no cross-time constraints on the parameter estimates are being made). When I discuss cross-group comparisons, I use a *g* as the subscript, but the basic idea is the same. When I work through a multigroup longitudinal example, I will use a *g* and an *o* as the subscripts when that part of the equation is allowed to vary freely across group and time.

Equation 5.1. The fundamental equations of SEM

a) $y_o = \mathbf{T} + \mathbf{\Lambda}_o \eta_o + \mathbf{\Theta}_o$

b) $E(y_o) = \mu_{y_o} = \mathbf{T}_o + \mathbf{\Lambda}_o \mathbf{A}_o$

c) $\mathbf{\Sigma} = \mathbf{\Lambda}_o \mathbf{\Psi}_o \mathbf{A}'_o \mathbf{\Theta}_o$

- o refers to the occasions of measurement.
- y are the scores on the indicators.
- $E()$ is the expectation operator.
- μ_y is the vector of means.
- $\mathbf{T}$ is the column vector of indicator means.
- $\mathbf{A}$ is the column vector of latent construct means.
- $\mathbf{\Sigma}$ is the model-implied variance–covariance matrix.
- η is the latent construct scores.
- $\mathbf{\Lambda}$ is the matrix of loadings or estimates of the indicator to construct relations.
- $\mathbf{\Psi}$ is the matrix of variances and covariances among the constructs.
- $\mathbf{\Theta}$ is the matrix of residual variances or unique factors and residual covariances among the indicators.
- $\mathbf{\Lambda}'$ is the transpose of the $\mathbf{\Lambda}$ matrix.

TABLE 5.1. Levels, labels, and model equations for longitudinal factorial invariance

Level	Labels used	Some key citations for labels	Definitional equations
0	**Configural Invariance** Pattern Invariance	Horn & McArdle, 1992 Horn, McArdle, & Mason, 1983 Meredith, 1993 Millsap, 1997	A) $y_o = \mathbf{T}_o + \mathbf{\Lambda}_o \eta_o + \mathbf{\Theta}_o$ B) $E(y_o) = \mu_{y_o} = \mathbf{T}_o + \mathbf{\Lambda}_o \mathbf{A}_o$ C) $\mathbf{\Sigma}_o = \mathbf{\Lambda}_o \mathbf{\Psi}_o \mathbf{\Lambda}'_o + \mathbf{\Theta}_o$
1	**Weak Factorial Invariance** Metric Invariance Loading Invariance	Little, 1997 Widaman & Reise, 1997 Steenkamp & Baumgartner, 1998 Horn & McArdle, 1992 Little, Card, Slegers, et al., 2007	A) $y_o = \mathbf{T}_o + \mathbf{\Lambda} \eta_o + \mathbf{\Theta}_o$ B) $E(y_o) = \mu_{y_o} = \mathbf{T}_o + \mathbf{\Lambda} \mathbf{A}_o$ C) $\mathbf{\Sigma}_o = \mathbf{\Lambda} \mathbf{\Psi}_o \mathbf{\Lambda}' + \mathbf{\Theta}_o$
2	**Strong Factorial Invariance** Scalar Invariance Intercept Invariance	Meredith, 1993 Steenkamp & Baumgartner, 1998 Little, Card, Slegers, et al., 2007	A) $y_o = \mathbf{T} + \mathbf{\Lambda} \eta_o + \mathbf{\Theta}_o$ B) $E(y_o) = \mu_{y_o} = \mathbf{T} + \mathbf{\Lambda} \mathbf{A}_o$ C) $\mathbf{\Sigma}_o = \mathbf{\Lambda} \mathbf{\Psi}_o \mathbf{\Lambda}' + \mathbf{\Theta}_o$
3	**Strict Factorial Invariance** Error Variance Invariance Residual Invariance	Meredith, 1993 Steenkamp & Baumgartner, 1998 Little, Card, Slegers et al., 2007	A) $y_o = \mathbf{T} + \mathbf{\Lambda} \eta_o + \mathbf{\Theta}$ B) $E(y_o) = \mu_{y_o} = \mathbf{T} + \mathbf{\Lambda} \mathbf{A}_o$ C) $\mathbf{\Sigma}_o = \mathbf{\Lambda} \mathbf{\Psi}_o \mathbf{\Lambda}' + \mathbf{\Theta}$

Note. In the definitional equations, o represents the occasions of measurement. When a matrix is subscripted with o, it means that the estimates in that equation are unique for each occasion of measurement (freely estimated, with no cross-time constraints). When o is not present, it means the estimates in the matrix are constrained to be equal across occasions of measurement. For a complete description of the elements of the equations, see Equation 5.1.

I've put the three equations from Equation 5.1 into Table 5.1 in the hierarchical sequence of factorial invariance. This sequence is a nested sequence, which means that the changes from one level of invariance to the next are meaningfully and statistically testable (I'll give more on this idea later). I've also assembled the different labels for the different levels of invariance that have been bandied about in the literature. The factorial invariance literature discusses a number of different levels of invariance, and, as you can see, the different levels of invariance go by many different names. In the table, I've put citations to the researchers who introduced or used the corresponding label. The common idea, however, is conveyed in the definitional equations that correspond with each level of invariance. In my discussions, I primarily stick with the terminology of *configural*, *weak*, and *strong invariance*, but I sometimes use *loading invariance* and *intercept invariance* when talking about weak and strong invariance, respectively. I also refer to strong invariance as evidence of *construct comparability*, *measurement equivalence*, or *measurement invariance*. These latter three terms are generally interchangeable and indicate that any observed changes in the constructs over time are true construct differences and not due to measurement artifacts or item biases (e.g., differential item functioning).

For longitudinal models, the issue of invariance applies only to the indicators and constructs that are measured at more than one occasion (or across more than one group). Any construct that is measured at only one time point or in only one group is not relevant to the definitional equations. Such lone constructs would not be addressed when evaluating invariance; they would simply be unconstrained or freely estimated constructs in the model. To simplify the rest of this discussion, I'll focus on the scenario where all indicators and constructs are measured at each time point. In fact, to help your imagination, picture two constructs measured with three indicators each at three time points (or take a second to jump ahead to the model in Figure 5.5, which is about midway through this chapter).

At level 0, the criterion for configural invariance is simply that the relations between each indicator and its construct should have the same pattern of fixed and freed loadings at each time point. That is, everywhere there is an estimate at one time point, there's a corresponding estimate at the next time point; and everywhere there's a fixed 0 (nonestimated parameter) at one time point, there's a corresponding fixed 0 in the other time point. This level of invariance is more qualitative than quantitative. The evaluation criteria for whether it holds are (1) the interocular test (i.e., Does the pattern look the same?) and (2) basic model-fit information (i.e., Does the model fit the data reasonably well? See Chapter 4). A key feature of the configurally invariant model is that each element of the SEM equations is estimated uniquely for each occasion of measurement. The configurally invariant model is primarily used as the baseline model to evaluate the degree to which the different levels of factorial invariance are supported by the data. If the configurally invariant model has an acceptable model fit (and no indication that changes to the model are needed to improve its fit), then the other levels of invariance can be imposed and evaluated in the sequence depicted in Table 5.1. The different levels of factorial invariance hold if the change in model fit from a lower level of invariance to a higher level of invariance is negligible.

If you look closely at the equations in Table 5.1, you'll notice that at each level of the factorial invariance assumption the subscript o is removed from one of the key elements of the equations. For example, when testing for weak factorial invariance, the loadings of the indicators on the constructs are estimated as a common set of parameter estimates that are used for all occasions of measurement. That is, the loadings contained in Λ are *not* allowed to vary across occasions of measurement. Here, you simply specify equality constraints on the corresponding loadings across all measurement occasions. All other elements of the equations are estimated uniquely (freely, independently) for each measurement occasion. Similarly, with strong factorial invariance, the corresponding intercepts of the indicators are constrained to be equal across all measurement occasions. This constraint is added to the already constrained loadings. The other elements of these equations are freely estimated for each of the measurement occasions. The third level of invariance, termed *strict factorial invariance*, adds the additional constraint that the residual variances of the corresponding indicators are the same across measurement occasions (a level of invariance that I do not endorse).

As the name implies, *weak factorial invariance* is weak evidence as to whether the constructs are comparable across time (or groups). The reason it is a weak test is that it is a relatively easy test to pass, even if I don't have truly invariant indicators. Good indicators of a construct will typically have uniformly high loadings. As a result of the uniformity, violations of invariance won't be easily revealed. Mean levels, on the other hand, vary quite a bit more across indicators. Adding the constraints on the intercepts to evaluate strong invariance thereby provides a strong test of the invariance assumption, because now both the loadings and the intercepts must show consistent relative relationships in order to conclude that the constructs are comparable.

One time, I was testing invariance and specified equality of the loadings across time, but I had accidentally selected the wrong indicators at Time 2 (indicators of completely different constructs!). My test of weak factorial invariance passed with flying colors. In this model, all the indicators loaded on their respective constructs at about the same level, and when I specified invariance, there was very little change in model fit. When I went on to test strong invariance, on the other hand, the test failed miserably. Surprised by this, I double-checked my syntax and found the error. The reason the strong invariance test revealed the problem is that the means of the indicators can vary quite a bit, both when they are measuring the same construct and when they are measuring different constructs. My point here isn't that a failure of invariance is due to sloppy programming. Instead, my point is that the ability to detect whether invariance requires both the loadings and the intercepts to conform to the expectations of invariance. Passing the strong test is harder (and therefore provides strong evidence) than passing the weak test.

From this perspective, you might think that adding strict invariance would be an even tougher test of the invariance assumption. As I mentioned earlier (see Table 5.1), strict invariance is tested when I also add the restriction that the unique factors must also be invariant across time. This test, in my view, is overly restrictive, and it does not provide "better" evidence of invariance. In fact, I strongly recommend that strict factorial invariance not be imposed when doing any kind of comparisons across time (or groups). I don't have a problem with testing for strict invariance, but I do have a problem with enforcing it when I move forward to test hypotheses about the nature of the constructs.

Why do I have a problem with enforcing strict invariance? The reason is that the variances of the indicator residuals contain both the indicator-specific information and the random unreliability of measurement. Strict factorial invariance is a test that the sum of these two sources of variance (indicator specific and random error) is *exactly* the same across time (or groups). Although it might be reasonable to assume that the indicator-specific information would be invariant across time (or groups), I don't think it is reasonable to assume that the amount of random error present in each indicator at each time point (or across groups) would be the same. In addition, the indicator-specific information in the indicators can contain trivial amounts of population misfit that might change over time (again, in trivial amounts). From this vantage point, even *testing* for strict factorial invariance has dubious theoretical grounds to begin with. Some might argue that testing for strict invariance isn't *that* problematic, but I would strongly argue that *enforcing* it during further testing *is* problematic because there is simply no place for the misfit and the differences in unreliability to go. In other words, the reason that enforcing the strict factorial invariance constraints during further testing is problematic is because if the sum of the two pieces (indicator specific and random) is not *exactly* equal, the amount of misfit that the constraints on the residuals would create must permeate all other estimated parameters of the model. Residuals are like the steam valve of a pressure cooker. If I don't open the valve to let off some of the steam, the whole pot (model) may become disfigured (biased estimates) or even explode (estimation problems).

A SMALL (NEARLY PERFECT) DATA EXAMPLE

Configural Factorial Invariance

Figure 5.1 is the same model I presented in Figure 3.10 in Chapter 3. It is the configural invariance model in that no constraints are placed on any of the parameter

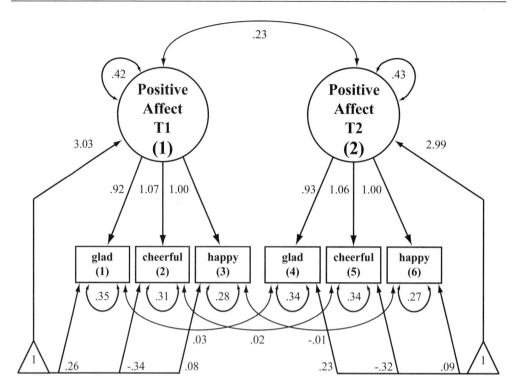

FIGURE 5.1. Estimates for two time points with positive affect: The configural invariance model. None of the loadings or intercepts are equated over time. Model fit: $\chi^2_{(n=823,\ 5)} = 18.41$; RMSEA = $.057_{(.031;\ .086)}$; CFI = .992; TLI/NNFI = .968.

estimates; only the same pattern of loadings is expected. Recall that I used the effects coding method of identification so the loadings would average 1 and the intercepts would average 0. Notice that the loadings of the indicators of positive affect at Time 1 are .92, 1.07, and 1.00. The first indicator has the smallest loading, the second has the largest, and the third is in the middle. At Time 2, the loadings follow the same pattern, with the first indicator having the smallest loading, the second having the largest, and the third being in the middle. The intercepts of the indicators also follow a consistent pattern across time. With the centering value of 0 across the three indicators, the mean of "glad" is slightly higher than 0, the mean of "cheerful" is lower than 0, and the mean of "happy" is near 0. This pattern is the same at both time points. In addition to this consistent pattern of the loadings and intercepts, the overall model fit is at acceptable to very good levels (again the RMSEA would not reject the acceptable-fit hypothesis, but the other fit indices are outstanding). As mentioned, this data example is nearly perfect with regard to testing for invariance. In practice, however, I almost never see as clean a case as I'm presenting here. Later in this chapter, I present a more realistic example.

Weak Factorial Invariance

Testing for weak factorial invariance involves making each corresponding loading mathematically equal; however, other parameters (particularly the variances) are allowed to change over time (i.e., are freely estimated at each time point). Figure 5.2 shows the model estimates with the constraint that the corresponding loadings are mathematically equal over time. I have superscripted the corresponding loadings with a, b, and c to show which loadings are specified to be equal over time. Notice that the loadings have changed only very slightly over time (in fact, most change is in the third decimal place, which is beyond the meaningful level of precision). Because this example is nearly perfect, these are pretty much the only estimates that changed between the two models. More often than not, however, the estimated variances of the constructs and the residual variances of the indicators will also change (in this example, the biggest change was in the residual of "happy" at Time 2, which changed from .27 in Figure 5.1 to .28 in Figure 5.2).

Keep in mind that all estimated parameters are free to change from one model to the next, because the model is being reestimated at each step; in the case of weak

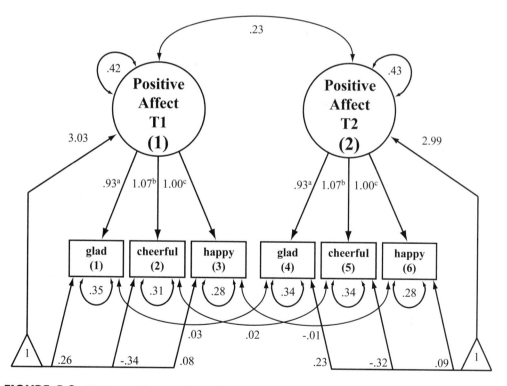

FIGURE 5.2. Estimates for two time points with positive affect: The weak factorial invariance model. Only the corresponding loadings (denoted [a], [b], and [c]) are constrained to be equal to one another over time. Model fit: $\chi^2_{(n=823,\,7)} = 18.51$; RMSEA = $.043_{(.020;\,.070)}$; CFI = .993; TLI/NNFI = .980.

factorial invariance, it is reestimated with the equality constraints on the loadings in place. With each new model, the estimator will attempt to find the best fit between the model-implied matrix (and mean vector) and the observed matrix (and mean vector). To accomplish this optimization of fit, other parameters must also change to accommodate the equality constraints. In other words, all estimated parameters of a model can change.

Regardless of scaling method (see Chapter 3), when the loadings are equated across time, the scaling constraint at Time 2 (and any additional time points) is no longer needed. Constraints at later time points are no longer needed because the scale for the estimates of the loadings and the variance of the construct at Time 2 (and later) are determined by the scaling constraint that is in place at Time 1. That is, the scale for the estimates of the construct at all measurement occasions is determined by the Time 1 scaling constraint (i.e., either the marker variable, fixed factor, or effects coded method).

Referring back to Figure 5.2, with the constraint that the loadings are invariant over time, the metric of the latent constructs' variances is now operationally defined in the same way. That is, the relative strength of each indicator is constrained to be the same at both time points. This constraint basically forces the loadings to be estimated as the optimal balance among the loadings both within time and across time. In this regard, information from both time points is used to find the optimal balance of information among the indicators. Using information from only one time point or the other (as we do with the configural invariance model) is not really an optimal solution because sampling error at a given time point is present. In this regard, using the information from across the time points provides a better population estimate of the true loadings for the construct. Thus, if weak invariance holds, the loadings are more generalizable than they would be if they were not equated across time. Because the loadings are equal across time, the scale for interpreting the variance and covariance estimates is the same. In other words, when the scale for the estimates of the loadings is mathematically the same over time, the estimates of the loadings are now based on a common metric.

You may have noticed that the change in degrees of freedom from the configurally invariant model to the weak factorial invariance model is only 2 degrees of freedom, even though there are three loadings that are equated across time. There are two possible reasons that the degrees of freedom gained do not equal the number of loadings that are equated across time (or across groups). Both reasons are related to the scaling constraint used to set the scale for the constructs. The first reason is that the scaling constraint is no longer needed at the second time point. The second reason is that the scaling constraint is already placed on one of the indicators, and so only two loadings are freely estimated at each time point. This idea is important to understand, and I continue to emphasize it as I walk through the examples. Later on, in Table 5.2, I report the estimates for this model using the three methods of scaling and identification. In the table, I've indicated which of the possible parameters are fixed for scaling purposes and which ones are constrained for invariance testing purposes.

In Figure 5.2, I present the results of the weak factorial invariance model using the effects coding method of scaling (scripts for each scaling method are available on *www.guilford.com/little-materials*). With the effects coding method of scaling, the constraint that the loadings average 1.0 is placed at Time 1. Here, I chose the first loading to be the constrained loading (remember, I could have chosen any of the loadings to constrain to enforce the effects coding constraint and gotten the same results; see Chapter 3 for details). When weak invariance is specified, the equality constraints across time will make the loadings at Time 1 equal to the corresponding loadings at Time 2. Because the loadings at Time 2 are equal to the loadings at Time 1, the scaling constraint at Time 1 provides the scale for all estimates across all times of measurement. As with any method of identification and scaling, the scaling constraint at Time 1 saves a degree of freedom. Making the loadings equal across time means that only two estimated parameters are, in fact, further constrained. With three indicators of the construct at both time points, the difference in model degrees of freedom between the configural and the weak invariance models will be 2, just as with the marker variable method. The constraint on the first loading of the construct at Time 2 is no longer a scaling constraint but is now a cross-time invariance constraint. It is specified to be equal to the first loading of the construct at Time 1, which *is* constrained to set the scale. This indicator at Time 2 is indirectly a part of the scaling process only because the loading at Time 2 is constrained to be equal to the loading at Time 1 (see Figure 5.2).

With the marker variable method of scaling, the first loadings of the construct at Time 1 and at Time 2 are fixed to 1.0 to set the scale. The variances of the constructs are freely estimated and, therefore, can be different at Time 1 and Time 2. When the weak factorial invariance constraint is placed on the loadings (i.e., equality of the corresponding loadings across time), the first loading, which is fixed to 1 to set the scale at both time points, is already "equated" across time. The second and third loadings, which are freely estimated at both time points, are the only two *estimated* parameters that are equated. As a result, the difference in the model degrees of freedom is only 2. I reiterate: the variances of the constructs at both time points are both freely estimated, as shown in the definitional equations of Table 5.1.

As mentioned, regardless of scaling method, when the loadings are equated across time, the scaling constraint at Time 2 (and any additional time points) is no longer needed and should be removed. The scale for the estimates of both the loadings and the variance of the construct at Time 2 is determined by the scaling constraint that is in place for the Time 1 version of a construct. With the marker variable method of scaling, because the first loading is fixed at Time 1, the equated loading at Time 2 becomes fixed again when it is specified to be the same as its Time 1 counterpart. This issue becomes more apparent when I use a different method of scaling, such as the fixed factor method.

Using the fixed factor method of scaling, the variance of the construct is fixed at both time points to set the scale for the constructs in the configural invariant model. When the loadings are equated across time, the three freely estimated loadings at Time 2 are now equal to their Time 1 counterparts. However, with the fixed factor method of identification, the fixed variance at Time 2 is no longer needed to set the scale for the loadings (see the definitional equation in Table 5.1 for weak invariance). Here, the variance of the construct should no longer be set to 1.0 at Time 2; instead, it should become a freely estimated parameter. If I neglect to free this constraint at Time 2, then I am asking two different kinds of questions *at the same time*! That is, I am testing the invariance of the loadings *and* the invariance of the latent constructs' variances across time. Invariance of the loadings is one question, whereas invariance of the latent constructs' variances is a second, separate, question.

With the other two methods of identification and scaling, the scaling constraint is in the loadings, while the variances are freely estimated at all times of measurement. Hence the need to relax the scaling constraint at Time 2 is not obvious (it is implicit). Relaxing the scaling constraint is necessary and explicit with the fixed factor method of identification and scaling. I reiterate: the three methods of identification and scaling will yield exactly the same answers in terms of model fit and change in fit (if specified properly) when I proceed from configural to weak to strong invariance.

Strong Factorial Invariance

Testing for strong factorial invariance works much the same way as testing for weak factorial invariance, but now the focus is on the observed means and estimated intercepts of the indicators. Here, each corresponding intercept is specified to be mathematically equal across groups. In Figure 5.3, I have superscripted the corresponding intercept estimates with d, e, and f to indicate which ones are specified to be mathematically equal.

For the effects coded method, the constraint that the intercepts center on 0 allows a latent mean to be estimated at both time points. When the constraint of cross-time invariance is placed on the intercepts, the difference in degrees of freedom would again be only 2 because the scaling constraint uses up 1 degree of freedom at Time 1. The cross-time equality constraints apply only to the two intercepts that aren't constrained. Stated another way, if a parameter is fixed or constrained at Time 1, it does not use a degree of freedom; equating a parameter at Time 2, which is already fixed or constrained, to be equal to the fixed or constrained parameter at Time 1 will result in the Time 2 parameter remaining fixed or constrained and therefore would not use up (or gain) a degree of freedom. When I equate two parameters that were freely estimated, on the other hand, I am making one parameter estimate that applies to two locations, and the cost is only 1 degree of freedom (see Figure 5.3).

With the marker variable method of identification, the intercept of the marker

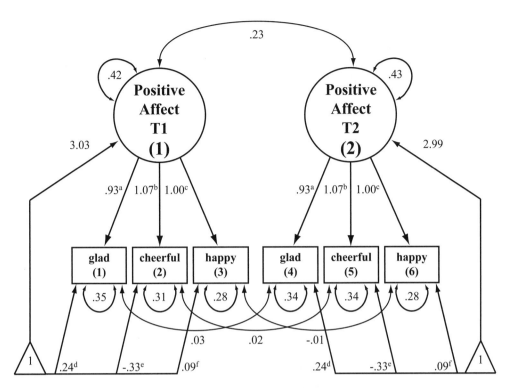

FIGURE 5.3. Estimates for two time points with positive affect: The strong factorial invariance model. Now, in addition to the corresponding loadings (denoted ᵃ, ᵇ, and ᶜ) being equated over time, the corresponding intercepts (denoted ᵈ, ᵉ, and ᶠ) are constrained to be equal to one another over time. Model fit: $\chi^2_{(n=823, 9)} = 20.25$; RMSEA = $.039_{(.016; .062)}$; CFI = .994; TLI/NNFI = .985.

variable should be set to 0 (although some users will fix the latent mean to 0, which is fine in terms of model fit, but the scale of things gets a bit wacky). If I stayed consistent with the method used for the loadings, I'd fix the marker variable's intercept to 0. The latent mean of the construct at both time points would then be estimated freely. Here, because I chose a marker variable to set the scale, the latent mean would simply reflect the mean of the chosen marker variable (again, an arbitrary scale—more on this later when I discuss Table 5.2).

When I use the fixed factor method of scaling, the means of the latent constructs are fixed at 0 to provide the scale for the mean-level information (intercepts and latent means) at both time points. Once the cross-time equality constraints on the indicators' intercepts are in place, however, the means of the latent constructs at the subsequent time points can now be estimated freely. The latent mean at Time 2, for example, will become the mean difference from Time 1. Because the latent mean at Time 1 is fixed at 0 to set the scale, the mean difference estimated at Time 2 and all subsequent time points is the difference from 0 (because 0 is the fixed scaling value I set on the mean of the construct at Time 1).

In order to see the differences in the identification and scaling constraints, I've fit this simple model using all three methods of scaling. The results are shown in Table 5.2 where I have put the value that corresponds to each of the labeled parameters from Figure 5.4 and the relevant fit information. Before you balk at the numbers in the table, I'd like you to let me walk you through some of the patterns that show up. In Table 5.2, I've put * by the parameter that is fixed to set the scale of

TABLE 5.2. Comparison of parameter estimates across the levels of invariance depending on the method of scaling

Parameter	Effects Coded Config	Weak	Strong	Marker Variable Config	Weak	Strong	Fixed Factor Config	Weak	Strong
$\lambda_{1,1}$	0.925^a	0.930^a	0.930^a	1.000^*	1.000^*	1.000^*	0.600	0.603	0.603
$\lambda_{2,1}$	1.075	1.068	1.069	1.162	1.149	1.150	0.697	0.693	0.693
$\lambda_{3,1}$	0.999	1.002	1.001	1.080	1.078	1.076	0.648	0.650	0.649
$\lambda_{4,2}$	0.934^a	0.930^b	0.930^b	1.000^*	1.000^b	1.000^b	0.610	0.603^b	0.603^b
$\lambda_{5,2}$	1.061	1.068^b	1.069^b	1.136	1.149^b	1.150^b	0.693	0.693^b	0.693^b
$\lambda_{6,2}$	1.004	1.002^b	1.001^b	1.075	1.078^b	1.076^b	0.656	0.650^b	0.649^b
$\psi_{1,1}$	0.420	0.420	0.420	0.360	0.363	0.364	1.000^*	1.000^*	1.000^*
$\psi_{2,2}$	0.427	0.427	0.427	0.373	0.369	0.369	1.000^*	1.016	1.016
$\psi_{2,1}$	0.234	0.234	0.234	0.202	0.202	0.202	0.553	0.557	0.557
$\theta_{1,1}$	0.349	0.348	0.348	0.349	0.348	0.348	0.349	0.348	0.348
$\theta_{2,2}$	0.306	0.309	0.309	0.306	0.309	0.309	0.306	0.309	0.309
$\theta_{3,3}$	0.278	0.276	0.277	0.278	0.276	0.277	0.278	0.276	0.277
$\theta_{4,4}$	0.336	0.337	0.337	0.336	0.337	0.337	0.336	0.337	0.337
$\theta_{5,5}$	0.343	0.341	0.340	0.343	0.341	0.340	0.343	0.341	0.340
$\theta_{6,6}$	0.274	0.275	0.276	0.274	0.275	0.276	0.274	0.275	0.276
$\theta_{4,1}$	0.031	0.032	0.032	0.031	0.032	0.032	0.031	0.032	0.032
$\theta_{5,2}$	0.018	0.018	0.017	0.018	0.018	0.017	0.018	0.018	0.017
$\theta_{6,3}$	-0.011	-0.011	-0.011	-0.011	-0.011	-0.011	-0.011	-0.011	-0.011
τ_1	0.260^a	0.247^a	0.245^a	0.000^*	0.000^*	0.000^*	3.069	3.069	3.067
τ_2	-0.338	-0.316	-0.331	-0.614	-0.600	-0.612	2.926	2.926	2.915
τ_3	0.078	0.069	0.086	-0.204	-0.197	-0.177	3.110	3.110	3.123
τ_4	0.231^a	0.249^a	0.245^b	0.000^*	0.000^*	0.000^b	3.026	3.026	3.067^b
τ_5	-0.319	-0.339	-0.331^b	-0.581	-0.620	-0.612^b	2.857	2.857	2.915^b
τ_6	0.088	0.095	0.086^b	-0.159	-0.168	-0.177^b	3.093	3.093	3.123^b
α_1	3.035	3.035	3.035	3.069	3.069	3.069	0.000^*	0.000^*	0.000^*
α_2	2.992	2.992	2.992	3.026	3.026	3.026	0.000^*	0.000^*	-0.066
χ^2	18.41	18.52	20.25	18.41	18.52	20.25	18.41	18.52	20.25
df	5	7	9	5	7	9	5	7	9
RMSEA	0.057	0.045	0.039	0.057	0.045	0.039	0.057	0.045	0.039
CFI	0.994	0.995	0.995	0.994	0.995	0.995	0.994	0.995	0.995
TLI/NNFI	0.983	0.990	0.992	0.983	0.990	0.992	0.983	0.990	0.992

Note. Config = results from configurally invariant model; weak = weak invariant model; strong = strong invariant model. *Indicates that the value is fixed to set the scale of the constructs' parameter estimates. "a" indicates that the estimate is constrained to set the scale of the construct's parameters. "b" indicates that the estimate is constrained to be equal to its Time 1 counterpart (e.g., $\lambda_{4,2} = \lambda_{1,1}$ under both the weak and strong invariant models, and $\tau_4 = \tau_1$ under the strong invariant model). Blocks of estimates highlighted with gray are exactly the same across the different methods of scaling and identification.

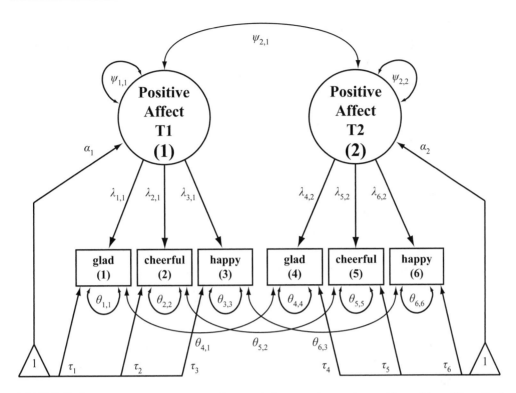

FIGURE 5.4. Model parameter labels in Greek for two time points with positive affect. Each parameter is labeled so that you can follow along with the different estimates that emerge using the three different methods of scale setting that are presented in Table 5.2.

the construct's parameter estimates and a superscripted ^{a} by the estimate if it is a constrained parameter that provides the scaling constraint. I have put a superscripted ^{b} by any estimate that is constrained to be equal to its Time 1 counterpart (e.g., $\lambda_{4,2} = \lambda_{1,1}$ under both the weak and strong invariant models and $\tau_4 = \tau_1$ under the strong invariant model).

With the configural invariant model, a scale is set for the constructs at both Time 1 and Time 2. For the effects coded method, one loading is constrained to be a function of the other two loadings. In this case, $\lambda_{1,1} = 3 - \lambda_{2,1} - \lambda_{3,1}$ for the construct at Time 1 and $\lambda_{4,2} = 3 - \lambda_{5,2} - \lambda_{6,2}$ for the construct at Time 2. For the marker variable method, $\lambda_{1,1}$ and $\lambda_{4,2}$ are fixed at 1.0. For the fixed factor method, the variances of the constructs (i.e., $\psi_{1,1}$ and $\psi_{2,2}$) are fixed to 1.0.

For the weak invariance model, each corresponding loading is equated across time ($\lambda_{4,2} = \lambda_{1,1}$, $\lambda_{5,2} = \lambda_{2,1}$, and $\lambda_{6,2} = \lambda_{3,1}$), and the scaling constraint for the variance–covariance information at Time 2 is removed. For the strong invariant model, each corresponding intercept is equated across time ($\tau_4 = \tau_1$, $\tau_5 = \tau_2$, and $\tau_6 = \tau_3$) in addition to the constraints already in place on the loadings. The scaling constraint for the mean information at Time 2 is also relaxed.

The first thing to notice about the numbers in Table 5.2 is that the fit information is exactly the same across each invariance test using the different scaling constraints. The fact that model fit is identical across the methods of scaling and identification means that the different methods are mathematically and statistically equivalent and would lead to the same conclusions about whether or not the invariance constraints are acceptable. That is, all three methods lead to isomorphic model fit information; only the scales of the estimated parameters and their associated standard errors vary.

The second thing to notice is that the variances of the latent constructs are allowed to vary across time when the weak invariance constraints are imposed (i.e., loadings are equated over time). That is, the variance at Time 2 can be different from the variance at Time 1, regardless of the scaling method. The means of the latent constructs are similarly allowed to vary across time when the strong invariance constraints are imposed (i.e., intercepts are equated over time).

The third thing to notice is that the residual variances of the indicators are exactly the same across the three different methods of scaling and identification. The fact that the residual variances are exactly the same also speaks to the mathematical and statistical equivalence of the three scaling methods. The three scaling methods are each equivalent ways to estimate the reliable bits of the latent constructs (the loading and intercepts of the indicators and the variances and means of the constructs). To borrow John Nesselroade's (2007) idea, if indicators are our worldly window into the latent space, then the scaling methods are simply different locations for the window. What we see when we peer in the window is essentially the same space, but the perspective shifts depending on where we locate the window. And, I would add, some perspectives are more revealing than others (more on this idea later).

Although there are other nuances you might notice in the pattern of numbers in Table 5.2, the final feature that I'd like to point out is the differences in the metrics that each method provides. The latent variance and latent mean of the constructs using the marker variable method are both a reflection of the information that the chosen marker variable contributes to the definition of the construct. As mentioned numerous times before, the choice of marker variable and the metric that it introduces are arbitrary and provide little in terms of meaningful units to discuss or interpret in terms of the construct's actual mean and variance.

With the fixed factor method, the latent variance and mean are fixed at 1.0 and 0.0, respectively, thereby standardizing the latent construct information. In the configural model, the association between the two constructs is a correlation of .553 because the variances at Time 1 and Time 2 are both fixed at 1.0. When I move to the weak invariant model, however, the association between the two constructs is now a covariance of .557. The estimate of the association between constructs in the weak invariant model (and the strong model, as well) is a covariance because the variances of the constructs at both time points are not exactly 1.0. When the two variance estimates involved are exactly 1.0, the association between them is a correlation. When one or both latent variances differ from 1.0 even by a trivial amount, the association between them is now a covariance. Granted, it is a covariance that is very close to being a correlation, but I cannot square it and get a true or precise estimate of shared variance, for example. This issue can be resolved by using phantom constructs, which I introduced in Chapter 3 and further exemplify in Chapter 7.

In terms of the means, the observed manifest variable means are 3.036 and 2.993 for the two time points. The latent means are 3.035 and 2.992, respectively. The difference between the two estimates of the constructs' means is that in the observed metric the mean is the average of the three indicators, where each indicator is weighted equally (i.e., by 1.0; see Equation 5.2a vs. 5.2b). For the latent mean, the indicators are weighted by the magnitude of the loading. Here, the mean information for the first indicator, "glad," is weighted by 0.930, whereas the mean of the second indicator, "cheerful," is weighted by 1.069. Finally, the mean of the third indicator, "happy," is weighted by 1.001. Also note that with the effects coded method of identification, the average of the τ's is 0. The loadings reflect the relative quality of the indicators as reflections of the underlying construct. The indicators with higher loadings are better indicators of the construct than are the indicators with lower loadings. In this example, the indicator "cheerful" had the strongest loading but also the lowest mean; thus, the latent mean is a smidgen lower than the manifest mean. Granted, in this example the difference doesn't show up until the third decimal place. In other data, however, the difference can be more noticeable if the indicators differ in their relative quality, especially in comparison to our "essentially

Equation 5.2. How the means are calculated

a) $\bar{\eta}_1 = \alpha_1 = \dfrac{\lambda_{11} \cdot y_1 + \lambda_{21} \cdot y_2 + \lambda_{31} \cdot y_3}{3} + \dfrac{\tau_1 + \tau_2 + \tau_3}{3}$

b) $\bar{Y} = \dfrac{1 \cdot y_1 + 1 \cdot y_2 + 1 \cdot y_3}{3}$

c) $\bar{y}_1 \approx \tau_1 + \lambda_{11} \cdot \alpha_1$

d) $\bar{y}_2 \approx \tau_2 + \lambda_{21} \cdot \alpha_1$

e) $\bar{y}_3 \approx \tau_3 + \lambda_{31} \cdot \alpha_1$

- η_1 is the calculated mean of the latent variable scores.
- α_1 is the estimated mean of the designated latent variable.
- λ is the loading of the subscript designated indicator.
- τ is the estimated mean of the designated indicator.
- These formulae assume that the construct has three indicators, as depicted in Figure 5.4.
- When the effects coded method of identification is used, the average of the τ estimates is 0.

perfect" example. And, in some instances, they can make a meaningful difference in the estimate of the mean.

Evaluating Invariance Constraints

In evaluating whether the assumption of invariance is tenable, few specialists would argue that a pure statistical decision rule must be applied. A statistical test is an exact test of no differences. Invariance tests, for the most part, are tests of approximate similarity (i.e., only trivial differences exist). Recall that all models are wrong, even in the population. Models are simply attempts to provide a useful and parsimonious approximation of the processes that give rise to the data. In this regard, the assumption of factorial invariance is a model that I think will provide a parsimonious approximation of the processes that give rise to the data. Because I am examining the general tenability of this model, consulting the changes in the relative model fit measures is warranted (see Little, 1997, for a more detailed discussion of the modeling rationale vs. the statistical rationale, which I also introduced and discussed in Chapter 4).

In one of the first Monte Carlo studies examining the performance of model fit measures for use in tests of invariance, Cheung and Rensvold (2002) concluded that three measures of model fit performed pretty well for judging the adequacy of the invariance assumption. In addition to gamma hat and McDonald's (1989) noncentrality index (NCI), the CFI performed very well. Although they had recommendations for change in gamma hat and NCI, the key recommendation that is relied on in the literature is their change in CFI guideline (see Chapter 4 for the calculation of CFI). Here, if the change in CFI is not more than .01, the assumption of invariance is tenable. That is, if the change in CFI is .01 or less, then invariance holds. If the change is more than .01, then the assumption of factorial invariance is not reasonable, and I would need to examine where the failure of invariance occurred (see my discussion of partial invariance in a later section). This criterion is applied in the step from configural to weak and then from weak to strong. Once strong invariance has been established, this model becomes the baseline model for all further comparisons, including tests of cross-time similarities or differences in the constructs.

More recently, Meade, Johnson, and Braddy (2008) conducted a follow-up Monte Carlo simulation. Their results indicated that the change in CFI should not be more than .002 to consider the deviations from perfect invariance as functionally trivial. They also provide a table of values for changes in McDonald's NCI that vary depending on the number of factors and indicators.

Both of these Monte Carlo simulations (i.e., Cheung & Rensvold's [2002] and Meade et al.'s [2008]) compared the performance of these alternative fit indices with the pure statistical criterion of the change in the χ^2 value. The statistical criterion performed very poorly in both simulations. One key point here is that strong Monte Carlo evidence indicates that questions of factorial invariance are best addressed by examining the changes in these alternative fit indices rather than relying on the χ^2 difference test. The χ^2 test is simply too sensitive to trivial fluctuations and differences in the context of invariance testing.

A second key point, which may not be so obvious, is that we still don't have good guidance on the criteria for determining lack of invariance using these alternative fit measures. Only two simulation studies have been conducted, and both have limitations. For example, Meade et al. (2008) developed their criteria based on very high power and very low error (e.g., a Type I error rate of .01). We have no guidance for a less rigorous .05 error rate, for example. In addition, Meade et al. did not include trivial misfit in the population generating model like Cheung and Rensvold did. Good simulations should include trivial misfit in order to mimic real world models. Both of the existing simulation studies examined the question of invariance across two groups. We have no guidance for three or more groups, and we have even less guidance for longitudinal invariance tests where things like stability of both the common and unique factors would likely have an influence on our ability to detect whether or not the invariance constraints are reasonable.

Another issue that remains to be addressed thoroughly in a Monte Carlo framework is what criteria for change in CFI would emerge if the CFI were calculated using an appropriate null model (see Chapter 3). The two simulation studies used the standard independence null model and did not incorporate information about the means or variances in the null model expectation. As mentioned, the baseline models used in the Meade et al. simulation don't vary in terms of the quality of overall fit (i.e., they are perfect models in the population). In practice, the configural invariant models that provide the baseline for how well a model fits with no constraints across time (or groups) will vary in terms of how accurately they reflect the true model and how the models then approximate the data.

Yet another consideration in this context is the difference in what Cheung and Rensvold's (2002) simulation examined versus what Meade et al.'s (2008) simulation examined. Meade et al. explicitly included lack of invariance as part of the simulation, whereas Cheung and Rensvold did not. Thus, Meade et al.'s simulation provides power and Type I error for detecting the lack of invariance that they included in the simulation. Cheung and Rensvold (2002) provide recommendations under conditions in which invariance is true.

The bottom line is that there's still a lot of work that needs to be done in this area, and I would strongly caution readers and reviewers not to get too excited by the current recommendations for determining invariance. In my personal view, however, the .01 criteria of Cheung and Rensvold (2002) has been a good rule of thumb across the many studies I have conducted and reviewed. At this point, I would recommend that one treat these guidelines as just that, *guidelines*. Guidelines are not hard and fast rules to which one must blindly adhere. As with model fit measures in general, I have to examine the whole set of measures and use wise judgment before pronouncing support or not for the invariance constraints. The wise judgment will consider the model fit as a whole, the expectations for invariance or noninvariance, the place in the literature of the project, and careful examination of potential local misfit (e.g., scrutinize the fitted residuals and modification indices carefully).

For longitudinal studies in particular, either the expectation of invariance is well supported by theory or the expectation of noninvariance is well supported by theory. During many developmental epochs, the measures and the constructs are age appropriate, and invariance would be expected. During such epochs, a lack of invariance would generally result only from some contextual influence rather than a developmental change in the meaning of a particular item or indicator. For example, an indicator of positive affect such as "great" might change its meaning if a popular TV advertisement used the word "great" as part of a campaign. During periods of developmental transitions, on the other hand, some items or indicators might be expected to change in their meaning across different age ranges. For example, a temper tantrum might fit as an indicator of aggressive behavior in toddlerhood but may "fall out" as an indicator of aggression during the preschool or early elementary school ages.

One caveat that I would offer here relates to the goals of the research and the kind of test that would be performed. For most tests of factorial invariance, the general expectation is that the measures are reasonably OK and have sufficiently invariant properties to allow me to examine the construct differences and similarities over time. In this context, the changes in the relative fit measures are quite adequate to evaluate the tenability of the invariance assumption. On the other hand, if my research questions are very specific about the behavior of a measure or set of items as they change over time, then I would use a stricter statistical test of those hypotheses. The change in χ^2 or noncentral χ^2 might be appropriate for strong theoretical tests, but I would adjust the alpha level (i.e., the p-value for controlling Type I error) to be less stringent given the likely power that I'd have in the statistical test.

Model Modification

Any changes to an initially specified model should be done with caution. For example, modification indices can suggest ways in which a model might achieve better model fit; however, if the overall model fit is already acceptable, then I should be cautious. Much like the song of the Sirens, the allure of modification indices should be resisted. Many times, the suggested modifications are due to sampling variability and not to a "real" process. Because any change to a model becomes a statement of theory, changes should make strong theoretical sense. If I make a change to the model, I am essentially saying "heretofore, if I collect data using these measures again, I will expect this modified parameter estimate to occur again." In other words, if I make the change, I am elevating the parameter in question to the level of nontrivial population parameter rather than relegating it to the category of a trivial sample-specific blip that can be ignored. On the other hand, making post hoc modifications can be seen as a symptom that one has abandoned theory and has joined an exploratory, atheoretical cult that flaunts its disdain for falsifiability and the scientific method. In other words, don't let data do the driving; they don't have a license!

Most SEM software provides some variation of a modification index. A modification index is an approximate estimate of the amount of change in the overall model's χ^2 that is expected to occur if the parameter of interest is freely estimated. Any potential relationship that is not being estimated in a given model will yield a modification index. Any parameter that is constrained to equality (e.g., when loadings are equated across time) will yield a modification index. Any parameter that is freely estimated, however, will not yield a modification index because the parameter is already optimized for fit given the other estimates (and constraints) in the model. Sometimes, the software will give a modification index for a parameter that is not modifiable. For example, the parameter that is fixed to set the scale will sometimes have a modification index associated with it, but this parameter cannot be changed because the scaling constraint is required. In longitudinal research, I often get a modification index for a variable or construct at a future time point having a predictive relationship to a variable or construct at a prior time point. Although some are tempted to interpret such an effect as evidence of a reciprocal process, it is not. Because the time-ordered relationship goes forward in time, this type of modification index is impossible. The software has no way of knowing that some estimated relationships are implausible given the constraints of logic and the design of the study. I address ways to handle reciprocal processes in Chapter 7.

When my model fit is already acceptable, my rules of thumb about whether to make a modification are somewhat simplistic and have not been tested in any way other than by personal experience. First, if my model fit is *already* at an acceptable level, a modification index should be "obvious" and/or "seriously large." "Obvious" means that the value pops out much like an outlier and has clear interpretation. "Seriously large," on the other hand, is a relative value; it should approach about 10% of the overall model χ^2. If my model χ^2 is 100, I'll take a serious look at modification indices that approach 10. If my model χ^2 is 1,000, I'll ignore the 10s and start taking a serious look at the modification indices that start to approach 100. When looking at the "serious" modification indices, the second level of heuristic for deciding to make or not make a change is based on the theoretical meaning and implications of the potential change. If I am looking at a suggested change and I'm scratching my head in bewilderment as to why there is a large suggested change, it probably is not a meaningful modification to make. On the other hand, if I thump my forehead with the palm of my hand and think to myself "duh!," then the modification is probably meaningful (and I probably should have thought of it to begin with).

Clearly, theory is the analyst's best friend. Ad hoc changes are like a deviant peer's influence: make good choices and you'll be OK.

Partial Invariance

Partial invariance occurs when one or more of the loadings and/or one or more of the intercepts cannot be constrained to equality across time (or across groups). For example, following the advice of Cheung and Rensvold (2002), when the change in CFI is less than or equal to .01, then the set of constrained parameters is fundamentally the same across time. If the change in CFI is greater than .01, on the other hand, then at least one of the constrained parameters is not like the others. In this situation, I have a problem in that at least one of the variables is not invariant over time.

Imagine a hot air balloon (the construct) with three baskets hanging from it (the indicators), each connected by two ropes (a loading and an intercept). When the winds of context, time, and maturation move the balloon, the indicators will follow—*if the baskets' ropes are securely attached to the balloon.* If a rope for one of the baskets is not securely attached, then when the balloon moves, the basket may not follow, or the winds might catch the basket and cause it to break away from the other baskets that are secured to the balloon. This loose basket would not be invariant across the changes that are pushing the balloon. If the rope slips a little bit but stays attached, I'd consider this situation OK and conclude I have invariance. If the rope slips a lot or becomes completely detached, I'd consider this situation a violation of the invariance assumption, and I'd have the situation of partial invariance.

If I have evidence of partial invariance, I would then proceed with a follow-up search to find the offending indicator—or, more precisely, the noninvariant loading or intercept parameter(s). You might ask, "Wouldn't that be easy to see?" Well, that depends. It depends on the method of scaling and identification that I use. If I use the marker variable method, identifying the noninvariant loading or intercept is very involved and very misleading. If I use the fixed factor method, the process is simpler and more efficient (see Lee, Little, & Preacher, 2011).

Although there are many methods recommended for finding the noninvariant parameter, my colleagues and I are pretty confident that a simple procedure can reveal the source of noninvariance, but it will depend on the method used when scaling the constructs! For example, I have relied on examining the model modification indices to identify the offending indicator(s), but only when I use the fixed factor method of scaling and identification. If I use the marker variable method (or the effects coded method for that matter), I run the risk of making errors in judgment as to which indicator(s) are not invariant. Jason Lee (2009) provides evidence that scaling method matters.

Specifically, Lee (2009; see also Lee, Preacher, & Little, 2011) conducted an extensive Monte Carlo simulation study to examine the performance of different criteria and methods for identifying the offending indicator in tests of partial invariance. He compared the ability to find the noninvariant indicator under the three different scaling methods (fixed factor, marker variable, and effects coding).

Contrary to what many would expect, the choice of scaling constraint does influence the ability to identify which indicator is noninvariant. Specifically, he found that only the fixed factor method provides a reasonable control for Type I error in finding the noninvariant parameter; in addition, if a Bonferroni-corrected χ^2 difference test is used as the decision criterion, then Type I error for the fixed factor method is almost eliminated, regardless of the type of item response (binary or ordinal), type of parameter tested (loading or intercept), or size of scale (6 or 12 items). In terms of power, the fixed factor method provided adequate power for detecting the noninvariant intercept parameter(s). Power for the marker variable method was adequate if and only if the item being used as the marker was invariant. Bottom line: if I have evidence of a failure of the omnibus test of invariance, I must switch to the fixed factor method of identification and scaling. I can set the nominal alpha at a value I think is appropriate (based on sample size considerations) and then correct the criteria for the number of comparisons.

Once I have identified the offending indicator(s), the question of what to do next emerges. Some researchers will remove the offending indicator from the analysis. I would not. Finding that an indicator changes its meaning over time is an interesting and perhaps even important outcome of the study. Hopefully, after careful consideration, the underlying reasons for which the indicator changes its meaning can be identified. Keeping the indicator in the model but relaxing the constraint of invariance would allow a comment on the possible reasons for the change in the indicator's behavior in the context of the other indicators and constructs. Generally speaking, if at least a majority of the indicators (i.e., two of three) are still invariant over each successive time point, I still have a reasonable basis for discussing changes in the underlying construct *as defined by the invariant indicators*. If it is two out of three indicators, the basis is stronger than if it were three out of, say, five. Regardless of the number of indicators for a construct, if only one of them is invariant over time, the basis for discussing changes in a common underlying factor is more challenging. Most would argue that there is no construct being measured but only a set of variables that each lack evidence of validity. On the other hand, and depending on the nature of the indicator that is invariant versus the ones that aren't, I might be able to argue for the prominence of this invariant indicator as a central indicator of the construct of interest and that its invariant properties over time allow me to examine differences in the construct (you may want to kiss the Blarney stone before you attempt this argument).

In general, partial invariance is not a problem if there aren't too many loadings or intercepts that change meaning over time. If I have too many indicators that show evidence of noninvariance, then perhaps the construct I thought I was measuring is not a cohesive construct after all. In this case, I would need to back up and reconsider what I am trying to measure and what measures would serve as sound indicators of it.

A LARGER EXAMPLE FOLLOWED BY TESTS OF THE LATENT CONSTRUCT RELATIONS

In this section, I introduce a larger example. This time I have two constructs, positive affect and negative affect, measured at three measurement occasions. The data that I use are still pretty good quality but not nearly as "perfect" as in the previous example. The sufficient statistics for this example are presented in Table 5.3.

In Table 5.3, I have also overlaid some thin dividing lines to demarcate where indicators of a common construct are located. You'll notice that within each triangle along the diagonal, the indicators of a common construct correlate quite highly with one another; this is a good thing. Correlations in the mid-.7 region indicate a high level of reliability (which easily translates to above .85 reliability for each construct at each time point) and good convergent validity among the indicators. Also notice that the nine correlations within each square below the diagonal are pretty uniform in the magnitude of their correlations. For example, the indicators of positive affect at Time 1 correlate in the −.1 region with the indicators of negative affect at Time 1.

I'm going to step through the tests of factorial invariance and then follow these tests with an examination of the latent construct information. With longitudinal data, I can examine a number of aspects of changes that may have influenced the constructs over time. In this example, I am now modeling parcels of items as the three indicators for each of the two affect constructs. As I discuss in Chapter 2, parcels have nice psychometric features. These data are still based on the 823 youths who completed the I FEEL questionnaire (see the sample description in the prologue). The parcels are the same parcels of positive and negative affect that I used to illustrate the psychometric advantages of parcels in Chapter 2.

Before I begin, let me start with a diagram of two constructs measured at three time points. To number the parameters in the path diagram shown in Figure 5.5, I start at the upper left corner, numbering each indicator for the first construct. I put all constructs' measures at the same time point in a column format. I then number top to bottom. Next, I move to the second time point, where all indicators and constructs are ordered in a column format again. Numbering continues from left to right and top to bottom within a measurement occasion (i.e., indicators 1–6 are measured at the first occasion, 7–12 are measured at the second occasion, and 13–18 are measured at the third occasion). Once each indicator and each construct has a unique number, all the parameters can be labeled. For example, $\lambda_{11,4}$ refers to the loading of the 11th indicator on the 4th construct.

The first step in this analysis is to specify the appropriate longitudinal null model. As mentioned in Chapter 4, the null model should include expectations of no change in the variances or the means of the constructs over time. Table 5.4 provides an illustration of what the null model is fitting for this example. You'll notice that no associations are estimated among all the indicators (i.e., the independence model). On the diagonal of this matrix, you'll see that the variances of the six indicators are

TABLE 5.3. Correlations, means, and standard deviations among the indicators of positive and negative affect for three measurement occasions: Grades 7 and 8 combined

	Measurement Occasion 1						Measurement Occasion 2						Measurement Occasion 3					
	Pos 1	Pos 2	Pos 3	Neg 1	Neg 2	Neg 3	Pos 1	Pos 2	Pos 3	Neg 1	Neg 2	Neg 3	Pos 1	Pos 2	Pos 3	Neg 1	Neg 2	Neg 3
Pos 1	1.00																	
Pos 2	0.76	1.00																
Pos 3	0.77	0.76	1.00															
Neg 1	-0.06	-0.07	-0.11	1.00														
Neg 2	-0.14	-0.05	-0.14	0.66	1.00													
Neg 3	-0.16	-0.12	-0.16	0.66	0.82	1.00												
Pos 1	0.46	0.45	0.41	-0.08	-0.12	-0.13	1.00											
Pos 2	0.44	0.46	0.40	-0.11	-0.10	-0.11	0.83	1.00										
Pos 3	0.43	0.46	0.43	-0.10	-0.13	-0.15	0.79	0.79	1.00									
Neg 1	-0.13	-0.08	-0.11	0.44	0.33	0.34	-0.17	-0.11	-0.16	1.00								
Neg 2	-0.13	-0.09	-0.15	0.42	0.34	0.34	-0.19	-0.19	-0.27	0.72	1.00							
Neg 3	-0.15	-0.11	-0.15	0.44	0.36	0.37	-0.20	-0.19	-0.26	0.75	0.77	1.00						
Pos 1	0.42	0.41	0.40	-0.05	-0.12	-0.01	0.45	0.42	0.41	-0.09	-0.06	-0.10	1.00					
Pos 2	0.42	0.45	0.42	-0.03	0.03	0.04	0.49	0.47	0.45	-0.10	-0.08	-0.12	0.78	1.00				
Pos 3	0.38	0.38	0.39	-0.07	-0.07	-0.08	0.40	0.37	0.39	-0.13	-0.10	-0.13	0.77	0.72	1.00			
Neg 1	-0.02	-0.01	-0.07	0.41	0.34	0.35	-0.02	-0.04	-0.05	0.42	0.42	0.39	-0.09	-0.01	-0.16	1.00		
Neg 2	-0.03	0.02	-0.04	0.38	0.34	0.33	-0.06	-0.06	-0.09	0.40	0.43	0.39	-0.20	-0.08	-0.26	0.75	1.00	
Neg 3	-0.04	-0.00	-0.08	0.37	0.30	0.30	-0.06	-0.05	-0.06	0.36	0.37	0.35	-0.19	-0.08	-0.25	0.74	0.76	1.00
Mean	2.99	2.90	3.11	1.71	1.45	1.45	3.00	2.91	3.13	1.70	1.54	1.58	2.89	2.85	3.06	1.72	1.58	1.64
STD	0.76	0.75	0.75	0.71	0.66	0.67	0.76	0.75	0.73	0.66	0.62	0.65	0.78	0.76	0.75	0.69	0.66	0.70
Var	0.58	0.56	0.56	0.50	0.43	0.45	0.58	0.56	0.53	0.44	0.39	0.42	0.61	0.58	0.56	0.48	0.44	0.49

Note. Total sample size is 823. I put the variances and standard deviations in the table for later comparison purposes.

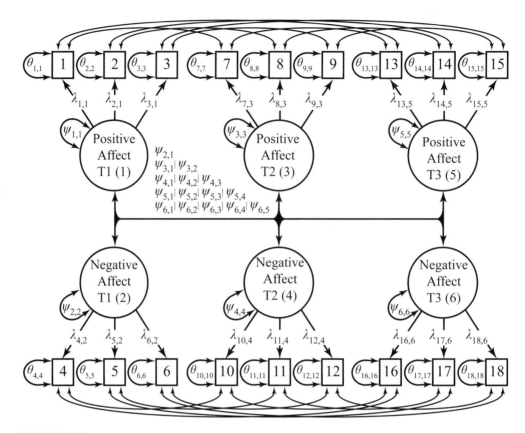

FIGURE 5.5. Parameter labels for three time points with positive affect and negative affect: The configural invariance model. The stylized covariance links among all the constructs represents the fact that each construct correlates with each other construct. The parameter labels for these 15 possible linkages are listed in matrix form on the figure. The residual variances among the corresponding indicators are allowed to associate over time.

equal to each other over time. In the mean vector at the bottom, the six indicators each have the same mean level over time. On the support pages for this book (*www.guilford.com/little-materials*), you'll find example scripts for longitudinal null models, as well as calculators for the CFI and TLI/NNFI based on the appropriate longitudinal null model χ^2 and degrees of freedom. I've put χ^2 and degrees of freedom from this longitudinal null model in Table 5.5, which is also a good example of reporting model fit information in an empirical write-up.

The second step is to fit the configural invariant model. Again, in this model, I specify the expected pattern of loadings on each construct at each occasion of measurement. In addition, the unique factors of the parallel indicators are allowed to correlate over time. That is, the same indicators that are measured at the different occasions would have their residual variances correlated across all possible time points (see the "spaghetti" of interconnected lines among the indicators at the top

TABLE 5.4. The estimated null model for the indicators of positive and negative affect for three measurement occasions: Grades 7 and 8 combined

	Measurement Occasion 1						Measurement Occasion 2						Measurement Occasion 3					
	Pos 1	Pos 2	Pos 3	Neg 1	Neg 2	Neg 3	Pos 1	Pos 2	Pos 3	Neg 1	Neg 2	Neg 3	Pos 1	Pos 2	Pos 3	Neg 1	Neg 2	Neg 3
Pos 1	0.59																	
Pos 2	0.00	0.57																
Pos 3	0.00	0.00	0.55															
Neg 1	0.00	0.00	0.00	0.47														
Neg 2	0.00	0.00	0.00	0.00	0.42													
Neg 3	0.00	0.00	0.00	0.00	0.00	0.46												
Pos 1	0.00	0.00	0.00	0.00	0.00	0.00	0.59											
Pos 2	0.00	0.00	0.00	0.00	0.00	0.00	0.00	0.57										
Pos 3	0.00	0.00	0.00	0.00	0.00	0.00	0.00	0.00	0.55									
Neg 1	0.00	0.00	0.00	0.00	0.00	0.00	0.00	0.00	0.00	0.47								
Neg 2	0.00	0.00	0.00	0.00	0.00	0.00	0.00	0.00	0.00	0.00	0.42							
Neg 3	0.00	0.00	0.00	0.00	0.00	0.00	0.00	0.00	0.00	0.00	0.00	0.46						
Pos 1	0.00	0.00	0.00	0.00	0.00	0.00	0.00	0.00	0.00	0.00	0.00	0.00	0.59					
Pos 2	0.00	0.00	0.00	0.00	0.00	0.00	0.00	0.00	0.00	0.00	0.00	0.00	0.00	0.57				
Pos 3	0.00	0.00	0.00	0.00	0.00	0.00	0.00	0.00	0.00	0.00	0.00	0.00	0.00	0.00	0.55			
Neg 1	0.00	0.00	0.00	0.00	0.00	0.00	0.00	0.00	0.00	0.00	0.00	0.00	0.00	0.00	0.00	0.47		
Neg 2	0.00	0.00	0.00	0.00	0.00	0.00	0.00	0.00	0.00	0.00	0.00	0.00	0.00	0.00	0.00	0.00	0.42	
Neg 3	0.00	0.00	0.00	0.00	0.00	0.00	0.00	0.00	0.00	0.00	0.00	0.00	0.00	0.00	0.00	0.00	0.00	0.46
Mean	2.96	2.89	3.10	1.71	1.52	1.56	2.96	2.89	3.10	1.71	1.52	1.56	2.96	2.89	3.10	1.71	1.52	1.56

163

TABLE 5.5. Model fit statistics for the tests of invariance in positive and negative affect across three waves

Model tested	χ^2	df	p	$\Delta\chi^2$	Δdf	p	RMSEA	RMSEA 90% CI	CFI	ΔCFI	TLI/ NNFI	ΔTLI	Pass?
Null model	11199.4	177	<.001	—	—	—	—	—	—	—	—	—	—
						Measurement model estimates								
Configural invariance	351.80	102	<.001	—	—	—	.053	.045;.059	.977	—	.961	—	Yes
Weak invariance	366.12	110	<.001	—	—	—	.052	.046;.058	.977	.000	.963	.002	Yes
Strong invariance	418.17	118	<.001	—	—	—	.055	.049;.060	.973	.002	.959	.004	Yes
						Latent model estimates								
Var/covar/stabilities	438.46	128	<.001	20.29	10	.027	.054	.048;.059	.972	.001	.961	+.002	Yes
Latent means	454.05	122	<.001	35.88	4	<.001	.058	.052;.064	.970	.003	.956	.003	No

and bottom of Figure 5.5). In this example, I have three time points. Thus, the six indicators of the two constructs at Time 1 would have residual correlations with their corresponding parallel indicators at Time 2 *and* Time 3. I should mention that, technically speaking, correlated residuals are actually covariances among the residual variances of the specific factors of a given indicator. Most everyone uses the term *correlated residual* in this context.

Keep in mind that these residual covariances should be estimated even if the estimated values are not significantly different from 0. The reason to estimate these residual covariances is that the indicator-specific variance that is reliable is likely to correlate with itself over time. There might be models in which the time course between measurement occasions would reduce the correlations among the indicator-specific residuals to essentially 0, and, if degrees of freedom were an issue (which they really shouldn't be), I could make an argument for not estimating these residual covariances. If these correlations are not exactly 0, however, the slight misfit that would occur would permeate the other parameter estimates of the model. Estimating these correlated residuals would always be justifiable; not estimating them should be done only after careful consideration.

The configural model is the best fitting model that I will specify in any longitudinal analysis. This model is an optimally fitting model because it has no constraints on any estimated parameters. This model allows all possible correlations among the latent constructs, allows all loadings and intercepts to be freely estimated, and makes no restrictions on the expected pattern of residual relationships. In this regard, the configural model becomes the baseline model against which the constraints of measurement invariance are evaluated. As seen in Table 5.5, this model shows acceptable levels of model fit. If you download the output file from this model, you'll see that the fitted residuals from this model are normally distributed and that the modification indices do not suggest any meaningful changes that would improve model fit in any appreciable way.

If the configurally invariant model does not suggest acceptable levels of model fit, however, the "fixes" to make the model fit adequate should be done on the configurally invariant model, before any additional tests of invariance are conducted.

If I decide to add a dual-factor loading or an additional correlated residual among the indicators, for example, the best candidates for such fixes are the ones that occur consistently across measurement occasions. A blind focus on the largest modification index will often overlook a theoretically more meaningful and consistent model modification. Modifications that are consistently suggested across the different measurement occasions are more likely to be a real phenomenon rather than a chance or sample-specific fluctuation (i.e., the initial misspecification replicates as a meaningful modification at each time point). Once all the necessary and theoretically meaningful adjustments are made, then I can proceed to test for invariance. If a model modification (other than the invariance constraint itself) is suggested after I impose one of the invariance constraints, it likely is not a real phenomenon but rather an artifact of the constraints. The constraints of invariance will give me modification indices for each constrained parameter that can be used to guide decisions about partial invariance (see my subsequent discussion of this idea). Modifications in locations other than where the invariance constraints are placed, however, are the ones I want to avoid. It's like constricting a balloon to form a desired shape but then discovering that the balloon has bulged in an unexpected place. If constricting the balloon creates a desired outcome with no unexpected bulges, then I am doing something right. If bulges occur, I'm probably not quite doing things correctly.

The next model listed in Table 5.5 is the weak invariance model. Here, the loadings of each corresponding indicator are equated over time. Figure 5.6 shows which corresponding loadings are constrained to equality using superscripted letters. This figure also shows the corresponding constraints on the intercepts for the test of strong invariance (to which I turn next). On the support pages for this book at *www.guilford.com/little-materials*, I've fit this model using all three methods of scaling and identification to further demonstrate that the model fit results are the same regardless of the scaling choice you make. As seen in Table 5.5, the change in model fit between the configural and weak models was negligible, and therefore the constraint of weak invariance passes very nicely. Again, this test supports the idea that the constructs of positive and negative affect are fundamentally the same across the measurement occasions represented in this sample.

For the test of strong invariance, the change in CFI of .004 is beyond the threshold recommended by Meade et al. (2008) though still within the criterion of Cheung and Rensvold (2002); however, I would still judge the test of invariance as passed. There's no reason to expect a developmental change in the item behavior when youths responded to simple mood items within this age range (ages 12–14; grades 6–8). Moreover, the fact that this model is based on parcels of mood items, in which the specific factors of the items have been reduced considerably, leads me to conjecture that the change in model fit is really a function of sampling variability, especially in this age range. The change in CFI of .004 for this test is also consistent with my general experience that constraining intercepts over time (or across groups) leads to greater change in fit measures than does constraining loadings over time.

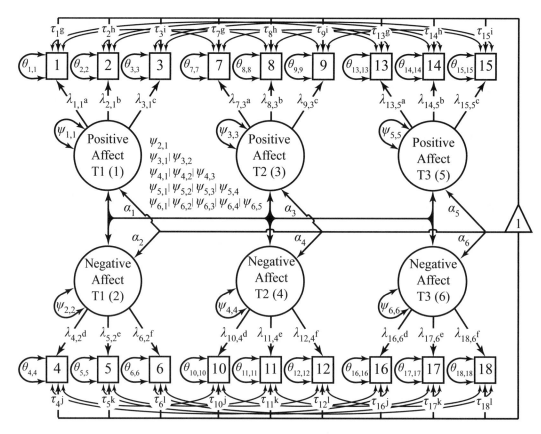

FIGURE 5.6. Parameter labels for three time points with positive affect and negative affect: The strong invariance model. The corresponding loadings and intercepts that are equated across time are designated by a common superscripted letter. The residual variances among the corresponding indicators are allowed to associate over time.

Stated more strongly, the model I am fitting is based on really good data in which invariance is essentially a given. The fact that a model for data such as these would be rejected by the Meade et al. (2008) recommendations suggests to me that their recommended criterion of .002 is too rigid for a real-world application of invariance testing.

Given that I have established strong factorial invariance, this model now becomes the new baseline model for further tests of the reliable latent-variable relationships. My colleagues and I have written about this before (Little, 1997; Little, Card, Slegers, et al., 2007). In my view, strong factorial or partial strong factorial invariance is the desired level of invariance to achieve before any consideration of latent parameters would come into play. There are two distinct issues or areas to be tested when making longitudinal comparisons. The first is whether the measures are factorially invariant over time (i.e., either strong factorial or partial strong factorial invariance holds). Satisfactory resolution of this issue establishes that the constructs are in fact comparable. By comparable, I mean that we can now examine the *constructs* for similarities or differences. In other words, the cross-time measurement invariance/equivalence means that any differences are true differences in the constructs and are not due to changes in the measurement properties of the constructs. Returning to the plant metaphor, we now are pretty sure that we are comparing the same variety of plant and not two different plants that we think are the same variety.

Figure 5.7 provides a depiction of the various nested model comparisons that are conducted when testing for factorial invariance (i.e., weak and strong measurement invariance) and structural invariance (i.e., the latent covariances or correlations, variances, and means). The tests of structural invariance should be conducted only when factorial invariance of the measurement model is supported.

Testing the Latent Construct Parameters

The next steps of testing for cross-time similarities and differences focus on the latent construct information. I can conduct these tests in a number of different orders and with different logic and rationales. In this section, I outline some logic and orders

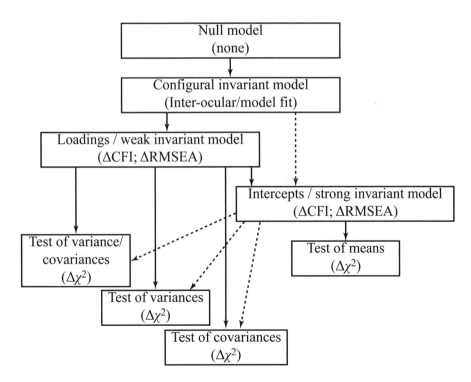

FIGURE 5.7. Nested model relationships among the various tests of invariance and the tests of omnibus hypotheses. The recommended criteria to evaluate the acceptability of the designated test is parenthetically referenced. Arrows designate which comparisons are nested. Dashed lines are one potential sequence and the solid lines are another possible sequence.

that I think make general sense; however, you should not treat my suggested order as a rule. In making tests of the latent construct parameters, I generally revert now to a statistical basis for making decisions. Because of the high power associated with an SEM model, in general, and longitudinal models, in particular, I set a less stringent p-value to determine significance. With sample sizes around 200–500, I generally use $p < .005$, and with samples greater than 500, I generally use $p < .001$. These p-values, however, are not rules, and you can choose to set the criterion for significance based on your own rationale. For example, a strong a priori theory might rely on $p < .05$ for significance. One important consideration here is effect size. I would focus less on the significance of parameters and more on their effect sizes.

When I start testing for similarities or differences in constructs, I generally start with an omnibus test of whether the variance and covariance information among the constructs is essentially the same within measurement occasions. Sometimes I will also include the stability covariances in this omnibus test, but not always. It depends on whether I expect a steady rate of the whole change process. If I do expect a steady rate, then I would include the stabilities. If I expect the rates of change between occasions to be different, I would test this expectation separately. In this example, I expected steady rates of change, so I tested the within-time variances and covariances to be equal at Times 1, 2, and 3 and the between-occasion associations to be equal between Times 1 and 2 and between Times 2 and 3.

Regarding within-time variances and covariances, the idea here is that if the set of variances and covariances do not differ across time, then performing multiple tests of the various elements would not be warranted. This logic is the same as that taught by the ANOVA school: follow-up comparisons are warranted only if the overall omnibus test suggests that there's enough meaningful difference. In Table 5.6, I report the variance–covariance matrix from the strong invariant model. In this

TABLE 5.6. Latent variance–covariance matrix and latent means from the two-construct three-wave example: Estimates from the strong factorial invariant model

Construct	Positive Affect 1	Negative Affect 1	Positive Affect 2	Negative Affect 2	Positive Affect 3	Negative Affect 3
Pos Aff 1	**0.433**	-0.163	0.552	-0.162	0.526	-0.036
Neg Aff 1	-0.062	**0.336**	-0.153	0.477	-0.028	0.443
Pos Aff 2	0.243	-0.059	**0.448**	-0.246	0.544	-0.072
Neg Aff 2	-0.059	0.153	-0.091	**0.305**	-0.128	0.514
Pos Aff 3	0.231	-0.011	0.243	-0.047	**0.446**	-0.200
Neg Aff 3	-0.014	0.151	-0.028	0.167	-0.079	**0.347**
Means:	3.00	1.52	3.01	1.61	2.93	1.64

Note. Results are based on the effects coded method of identification in which the loadings and intercepts are invariant across time. **Bold** numbers on the diagonal are the estimated variances. Covariances are below the diagonal and correlations are above.

sample, positive and negative affect correlate around −.20 within each measurement occasion. In terms of the stability of the constructs, these constructs have about .50 stability correlations over time. A .50 correlation means that only about 25% of the variance overlaps; that is, 25% of the individual differences remain stable over these intervals of measurement.

Table 5.5 shows that the set of equality constraints testing homogeneity of the variances and covariances and the stability of change was nonsignificant. This outcome suggests that no external factors have influenced the relationships among the constructs or affected the rate of change in the constructs. In other words, time of measurement has not had a moderating influence on the associations among the constructs, either within each measurement occasion or between each pair of measurement occasions. The finding of no differences in the change relationships (cross-time correlations) between each construct also implies that the predictive relations (autoregressive and cross-lagged) between each consecutive time point will statistically be the same (see Chapter 6 for details).

Finally, Table 5.5 shows the results of testing the means of positive and negative affect for equivalence over time. This test did not pass (i.e., the means of the constructs show evidence of change over time). These means are shown in the bottom of Table 5.6. To do the follow-up tests, I first equated the three positive affect means over time. This test leads to a significant change in χ^2 on 2 degrees of freedom ($\Delta\chi^2_{(2)} = 13.33$, $p < .001$). A significant difference indicates that one or more of the three mean levels are different (have changed). Once in a while, however, you may find situations in which no individual means are different, yet the omnibus test is significant. In this example, further follow-up testing comparing Time 1 with Time 2 shows that these two means are statistically equivalent $\Delta\chi^2_{(1)} = 0.28$, $p = .59$, but that Time 3 is significantly lower than both Time 1 ($\Delta\chi^2_{(1)} = 8.29$, $p = .004$) and Time 2 ($\Delta\chi^2_{(1)} = 11.76$, $p < .001$). For negative affect, the overall test also reveals that one or more of the means differ across time ($\Delta\chi^2_{(2)} = 29.56$, $p < .001$). Follow-up comparisons show that negative affect at Time 1 is lower than at Time 2 ($\Delta\chi^2_{(1)} = 14.48$, $p < .001$) and Time 3 ($\Delta\chi^2_{(1)} = 28.55$, $p < .001$), whereas the means of negative affect at Time 2 and Time 3 are essentially the same ($\Delta\chi^2_{(1)} = 3.75$, $p = .053$).

If I have strong theory about where the means might differ, I can specify a priori planned comparisons that I would make to test my theory. Because I don't have strong theory, I proceed with a series of comparisons. As with multiple comparisons in any testing context, I could use a family-wise error correction for the p-value used as the criterion for significance. On the other hand, because I have so much power with a sample size of 823, I would use a fairly stringent p-value anyway. In this context, the significances of the differences are less meaningful than the effect size comparisons. The effect sizes for these comparisons are in the small to medium range, with the largest effect size being the one for negative affect between Time 1 and Time 3 ($d = .21$).

Equation 5.3 shows two ways to calculate Cohen's d as a measure of effect

Equation 5.3. Calculating effect size: Cohen's *d*

a) Manifest Cohen's $d =$

$$\frac{m_2 - m_1}{\sqrt{(n_1 \cdot Var_1 + n_2 \cdot Var_2)/n_1 + n_2}}$$

b) Latent Cohen's $d =$

$$\frac{\alpha_2 - \alpha_1}{\sqrt{(n_1 \cdot \Psi_1 + n_2 \cdot \Psi_2)/n_1 + n_2}}$$

- m_2 and m_1 are estimated means in manifest metric. These can be independent means, as in comparing two groups, or they can be dependent means, as in comparing the same construct across two time points.
- n_2 and n_1 are the sample size associated with m_2 and m_1, respectively.
- Var_2 and Var_1 are the estimated variances of the distributions around the means of m_2 and m_1, respectively.
- α_2 and α_1 are the estimated means in latent-variable metric.
- ψ_2 and ψ_1 are the estimated latent variances of the distributions around the latent means of α_2 and α_1, respectively.
- Method of identification does not affect these calculations.

size. In manifest metric the observed variances are used, and in latent metric the estimated latent variances are used. As a result, effect sizes in latent-variable metric are always larger than they are in manifest-variable metric because the pooled standard deviation is based on only the reliable variance when calculated using the latent-variable variances. In manifest metric the error information is contained in the estimate of the pooled standard deviation, making it a larger value than it should be. Hence, when the mean difference is expressed as a proportion of the pooled standard deviation, it will be underestimated in manifest metric and correctly estimated in latent metric.

AN APPLICATION OF A LONGITUDINAL SEM TO A REPEATED-MEASURES EXPERIMENT

The longitudinal CFA model can also be useful for testing experimental data, such as a repeated-measures, pre–post design. In this section, I'll walk through an example from an undergraduate thesis by Sandy Sola (nee Carpenter). Sandy participated in our undergraduate social and behavioral sciences methodology minor at KU.

For her honors thesis, Sandy wanted to know what effect the testing environment might have on the quality of the data that are collected, particularly in questionnaire studies using undergraduates. She selected an initial sample of about 300 students, who took a battery of tests using an online data collection protocol. She then randomly assigned these students to take the same battery again 1 week later either in a group classroom environment, a private lab cubicle environment, or again online. The design, therefore, is a 3-by-2 repeated-measures design. Although she tested a number of different constructs, I focus on the findings for positive and negative affect.

Table 5.7 shows model fit statistics from testing factorial invariance across time and across groups. For the null model, Sandy specified the null expectation that neither the variances nor the means change over time or across the three experimental conditions. As you can see in the model fit information presented in Table 5.7, strong factorial invariance holds for these data (I used *Loading Invariance* and *Intercept Invariance* as the terms in the table to reinforce the idea that the levels of invariance go by many synonymous names). You'll notice that the RMSEA for these models is below the common threshold for acceptable model fit. I have found that the RMSEA is not a good index of model fit when I have only a couple of constructs and each is just identified. The CFI and TLI/NNFI, on the other hand, are in the good to very good range. Given the nature of these mood constructs, I attribute the lack of fit to simple sampling variability and not to model misfit. Positive and negative affect are two unidimensional constructs that have straightforward operational characteristics. From a pure face validity perspective, the only source of error is sampling variability when using constructs such as these.

In Table 5.8 I have put all the latent-variable information about the constructs from the strong invariant model fitted with phantom constructs. That is, the table contains the means, the standard deviations, and the correlations among the constructs. Recall that phantom constructs are simply estimation devices to convert the variance information into a standard deviation estimate and to then estimate the associations among the constructs in correlational metric.

The full model that produces the estimates contained in Table 5.8 is diagrammed in Figure 5.8. In this figure, the latent standard deviations are estimated as the links between the phantom constructs and the lower order constructs. These paths are labeled $\beta_{1,5}$, $\beta_{2,6}$, $\beta_{3,7}$, and $\beta_{4,8}$. The other noteworthy aspects of Figure 5.8 are that the variances of the lower order constructs are fixed at 0 (i.e., $\psi_{1,1}$, $\psi_{2,2}$, $\psi_{3,3}$, $\psi_{4,4}$), whereas the variances of the phantom constructs (i.e., $\psi_{5,5}$, $\psi_{6,6}$, $\psi_{7,7}$, $\psi_{8,8}$) are fixed

TABLE 5.7. Model fit statistics for the tests of invariance in positive and negative affect across two repeated measures and three groups

Model tested	χ^2	df	p	RMSEA	RMSEA 90% CI	CFI	ΔCFI	TLI/ NNFI	ΔTLI	Pass?
Null model	3961.98	258	<.001	---	---	---	---	---	---	---
Configural invariance	298.64	126	<.001	.105	.087;.124	.959	---	.935	---	Yes
Loading invariance	354.82	146	<.001	.110	.093;.127	.950	.009	.933	.002	Yes
Intercept invariance	394.95	166	<.001	.108	.096;.123	.946	.004	.935	.002	Yes

TABLE 5.8. Freely estimated latent parameters across condition and time (pre–post design)

Estimate	Positive Affect 1	Negative Affect 1	Positive Affect 2	Negative Affect 2
Online condition				
Pos Aff 1	1.000			
Neg Aff 1	-0.029	1.000		
Pos Aff 2	0.772	-0.041	1.000	
Neg Aff 2	-0.070	0.771	0.042	1.000
Latent Means	2.972	2.253	2.969	2.042
Latent Std. Dev.	0.926	0.925	0.926	0.909
Lab condition				
Pos Aff 1	1.000			
Neg Aff 1	0.274	1.000		
Pos Aff 2	0.559	-0.121	1.000	
Neg Aff 2	-0.016	0.715	0.147	1.000
Latent Means	3.175	2.299	3.094	1.944
Latent Std. Dev.	0.928	0.917	0.936	0.907
Class condition				
Pos Aff 1	1.000			
Neg Aff 1	-0.056	1.000		
Pos Aff 2	0.850	0.018	1.000	
Neg Aff 2	-0.180	0.793	-0.075	1.000
Latent Means	3.029	2.035	3.083	1.731
Latent Std. Dev.	0.936	0.947	0.834	0.899

Note. Results are based on the effects coded method of identification with the loadings invariant across time. Phantom constructs were used to convert covariance information into estimates of the correlations among constructs and their respective latent standard deviations.

at 1.0. These two sets of constraints are necessary to set the standardized metric for calculating the associations among the phantom versions of the constructs (i.e., $\psi_{6,5}$, $\psi_{7,5}$, $\psi_{7,6}$, $\psi_{8,5}$, $\psi_{8,6}$, and $\psi_{8,7}$) as correlations. That is, the variances of the lower order constructs must be fixed at 0 so that all the common variance captured in the indicators is transported to the higher order construct, and the variances of higher order phantom constructs must be fixed at 1.0 in order to transform the variance information into the standard deviation metric represented in paths $\beta_{1,5}$, $\beta_{2,6}$, $\beta_{3,7}$, and $\beta_{4,8}$ and the associations as correlations.

I think you can see how this works by using the tracing rules I described in Chapter 3. Let's take positive affect at Time 1. The original variance of the first-order constructs is reproduced by tracing the path labeled $\beta_{1,5}$ (start at the arrowhead and trace down to the phantom construct), tracing the variance of the phantom construct, $\psi_{5,5}$, and then tracing back to the first-order (lower order) construct through $\beta_{1,5}$ again. In other words, the original variance of the first-order construct that was

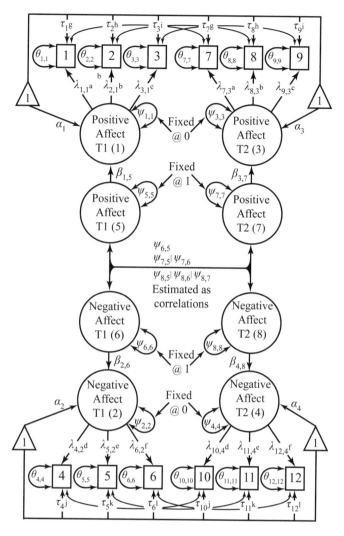

FIGURE 5.8. Full model for one group with phantoms. The equality constraints on the loadings and intercepts would also be placed across all three groups.

contained in $\psi_{1,1}$ has now been transformed into $\beta_{1,5} \cdot \psi_{5,5} \cdot \beta_{1,5}$. Similarly, the association between any two constructs can be "traced" by following from a lower order construct through a β path linking the second-order phantom construct with the first-order construct and then through any one of the paths linking the second-order constructs (i.e., $\psi_{6,5}$, $\psi_{7,5}$, $\psi_{7,6}$, $\psi_{8,5}$, $\psi_{8,6}$, or $\psi_{8,7}$) and finally back down a β path. The method of scaling that you would apply to the lower order construct does influence the interpretability of the parameter estimates. Here, effects coded scaling of the loadings and intercepts provides the metric that allows us to interpret the latent estimates in their meaningful metric.

Now, if you make a casual read of the information contained in Table 5.8, it appears that the means of negative affect have gone down at the second testing occasion. It also looks as though the variances of positive and negative affect have decreased at the second assessment occasion. To test whether these casual observations are statistically significant differences, a series of nested log-likelihood ratio tests would be conducted. The results of all these tests are presented in Table 5.9.

The first set of tests in Table 5.9 focus on the simultaneous tests of the variances and covariances. If this test showed no differences across the groups, then there would be little utility in modeling the data as a multiple-group comparison. This first test is also referred to as a test of the homogeneity of the variance–covariance matrix. Some authors recommend testing the homogeneity of the variance–covariance

TABLE 5.9. Tests of differences in positive and negative affect across three groups and two times of measurement (pre–post experiment)

Model tested	χ^2	df	p	$\Delta\chi^2$	Δdf	p	Decide?
Tests of (homogeneity of) variances and covariances							
Omnibus	471.88	189	<.001	76.93	23	<.001	Diff
Group	427.30	186	<.001	50.53	20	<.001	Diff
Time	447.15	175	<.001	52.20	9	<.001	Diff
Tests of latent variances							
Omnibus	438.47	176	<.001	43.53	10	<.001	Diff
Group	408.25	174	<.001	13.30	8	.102	Same
Time	435.87	172	<.001	40.93	6	<.001	Diff
Online	399.40	168	<.001	4.45	2	.108	Same
Lab	399.48	168	<.001	4.53	2	.104	Same
Class	426.82	168	<.001	31.87	2	<.001	Diff
Pos Aff	414.35	167	<.001	19.40	1	<.001	Diff
Neg Aff	406.54	167	<.001	11.59	1	<.001	Diff
Tests of latent correlations							
Within occasion	408.76	171	<.001	13.81	5	.017	Same
Between occasions	412.74	174	<.001	17.79	8	.022	Same
Tests of the latent means							
Omnibus	457.44	176	<.001	62.49	10	<.001	Diff
Group	408.87	174	<.001	13.92	8	.084	Same
Time	444.72	172	<.001	49.77	6	<.001	Diff
Pos Aff	397.35	169	<.001	2.4	3	.494	Same
Neg Aff	442.18	169	<.001	47.23	3	<.001	Diff
Online	403.68	167	<.001	8.73	1	.003	Diff
Lab	415.58	167	<.001	20.63	1	<.001	Diff
Classroom	412.71	167	<.001	17.76	1	<.001	Diff

matrix among the indicators of all the constructs rather than the latent construct variance–covariance matrix. I generally prefer doing this test on the latent construct variances because I want to have the differences in unreliability of the measurement process removed from consideration. I also want to ensure that factorial invariance is tenable when making this test. Because of measurement error, sampling variability, and lack of guidance on any criteria for judging the homogeneity of the variance–covariance matrix among the indicators, I feel this step is fundamentally meaningless when done at this level. When done at the level of the latent construct information, this test is meaningful, and I think the log-likelihood ratio test (i.e., χ^2 difference test) is reasonable to use.

In these data, this test did not pass ($\Delta\chi^2_{(23)} = 76.93$, $p < .001$). The test results also indicate enough difference across the groups ($\Delta\chi^2_{(20)} = 50.35$, $p < .001$) and time ($\Delta\chi^2_{(9)} = 52.20$, $p < .001$) to warrant looking more closely at where the differences lie. So the next set of tests in Table 5.9 focus only on the variances of the variables. This omnibus test indicates that one or more of the variances differ across time. When testing all of the constructs' variances across all the groups simultaneously, the data do not indicate a significant difference. When testing the constructs across time, however, the results indicate that the variances in one or more groups have changed across time. Now, I can follow up even more specifically. First, looking at changes in the variances across time for the online and lab conditions, the evidence indicates that the variances did not change. In the classroom condition, however, one or more of the variances changes over time ($\Delta\chi^2_{(2)} = 31.87$, $p < .001$). In fact, both positive and negative affect became more homogeneous at the second testing occasion when the testing was done in a group classroom format (see Tables 5.8 and 5.9).

Interestingly, these data show evidence of an experimental manipulation that produced a significant interaction by changing the variance of the constructs—that is, it reduced the response patterns for a group of individuals! Very few experimentalists postulate about the impact of a study changing the variance of a distribution. In Sandy's honors thesis, it appears that the group atmosphere has a homogenizing influence on both the reported positive and negative affect of the students in this study.

Because of the differences in variances across time in the classroom condition, the tests of the strength of the associations among the constructs were done on the correlations among the phantom constructs (see Figure 5.8). These tests would not yield the same results if they were done on the covariances among the constructs because the covariances are based on different metrics, particularly in the classroom condition. In fact, the differences in metrics for some constructs can lead to rather dramatic differences in the strength of an association.

In Chapter 3, I showed a hypothetical example that demonstrated the usefulness of phantom constructs. In that example, when phantom constructs are introduced, the strength of the association between the two hypothetical constructs is in fact quite different (i.e., the correlations were .52 vs. .66, which is a difference in shared variance of 16%). The main point of that example is that when the variances of the constructs differ either across groups or across times, the metric of the association is not comparable unless one uses phantom constructs to estimate the strength of the association on a common metric. This "trick" of adding phantom constructs to the model allows one to directly estimate the association as a parameter of the model. As such, this parameter would be something that one could then directly test using any form of model constraint (equating across groups or time, fixing to 0, fixing to a nonzero value, etc.) and then evaluating the change in model fit.

Returning to the analysis of Sandy's experiment, she did not find any evidence that the strengths of the associations differ either within time or between the two measurement occasions (see Table 5.9 for tests of the latent correlations).

Lastly, I can examine mean-level changes in the constructs. Had Sandy analyzed the data from this experiment with a traditional manifest-variable approach, a simple 3 (groups) by 2 (time points) ANOVA would have been conducted, and only the means would have been examined. The homogeneity assumption about the variances may have been tested to adjust the mean comparisons accordingly. In the SEM framework, the variance information is an outcome of the study, and any tests of the means are not dependent on whether the variances are equal or not. The means are being tested as maximum likelihood estimates using the log-likelihood function as the basis for determining significance. As seen in Table 5.9, as I progress through the tests of the means, there is evidence of a main effect only for time. There was no evidence of group differences in the means or of an interaction between group and time. In all conditions, the mean of negative affect decreased at the second testing occasion. The interpretation of this effect has to do with the way in which students at our university are recruited for experiments. Our undergraduate pool is not informed about the specific details of a study. They are simply given generic information about how long the study will take and how much credit the study is worth. When students signed up for this study, they were naïve to what the study was about, and they probably had some anxious thoughts about what kind of "experiment" they would experience. At the second occasion of measurement, the students knew what the study entailed and participated without the anxiety of the unknown.

SUMMARY

In this chapter, I presented a lot of detail regarding the longitudinal CFA or measurement model. I covered factorial invariance, testing means, and using phantom constructs to test correlations. With these last topics now in hand, I have fully covered all the elements of the knowledge tree's trunk. I have done nothing yet regarding tests of any structural models; these branches are the focus of the remaining chapters of this book.

Recall that the goal of the longitudinal CFA is to establish that the constructs under scrutiny are measured in a psychometrically sound manner. I can also use this model to test simple hypotheses and provide descriptive information about changes in the constructs. In Chapter 6, however, I move into the realm of testing directed predictive relationships among the constructs that are established as comparable in the CFA. In other words, everything that I have described and discussed prior to Chapter 6 is a necessary foundation for testing a hypothesized SEM model. In Chapter 6, I depict a number of models that have predictive relationships among the latent constructs; all of them are predicated, however, on a well-constructed and acceptably fitting CFA model, etc.

KEY TERMS AND CONCEPTS INTRODUCED IN THIS CHAPTER

Construct comparability, measurement equivalence, measurement invariance. All three of these terms are interchangeable. They are used when one has tested the factorial invariance of the indicators and demonstrated that the indicators have strong factorial invariance properties. The properties are that the intercepts and the loadings of the indicators on the constructs can be equated over time with negligible loss in model fit.

Effect size and Cohen's d. Effect sizes in latent-variable metric are always larger than they are in manifest-variable metric because the pooled standard deviation is based on only the reliable variance when calculated using the latent-variable variances. In manifest metric the error information is contained in the estimate of the pooled standard deviation, making it a larger value than it should be. Hence, when the mean difference is expressed as a proportion of the pooled standard deviation, it will be underestimated in manifest metric and correctly estimated in latent metric.

Homogeneity of variances/covariances. In longitudinal models, homogeneity is present when the variances of corresponding constructs are the same across time and the within-time covariances are the same. When longitudinal homogeneity is supported, it indicates that the effects of time or other time-varying factors have not had a moderating influence on the relations among the constructs.

Invariance. Invariance basically means that something does not change. In SEM, invariance is a matter of degree. For the measurement of constructs, we focus on change in model fit to determine whether constructs are factorially invariant over time (or across groups). For other parameters of the constructs (construct means, variances, covariances/correlations), we focus on more precise statistical rules to determine whether two or more parameters are invariant.

Modification index. An approximate estimate of the amount of change in the overall model's χ^2 that is expected to occur if the parameter of interest is freely estimated. Only fixed or constrained parameters will have a legitimate modification index. Parameters that are fixed to set the scale of a construct will often have a modification index associated with them, but this modification index is not legitimate, because the scaling constraint is necessary to set the scale and identify the parameters of the model.

Nested model. Model B is said to be nested within Model A when Model B is derived by placing one or more constraints on Model A. Model A has fewer degrees of freedom and is less parsimonious than Model B. Relative to Model A, Model B gains back one or more degrees of freedom by virtue of the constraints placed on Model A. When all the regularity assumptions hold, the difference in the two models' χ^2's ($\Delta\chi^2$) is distributed as a χ^2 with degrees of freedom equal to the difference in the degrees of freedom of the two models. Model B is the more parsimonious model (because it has theoretically meaningful constraints in place). Model B will always yield a χ^2 that is larger than the χ^2 of Model A (unless the parameter constraint yields an exactly 0 change, which is nearly impossible). The adequacy of the more parsimonious model can be determined based on the significance of the $\Delta\chi^2$. If the change in χ^2 is significant, then the constraints are not reasonable, and Model A would be considered the better model. If the change is nonsignificant, then the constraints are acceptable, and Model B would be deemed the better model.

Omnibus tests. These tests involve simultaneous testing of a set of like parameters for significance. The motivation for such tests is to guard against Type I error that can occur if each individual parameter is tested in a multiple-comparison manner. If the omnibus test is significant, it indicates that one or more of the constrained parameters in the set is significantly different, and follow-up comparisons would be allowed and adjustments for multiple comparisons would not be needed. If the omnibus test is nonsignificant, then follow-up comparisons would not be warranted. An omnibus test can be bypassed if one has strong theory about which parameters are expected to differ. The weaker the theory, however, the more one would want to guard against Type I error by either incorporating a *p*-value correction for multiple comparisons or conducting an omnibus test of significance.

Partial invariance. When testing for factorial invariance, it is not an all-or-none proposition. When the omnibus test of invariance fails, one can proceed with post hoc follow-up tests to identify which of the indicators are the offending ones. When only a few of the loadings and intercepts of a construct show a lack of invariance (while the majority of the indicators are consistent with invariance), one can generally proceed with making comparisons of the constructs' key parameters (construct means, variances, and covariances/correlations). Most scholars of partial invariance suggest that a majority of the loadings and intercepts should be invariant. The few offending indicators would need to be discussed as to why they are not invariant and what the developmental implications would be for the offending indicators and the constructs involved.

Second-order, higher order constructs versus first-order, lower order constructs. These terms refer to kinds of constructs we can estimate. First-order and lower order constructs refer to constructs with which measured indicators are directly associated. That is, any construct that predicts the common variance of a manifest indicator (a box in our diagrams) is a first-order/lower order construct. Any construct that lacks a measured indicator is a second-order/higher order construct. These kinds of constructs capture variance from other constructs and not directly from a measured indicator. The phantom constructs I introduced in Chapter 3 and used here in Chapter 5 are a form of second-order or higher order construct. Multiple levels of higher order constructs are possible, but only one level can be termed the first-order level.

RECOMMENDED READINGS

Factorial Invariance

Little, T. D. (1997). Mean and covariance structures (MACS) analyses of cross-cultural data: Practical and theoretical issues. *Multivariate Behavioral Research, 32,* 53–76.

Little, T. D., Card, N. A., Slegers, D. W., & Ledford, E. C. (2007). Representing contextual effects in multiple-group MACS models. In T. D. Little, J. A. Bovaird, & N. A. Card (Eds.), *Modeling contextual effects in longitudinal studies* (pp. 121–147). Mahwah, NJ: Erlbaum.

> The issues and, for the most part, the recommendations I wrote about in 1997 are still relevant and lay out the rationale for thinking about the different kinds of invariance that can be tested. Although I made the recommendation to use the change in TLI/NNFI to determine invariance in this paper (which I have since retracted given the Monte Carlo work since conducted), most everything else is still a succinct depiction of my thinking about the issues and logic of invariance testing. Little et al. (2007) updates things and provides different examples.

Meredith, W. (1964). Notes on factorial invariance. *Psychometrika, 29,* 177–186.

Meredith, W. (1993). Measurement invariance, factor analysis and factorial invariance. *Psychometrika, 58,* 525–543.

> Both of these papers provide the definitive theoretical and mathematical basis for understanding when and how factorial invariance will hold. Neither of these papers is particularly easy to read, but they are the core sources you'll need to read. Also, the pithiness of a Meredith article is worth the effort.

Evaluating Invariance Constraints

Cheung, G. W., & Rensvold, R. B. (2002). Evaluating goodness-of-fit indexes for testing measurement invariance. *Structural Equation Modeling, 9,* 233–255.

Meade, A. W., Johnson, E. C., & Braddy, P. W. (2008). Power and sensitivity of alternative fit indices in tests of measurement invariance. *Journal of Applied Psychology, 93,* 568–592.

> Both of these papers report on important Monte Carlo studies that provide guidelines for using alternative fit statistics to examine and determine whether constructs are measurement equivalent.

6

Specifying and Interpreting a Longitudinal Panel Model

In Chapter 5, I covered the basics of the longitudinal CFA model—the so-called measurement model of a longitudinal SEM. In this chapter, I focus on how to specify and interpret a longitudinal panel model. This chapter covers topics related to model building and includes discussions of the simplex structure of many longitudinal datasets, the process of model pruning, how to estimate indirect effects, and ways to include covariates. I present a number of examples from both published and unpublished projects.

I use the terms *panel model* and *longitudinal SEM* interchangeably. The longitudinal SEM/panel model examines the predictive (directed regression) relations among the latent constructs over time. The panel model does not explicitly address any information or hypotheses about the mean levels of the constructs; instead, it focuses on fitting a model to the system of relations among the variables' patterns of covariation over time. The longitudinal SEM model is typically a restricted model in that not all of the possible associations are estimated directly. This model is in contrast to the CFA model, which specifies all possible covariances (nondirectional associations) among the constructs. In other words, the CFA model simply estimates the magnitude of all the possible associations among the constructs. In this regard, the CFA model is a saturated structural model; there are as many estimates of latent associations as are possible given the number of latent constructs. A longitudinal SEM/panel model addresses questions about the predictive regression relations. These relations are represented as direct and indirect effects among the latent variables over time, while within-time relations usually remain as covariance (nondirectional) estimates.

In panel models, the mean levels of the constructs are typically examined in the CFA model when strong factorial invariance is specified. In panel models, mean levels are typically tested for differences without fitting a specific model to the means. Latent growth curve models, on the other hand, explicitly attempt to fit a model to the mean levels of the constructs. Latent growth curve models and their variations are beyond the scope of what I cover in this chapter, but I do address them in Chapter 8. You can get very thorough coverage of these kinds of models in Preacher et al. (2008) and in Curran and Bauer (in press). In panel models, the means of the latent constructs are only estimated as the intercept locations for the latent regressions that predict the individual-difference standings on the latent constructs at different time points (i.e., different waves of assessment after the first wave of measurement).

In longitudinal panel models, the predictive regression relationships have a causal flavor to them but must be interpreted with caution. Specifically, with many (if not most) panel models, statements about causality are not possible because the data are not controlled experimentally. Causality is implicated, however, to the degree that reliable predictive effects emerge over time. With panel models, the temporal separation between measurement occasions guides the direction of the predictive effects (e.g., predictive effects cannot go backward in time). In addition, paths that allow for control of the individuals' prior standings on a given construct are included (i.e., the autoregressive paths).

Keep in mind that the panel model is a statistical model for data. To demonstrate causality, the *data* need to be collected with appropriate controls in place and rigorous experimental manipulation to allow a causal inference from them. Once appropriate data are collected, the appropriate statistical model needs to be specified for the data to test any causal hypotheses. The appropriate model may or may not be a panel model. For many quasi-experimental datasets, the panel model is an ideal statistical model, and, with additional support and reasoned arguments, the results of a panel model can prove very useful for adding new knowledge and moving science forward. Here, arguments based on theory, prior research, and the statistical control of plausible confounds to the validity of a panel model lend strong implications for drawing a valid causal conclusion.

One key to valid inference is the statistical control of potential confounding variables. In Chapter 1, I mentioned the various ways that covariates can be included in a model to account for their influence. In this chapter, I illustrate a number of different ways and discuss the interpretations that unfold.

In the next section of this chapter, I walk through the various steps and discuss some of the nuances of fitting a basic panel model. This demonstration dataset builds on the positive and negative affect data from Chapter 5. At the end of this chapter, I use other datasets and other constructs to highlight the idea of the simplex process that can govern many longitudinal change processes. I also show how this simplex process can be used to describe the relations among constructs that are ordered along a continuum. In a final example, I introduce some new constructs and build a model that highlights how a panel model can reveal the direction of predictive influence among two or more constructs over multiple waves of data.

BASICS OF A PANEL MODEL

To begin a panel model, most of the cross-time nondirectional associations of the CFA model are converted into directed regression relationships, or the linkages among the constructs are removed (i.e., fixed to 0). When the cross-time associations are specified as regression paths (diagrammatically: lines with a single arrow head), the longitudinal associations are thereby estimated as unique effects controlling for all other specified regression pathways. Only the within-time associations are typically still specified as nondirectional covariance relationships (double-arrow-headed curved lines). Some researchers attempt to estimate directed regression relationships among constructs that are measured at the same point in time. This attempt is not warranted on a number of grounds. If I take the time to collect longitudinal data, it does not make sense to muddy the waters by having directed relations within a given measurement occasion (there is no temporal separation to indicate which construct is a predictor or an outcome). Instead, the design of the study should have allowed for the separation of time needed to use the time-ordered nature of the data to support specifying a directed relationship. Stated more plainly, a poor data collection design cannot be remedied with wishful estimation of directed associations within the same time point.

In a longitudinal model, the covariances among the variables at Time 1 are often zero-order associations (i.e., when no covariates are controlled for). At later time points, the within-time associations are referred to as residual associations or, sometimes, covariances among so-called disturbance factors. A disturbance factor is nothing more than the residual variance of a construct after the effects of the prior time point(s) are estimated. Such disturbance factors are essentially phantom constructs, with the scaling constraint being a fixed 1.0 regression parameter that links the disturbance factor with the construct. In Chapter 7, I again show how to use phantom constructs (which I introduced in Chapter 3 and used in Chapter 5) with an alternative scaling constraint to allow veridical comparisons of latent associations across two or more groups. For now, I'll focus on models without disturbance factors/phantom constructs.

Figure 6.1 displays a simple path diagram of a panel model with the various effects labeled. In Figure 6.1, a path that links a latent variable at Time 1 with itself at Time 2 is termed an *autoregressive path*. *Regressive* means that the path is a directional linearly predictive path, and *auto* means that the path is for the "self" or "same" construct. The longitudinal or cross-time linkages between the two constructs are referred to as *cross-lagged* effects. The term *cross* refers to the fact that a regression path crosses over from one construct to the next (and visually the diagram shows crossing paths). The term *lagged* refers to the fact that the constructs are separated by some amount of time lag. Cross-lagged paths and autoregressive paths are both predictive effects in which the effects of any other estimates leading to the same construct are controlled. For example, a cross-lagged effect is the unique effect controlling for the autoregressive effect. In Figure 6.1, the autoregressive path represents the amount of variance explained by the prior levels of a construct, controlling for the amount of variance explained by the individuals' standings on the other construct at the first time point. Similarly, the cross-lagged effect is the amount of change variance explained in the latent construct after controlling for the stability information from the prior measurement occasions. The autoregressive

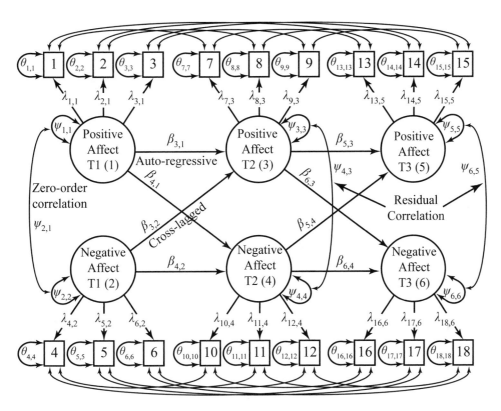

FIGURE 6.1. Parameter labels for three time points with positive affect and negative affect: A basic directional panel analysis. As always, the residual variances among the corresponding indicators over time are allowed to associate.

path typically would also reflect the common variance shared between the earlier constructs. In other words, the zero-order correlations between Time 1 and Time 2 are decomposed into unique and common influences—they are now represented as a combination of the directed pathways that are being estimated in the structural model.

With multiple waves of data, a large number of possible relationships can be estimated over time. When all possible directed regression paths (i.e., structural paths) from an earlier time point to all later time points are estimated, the longitudinal model is said to be saturated. A saturated structural model is generally not very informative because it does not reflect a parsimonious representation of how the predictive associations unfold over time. In this regard, the goal of a longitudinal SEM is to find a reduced set of structural paths that can explain the pattern of associations in the data over time just as well as the saturated model (i.e., the CFA measurement model, which is also a saturated model because all possible associations among the constructs are specified). The reduced set of structural paths represents a more parsimonious and theoretically meaningful model of the processes that may underlie the data. Choosing an appropriate theoretical model to fit to the data can be challenging. Ideally, two or more alternative models are compared and contrasted so that the set of competing ideas can be evaluated against one another and a better model can be determined. The problem of equivalent or nearly equivalent models is very relevant to longitudinal models, so finding a model that fits the data well is not a cause for celebration. It must withstand the test of scrutiny by both the researcher who is building the model and the professionals in the field who digest the results of the published model.

THE BASIC SIMPLEX CHANGE PROCESS

One potential model that represents a pretty good starting point for many longitudinal panel models is the simplex model. The idea of the simplex structure underlying longitudinal data is straightforward. Simply stated, if individuals are changing at a steady rate and any outside influences (contextual influences) affecting the rate of change are minimal, the pattern of correlations from one time point to the next will follow an expected simplex pattern. Or, as Humphreys and Parsons stated it (1979, p. 325), "since the cross-lagged [i.e., panel] methodology is used in the expectation that there will be change in the rank order of individual differences in the functions measured with the passage of time, one should also expect that the intercorrelations of each of the two or more measures over multiple occasions will show the simplex pattern." In other words, the simplex pattern is the pattern of correlations that one would expect when change is steady. It is the by-product of gradual and consistent change across ordered constructs (Jöreskog, 1970). Table 6.1 gives two examples of the simplex correlation pattern.

Early cognitive development, for example, appears to unfold at a pretty steady rate, and the environmental influences on the rate of development are minimal (see

TABLE 6.1. Example of two simplex correlation structures

	Time 1	Time 2	Time 3	Time 4	Time 5	Time 6	Time 7	Time 8
Time 1	--	.528	.279	.147	.078	.041	.022	.011
Time 2	.800	--	.528	.279	.147	.078	.041	.022
Time 3	.640	.800	--	.528	.279	.147	.078	.041
Time 4	.512	.640	.800	--	.528	.279	.147	.078
Time 5	.410	.512	.640	.800	--	.528	.279	.147
Time 6	.328	.410	.512	.640	.800	--	.528	.279
Time 7	.262	.328	.410	.512	.640	.800	--	.528
Time 8	.210	.262	.328	.410	.512	.640	.800	--

Note. The simplex correlations above the diagonal are based on the card shuffling analogy with a .528 autoregressive correlation. The correlations below the diagonal are a hypothetical simplex structure assuming a very stable individual-differences change process (i.e., an autoregressive correlation of .80).

Blaga et al., 2009). In such situations, measured constructs would be expected to show a simplex structure. On the other hand, measures of social adjustment in elementary and middle school are likely to be strongly influenced by context and environmental influences, which would disrupt the rates of change. Such disruptions would create perturbations in an otherwise smoothly changing system. Think of a river flowing steadily along a valley floor as a metaphor of the steady rate-of-change process. For a nonsteady rate of change, think of a mountain river that tumbles over a waterfall and pools before the next waterfall as the river cascades out of the mountains. This waterfall image is a good one to think of as a metaphor for a change process that is strongly influenced by environmental characteristics, whereas the meandering of a river across a valley floor would reflect the steady "flow" of change.

Many developmental change processes typically start with the assumption of a steady change process (Humphreys & Parsons, 1979). The resulting covariance pattern from such a change process is described as a Guttman simplex structure (e.g., Guttman, 1955), a perfect or quasi simplex, or just a simplex structure (Jöreskog, 1970). The simplex idea is a simple one that has some known properties that can often be used as a baseline expectation for a model of developmental change, as well as other constructs that are hypothesized to lie along a continuum (Walls & Little, 2005).

To understand steady change and the simplex structure, imagine a deck of cards and a shuffling machine that can cut the deck exactly in half and interleave the cards one on top of another. If I code the "standing" of each card in the deck before the shuffle (i.e., the individual-differences standing in the distribution) and then correlate that standing with the rank-ordered standing of the cards in the deck after the shuffle (the standing in the distribution at Time 2), the correlation would be .528. If I then took that deck and again did a perfect shuffle, the correlation between the order in the second deck and the third deck would again be .528. Here, the stability coefficient for shuffling a deck of cards is .528. The correlation between the order of the cards in the first deck and the order in the third deck, however, would now be .279, because two shuffles have occurred (see Table 6.1 and Figure 6.2). With a perfect shuffle of the deck on each of these three shuffles, the correlation between each contiguous deck would be .528, and the correlation between every two orders of the deck would be .279. If I did a perfect shuffle again, the correlation between the first deck and the fourth deck would now be .147, because three perfect shuffles have now taken place. For those of you who play cards, it may interest you to know that given this degree of stability from one shuffle to the next, it takes about seven shuffles to get back to an essentially random order in the deck of cards, where the correlation is statistically 0.

In Table 6.1, I have depicted the simplex correlation structure for the deck of cards after seven shuffles. I have tabled these correlations in the upper quadrant above the diagonal. In the lower quadrant below the diagonal, I have tabled a simplex structure that is based on a much stronger initial stability relationship of .80.

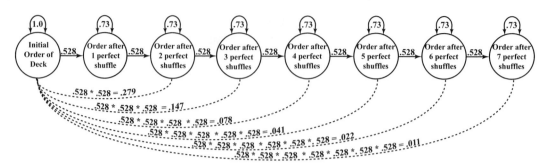

FIGURE 6.2. Standardized parameter estimates from the simplex model of consecutively shuffled decks of cards. These parameter estimates are from a model fit to the data in Table 6.1. This model has 21 degrees of freedom and perfect model fit. The correlations between the decks separated by more than 1 shuffle are reproduced by tracing the regression paths between each consecutive deck. The dashed lines show the reproduced correlations with the initial order of the deck.

The purpose of these two sets of correlations is to demonstrate the "rate" of reduction in the cross-time correlations depending on the level of stability between adjacent time points and, by implication, the length of time that intercedes between each measurement occasion.

If the measurement occasions correspond with the speed of the shuffling machine, the estimated change model would accurately capture the rate of change as indexed by the .528 stability coefficient. Figure 6.2 is, in fact, the estimated model when fit to the upper diagonal correlations in Table 6.1. Figure 6.2 displays a simple autoregressive longitudinal model that, when estimated, reproduces all the correlations depicted in the upper triangle of Table 6.1. That is, Figure 6.2 is the estimated longitudinal model for the expected card shuffle simplex structure. The correlation table and figure highlight the importance of accurately timing the measurement occasions in order to properly capture the change process under scrutiny.

If I mistimed the measurements and instead captured the individual-differences shuffle after every two shuffles, the model would estimate a rate of change that is lower than .528. Instead, I would observe an estimated stability of .279. If one investigator used the shorter lag and another used the longer interval, the estimated stability coefficients would differ. In fact, many of the differences in lagged relationships from developmental studies can be attributed to the timing of the measurements and not the rate of change in the constructs. All other things being equal, if one study uses 6-month intervals and another uses 1-year intervals, the estimated stability or autoregressive paths would typically be higher for the study using 6-month intervals than the one using 12-month intervals, especially if the process being measured is a steady change process. In such situations and if enough studies are done with enough different lags, a meta-analytic combination of the information might be able to yield a proper sense of the true change process and the rate of change in the construct. A better plan, however, might be to design each study to optimally time the associations or intentionally vary the time lags in order to estimate the nature of the lagged effects.

Returning to the correlations in the lower diagonal of Table 6.1, the stability from one time point to the next is quite high, with adjacent correlations of .80 at each successive time point. When more time has passed between measurements, however, the correlation between nonadjacent time points is lower—not just lower, but lower by an expected and predictable amount. In the lower diagonal pattern of Table 6.1, the correlation between Time 1 and Time 3 would be .64; the correlation between Time 2 and Time 4 would also be .64, as would the correlation between Time 5 and Time 7 or any bicontiguous pair of time points. In this example, the correlation between the longest lags—that from Time 1 to Time 8—would still be a small positive correlation of .210 (with more time points, this correlation would eventually approach 0). In the second pattern of simplex correlations shown in the upper triangle, the stability between adjacent time points is lower, with a .528 correlation; bicontiguous time points correlate at .279, and the longest lag from Time 1 to Time 8 yields a correlation of .011, or essentially 0. Both patterns of correlations in Table 6.1 reflect a steady rate of change and would be optimally fit with a simplex autoregressive model.

A simple autoregressive model can reproduce all the correlations because of the indirect effects contained in such a model. In this simple autoregressive model, the influence of Time 1 on Time 8 is indirectly carried by the direct influences of Time 1 on Time 2 and then Time 2 on Time 3 and then Time 3 on Time 4 and so on. Tracing rules can be applied to a model such as this to see how the correlation pattern in Table 6.1 is reproduced.

In Figure 6.1, I have labeled the first direct autoregressive paths as $\beta_{3,1}$ (for positive affect) and $\beta_{4,2}$ (for negative affect). The subscripts are read as the third construct is regressed on to the first construct (i.e., construct 3 on 1) and the fourth construct is regressed onto the second construct. That is, the first number refers to the construct that has the arrowhead pointing to it, and the second number is the construct where the line begins (construct 3 from 1 and 4 from 2). The autoregressive paths between Time 1 and Time 2, therefore, are labeled $\beta_{3,1}$ and $\beta_{4,2}$.

If I were to remove the cross-lagged paths ($\beta_{3,2}, \beta_{4,1}, \beta_{5,4},$ and $\beta_{6,3}$) and keep only the autoregressive paths, then I would be fitting the simplex model to both constructs (a bivariate simplex model). In this type of model, the correlation between adjacent time points is reproduced as the direct autoregressive path coefficient. The nonadjacent paths, however, are reproduced by tracing the direct pathways and multiplying the path coefficients. So the correlation between Time 3 and Time 1 for the construct at the top of Figure 6.1 would be the product of $\beta_{3,1}$ and $\beta_{5,3}$. Similarly, the correlation between Time 3 and Time 1 for the construct at the bottom of Figure 6.1 is the product of $\beta_{4,2}$ and $\beta_{6,4}$, assuming that the cross-lagged paths are removed (e.g., if they were nonsignificant). If the cross-lagged paths are significant, then they would contribute to the process of reproducing the correlation between time points, and the change process would no longer be considered a true simplex change process.

The model in Figure 6.2 is a univariate simplex model because I have only one construct in the model, which is represented at multiple time points (note that strong factorial invariance of the measurement model would be tested and enforced and the corresponding residuals would have correlated uniquenesses over time for each occurrence of the same indicator). The path coefficients in this model reproduce perfectly the correlations in the top half of Table 6.1. This same model, when fit to the other set of correlations in Table 6.1, also would perfectly reproduce the correlation pattern. The direct effects at each adjacent time point would be .8, and the indirect effect would be the multiple products of the direct path coefficients.

As a caveat, a simplex structure is also called a first-order discrete-time autoregressive structure of lag 1 (AR1). There are a number of other potential autoregressive structures that have been discussed in various statistical literatures. For example, if the correlation between every other deck of cards was higher than predicted by an AR1 process, the data are said to have a second-order autoregressive structure (AR2). The simplex structure is probably the most common change model in the social and behavioral sciences for assessing groups of individuals repeatedly over time. Although I demonstrate a couple of longitudinal models that have an AR2 (and higher) structure to them, my view is that the baseline developmental process of change in the social and behavioral sciences is the simplex process. In the examples that follow, I interpret the AR2 influences as context effects that influence every other occasion of measurement. I think the context interpretation is very reasonable in the social sciences. In fact, I have not yet seen an example of other autoregressive structures that cannot be described as a simplex process with another context effect (or multiple effects) superimposed upon it. Regardless of the true underlying structure, the various statistical models that I describe in this chapter and in later chapters can handle most change processes that might be encountered. Good theory, better measurement, and improved designs will help clarify what changes and how it changes; for now, I think I can proceed with little loss of generality.

In Table 6.2, I've depicted a couple of different correlation patterns that would *not* be consistent with the pure simplex structure. In the first pattern of correlations on the bottom of Table 6.2, some of the lagged correlations are higher than would be expected by the simplex pattern. This pattern of correlation would result in a need for a direct path from Time 1 to Time 3 and from Time 3 to Time 5; such a direct effect path would be called an AR2 pathway. This type of pattern would suggest that there is some common influence or consistent context effect at Time 1 and Time 3; this influence is creating a stronger than expected stability relation. A similar pattern between Time 3 and Time 5 suggests that these two measurement occasions also share a common influence that is creating a stronger than expected cross-time relation. In these data, an AR2 pathway would be needed, and it would be positive in

TABLE 6.2. Examples of two correlation structures that contain deviations from the simplex expectation

	Time 1	Time 2	Time 3	Time 4	Time 5	Time 6	Time 7	Time 8
Time 1	--	.528	.079	.041	.022	.011	.001	.000
Time 2	.800	--	.528	.079	.041	.022	.011	.001
Time 3	.750	.800	--	.528	.079	.041	.022	.011
Time 4	.512	.640	.800	--	.528	.079	.041	.022
Time 5	.550	.512	.750	.800	--	.528	.079	.041
Time 6	.328	.410	.512	.640	.800	--	.528	.079
Time 7	.400	.328	.550	.512	.750	.800	--	.528
Time 8	.210	.262	.328	.410	.512	.640	.800	--

Note. The correlations below the diagonal show an additional influence at Times 1, 3, 5, and 7 that lead to higher correlations than expected by the simplex structure. This influence can be modeled as an AR2 process or as a common construct (e.g., a fall construct). Above the diagonal, the correlations are all lower than expected but due to a consistent AR2 process.

value. If this influence is due to another measured construct, then it can be estimated and controlled for—and the AR2 pathway would no longer be needed. In the upper half of Table 6.2, I have depicted a pattern in which relationships are lower than expected from a simplex process. Here, the AR2 pathway would be negative because the correlation is lower than would be predicted by the AR1 pathway.

BUILDING A PANEL MODEL

The starting point for a panel model will depend on your theoretical expectations and the guidance of past work. The more theory you have about which effects will be direct and which ones will be adequately captured as indirect relations, the better. One starting point is to review the literature to see what relationships have emerged in other work with the same or similar constructs. You will need to consider carefully the similarities or differences in the samples, the time lags used, and the nature of the other ancillary constructs when crafting your first model specification.

Pragmatically speaking, it is difficult to have strong theory about all the relationships that will emerge in a longitudinal model for the simple reason that many of the relations will be new and novel in the context of a given study and in the context of the particular set of constructs that have been included in the analysis. In most applications of a longitudinal SEM model, I am trying to build upon and extend prior work. If prior work has shown an association between Construct A at Time 1 and changes in Construct C at Time 2, it does not necessarily follow that your model will show the same association. Your model will likely build on this work by adding a third construct (Construct B). If Construct B is also expected to predict changes in Construct C, the unique effect of Construct A on Construct C may no longer be significant. One modeler may be tempted to specify the A-to-C and B-to-C paths in the initial a priori model and let the data determine whether both paths are needed or not. Another modeler, after considering carefully the context of all three constructs together, may come up with a different theoretically derived expectation. For example, this modeler may think that when Construct B is in the model, it will have a significant unique effect on Construct C but the A-to-C linkage will no longer be needed. Both modelers will most likely need to make some model modifications, although I suspect the second one, by virtue of carefully considering the context of all three constructs together, would have fewer post hoc changes. The fewer the post hoc changes to an initial SEM model, the better.

In the absence of strong theory, the model-building process can start with a minimal set of paths and then add paths as suggested by the data and the model modification indices. Alternatively, the model building can begin with a mostly saturated set of directed path coefficients, and the nonsignificant pathways can be subsequently removed, or pruned from the model. I am not advocating these approaches per se; I am simply pointing out that model building (in the absence of strong theory) can be approached in one of these two general ways. Developing a strong theory before the model-building process begins, however, may involve less effort in the long run and certainly would be more useful than diving into a model-building enterprise with little guidance. In other words, thoughtful planning beforehand will pay dividends during the model-building process.

Covariate/Control Variables

The role that a variable plays in a given model is generally a matter of choice and justification on the part of the investigator; in addition, the label used to describe the role of a variable is different across the various life science disciplines. In traditional regression analysis, one variable is typically designated as the dependent variable. Sometimes, this variable is called the outcome variable. It's also called an endogenous variable. One or more other variables are selected and labeled as independent variables or predictor variables. These variables are also called exogenous variables. Then there is the third class of variable that is selected and included. This class of variable is sometimes called a control variable or simply a covariate (see Table 1.4 for a general taxonomy and their associated names). In some disciplines, the predictor variables are labeled covariates, and the control variables have other names or functions (e.g., instrumental variables). In this section, I refer to control variables as covariates, and I use the terms *predictor variables* and *outcome variables* to describe the other two variable types.

Covariates come in a couple of different forms. There are the static covariates, such as age, grade, ethnicity, gender, or any other demographic-like variable that does not change during the course of a study. Such variables are entered into a model to control for differences related to individuals' standings on these covariates so that relations among the focal constructs are not confounded. Be very mindful of the fact that covariates control only for mean-level differences related to the covariate.

Covariates do not account for or correct for any moderating influences (see Chapter 9 for a discussion of moderation and mediation). A second type of covariate is referred to as a time-varying covariate. As the name implies, a time-varying covariate can change over time. An example of a time-varying covariate would be the amount of an intervention received during the period of time preceding an assessment of the focal variables or constructs. I discuss the different ways that covariates can be included into an SEM model later in this chapter.

Building the Panel Model of Positive and Negative Affect

In Chapter 5, I fit the CFA model for the positive and negative affect model in adolescent youths. Here, I turn to fitting a longitudinal SEM model to these data. The starting point for this model is to remove the cross-time covariance relations among all the constructs from the CFA model and convert some of these relations into directional arrows. Because of the temporal precedence of causal directions, the directional arrows go forward in time. Figure 6.1 shows a standard panel model with all possible directional arrows between Time 2 and Time 1 and between Time 3 and Time 2. This model is a reasonable starting point for a longitudinal model in the absence of more information about possible context effects or other mitigating influences.

For these affect data, however, the times of measurement related to Time 1 and Time 3 coincide with the beginning of a school year, whereas Time 2 occurs in the spring of the school year. The constructs that I assessed are positive affect and negative affect. These constructs are not only sensitive to diurnal fluctuations but also pick up on or are reflective of day of the week and time of the year. In this case, the time of the year that is repeated in the study is the beginning of a school year, which is expected to have an influence on affect at Time 1 and at Time 3. I hypothesize, therefore, that the affect reactions at Time 3 will be related to the affect reactions of Time 1 above and beyond the steady change process of affect change. To test this a priori hypothesis, my initial SEM model would also include a directional path from Time 1 to Time 3 for both positive affect and negative affect.

The cross-lagged paths represented in Figure 6.1 are meant to model the possible bidirectional influences between the two constructs. Given the time scale of these data, the likelihood that positive affect would influence or predict negative affect over a 6-month time span is remote at best. Given that affect is primarily a moment-to-moment change process (which is susceptible to context influences), any bidirectional change influence of one affect state predicting or influencing the other affect state would happen in a matter of minutes, hours, or days rather than in a matter of months. Given this characteristic of the constructs and the measurement span in this example, I would hypothesize that neither affect construct predicts the other affect construct over time. That is, I would specify the model with no cross-lagged linkages. Cross-lagged linkages from Time 1 to Time 3 would also be excluded from this model. Only the covariance and residual covariance between the two constructs within each time point would be specified on an a priori basis.

The fit of this initial model is very good. The key considerations in evaluating whether this model is the optimal best fitting SEM model for these data are twofold. First, is the fit of the model at the same levels of model fit as the CFA model upon which it is built? I chose to use the strong invariance CFA model to build the SEM model. As indicated in Table 6.3, the fit of the strong invariance CFA model is quite good, with $\chi^2_{(118, n=823)} = 418.17$, RMSEA $= .055_{(.049; .060)}$, CFI $= .973$, and TLI/NNFI $= .959$. The fit of the structural SEM model is also quite good, with $\chi^2_{(124, n=823)} = 440.92$, RMSEA $= .055_{(.049; .060)}$, CFI $= .971$, and TLI/NNFI $= .959$. Second, are there any theoretically justified indications that a model modification would add appreciably to the overall model fit? The strong invariant CFA model was already deemed the best fitting measurement model (see Chapter 5). As such, there are no further modifications to the measurement model that could improve the model fit. This model becomes, therefore, the best fitting baseline model against which I can evaluate the performance or fit of the reduced set of structural equations that I specified. Thus, the only parameters that I would evaluate for potential improvement to the model would be the omitted structural paths.

With these two criteria in mind, I would use a p-value for the change in χ^2 of less than .001 (or perhaps use the Meade et al. [2008] criterion of a change in the CFI of greater than .002) as my criterion for determining whether I have lost too much model fit because of the very large sample size of 823. Clearly, I have a tremendous amount of power to detect even trivial differences with a sample size this large. In addition to these criteria for evaluating overall model fit change, I may want to evaluate whether any of the nonhypothesized (omitted) structural paths from Time 1 to Time 2, Time 2 to Time 3, or Time 1 to Time 3 are significant (again, probably at

TABLE 6.3. Model fit statistics for the various tests with positive and negative affect across three waves

Model tested	χ^2	df	p	$\Delta\chi^2$	Δdf	p	RMSEA	RMSEA 90% CI	CFI	ΔCFI	TLI/ NNFI	ΔTLI	Pass?
Null model	11199.4	177	<.001	---	---	---	---	---	---	---	---	---	---
					Measurement model estimates								
Configural invariance	351.80	102	<.001	---	---	---	.053	.045;.059	.977	---	.961	---	Yes
Weak invariance	366.12	110	<.001	---	---	---	.052	.046;.058	.977	.000	.963	.002	Yes
Strong invariance	418.17	118	<.001	---	---	---	.055	.049;.060	.973	.002	.959	.004	Yes
					Latent model estimates								
Var/covar/stabilities	438.46	128	<.001	20.29	10	.027	.054	.048;.059	.972	.001	.961	+.002	Yes
Latent means	454.05	122	<.001	35.88	4	<.001	.058	.052;.064	.970	.003	.956	.003	No
					Longitudinal structural model								
Initial SEM	440.92	124	<.001	22.75	6	.001	.055	.049;.060	.971	.002	.959	.000	Yes

Note. These values are the same as I presented in Table 5.5 with the exception of the information regarding the longitudinal structural model. When evaluating the latent parameters for differences, the criterion for determining too much loss in fit, given the power of the sample size, is a p-value less than .001 (other possible criteria include change in CFI greater than .002 or a point estimate of the RMSEA that falls outside the confidence interval of the strong invariance model—these latter two criteria need to be studied in more detail).

a p-value level of .001 or less). I would accomplish this determination by simply adding the nonhypothesized effects one at a time to see whether the pathway attained a level of significance and a meaningful effect size that would warrant keeping it in the model. Because I have strong theory for my tested expectations, I can use a strong set of criteria to gauge how adequate this final model is for representing the longitudinal pathways.

The final model for these data happens to be my initial SEM model. Achieving a satisfactory level of model fit for the initial longitudinal SEM model will ordinarily involve making some changes to the initial model. Some nonhypothesized pathways may need to be added, and some of the hypothesized pathways may need to be removed if they are not significant. For these data, I had very strong theory and was successful at obtaining an acceptable level of model fit for the initial model, which therefore becomes my final SEM model. The parameter estimates for this final model are presented in Figure 6.3. I have reported the unstandardized parameter estimates because the scale of the constructs is meaningful. Specifically, I used the effects coding method of identification for this model, which means that the estimates of all parameters are in the metric of the scale that was used to collect the data, which was a scale of 1–4 (*almost never* to *almost always*).

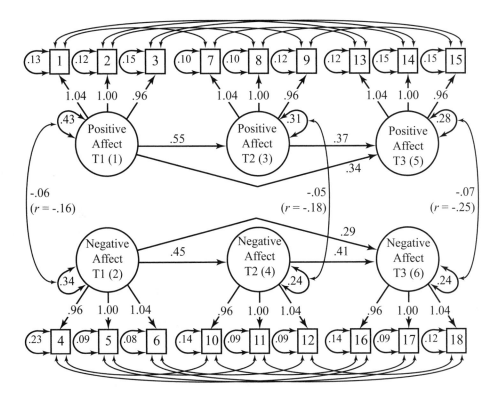

FIGURE 6.3. Parameter estimates for three time points with positive affect and negative affect: A basic directional panel analysis.

The parameter estimates in Figure 6.3 are unconditioned. That is, I have not included any covariates in the model in order to evaluate whether any of the effects would change noticeably once any potential covariate's influence is controlled. The choice of which covariate(s) to include in any model should be based on theoretical considerations rather than blindly throwing lots of variables into a model. Without theory, the covariate controls have little interpretive meaning. Age, gender, and ethnicity are common covariates that are included in longitudinal models. These covariates reflect contextual influences that can affect developmental processes. As I mentioned earlier, there are a number of different ways in which covariates such as these can be included into a model. I demonstrate four of the different ways here. In Table 6.4, I have reestimated the model and reported the model fit statistics with five additional variables: grade (8 vs. 7); female; and black, Hispanic, and other (the last four dummy-coded so that 1 reflects the name of the variable, 0 otherwise).

A word about overcontrol: as I mentioned, covariates (control variables) should be included based on a reasonable and sound theoretical basis. Overcontrol occurs in a couple of different ways. First, by including too many variables in an effort to control for extraneous influences, the effects of interest can be attenuated. By way of illustration, if I created truly random variables and then included them in a model as control variables, by chance alone the random variables can have an association with the variables of interest, including the common variance among a set of substantively interesting variables. In this situation, including more variables as "controls" can result in effects that become unintentionally attenuated.

Overcontrol can also occur if we estimate all the effects of focal constructs

TABLE 6.4. Fit information for the positive and negative affect SEM model with covariates included three ways

Model tested	χ^2	df	p	$\Delta\chi^2$	Δdf	p	RMSEA	RMSEA 90% CI	CFI	ΔCFI	TLI/ NNFI	ΔTLI	Pass?
Null model	11451.3	277	<.001	---	---	---	---	---	---	---	---	---	---
Comparisons for first three ways of including covariates in the model													
Strong invariance	529.24	178	<.001	---	---	---	.048	.043;.053	.969	---	.951	---	Yes
Covariate Type I	556.20	184	<.001	26.95	6	.0001	.048	.043;.053	.967	.002	.950	.001	Yes/No
Covariate Type II	554.57	184	<.001	25.33	6	.0003	.048	.043;.053	.967	.002	.950	.001	Yes/No
Covariate Type III	623.23	204	<.001	94.00	26	.0000	.049	.048;.059	.962	.007	.949	.002	No
Comparisons for adding covariates in a model at the level of the indicators													
Strong invariance[1]	392.11	118	<.001	---	---	---	.052	.046;.058	.975	---	.942	---	Yes
Covariate Type IV	418.99	124	<.001	26.88	6	.0002	.053	.047;.058	.974	.001	.941	.001	Yes/No

Note. The basic SEM model is the same as Figure 6.3 except that five covariates have been added and specified in four different ways. Type I is a full partial control in which all constructs are regressed on the covariates. Type II is a semipartial control in which only the last wave of constructs are regressed onto the covariates. Type III is an indirect control whereby only the first wave of constructs are regressed onto the covariates and the effects of the covariates are estimated as indirect effects downstream. Type IV is also a full partial approach, but the covariate effects are removed from all indicators of the constructs. The criteria for determining too much loss in fit, given the power of the sample size, is a *p*-value less than .001, a change in CFI greater than .002, or a point estimate of the RMSEA that falls outside the confidence interval of the strong invariance model.
[1]To test the adequacy of the SEM model, the appropriate comparison CFA would have the covariate controls on the indicators.

being regressed onto the control constructs and leave all nonsignificant parameter estimates in the model. The nonsignificant parameters can, again, soak up variance that may in fact be random perturbations. Some researchers may argue that these effects should remain in the analysis because one desires to remove all reliable sources of variance that are related to the influence of the covariates, regardless of the levels of significance. Such an argument is based on a "conservative" school of thought. As I have mentioned elsewhere, research should not be conservative or liberal; instead, it should be as accurate as possible. In the absence of theoretical expectations for most of the effects that are estimated, I argue that the more accurate approach is to remove the estimated effects that are not contributing significantly to the prediction of the construct variability; here, marginally significant effects (e.g., $p < .10$) could be left in a model.

The first way in which I have included the covariates into the basic model is by regressing each of the constructs at each of the time points onto each of the five covariates. This method provides full control of the covariate influences. In other words, the covariate influences are controlled from both the exogenous (predictor) constructs and the downstream endogenous (outcome) constructs (i.e., the construct associations are partial correlations controlling for the covariates). In Table 6.4, I have put the model fit information for each way in which covariates can be included in a longitudinal model, and in Table 6.5 I have entered the estimates for the three methods that control for covariates at the latent-variable level. As displayed in Table 6.4, I respecified both the null model and the strong invariance model to include the five covariate variables. With the covariates in the model, the model fit for the SEM model is right on the edge of being acceptable. The p-value is below the .001 level, but because the change in CFI and RMSEA are within acceptable bounds, I would give this model an overall pass. In addition, there are no pronounced parameter estimates that would improve model fit in a meaningful way. That is, none of the modification indices or residuals is particularly noteworthy, and my theoretical expectations for these data are sound. In Table 6.5, I have put the unstandardized estimates of the covariate relationships. Only six of the parameters were significant (which are designated in bold italic font).

The second way in which I have included covariates is as semipartial controls, where they predict only the Time 2 and Time 3 versions of the constructs. The covariates would still have nondirectional covariance relationships with the Time 1 constructs. Time 1 and the covariates are all treated as exogenous constructs in this case. In terms of model fit and interpretation of the SEM final model, not much is different between the first way and the second way. The only real difference is conceptual. What is the status or role of a time-invariant covariate in a longitudinal SEM model? Personally, I think it is reasonable to assume that time-invariant covariates like gender, cohort, and ethnicity are exogenous to the modeled constructs. From this perspective, having the covariates also predict the Time 1 constructs makes sense. On the other hand, with the assumption of exogeneity in question, treating all

TABLE 6.5. Comparison of estimates for three different ways of including covariate/control variables in a longitudinal panel model of positive and negative affect

Construct	Grade	Female	Black	Hispanic	Other
Control for covariates at each time point (full partial)					
Positive Affect T1	*-.11*	.07	-.15	-.01	-.15
Negative Affect T1	-.06	.07	.01	-.09	.01
Positive Affect T2	-.08	*.14*	*.24*	-.01	-.06
Negative Affect T2	.07	.06	-.08	.03	.01
Positive Affect T3	-.03	-.03	-.06	*-.17*	-.13
Negative Affect T3	*.09*	.00	.14	.07	*.26*
Control for covariates at endogenous time points (semi partial)					
Positive Affect T1	.--	.--	.--	.--	.--
Negative Affect T1	.--	.--	.--	.--	.--
Positive Affect T2	-.08	*.14*	*.24*	-.01	-.06
Negative Affect T2	.07	.06	-.08	.03	.01
Positive Affect T3	-.03	-.03	-.06	*-.17*	-.13
Negative Affect T3	*.09*	-.01	.14	.07	*.26*
Control for covariates at first time point (indirect thereafter)					
Positive Affect T1	*-.11*	.08	-.14	-.01	-.16
Negative Affect T1	-.06	.07	.02	-.09	.02
Positive Affect T2	-.06	.05	-.08	-.01	-.09
Negative Affect T2	-.02	.03	.01	-.04	.01
Positive Affect T3	-.03	.05	-.08	-.01	-.09
Negative Affect T3	-.03	.03	.01	-.04	.01

variables that are measured at the first measurement occasion as exogenous is also a defensible position. Mathematically, the difference in the effects is rather trivial. In Table 6.4, the model fits are about the same, and the conclusions regarding the SEM model would be about the same. In Table 6.5, the information about the covariate influences that are presented would differ meaningfully only for the Time 1 constructs.

This second way in which I included covariates is analogous to how covariates are controlled for in traditional regression analysis. In traditional regression analysis, covariates are entered first into a regression model to predict variance in the outcome variable of interest. Then the primary variables of interest are entered after the covariates to see whether they account for an additional and significant amount of variance in the outcome variables above and beyond the influence of the covariates. Here, the outcome variables are the Time 2 and Time 3 versions of the constructs.

The third way to include the covariates in a longitudinal model is to estimate their direct effects only on the Time 1 constructs and thereafter "estimate" or control for the covariate effects downstream as indirect effects. This way of including covariates has some appeal for longitudinal models because it assumes that once the initial differences in the covariates are accounted for, the downstream effects begin to dissipate as time continues to pass, and the constructs achieve equilibrium in their relations over time. In other words, this way of including covariates assumes that the impact that produced the differences due to the covariates has already happened. The only effects of the covariates that remain are lingering and dissipating with time as the constructs themselves undergo further change. Think of a rock hitting a pond. The rock causes a ripple. This ripple radiates out over time, but gets less and less powerful as it gets farther and farther from the origin of the event that caused the ripple to begin with.

The fourth way in which I have included covariates in this basic SEM model is as a full partial but at the level of the indicators (as opposed to the construct level). For most constructs, it makes more sense to control for covariate influences at the level of the construct instead of at the level of the indicators. At the latent-variable level, the variance information contains the reliable variance related to the focal construct of interest. Covariate influences are usually expected to affect the true-score (construct) variance and not the specific (indicator-level) variance. If covariates have the possibility of pronounced influences at the level of the specific variances among the indicators of a construct, then controlling for their influence at this level of specification is probably warranted.

I can think of one notable example where controlling for gender differences would be best done at the level of indicators rather than at the level of the construct. Specifically, achievement is a construct that is often represented by two indicators: math performance and verbal performance. If I want to control for gender differences in a model that contains achievement, I would not control for it at the latent level but instead would control for it at the level of the indicators. Math performance often favors boys and verbal performance often favors girls (depending on the age range of the study). Thus, the gender differences are not in achievement but in the specific variances of the indicators that are used to represent achievement. In this achievement example, the gender differences in the indicators would likely cancel each other out at the latent-variable level because the gender effects go in opposite directions at the level of the indicators.

A fifth and related way to control for covariate influences is to calculate the partial covariances among all the indicators and fit the CFA and SEM models to the partial covariances. The drawback to this method is that you lose all the mean-level information about the indicators and the constructs. As a result, the information needed to test for strong factorial invariance or to test the constructs for mean-level changes over time is no longer available. Because of these drawbacks, this fifth method is rarely used.

Given these general considerations, my recommendation is to include covariates selectively and to prune the nonsignificant effects. Table 6.6 shows the covariate

TABLE 6.6. Pruned covariate effects for the full partial method of including covariates

Construct	Grade	Female	Black	Hispanic	Other
Control for covariates at each time point (full partial)					
Positive Affect T1	-.13	.--	.--	.--	.--
Negative Affect T1	.--	.--	.--	.--	.--
Positive Affect T2	.--	.15	.22	.--	.--
Negative Affect T2	.--	.--	.--	.--	.--
Positive Affect T3	.--	.--	.--	-.14	.--
Negative Affect T3	.09	.--	.--	.--	.21

Note. The pruned model fits as well as the saturated covariate model: $\chi^2_{(24, n=823)} = 39.05, p = .054$.

effects for the full-partial method but only for the significant influences. These pruned covariate effects fit the data essentially as well as when all the parameter estimates were included in the model: $\chi^2_{(24, n=823)} = 39.05, p = .054$. With the power of my sample size ($n = 823$), I would not consider this p-value a significant or meaningful difference. This pruned set of covariates would be reasonable to keep in the model to evaluate the impact of their influences on the parameters of the model.

In Figure 6.4, I have put the estimated parameters from this final model with the covariate effects removed. I have also added the mean vector so that the intercept for each of the regression equations predicting each time point are clearly noted. The total equation for predicting the scores at a given time point is the intercept value of the latent construct plus the regression weights that directly predict the individual differences.

A careful inspection of the estimates in Figure 6.4 versus Figure 6.3 reveals only a handful of differences in the parameter estimates, and in this case, no change is greater than .01. This small degree of change simply indicates that the covariates in this case account for very little of the variance in the constructs and therefore their effects are relatively minor. Nonetheless, the estimates in Figure 6.4 reflect the best estimates because the few significant covariate influences are controlled.

ILLUSTRATIVE EXAMPLES OF PANEL MODELS

A Simplex Model of Cognitive Development

The first illustrative example of a simplex model is from a panel model of cognitive development that I assisted with (Blaga et al., 2009; the data come from John Colombo's infant cognition lab: *www.people.ku.edu/~colombo/*). In this study, over 200 infants were assessed semiannually using a variety of cognitive tests. At 12, 18, and 24 months they received the Mental Development Index subscale of the

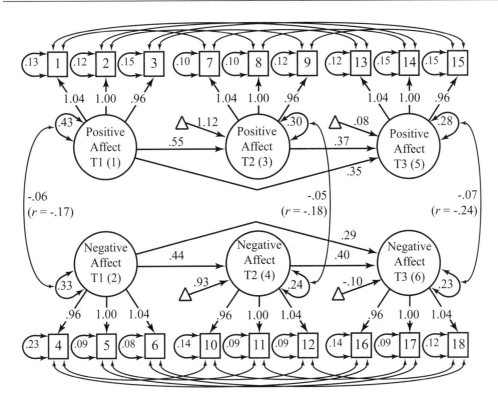

FIGURE 6.4. Parameter estimates for three time points with positive affect and negative affect: After covariate controls.

Bayley Scales of Infant Development and the Words Produced scale of the MacArthur–Bates Communicative Development Inventory. At 30 months, a different set of age-appropriate measures of infant cognition were used—namely, the Stanford–Binet Intelligence Scales and the Peabody Picture Vocabulary Test. The first step in the analysis was to specify a CFA for these various instruments and to test the measurement structure for factorial invariance over time. In the initial longitudinal CFA, early cognition was represented by the Bayley Scales and the MacArthur–Bates inventory to form a unidimensional measure of cognition. Two constructs were expected to underlie the cognitive battery after 30 months: nonverbal cognition (four indicators) and verbal cognition (five indicators). In the process of testing for factorial invariance across time, the Words Produced scale of the MacArthur–Bates inventory at 12 months of age was not invariant across time. At 12 months of age, word production is not an indicator of cognition in the same way that it is at later ages. As I mentioned in Chapter 5, having an exception or two in the process of examining the factorial invariance of a set of variables is not that uncommon and does not pose a problem in the interpretation of the relationships among the latent constructs.

The next step, after the CFA model was supported, was to specify the expected simplex structure to the relations among the latent constructs. Figure 6.5 displays the standardized parameter estimates from fitting the simplex model to the seven occasions of measurement. A couple of features of the figure bear mentioning. First, I have omitted the measurement model. I generally will omit the measurement model information from any figures in order to keep the figures clear and focused on the construct information at hand. Usually, I will create a table in which the information about the measurement model is placed. Table 2 in Blaga et al. (2009) is an example of such a table, and I have included an example in Chapter 9.

The results from fitting this simplex model indicate strong continuity across the entire period of toddlerhood (up to 4 years old). In other words, the data evince an elegant simplex process. A notable feature of this model is that the data showed very clear continuity in the constructs that were measured with the same instruments (as one would generally expect). Between 24 and 30 months, however, when different, age-appropriate measures of infant cognition were used, the simplex regressions showed smooth and robust relationships with little evidence of any disruption or discontinuity in the process. These results provide strong support that cognitive development during this period is a process that demonstrates steady change with a high degree of individual-difference stability. Because the period between toddlerhood and preschool has been suspected to be a period of discontinuity and reorganization, the results of the simplex model provide unequivocal evidence for continuity of intellectual functioning during this age range. In other words, the model is compelling, and the data have spoken. For more information see Blaga et al. (2009).

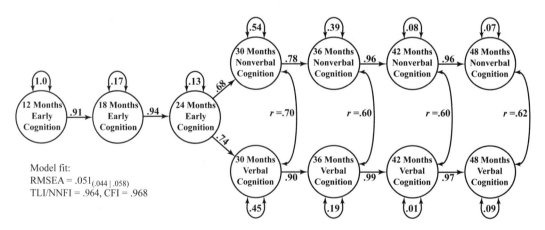

FIGURE 6.5. Standardized parameter estimates from the simplex model of intellective functioning. This figure was reproduced with permission from the journal *Intelligence* and my coauthors. For details of the study, see Blaga, Shaddy, Anderson, Kannass, Little, & Colombo (2009).

Two Simplex Models of Nonlongitudinal Data

The next example is meant to provide an illustration of ordered constructs that are not ordered by time but instead are sequentially related by their theoretical position on an underlying theoretical continuum. This example comes from Pat Hawley and her work on social dominance. The question at hand related to one's preference for different types of sexual fantasy. These sexual fantasies varied along a continuum from a neutral interaction to a highly dominating interaction. These fantasies were set up in the form of vignettes that were rated for the degree of personal appeal each fantasy vignette conveyed. The degree to which it matched an ideal fantasy was also assessed, but I present only the data for "appeal" ("ideal" showed nearly identical results). These appeal (and ideal) ratings were made using a 9-point Likert scale.

For the neutral encounter the vignette portrayed a simple boy-meets-girl or girl-meets-boy encounter; they exchange pleasantries, they have a mutual attraction to one another. The vignettes then added elements of sexual dominance or submission in these heterosexual encounters; in one set of vignettes the male dominates the female, and in a parallel set of vignettes the female dominates the male. In the low-dominance vignette, one of the characters in the vignette puts a move on the other. In the medium-dominance vignette, one character is now clearly the sexual dominator, while the other displays a clearly submissive posture. In the high-dominance vignettes, the degree of sexual dominance is the stuff of romance novels and letters to adult magazines. These vignettes were developed to assess points along a continuum on which the dominance–submission distance increases. Thus, the constructs are ordered along a continuum.

To test the theoretical expectation of the ordered simplex structure among the vignettes, a "longitudinal SEM" model can be fit to the data. Figure 6.6 shows the results of fitting an SEM longitudinal model to the response ratings. This model has some unique characteristics over and above a simple simplex model that can be fit to other ordered variables (e.g., self-determination constructs). First, the vignettes actually create two different continua that have as the central starting point the neutral encounter. One ordered continuum goes from neutral to low to medium to high, with the male dominating the female, and a similar neutral, low, medium, to high order, with the female dominating the male, extending in the opposite direction.

After fitting this model to the data, we found an unexpected set of relations in the data that, upon further reflection, had clear interpretive merit. The two low-dominance vignettes had shared variance that we interpreted as preference for low dominance regardless of the gender of the dominant protagonist—a pure low-dominance preference. We created a construct of low dominance where the loadings on low dominance: male < female and low dominance: male > female were equated. These loadings had to be equated because the "pure" low-dominance construct would not otherwise be identified. Similarly, a pure medium-dominance construct and a pure

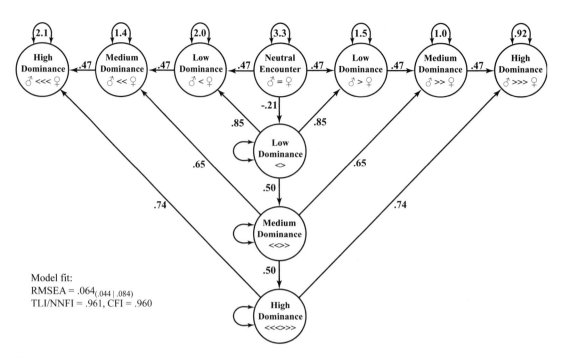

FIGURE 6.6. Unstandardized parameter estimates from the simplex model of sexual submission from a two-group model (males ♂ vs. females ♀): Appeal. All parameter estimates are equal across males and females, $\chi^2_{(36,\ n=470)} = 17.67$, $p = .007$. For details of the study for which this measure was developed, see Hawley & Hensley (2009).

high-dominance construct were evident in the data. The respective loadings were also equated in order to identify the parameter estimates. These latter three constructs have only two sources of information that serve as the indicators of each of the "pure" constructs, and in such situations the additional identification constraint is required. These pure constructs are derived from the residual variance of the gendered versions after controlling for the prior location on the respective gendered continuum. For this simplex model, the direction of the arrows does matter. With the neutral vignette as the starting point, the directions move out to the greater extremes of dominance. Theoretically, it does not make as much sense to have the extremes be the starting point and have the arrows directed toward the neutral vignette. For other constructs that lay along a single continuum, the direction of the arrows is less important.

As a specific example of this direction irrelevancy, self-determination is another theory that has constructs ordered along a continuum. In this case, self-determination theory posits that motivation varies along a continuum from intrinsic to extrinsic motivation (Deci & Ryan, 1985; Ryan & Deci, 2000). The Deci and Ryan research group has collected lots of data relating these motivational orientations to various well-being and performance outcomes. A key assumption of their theoretical model, however, is that the different motivational orientations fall along a continuum. In a paper with Ted Walls (Walls & Little, 2005), we tested the continuum hypothesis by fitting a simplex model to the constructs ordered as extrinsic > introjected > identified > intrinsic. This simplex longitudinal model fit the data extremely well and provided strong theoretical support to the continuum idea that underlies their model of motivation. With this set of constructs, however, we also could have fit the model in the exact opposite direction and achieved the same level of model fit and had the same support for the continuum. The direction of the arrows (left to right vs. right to left) does not have the same required directionality in the case of a single-order continuum of constructs (such as motivation orientation) as we would have for time-ordered longitudinal data. The only real issue with ordered constructs of this nature is that the variables are placed in the order in which they are expected to fall along the continuum. The simplex model of sexual dominance is an exception given the multiordered structures implied in the data.

A Panel Model of Bullying and Homophobic Teasing

This example is compliments of Dorothy Espelage (see the prologue for a description of the sample and the measures). The data are from a longitudinal study examining the relationships between bullying behavior and homophobic teasing. Five times of measurement separated by 6 months are represented in the dataset. The sample consists of 1,132 students from four Midwestern middle schools (Grades 6, 7, and 8; 49.8% female; spanning ages 10–15 years). These students completed a survey protocol that gathers information about their attitudes and their experiences with both physical and sexual violence. The survey is part of Espelage's research project, which was funded by the Centers for Disease Control and Prevention. At each measurement occasion, they measured bullying behavior and homophobic teasing. The key question for these data is, Does bullying positively predict changes in homophobic teasing or not? An ancillary question is whether the teasing would predict changes in bullying. The theory guiding this work hypothesizes that the bullying behavior will predict changes in homophobic teasing but not the reverse. This type of question is perfectly suited to be addressed as a panel design.

Before testing the hypothesized model, we first tested the longitudinal factorial invariance of the constructs by starting with a longitudinal null model. We then proceeded with the tests of invariance (configural, weak, and strong) over time. An important supplement to this analysis was learning whether there were any meaningful differences across the middle schools that were sampled for this project. In the supplemental analysis, a multiple-group model was used to test for invariance of the measurement space, as well as homogeneity of the variance–covariance matrix

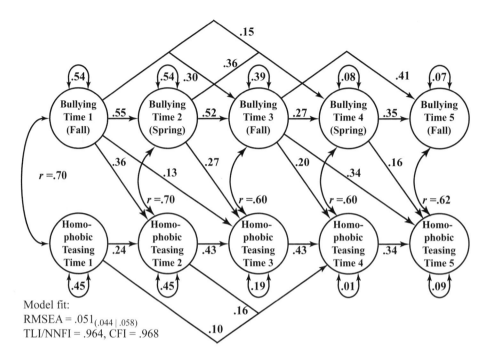

FIGURE 6.7. Standardized parameter estimates from the panel model of the relations among bullying and homophobic teasing. This figure is based on data from Dorothy Espelage.

among all the latent constructs. I present details of this supplemental analysis in Chapter 7 when I use these data to do a multiple-group panel model.

The results of the longitudinal SEM model are displayed in Figure 6.7. The primary hypothesis was that being bullied at an earlier time point would be positively associated with the degree of homophobic attitude reported by the adolescents at later time points. As can be seen in Figure 6.7, the model contained some additional autoregressive pathways. In fact, for bullying, a consistent AR2 emerged, as well as an AR3 from Time 1 to Time 4. For homophobic teasing, the additional autoregressive paths are less consistent and quite small. The weak autoregressive effects were found only at Time 4 from Times 1 and 2. In terms of the most critical substantive findings, the effect of bullying on changes in homophobic teasing was very consistent, with each contiguous cross-lagged path being significant; in addition, cross-lagged effects from Time 1 to Time 3 and from Time 3 to Time 5 emerged. These additional effects are also positive, which indicates a cumulative increase in the amount of homophobic teasing if one has engaged in bullying behavior at earlier time points.

In terms of indirect effects, the longitudinal model contains a large number of pathways by which bullying at Time 1 predicts homophobic teasing at Time 5. In fact, there are 11 different indirect pathways by which bullying at Time 1 affects homophobic teasing at Time 5. Typically, hypotheses about the significance of a specific pathway are not very common. Usually, indirect effects are summarized as a sum of the indirect pathways that emanate from a given construct. It is possible, however, to test specific pathways by using definition variables and alternative parameters. These are topics that I cover in more detail in Chapter 9.

SUMMARY

In this chapter, I have covered the steps and many of the issues that are associated with fitting a standard panel model to longitudinal data. I also showed how the logic of the SEM longitudinal model is also appropriate for other data structures that are ordered along some theoretical continuum. With longitudinal data, the continuum along which the constructs are ordered is time. With other constructs, the continuum can be any theoretically meaningful dimension along which constructs can be ordered.

The basic panel models that I tested here are just a few of the types of models that can be fit to panel data. In Chapter 7, I cover multiple-group versions of the structural panel model. I spend parts of Chapter 8 on multilevel versions of the panel model. In Chapter 9, I discuss mediation and moderation in the context of latent-variable panel models. Finally, Chapter 10 provides a survey of various special models that can be applied in the context of panel models.

KEY TERMS AND CONCEPTS INTRODUCED IN THIS CHAPTER

Autoregressive path/effect. An autoregressive (AR) path is a directed regression path where a construct or variable predicts itself at the next ordered measurement occasion or interval. An AR1 path specifies direct linkages between successive occasions or intervals. An AR2 path specifies a direct linkage between occasions or intervals where one occasion or interval of measurement intercedes. That is, an AR2 "jumps" or bypasses an occasion or interval of measurement. An AR3 path would skip two time points, and AR4 would skip three occasions, and so on.

Continuum. A continuous process or ordered succession. As such, the parts of an underlying continuum cannot be distinguished from neighboring parts except by creating divisions. These divisions can be (and often are) arbitrary, or they can be based on some principle or logic that allows one to examine features of the continuum at select intervals. With time as a continuum, the divisions are the chosen occasions of measurement. With theoretical continua, the divisions are often based on points along the continuum that have unique psychological meaning.

Cross-lagged path/effect. A cross-lagged (CL) path is a directed regression path on which one construct predicts a different construct at the next ordered measurement occasion or interval. Like an AR path, a CL path can be a CL1, where the next successive time point is predicted, or a CL2, where an occasion of measurement is skipped or bypassed.

Direct effect/path. A direct effect occurs when a construct or variable is directly regressed onto another construct or variable. In longitudinal models, direct effects move forward in time. A direct effect indexes the amount of information in a subsequent construct that is directly associated with another variable or constructs. A direct effect is a transformation of the bidirectional covariation information. With only two variables, the direct effect is the same as the bidirectional effect. With more variables, the direct effect reflects the unique contribution of a variable to the prediction of another (downstream) variable.

Indirect effect/path. Occurs when a construct or variable is related to a subsequent time point, but only through an intervening variable or construct. An indirect effect is a measure of association that is the result of the product of two or more direct effects. Most longitudinal panel models have a number of indirect pathways that are possible. Each indirect pathway is indexed as the product of each direct pathway that links constructs or variables together. The total indirect effect is the sum of all possible indirect pathways.

Panel data. These result when one collects data at discrete intervals of measurement. The individual differences in the units measured (typically persons) are summarized as sufficient statistics within and between each of the discrete measurement occasions.

Panel models. Statistical models that attempt to represent the pattern of individual differences (and sometimes mean level) changes at each discrete occasion of measurement. That is, they are models of the individual differences expressed as changes over time.

Simplex structure. The expected covariance structure generated by a first-order nonstationary autoregressive process (Jöreskog & Sörbom, 2001). That is, the pattern of correlations that one would expect is a by-product of gradual and consistent change across ordered constructs. A variety of simplex structures exist (Jöreskog, 1970), including perfect (when the observed variables have no error and conform to a simplex) and quasi (when the simplex is a property of the latent variables). *Markov simplex* refers to simplex structures that are scale-free, whereas the Wiener simplex is scale-dependent. Latent variables are arbitrarily scaled and typically reflect the scale-free nature of the Markov simplex structure.

Unstandardized–standardized parameter estimates. The parameters of a panel model, as in traditional regression analysis, are estimated in the metric defined by the method of scale setting (see Chapter 3). The method of scale setting can vary, but the estimates and standard errors are in this metric. This metric is termed the *unstandardized solution*. Standardized estimates are usually obtained as a postestimation transformation of the unstandardized parameter estimates and are put on a roughly correlational metric. It is possible to specify the method of scale setting such that the parameters of a model are estimated in the standardized metric, and postestimation standardization is not necessary. To do so requires adding phantom variables (see Chapter 3 and an example in Chapter 7).

RECOMMENDED READINGS

General Overview of Longitudinal Models

Collins, L. M. (2006). Analysis of longitudinal data: The integration of theoretical model, temporal design, and statistical model. *Annual Review of Psychology, 57*, 505–528.

> Linda provides a very thoughtful and compelling argument for seamlessly integrating the theory of change and the temporal design to capture change and for choosing the right statistical model to address the question at hand. In this regard, the panel design that I discuss throughout this book is but one of a number of statistical models that can be applied to longitudinal data.

Little, T. D., Bovaird, J. A., & Slegers, D. W. (2006). Methods for the analysis of change. In D. K. Mroczek & T. D. Little (Eds.), *Handbook of personality development* (pp. 181–211). Mahwah, NJ: Erlbaum.

> My coauthors and I did a good job, I think, in providing a broad overview of the different models for analyzing change and, in so doing, giving a clear perspective on where panel models fit in this broader framework. It may help clarify what kinds of questions can be answered by panel models and what ones cannot.

McArdle, J. J. (2009). Latent variable modeling of differences and changes with longitudinal data. *Annual Review of Psychology, 60*, 577–605.

> Jack provides a terrific integration of the various statistical models that can be used for longitudinal data, particularly as latent-variable formulations. He also shows the parallels to classical procedures.

Rosel, J., & Plewis, I. (2008). Longitudinal data analysis with structural equations. *Methodology, 4*, 37–50.

> These authors provide comprehensive integration of many different types of longitudinal models. It is a high-level overview and quite comprehensive. It's more of a guide to the forest, with lots of figural representations of the various longitudinal models.

A Published Empirical Example of the Simplex Structure

Blaga, O. M., Shaddy, D. J., Anderson, C. J., Kannass, K. N., Little, T. D., & Colombo, J. (2009). Structure and continuity of intellectual development in early childhood. *Intelligence, 37*, 106–113.

> This paper provides details of the theoretical rationale for the study, as well as the theoretical implications of the findings. Continuity is a good way to think of the simplex processes.

Developments Specific to the Panel Model

Little, T. D., Preacher, K. J., Selig, J. P., & Card, N. A. (2007). New developments in latent variable panel analysis of longitudinal data. *International Journal of Behavioral Development, 31*, 357–365.

> Some of the ideas presented in this chapter, as well as earlier chapters, originally appeared in this article, which is devoted to developments in panel models.

7

Multiple-Group Models

Chapter 6 covered the foundations of a longitudinal panel SEM. This chapter addresses fitting longitudinal panel models in the context of multiple groups. I touched on the multiple-group CFA component at the end of Chapter 5. In this chapter I focus in more detail on the multiple-group aspect of a longitudinal model. In Chapter 8, I address multilevel SEM models in detail. Both multiple-group and multilevel models are ways to handle nested or clustered data (i.e., when a set of observations are contained in a larger setting, unit, or context; see the examples that follow).

Multiple-group models are useful when the number of groups is relatively small (under 20 or so) and the parameters that characterize a group are treated as fixed effects. That is, a parameter describes each group's overall value (a group's mean or a correlation between two variables in a given group), and these values are compared across the groups. For example, the mean score for boys would be compared with the mean score for girls, or the correlation between two constructs would be compared across different ethnic groups. In multiple-group comparisons, groups are generally defined by discrete characteristics, such as gender, cohort, school, country, experimental condition, disability type, and the like. Ordinal or otherwise continuous characteristics, such as age, SES, intelligence, and so on, would generally not be used to create groups based on levels. Continuous variables such as these would be included in a model as continuous variables and examined as predictors, moderators, or both (see Chapter 9 for a discussion of moderation in longitudinal SEM).

Multiple-group models are powerful ways to test core assumptions, such as whether the constructs are factorially invariant across groups. When groups are potential sources of confound, these models can determine whether the grouping variable introduces differences that may influence the conclusions about the associations among variables. They are also the preferred approach to testing key hypotheses about potential between-group differences. As I detail in Chapter 8, multilevel models are useful when the number of groups is relatively large (e.g., around 30 or so groups) and the parameters that characterize the groups are treated as random effects (i.e., each parameter has a mean and a distribution across the groups, and such random effects can now be predicted by other variables or parameter distributions). As mentioned, when the number of groups is small, multiple-group models are the preferred approach.

MULTIPLE-GROUP LONGITUDINAL SEM

Multiple-group SEM is a relatively straightforward extension of the single-group approach I presented in Chapter 6. The details of the process of conducting such an analysis, however, are a bit more nuanced than in the single-group case. I step through these issues in an order that makes logical sense. This order is not meant to be the only order that can be considered. For this example, I use the bullying data that Dorothy Espelage has kindly allowed me to use. Recall that these data have a consistent cross-lagged effect from bullying to homophobic teasing when fit to the overall sample (see Figure 6.7). The question that I address is whether the effects are the same for boys and for girls. To address this question, I also need to make sure that the data are appropriately treated for a multiple-group comparison and that the constructs are factorially invariant across each group in the model. Equation 7.1 shows the fundamental equations of SEM with an additional subscript added, g, to reflect group membership. These equations thus start with all necessary parameter estimates being freely estimated at each measurement occasion and within each

Equation 7.1. Multiple-group longitudinal equations for SEM

a) $y_{og} = \mathbf{T}_{og} + \mathbf{\Lambda}_{og}\eta_{og} + \mathbf{\Theta}_{og}$

b) $E(y_{og}) = \mu_{y_{og}} = \mathbf{T}_{og} + \mathbf{\Lambda}_{og}\mathbf{A}_{og}$

c) $\mathbf{\Sigma}_{og} = \mathbf{\Lambda}_{og}\mathbf{\Psi}_{og}\mathbf{\Lambda}'_{og}\mathbf{\Theta}_{og}$

- o refers to the occasions of measurement.
- g refers to the group membership.
- y are the scores on the indicators.
- $E()$ is the expectation operator.
- μ_y is the vector of means.
- $\mathbf{T}$ is the column vector of indicator means.
- $\mathbf{A}$ is the column vector of latent construct means.
- $\mathbf{\Sigma}$ is the model-implied variance–covariance matrix.
- η is the latent constructs' scores.
- $\mathbf{\Lambda}$ is the matrix of loadings or estimates of the indicator to construct relations.
- $\mathbf{\Psi}$ is the matrix of variances and covariances among the constructs.
- $\mathbf{\Theta}$ is the matrix of residual variances or unique factors, and residual covariances among the indicators.
- $\mathbf{\Lambda}'$ is the transpose of the $\mathbf{\Lambda}$ matrix.

group; that is, the parameter estimates in each group and at each time of measurement are freely estimated. When the invariance tests are conducted, sets of the parameters are equated across groups, g, and across time, o. More specifically, Λ_{og} is constrained to be equal across time and groups (becoming Λ with no subscripts) to test for weak factorial invariance, and T_{og} is constrained to be equal across time and groups (becoming T with no subscripts) to test for strong factorial invariance.

Generally speaking, I recommend that all modeling and data preparation considerations be done at the group level rather than the whole-sample level. In other words, determine beforehand whether grouping variables like gender or grade will be a key theoretical focus (or any other group variable that would be meaningfully compared and reported for publication). Other demographic variables or nontheoretically relevant grouping variables (e.g., schools, districts, states, and cities) can be represented as sets of dummy codes and control variables. Be mindful that group sizes can become too small to allow meaningful comparisons. Group sizes below 50, for instance, can begin to create problems both for missing data estimation by group and for multiple-group SEM analyses. For the example that I work through here, *gender* is the meaningful group, and *school* is the nontheoretically meaningful grouping variable.

Step 1: Estimate Missing Data and Evaluate the Descriptive Statistics

This step may seem obvious, but I constantly have to ask researchers to provide this information. Even if FIML is to be used for the SEM estimation, getting descriptive statistics based on imputation is still useful because the means and variances of the imputed variables are the best population estimates given that some data are missing (note I would report the range of scores from the unimputed data, because the range is not a sufficient statistic about the sample). As I just mentioned, in this step, the missing data should be addressed by imputing the missing information within each group in order to maintain as much as possible the potential between-group differences. If the data are imputed at the combined (whole sample) level, any differences in covariance relations as a function of group will be reduced. It is possible to create a gender dummy code *and* to create all possible interactions of this dummy code with variables on the dataset to effectively capture the between-group differences in covariances. It's usually easier just to impute the missing data at the group level that will be analyzed. In this example, I would impute for boys and girls separately.

In addition to calculating the percent missing, it's informative to also report the fraction missing. As I mentioned in Chapter 2, fraction missing is an index of how recoverable the missing information is for each variable in the imputation set. Fraction missing is characteristic of each variable's missing-data pattern (or each parameter if FIML estimation is used) for estimating the mean and the variance. Reporting each estimate of fraction missing would be unnecessary; however, reporting a histogram of these values for all the variables or describing the range and mean would be useful (details of this information can be placed on a web page). I also strongly encourage a thorough examination of predictors of the missing data and reporting these predictors either in the text of the manuscript being prepared or on a web page. The more information that the field can get about the predictors of missingness, the better the field can prepare to handle missing data when the mechanism is MAR (see Chapter 2 for a more thorough discussion of missing data issues; see also Enders, 2010). For a guide to calculating and reporting fraction missing, see *www.guilford.com/little-materials*. In reviewing the descriptive statistics, the key is to look for consistency in the information within each time point. Do the indicators correlate with each other to about the same degree? Table 5.3 in Chapter 5 provides an example of this kind of information.

Step 2: Perform Any Supplemental Analysis to Rule Out Potential Confounds

As I mentioned in Chapter 6, an important step in any modeling endeavor is to examine potential confounds. In this example, the data were collected from four Midwestern middle schools. The students are nested within each school and, as a result, may have different associations among the constructs. That is, the different school contexts and cultures may moderate the relations among the constructs. To assess this possibility, a four-group CFA of the constructs would be performed. A multilevel approach is not feasible because there aren't enough schools to treat the school influences as a random effect; to treat schools as a random effect, a large number of schools would be needed. At this point, clear guidance on how many are needed is lacking, but somewhere between 15 and 30 or so different schools (Level 2 units) would be needed in order to attempt a multilevel analysis. With only a few schools, such as here, a fixed effects approach is preferred. Each school is treated as its own group in the four-group analysis, and any differences between schools are tested. If the differences are trivial, then I can collapse the data across schools (i.e., I can ignore the school clusters and treat all students as independent observations). If the differences are pronounced, I would need to keep school as a grouping variable in the analyses.

Table 7.1 presents the fit statistics for testing the school-level differences. The first entries in this table are the tests for factorial invariance across schools. Then I conducted the two key tests to examine school-level impacts on the latent constructs. As seen in Table 7.1, the tests for configural, weak, and strong factorial invariance in this supplemental analysis are, as expected, easily supported using Cheung and Rensvold's (2002) recommended criterion of the change in CFI of .01 or better (see Chapter 5). All the steps that I took in examining the school differences to determine whether there is any reason to control for school differences in the gender comparisons are the same steps that I will take when I subsequently conduct the gender comparisons. The main distinction between the tests in Table 7.1 and the

TABLE 7.1. Supplemental tests of differences across the four schools

Model tested	χ^2	df	$\Delta\chi^2$	Δdf	p	RMSEA	RMSEA 90% CI	CFI	ΔCFI	Pass?
Null model	27719.3	1968				---	---			---
Configural invariance	2933.6	1200				.075	.071;.079	.933		Yes
Weak invariance	3165.6	1260				.077	.073;.081	.926	.007	Yes
Strong invariance	3325.5	1320				.077	.073;.081	.922	.004	Yes
Homogeneity var/cov	4031.6	1485	706.1	165	<.001	---	---;---	.901	.021	No
Variances	3510.9	1350	185.4	30	<.001	---	---;---	.911	.012	No
-Variances w/ fixes	3374.8	1344	49.3	24	.002	---	---;---	.919	.003	Yes
Covariances	3758.1	1455	432.6	135	<.001	---	---;---	.916	.006	No
-Covariances w/ fixes	3532.8	1442	207.3	122	<.001	---	---;---	.921	.001	Yes
Means	3404.5	1350	79.0	30	<.001	---	---;---	.920	.002	No
-Means w/ fixes	3370.4	1346	44.9	24	.012	---	---;---	.921	.001	Yes

Note. For the measurement model tests of invariance, a change in CFI of .01 or less is used. The criteria for determining too much loss in fit in the latent space, given the power of the sample size, is a *p*-value less than .001 or a change in CFI greater than .002. In the case of the covariances with fixes, no further estimates lead to a significant decrease in model fit, indicating no meaningful differences between the four schools.

ones I report in Table 7.2 is that the school comparisons are not theory-based and are done to rule out school differences as a possible confound when I conduct the theoretically motivated comparisons by gender. If the study had been done in a large number of schools, I could use a multilevel SEM model to control for the school differences while focusing on gender differences. Because there are only four schools, the potential confound of school effects can be examined only by using the multiple-group framework.

TABLE 7.2. Model fit statistics for the gender comparisons of homophobic teasing and bullying

Model tested	χ^2	df	p	$\Delta\chi^2$	Δdf	p	RMSEA	RMSEA 90% CI	CFI	ΔCFI	TLI/ NNFI	ΔTLI	Pass?
				Invariance tests for gender comparisons									
Null model	32997.8	1380	<.001	---	---	---	---	---	---	---	---	---	---
Configural invar.	1958.09	840	<.001	---	---	---	.046	.043;.049	.971	---	.952	---	Yes
Weak invariance	2149.92	876	<.001	---	---	---	.048	.045;.051	.967	.004	.948	.004	Yes
Strong invariance	2379.74	912	<.001	---	---	---	.051	.048;.053	.962	.005	.942	.006	Yes
				SEM comparisions across gender									
Means - omni	2474.73	922	<.001	94.99	10	<.001	---	---;---	---	---	---	---	No
Means - Bullying	2387.99	917	<.001	8.25	5	.14	---	---;---	---	---	---	---	Yes
Means - HomPhAt	2422.60	917	<.001	42.86	5	<.001	---	---;---	---	---	---	---	No
Homogeneity[a]	2709.81	1048	<.001	330.08	136	<.001	---	---;---	---	---	---	---	Yes
Homogeneity[b]	2672.14	1047	<.001	292.40	115	<.001	---	---;---	---	---	---	---	Yes
Homogeneity[c]	2630.50	967	<.001	250.76	55	<.001	---	---;---	---	---	---	---	No
Variances only	2432.85	922	<.001	53.11	10	<.001	---	---;---	---	---	---	---	No
Final SEM	2523.55	1037	<.001	143.81	125	.11	.048	.040;.050	.953	.009	.937	.005	Yes

Note. [a]The covariates are included in the homogeneity test. [b]The covariates are not included in the homogeneity test. [c]The covariates are controlled for in the homogeneity test; the covariates were also controlled for in the tests of the means, the variances, and in the final SEM. Nonsignificant covariate effects were pruned. For the final SEM, all parameters are significant, and no further modifications were indicated. Sample sizes are 556 females and 576 males.

The next important step in the supplemental analysis is to test for the homogeneity of the variance–covariance matrix. Here, each variance and covariance is set to equality across each of the groups to evaluate whether there is sufficient evidence for moderation by school. This test is an omnibus test of whether the relations among the constructs are sufficiently similar within each school. Large differences would indicate that different SEM models for two or more of the schools would likely be needed to explain the relations among the constructs. If one of the schools, for example, was in the middle of an antibullying campaign, the relations between bullying and homophobic teasing would likely be different in that school as compared with schools that did not have antibullying programs in place.

Small differences would indicate that the same SEM model would work in each of the schools and that the school context does not have any meaningful impact. This outcome would suggest that the set of features defining each school (e.g., catchment region, bullying prevention efforts, extracurricular activities) do not differentially affect the associations among the constructs in this model. Modest differences among the schools would necessitate a closer examination of which elements of the variance–covariance matrix are different and a determination of whether the pattern is sufficiently systematic to cause concern.

As seen in Table 7.1, this test shows a modest change in model fit. This modest change prompted some follow-up tests to locate where the modest differences might be. The first follow-up test is to isolate the test of the variances from the test of the covariances. The initial test of the variances shows that some differences exist. The test of variances with fixes reports the results of my examination of the constraints, which found that *one* of the variances was responsible for the overall test being untenable. Inspection of the variances indicated that Schools 1 and 4 had similarly high variances, whereas schools 2 and 3 had similarly low variances. When I constrained Schools 1 and 4 to be equal and Schools 2 and 3 to be equal, the model fit was acceptable. That is, the tests for similarities across schools and time are reasonably supported. Given the unsystematic nature of where the one variance difference emerged, I would deem this difference as ignorable, particularly because it has no theoretical basis.

Next, the covariances are examined in isolation from the variances (i.e., the variances are freely estimated). The initial test of homogeneity among the covariances indicates some modest deterioration in fit. As with the variances, I examined the covariances and the model fit information to see where the lack of fit might be. Given that there are $(30 \cdot 29)/2$ unique covariances in each school, I would expect by chance alone that around 4 covariances in each group would be significantly different from the others. And this expectation was supported. Three covariances in School 4, 5 in School 3, 2 in School 2, and 5 in School 1 showed significant differences. When I freely estimated these 15 covariances out of the 1,740 possible covariances, the model fit was now similar to the strong invariant model fit. Again, given the smattering of differences, their unsystematic nature (e.g., none of the freed covariances involved contiguous time points or showed any consistency within or between construct relationships), and their lack of any theoretical interpretation, I would deem these differences as ignorable. These two sets of analyses indicate that there is no meaningful moderation of the associations among the constructs as a function of school context.

The next comparison listed in Table 7.1 is the mean-level test. Here, I set the latent construct means to be equal over time. This test shows some evidence of mean-level differences on one or more constructs across one or more schools. To follow up on this finding, I examined the means across the groups and looked at the modification indices to see which means are indeed different. The follow-up revealed that Schools 1 and 2 had a lower mean-level bullying score at Time 1 (1.41) than did Schools 3 and 4 (1.52). In addition, School 1 had a lower mean score on homophobic teasing at Time 1 (1.63) than did Schools 2–4 (1.78). These mean differences are enough to warrant including school dummy codes in the analysis model when the focal comparison by gender is conducted.

Step 3: Fit an Appropriate Multiple-Group Longitudinal Null Model

Because model fit will be an important consideration for the substantive model being tested, I need to know the null model χ^2 value and its degrees of freedom. The null model provides an index of the amount of information contained in the analyzed dataset. This index of information comes in the form of a very large χ^2 value (recall that the null model χ^2 and degrees of freedom are needed to calculate the relative fit indices; see Chapter 4). The null model specifies a reasonable *null* expectation for the dataset, and, therefore, it should produce a large χ^2 value. This χ^2 value represents the total amount of modelable information contained in the data. Note that I also fit a multiple-group longitudinal null model for the supplemental tests of school differences in Step 2.

The null-model expectations in the longitudinal and multiple-group case are the following: (1) The measured variables have a 0 association with one another within each time of measurement and across all times of measurement (the so-called independence model that is the default null model for most SEM packages). (2) The variances of the corresponding measured variables (e.g., verbal bullying at each of the five time points) do not change over time (i.e., the variances are equated to be equal over time). (3) The means of the corresponding measured variables also do not change over time (i.e., the corresponding intercepts or indicator-level means are equated to be equal over time). In addition to these longitudinal expectations, I would add the additional constraint that the variances and means of the corresponding variables are equivalent across each group in the multiple-group model (in this case, I have only two groups). The constraints represent the null expectation of no changes over time and no differences between groups. Essentially, the null model (with these constraints in place) is a modeling device that allows me to obtain an overall χ^2 value with its associated degrees of freedom that characterizes the amount of modelable information in the data that I am analyzing. I use this information to calculate the relative fit statistics that I want to examine. When I start the process of modeling the changes in the constructs over time and across groups, I will be able to gauge how much of this information I am able to recover or "fit" with my theoretically derived substantive model. This information is represented in the value of the CFI and the TLI/NNFI that I would calculate.

For this model, I have two constructs—each with three indicators. Each construct is measured at five times of measurement for both groups. The number of unique sufficient statistics that I have is easy enough to calculate. I first need to figure out the number of variables in the dataset. The number of unique sufficient statistics represents the number of unique bits of information that I have available for estimating a model's parameters. The first question is how many variables are there in each group. Because each time of measurement is treated as a unique occasion of assessment, the six variables that are measured at Time 1 are repeatedly assessed at other time points. So the number of variables is 6 · 5 or 30 plus 6 covariate variables for a total of 36 variables. The number of unique variances and covariances in this 36-variable matrix is (36 · 37)/2, or 666. The number of unique indicator means is 36; hence the total number of sufficient statistics that are unique is 702. Because I have two independent groups, each group has its own set of unique sufficient statistics, so the grand total for this two-group longitudinal model is 1,404. The null model estimates only the variances and the means of the six indicators of the Time 1 constructs in Group 1. The six variance estimates are equal over time and across groups. The six means are also equal over time and across groups. The variances and means of the six covariates are estimated in Group 1 but equated in Group 2. This null model, therefore, makes only 24 estimates (six variances and six means for the main indicators, and six variances and six means for the covariates). The degrees of freedom for this null model would be the total number of sufficient statistics minus the number of parameter estimates, which is $1404 - 24 = 1380$.

When I fit this null model to the data, I obtain $\chi^2_{(1380, n=1132)} = 32997.8$. I put this information as the first entry into my table of model fit information (see Table 7.2). By the way, if you choose to use FIML estimation to handle missing data when you fit your substantive models, you can use this null-model fit information to calculate the CFI and TLI/NNFI in the presence of missing data using FIML. That is, fit this null model using FIML and use the χ^2 and degrees of freedom to calculate the relative fit measures based on the χ^2 and degrees of freedom of the FIML estimated substantive models. Most software will not provide this information when FIML is chosen as the estimator.

Step 4: Fit the Configural Invariant Model across Time and Groups

I am choosing to fit the configural invariant model to both groups simultaneously because I have strong theoretical reasons to expect that these two constructs will be configurally invariant across time and gender. I'm primarily interested in establishing a baseline of model fit for the subsequent substantive models that I would like to estimate (e.g., tests of measurement invariance, tests of latent equivalence, the structural SEM). The configural invariant model provides the best fitting model that I have in mind for these data because it estimates all loadings, intercepts, and latent-variable parameters as free parameters across time and across groups. In this regard, it is also the least parsimonious model. The goal in this model-building enterprise is to move from a nonparsimonious model such as the configural invariant model to a more rigorous model (i.e., the strong factorially invariant model) and even further to a reduced parameter structural model.

This fourth step is already a step in which I could conduct things in a more fine-grained set of steps. If I were really concerned about the nature of the model and its fit across boys and girls, I could fit the configural invariant model separately for boys and for girls to evaluate more independently the model fit information within each group. When I fit the model as a multiple-group model, the fit statistics are based on the combined information (as implied by the earlier discussion about how the null model is to be fit). If I did want to fit the models separately for boys and for girls, I would also need to calculate an appropriate null model for each subgroup. Here, I would fit the longitudinal null model (i.e., variances and means don't change over time, and no associations are allowed among all indicators) to allow me to evaluate fit within each group. As I mentioned, I would do such a detailed subanalysis only if I were really concerned about the behavior of the indicators within one or more of the groups. For example, I might have this level of concern if I translated a set of measures from one language into another and wanted to make sure that the translated instrument fit the data of the new culture at reasonably good levels.

The fit of the configural invariant model is usually evaluated as a combined overall assessment; however, most software will also provide some indication of the fit within a given group. For example, the percentage of the contribution to the overall χ^2 indicates whether the contribution is evenly distributed across groups. This information gives some confidence that the overall model fit is a good approximation for both groups. For the current example, the model fit of the configural invariant model is quite good, indicating that the constructs are maintaining their general measurement integrity across time and groups (see Table 7.2).

Step 5: Test for Weak Factorial (Loadings) Invariance

This step can be conducted based on a few different rationales and perspectives. That is, the tests of weak factorial invariance can be conducted in increments or as an overall omnibus assessment. From one perspective, when the expectation for invariance is very reasonable, the assessment can be conducted as an omnibus evaluation, whereby the loadings are constrained to be equal both across time and across groups simultaneously. Such an omnibus test would be reasonable when the instruments are age appropriate and the groups are based on relatively homogeneous characteristics (e.g., age cohorts, genders, schools).

If there is reason to believe that the constructs may not be factorially invariant, either across time or across groups, then the tests of weak factorial invariance could proceed in a more measured manner. Depending on which dimension I am worried about, I would continue with the test on the more worrisome dimension first. For example, if I had two samples from different cultures, I would want to make sure that the invariance tests across groups are tested without placing invariance constraints across time. I could then evaluate the tenability of the cross-group constraints unconfounded with constraints across time. I would then add the cross-time constraints on top of the cross-group constraints in a situation such as this.

I would be perfectly justified in testing for invariance across time and across groups as separate comparisons, using the change in CFI criterion for each. I could then fit the omnibus test where the constraints hold across groups and time and allow for a more relaxed evaluation of constraints. For example, I can adjust the change in CFI criterion. If the sum of the two constraints is not double the usual .01 criterion for the change in the CFI, then the set of constraints of invariance are tenable, and I can proceed with the next steps. As with any tests of invariance, I need to evaluate the residuals and modification indices very carefully. When modification indices are consistent across time or across groups, then the modification is more likely to be a real effect that should be carefully considered. Inconsistent modifications are more likely to indicate perturbations due to sampling variability.

For the working example here, the model fit was extremely good and showed only modest changes in model fit between the configural invariant model and the weak factorial invariant model. Table 7.2 contains the relevant information for this step of invariance testing.

Step 6: Test for Strong Factorial (Intercepts) Invariance

The next critical test in establishing measurement equivalence across groups and across time is the test of strong factorial invariance. As with the tests for weak factorial invariance, the order in which these tests are conducted can vary depending on the expectations of the researcher. Generally speaking, however, the order and manner in which strong factorial (intercepts) invariance is tested should mirror the order and manner in which weak factorial (loadings) invariance is tested.

Once this test of invariance is completed and assuming it passes, then the conclusion is that the measurement characteristics of the indicators (as they relate to their respective constructs) are unchanged by the passage of time and that they are universally relevant in the groups that are represented. Measurement equivalence is a key assumption that is tested in SEM models, and, when supported, the constraints of invariance on these measurement parameters provide important validity assurances. First, the constraints ensure that the operational characteristics of the indicators are defined in a common manner that is exactly the same for each time of measurement and across each group. Second, the constraints ensure that when tests of differences in the latent constructs' parameters are conducted, the defining characteristics of the indicators will remain tied in place. That is, the loadings in one group cannot change to be different values in a compensatory manner when constraints are placed on the latent constructs' parameters. The measurement invariance constraints provide the stable baseline for making meaningful construct comparisons. Third, the constraints assure us (when the model fit is relatively unchanged) that we have no evidence of differential item functioning or other measurement anomalies. In this regard, multiple-group tests of measurement equivalence are the continuous-variable analogue to categorical tests of differential item functioning in the item response theory (IRT) framework. In SEM, the loadings are the discrimination parameter and the intercepts are the difficulty or likeability level of the indicator. The analogous theta parameter of IRT is the latent construct score.

At both the weak and the strong levels of invariance testing, some of the constrained parameter estimates may not be acceptable. In the multiple-group longitudinal framework, the lack of invariance for a given parameter has a better chance to replicate either across groups or across time because of the additional replications of the same indicators being measured. If a loading or an intercept does not show an invariant relationship across groups or across time, it can be freely estimated. As mentioned, when a majority of indicators are invariant, the partially invariant construct can be examined with little loss of generality in the conclusions that can be drawn about the nature of the latent construct. In a situation of partial invariance, I can also get fancy and add a uniqueness factor to the offending indicator and then estimate the loading or intercept of the uniqueness factor to estimate the amount of deviation from factorial invariance that the offending indicator has (see Grob, Little, Wanner, Wearing, & Euronet, 1996, for an empirical example that estimated a uniqueness mean).

For the working example here, the model fit was extremely good and showed only modest changes in model fit between the configural invariant model and the weak invariant model, as well as between the weak invariant model and the strong invariant model. Table 7.2 contains the relevant information for this step of invariance testing. In other words, measurement invariance holds for these constructs across both time and gender. In these tests of factorial invariance, the covariates are included in the analysis model, but they are not included in the invariance constraints, and they are not used to condition the constructs (i.e., they do not predict the constructs at this point in the model-building process). In addition, their variances and means are freely estimated in both groups. After establishing invariance, I can then examine the predictive effects of the covariates by regressing each of the focal constructs onto the covariates. As I have mentioned before, I generally prune the nonsignificant covariate effects in an effort not to overcontrol when including covariates in an analysis such as this.

Step 7: Test for Mean-Level Differences in the Latent Constructs

I can conduct this test right after I have established strong factorial invariance or strong partial invariance of the constructs. These tests of the latent means examine not only the mean-level changes over time but also potential mean-level differences across groups. As before, these tests can be conducted in a number of different phases. One method, which I described in detail in Chapter 5, involves conducting an omnibus test of no latent mean changes across time and across groups. I can also perform specific comparisons if I have strong theory that guides which means would be expected to differ. For this example, I did the omnibus tests first. As shown in Table 7.3, the means of the bully constructs appear to be similar, but the means for homophobic teasing appear to be different. I first conducted an omnibus test but found that it was significant as evidenced by the χ^2 difference test (Table 7.2). The test of the set of means for bullying, on the other hand, showed that these means are not significantly different across boys and girls, $p = .14$. The means of homophobic teasing were different across boys and girls (see Table 7.2). Note that in these tests

TABLE 7.3. Correlations, means, and variances for the bullying and homophobic teasing constructs at five time points by gender

	Time 1		Time 2		Time 3		Time 4		Time 5	
	Bul1	Hom1	Bul2	Hom2	Bul3	Hom3	Bul4	Hom4	Bul5	Hom5
					Girls					
Bul1	1.00									
Hom1	0.81	1.00								
Bul2	0.58	0.51	1.00							
Hom2	0.63	0.65	0.69	1.00						
Bul3	0.64	0.52	0.77	0.61	1.00					
Hom3	0.60	0.54	0.71	0.73	0.78	1.00				
Bul4	0.51	0.44	0.66	0.57	0.61	0.59	1.00			
Hom4	0.52	0.51	0.59	0.61	0.61	0.77	0.63	1.00		
Bul5	0.52	0.44	0.57	0.35	0.58	0.50	0.58	0.46	1.00	
Hom5	0.61	0.53	0.64	0.52	0.67	0.59	0.57	0.62	0.75	1.00
Mean	1.47	1.69	1.45	1.76	1.45	1.79	1.38	1.72	1.42	1.61
Var	.21	.53	.25	.57	.22	.60	.10	.43	.16	.28
					Boys					
Bul1	1.00									
Hom1	0.75	1.00								
Bul2	0.50	0.47	1.00							
Hom2	0.49	0.47	0.67	1.00						
Bul3	0.53	0.42	0.60	0.48	1.00					
Hom3	0.45	0.40	0.58	0.68	0.72	1.00				
Bul4	0.48	0.50	0.60	0.48	0.60	0.52	1.00			
Hom4	0.47	0.47	0.54	0.64	0.66	0.72	0.72	1.00		
Bul5	0.40	0.37	0.54	0.35	0.65	0.55	0.61	0.55	1.00	
Hom5	0.39	0.38	0.57	0.42	0.63	0.56	0.62	0.71	0.75	1.00
Mean	1.47	1.81	1.45	1.98	1.51	2.03	1.38	1.84	1.38	1.81
Var	.27	.62	.27	.82	.31	.78	.12	.53	.14	.33

Note. The estimates are from the strong invariant CFA model with effects coded method of identification. Girls $n = 556$, boys $n = 576$.

of mean-level differences across boys and girls, I did include the covariate effects in the models.

Step 8: Test for the Homogeneity of the Variance–Covariance Matrix among the Latent Constructs

This step is an important one. If the variance–covariance matrix among the latent constructs is not different across boys and girls, then there is not much of a basis to go forward and fit the SEM model separately for boys and girls. If the variance–covariance matrices are the same for boys and girls, it means that the same SEM model would fit equally for boys and girls. This test, therefore, would indicate whether or not the two samples of youths can be combined into a single sample analysis, like the one I reported in Chapter 6. If the two matrices are sufficiently different from one another, it implies that different relations among the constructs exist and that different SEM models of the longitudinal relations among the constructs would likely emerge. This situation would warrant continuing to Step 9 and fitting the hypothesized longitudinal model for boys and for girls as a two-group model (while still keeping the invariance constraints in place).

In this example, I conducted the homogeneity tests in three different ways. In the first test, I included the covariates as part of the variance–covariance matrix. This test would mix the variance–covariance information about the focal variables with the variance–covariance information about the covariates. In these data, I had three dummy codes for school, one ordinal code for grade (Grades 6, 7, and 8), and two dummy codes for ethnicity. In my view, this test of the homogeneity of the information across the two groups is not very informative because it mixes the two sources of information (i.e., information due to the focal indicators of the constructs vs. information due to the relations among the covariates). One way to fix this confounding of information is to freely estimate the variances and covariances among the covariates but to place equality constraints on the remaining variances and covariances that involve the focal indicators. These constraints could include the covariances between the focal indicators and the covariates, or you could leave these covariances as freely estimated. I constrained them in this test, as I report in Table 7.2.

The third test of the homogeneity of the variance–covariance matrix is actually a test of the residual variance–covariance among the focal variables after controlling for the covariate effects. That is, each of the indicators of the two constructs across the five measurement occasions is regressed on to each of the covariate variables. The residual matrix is then compared across the two genders. I generally prefer this third way because the matrix that is conditioned on the covariates is the matrix that would have the SEM model fit to it. It could be that the unconditioned variance–covariance matrix among the focal indicators is different but that the residual matrix (conditioned on the covariates) is not different. As shown in Table 7.2, all three ways of testing the homogeneity of the variance–covariance matrix revealed significant differences between the genders.

I conducted a follow-up test of just the variances to evaluate whether the metric of the relations among the constructs is comparable across the two genders. If the variances differ to any appreciable degree between the two genders, then the structural relations that I would model would be on very different metrics. In this case, I would need to include phantom constructs to standardize the structural relations that I would be modeling (see Chapter 3 for my discussion of phantom constructs and why they are used). As seen in Table 7.2, the omnibus test of the variances indicates that there are significant differences between the genders. A casual inspection of the variances in Table 7.3 shows that boys vary more than girls in terms of reported bullying and in reported homophobic teasing, with some of these differences more pronounced (e.g., homophobic teasing at Times 3 and 5) and some nearly nonexistent (e.g., bullying at Times 4 and 5). Given that some of these variances are different and would produce unstandardized estimates that are on different metrics, the next step in building the longitudinal SEM in both groups would be conducted using the phantom constructs. Recall that phantom constructs provide a way to estimate the SEM model in a common metric across the two groups, which allows us to test the parameters of the SEM model for similarities and differences across the two genders.

Step 9: Test the Longitudinal SEM Model in Each Group

In this step, the hypothesized longitudinal SEM models for boys and for girls (because they are expected to be different) are fit simultaneously using the boys' data and the girls' data. This longitudinal SEM model for the two groups would be very similar to the model in Figure 6.7, but some of the additional AR2 and AR3 paths would not likely be included at this initial specification of the longitudinal SEM model. It is also possible that, with strong theory, the model for the boys may look quite different from the girls' model. Even if the models for the boys and for the girls are identical in terms of which paths are being estimated and which paths are fixed to 0, important differences between the groups could emerge. Specifically, the differences would be seen in the magnitudes (and perhaps directions) of the relations. For example, the cross-lagged path from bullying to homophobic teasing at each successive time point may be a large positive value in boys but a significantly lower positive value in girls. At this step, the key goal is to develop a longitudinal SEM model for each group such that the fit of the overall model does not differ significantly from the strong factorially invariant model.

The strong invariant model is the optimal best fitting model to use as the baseline for comparing the parsimonious restrictions that are placed when specifying the longitudinal SEM model. It is optimal because factorial invariance constraints are in place, which ensures that the constructs are identically defined in both groups and across time. It is also optimal because there are no restrictions on the relationships among the constructs. That is, the variances and covariances among the constructs are all freely estimated in the strong invariant model. When the cross-time covariances are converted to directed regression relations and many of them are removed (i.e., set to 0), the model fit will be degraded to some degree. The key, of course, is making sure that the degree of degradation is not too much. If it is too much, then there are still important relations among the variables that need to be estimated. Figure 7.1 displays the results of the two-group longitudinal comparison across genders.

This final model was built by individually testing each path for differences between the genders. To compare the parameters and to test them for differences across the genders, I used phantom constructs. If a path was significant in one group but not significant in the other group, the two paths were still tested for differences between groups. Just because a path is not significantly different from 0 does not mean that it is significantly different from that (significant) path in the other group. If

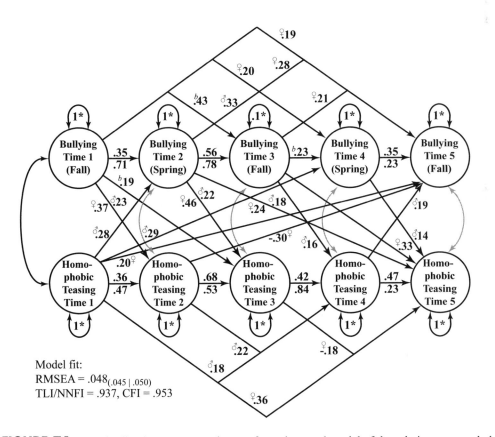

FIGURE 7.1. Standardized parameter estimates from the panel model of the relations among bullying and homophobic teasing. For the autoregressive paths the boys' parameter estimates are above the line and the girls' are below. ♀ = females, ♂ = males. b = parameter set to be equal in both groups. Within-time correlations are described in text.

the two paths are different from each other and one path is not different from 0, then the nonsignificant path would be pruned from the one group, and the path would be estimated only in the other group. If the two paths do not differ from each other and the constrained path is significant, then the cross-group equality constraint would be included in the final SEM model. In Figure 7.1, then, all paths are significantly different from 0. A value placed on the path is indicated by ^{b} if it was the same for both males and females; ♀ indicates females; and ♂ indicates males. If two values are shown for a given path, it means that the boys' path coefficient differed significantly from the girls' path coefficient, with the path for the boys listed above the line.

For this model, I was primarily interested in the directed regression relations. I did test the within-time correlations for similarities or differences but did not constrain them to be equal in the final model. My rationale for not constraining them to be equal is that these are residual correlations—or the relative association between the constructs after controlling for all directed regression effects. These values and the variance explained are not the kinds of parameters that I would necessarily hold constant across groups, as holding them constant would potentially influence the regression paths, which are the parameters of focal interest.

Table 7.4 presents the magnitude of the correlation between bullying and homophobic teasing at each of the five time points. The magnitude of these correlations did not differ between males and females at Times 1 and 2 but did differ between the genders at Times 3–5. The variance explained in each construct by the set of pathways shown in Figure 7.1 is also listed in Table 7.4. One feature of note is that more variance was explained in the homophobic teasing construct than in the bullying construct for both genders. This feature is consistent with the generally larger regression paths in Figure 7.1 for homophobic teasing versus bullying. A second feature of note in Table 7.4 is that overall more variance was explained in both constructs in the model for females than in the model for males. That is, the stability and predictability among the constructs is higher for females than it is for males.

TABLE 7.4. Correlations among the two constructs and the variance explained from model in Figure 7.2

	Time 1	Time 2	Time 3	Time 4	Time 5
Females:					
$r_{\text{Bullying-HomPhTeas}}$	.75	.52	.42	.36	.57
r^2 Bullying	---	.33	.61	.43	.46
r^2 HomPhTeas	---	.38	.61	.64	.52
Males:					
$r_{\text{Bullying-HomPhTeas}}$	.77	.55	.55	.56	.48
r^2 Bullying	---	.26	.46	.40	.43
r^2 HomPhTeas	---	.24	.53	.54	.48

Note. These tabled values correspond to Figure 7.2. HomPhTeas = Homophobic Teasing. r^2 is the variance explained, and r is the within-time correlation between bullying and homophobic teasing.

In complex models such as this one, a number of problems can emerge. First, providing accurate start values is very important to allow the model to successfully converge. When I use LISREL, I typically output the estimated results from a preceding model to read in as start values for the next subsequent model. There is a guide on our *www.guilford.com/little-materials* web page that further discusses some of the nuances for reading in start values. In other software such as Mplus the start values need to be hand entered as part of the syntax file. Although this process can take time up front when writing a program, the time it will save down the road when you are doing successive tests of parameters, for example, is well worth the initial investment.

A second problem can emerge if the ML estimator veers off course and ventures into the negative-numbers area. Sometimes loadings will show up in the output file as negative values. The absolute values of the loadings are correct optimal estimates for a given model, and model fit is unaffected when this happens. What does become problematic is the fact that the construct for which the loadings are now negative is effectively reverse-coded. When a construct is reverse-coded, the high scores no longer mean more of the construct but now are interpreted as less of the construct. Moreover, the signs of the relations among constructs would now be in the opposite direction than I may have expected. For any given run of an SEM model, it is important to take at least a cursory glance at the loadings to make sure that none of the constructs has reversed its meaning. The better the start values are, the lower the likelihood is of the reverse-sign problem. As I have mentioned earlier, good start values for the loading and the construct relations are very important, but putting higher residual values in as start values is often helpful because the ML estimator can avoid getting too close to the boundary conditions of 0 or even negative values for the indicators' residuals.

When phantom constructs are employed in a model such as this, the reverse-coding problem can also occur in the regression parameter that links the first-order construct with its associated phantom construct. As with the loadings, providing accurate start values for these linking regression paths is a good way to avoid the reverse-coding of a construct. To illustrate the reverse-coding problem that can sometimes emerge, I created Figure 7.2, which has four mathematically identical solutions.

Panel A in Figure 7.2 is the correct solution. In Panel B, the regression path linking the lower order construct with the phantom construct came up negative in the estimation process. When an estimate comes out negative like this, it effectively reverse-codes the construct. That is, the high scores that would have indicated more of the construct are now the low scores. Thus, higher scores on the construct now mean "less" of the construct. Moreover, the relations of this reverse-coded construct are now in the opposite direction of the intended scoring. This same phenomenon occurs in Panel C, when the loadings of the indicators on the lower order construct are estimated in the negative direction. The lower order construct is now reverse-coded, and the regression on the phantom construct carries this reverse-coded

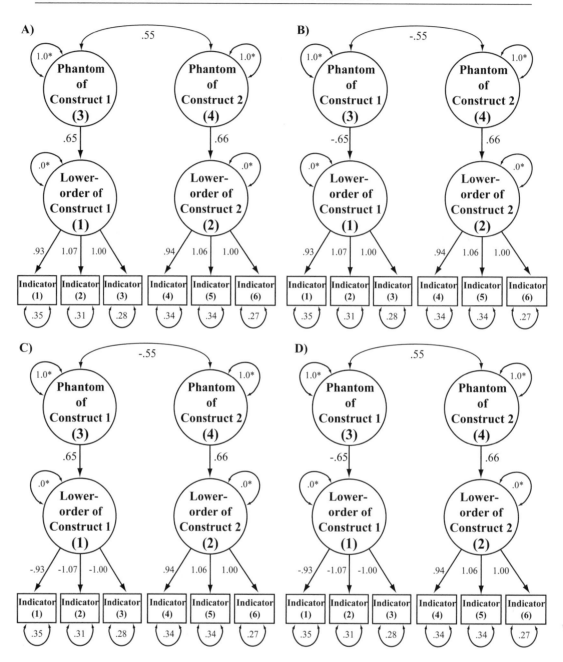

FIGURE 7.2. The correct solution (A) and the incorrect solutions with "reverse" coding by estimation ano-moly (B–D). Each model is mathematically the same in terms of the reproduced variance–covariance matrix and model fit. Solutions B–D can emerge by ML estimation. In B, the regression of the phantom variable was reverse-coded, causing the correlation to be incorrectly negative. In C, the loading on the lower order construct went negative, causing the reverse coding and a negative correlation. In D, both the loadings and the phantom regression estimated as negative. This happy accident results because a negative multiplied by a negative is a positive.

information up to the phantom level, which leads to the correlation between the constructs coming out negative again. In Panel D, a happy accident occurs. The loadings are estimated as negative, but so too is the regression parameter linking the lower order construct with the phantom construct. This second negative effectively "re-reverse-codes" the construct scores back into the meaning of their original raw metric.

When and how values "reverse" themselves is nearly impossible to predict ahead of time, and it can happen when only a small tweak is made to a model. Therefore, I strongly encourage you to take a quick glance at the loading parameters after each estimated model to make sure the loadings have not reversed. Similarly, if you use phantom constructs, glance at the regressions that link the lower order and phantom constructs to make sure they are also positive.

This section covered a two-group longitudinal model examining gender differences in the linkages between bullying and homophobic teasing. In the next section, I further demonstrate the use of multiple-group comparisons and the use of phantom variables. I use the context of dynamic P-technique SEM to introduce this general form of longitudinal model, as well as to show the striking parallels in fitting a panel model to groups of individuals and fitting a dynamic P-technique model to the intensive measures taken on a single person or a small handful of persons.

A DYNAMIC P-TECHNIQUE MULTIPLE-GROUP LONGITUDINAL MODEL

I mentioned in an earlier chapter that SEM models can generally be fit to the sufficient statistics: variances, covariances, and means. These sufficient statistics can be generated more ways than just by sampling lots of people and calculating the covariances among the variables. In fact, Cattell (1952) introduced his data box in order to help us "think outside the box" regarding how data can be collected and analyzed. Figure 7.3 is a graphic rendering of the box or cube. The idea here is that I can sample any one of these dimensions to create a dataset that can be modeled using mean and covariance structures techniques. Cattell talked about the data box in terms of exploratory factor analysis. More recently, people such as John Nesselroade have discussed the data cube in terms of SEM and introduced the idea of dynamic P-technique analyses. In Figure 7.3, the three primary dimensions are persons (or entities), variables, and occasions. In terms of a data matrix, we typically think of rows and columns, with the rows being the observational record and the columns being the things that we wish to understand the relations among. Cattell's data box works with this idea. The box or cube can be rotated to make any dimension the column and any other dimension the rows. Cattell labeled the different orientations using an arbitrary letter scheme. R-technique uses variables in columns and persons in rows. This data setup is the common one that I have been describing. It addresses the question of what the associations are among the

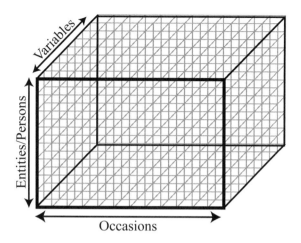

FIGURE 7.3. Cattell's data box/cube.

variables that tell us something about persons. In Q-technique persons are used in columns and variables in rows. Q-technique looks for similarities among persons in their profiles of scores on the measured variables—a form of cluster analysis. P-technique is a form of time-series modeling. Here, a single person is repeatedly observed over hundreds of occasions.

In the latter half of this chapter I demonstrate a multiple-group analysis of dynamic P-technique data. Because dynamic P-technique data are particularly useful for many kinds of developmental change questions, I first give a description of this kind of data before I go to the next step of analyzing them in a multiple-group model. Figure 7.4 shows the first few scores from a single person's responses to a mood questionnaire given every day for more than 100 days. These data are provided by Mike Lebo and John Nesselroade. Five pregnant women participated in the daily mood assessments. I have selected six of the adjectives that were rated by the women: *active, peppy, lively, sluggish, tired,* and *weary.* A priori, I expect two constructs to emerge from these adjectives: positive energy and negative energy.

In Figure 7.4, the first 7 days and the last 3 days are presented. Table 7.5 shows the correlations among the six variables across the 102 days. As seen in Figure 7.4, the mood reports for the first three variables are consistent with each other, and the scores for the second set of three variables are consistent with each other. The consistency in the patterns shows up in the correlation matrix presented in Table 7.5. The first three variables correlate with each other in the upper .80's; the second set of three variables also has a high positive correlational manifold. In the lower left quadrant of the matrix, the set of nine cross-construct correlations are all negative. This pattern of correlation among the six variables is consistent with the a priori expectation of two underlying constructs for these data: positive and negative energy.

Participant 1	Day	Lag 0 A L P S T W
Data from day 1	1	1 1 1 2 1 2
Data from day 2	2	3 3 3 0 1 1
Data from day 3	3	1 1 1 3 3 3
Data from day 4	4	3 3 3 0 1 1
Data from day 5	5	2 3 3 1 1 1
Data from day 6	6	3 3 3 1 1 1
Data from day 7	7	3 4 4 0 0 0
•••		•••
•••		•••
•••		•••
Data from day 100	100	3 4 3 1 1 1
Data from day 101	101	3 3 4 1 1 1
Data from day 102	102	1 1 0 3 4 3

FIGURE 7.4. Data for one person. A = Active, L = Lively, P = Peppy, S = Sluggish, T = Tired, W = Weary.

Figure 7.5 is an idealized ebb and flow of three indicators of the same construct over time. The scores on the three variables mirror one another as the construct goes down and up and down over time. This synchrony in the variables over time is what produces the high correlation among the three variables. In this case, the correlation is not generated by consistent scores across persons but instead by consistent scores across time for a given individual. If the variables are each good indicators of a given construct, then they will follow such a consistent pattern, and an SEM model can be easily fit to the resulting covariance matrix. If one or more of the variables display marked differences in their ebb and flow pattern over time, then the variables would

TABLE 7.5. Correlations among the six mood items for one person across 102 days

	Positive Energy			Negative Energy		
	A	L	P	S	T	W
Active (A)	1.00					
Lively (L)	.849	1.00				
Peppy (P)	.837	.864	1.00			
Sluggish (S)	-.568	-.602	-.660	1.00		
Tired (T)	-.575	-.650	-.687	.746	1.00	
Weary (W)	-.579	-.679	-.724	.687	.786	1.00

Note. These are the obtained correlations among the affect responses depicted in Figure 7.4.

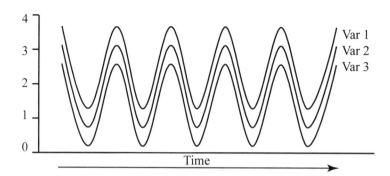

FIGURE 7.5. The ebb and flow of three indicators of the same construct over time in an idealized multivariate time series.

not correlate very well with each other, which would not be consistent with a coherent construct underlying the observed data patterns.

Figure 7.6 presents a diagram of the two-construct SEM model that I fit across the 5 participants. This model uses the phantom variables so that I can estimate the latent construct relations in a common metric across each of the 5 participants, because each participant is treated as a "group" in this multiple-group framework.

Table 7.6 presents the fit information that I obtained by testing this two-construct CFA model for factorial invariance across all 5 participants. In Table 7.6, I report the results of the null model that I specified and fit, just as I have done for each of the multiple-group models I've presented thus far in this chapter. The next model reported in Table 7.6 is the test of configural invariance. When I inspected the model parameter estimates for this model, I found that the first indicator of negative energy, "sluggish," did not load onto the negative energy construct for Participant 5. The low loading was due to the fact that the correlations of the variable "sluggish" with the other indicators of negative energy were at trivial levels and that the variance in the responses was minimal. Clearly, Participant 5 had an ideographic reaction to rating "sluggish" as an affect-related indicator. Perhaps the term is too colloquial, or perhaps the word was misinterpreted as being suggestive of aggressive behavior (i.e., sluggish as a feeling of wanting to slug someone or something). Because of this lack of a relationship, I fixed the loading of the "sluggish" indicator to 0 in the "group" that represents the model for Participant 5.

With this adjusted configural invariance model as the starting point, I then tested the loadings for weak factorial invariance across the 5 participants. Equating the loadings across the 5 participants led to a change in the CFI of .011. Even though this value of change in CFI is not less than the .01 general guidelines for evaluating invariance constraints, I inspected the loadings and the modification indices across the five groups. I found that all the invariance constraints across groups had minimal misfit except for two. More specifically, none of the modification indices was larger

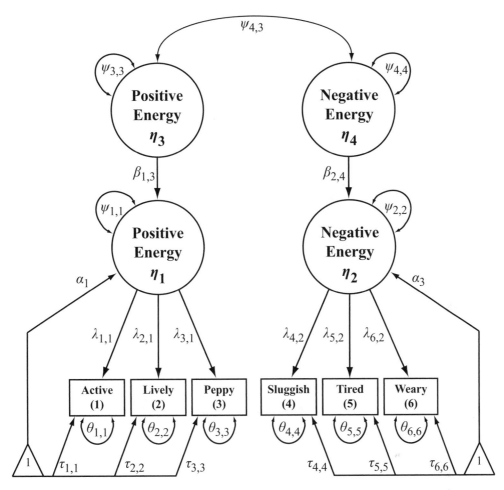

FIGURE 7.6. Parameter labels for the multiple-group model across five participants. Table 7.7 contains the estimates for these parameters under configural and partial invariance.

than 3 except for the loading of "peppy" on the positive energy construct in Participants 4 and 5. For these two participants, the loadings for "peppy" were clearly larger in relative magnitude than for the other three participants.

Table 7.7 contains the parameter estimates of the model that I fit to test for factorial invariance across these 5 participants. The first five columns of numbers correspond to the configural invariant model for each of the 5 participants. I used the fixed factor method of identification for these models because I anticipated that relationships of the indicators to the constructs may only provide partial measurement invariance. The fixed factor method of identification is appropriate to use when you have reason to anticipate that invariance of all loadings and intercepts may not hold. The fixed factor method will allow an unbiased search for the loadings and intercepts that are noninvariant. With the marker variable method and the effects coded

TABLE 7.6. Model fit statistics for tests across five participants with P-technique SEM models

Model tested	χ^2	df	p	RMSEA	RMSEA 90% CI	CFI	ΔCFI	TLI/ NNFI	ΔTLI	Pass?
Null model	3279.5	123	<.001	---	---	---	---	---	---	---
Configural invar.	54.38	41	= .08	.052	.000;.090	.996	---	.987	---	Yes*
Weak invariance	103.80	56	<.001	.085	.050;.113	.985	.011	.969	.018	No**
Strong invariance	225.29	71	<.001	.135	.113;.156	.951	.034	.915	.072	No
Partial invariance	127.05	68	<.001	.090	.065;.116	.981	.015	.966	.024	Yes

Note. Although the initial SEM had a nonsignificant *p*-value, some parameters were nonsignificant, and modification indices indicated that additional parameters were warranted. For the final SEM, all parameters are significant and no further modifications are indicated.
*The loading of "sluggish" was nonsignificant for Participant 5 and was fixed to 0 as part of the configural model.
**Two loadings showed evidence of significant differences even though the change in CFI was within the tolerance of .01 for the step from configural to weak. The partial invariance model is compared with the configural model, and the tolerance value is .01 + .01 or .02, as it is the sum of the two steps.

TABLE 7.7. Comparison of parameter estimates across the five participants under configural invariance and partial invariance

	Configural invariance					Final partial invariance				
	P1	P2	P3	P4	P5	P1	P2	P3	P4	P5
$\lambda_{1,1}$	0.506	1.014	0.933	0.891	1.000	0.467	0.467	0.467	0.467	0.467
$\lambda_{2,1}$	0.443	1.068	1.069	0.984	1.149	0.477	0.477	0.477	0.477	0.477
$\lambda_{3,1}$	0.367	0.845	1.001	1.049	1.078	0.381	0.381	0.381	0.525	0.525
$\lambda_{4,2}$	0.537	1.095	0.930	0.960	1.000	0.577	0.577	0.577	0.577	0.00*
$\lambda_{5,2}$	0.850	1.220	1.069	1.073	1.149	0.735	0.735	0.735	0.735	0.735
$\lambda_{6,2}$	0.611	1.242	1.001	1.025	1.078	0.672	0.672	0.672	0.672	0.672
$\beta_{1,3}$	1.00*	1.00*	1.00*	1.00*	1.00*	1.00*	2.235	1.975	1.998	2.222
$\beta_{2,4}$	1.00*	1.00*	1.00*	1.00*	1.00*	1.00*	1.758	0.857	1.517	1.812
$\psi_{3,4}$	-0.631	-0.651	-0.423	-0.799	-0.602	-0.660	-0.652	-0.423	-0.796	-0.627
$\theta_{1,1}$	0.094	0.398	0.389	0.214	0.340	0.112	0.392	0.388	0.212	0.389
$\theta_{2,2}$	0.183	0.046	0.190	0.156	0.550	0.183	0.053	0.208	0.163	0.487
$\theta_{3,3}$	0.182	0.197	0.343	0.152	0.622	0.191	0.202	0.335	0.150	0.604
$\theta_{4,4}$	0.213	0.706	0.133	0.466	0.173	0.207	0.739	0.130	0.492	0.173
$\theta_{5,5}$	0.079	0.220	0.093	0.274	0.540	0.154	0.193	0.098	0.260	0.938
$\theta_{6,6}$	0.126	0.204	0.090	0.324	1.137	0.109	0.254	0.103	0.328	1.175
τ_1	2.221	2.426	2.634	2.901	2.281	2.223	2.223	2.223	2.223	2.223
τ_2	2.008	2.152	2.280	2.906	2.269	1.931	1.931	1.931	2.208	2.208
τ_3	1.388	1.751	1.831	2.772	1.934	1.485	1.485	1.485	1.974	1.974
τ_4	1.452	1.895	1.210	2.608	1.054	1.441	1.441	1.441	1.441	1.05~
τ_5	1.679	2.005	1.327	3.045	2.893	1.620	1.620	1.620	1.620	1.620
τ_6	1.448	1.981	1.299	2.878	2.094	1.498	1.498	1.498	1.498	1.498
α_1	0.00*	0.00*	0.00*	0.00*	0.00*	0.00*	0.492	0.809	1.485	0.064
α_2	0.00*	0.00*	0.00*	0.00*	0.00*	0.00*	0.616	-0.352	1.991	1.394

Note. *indicates a fixed parameter. I used the fixed factor method to set the scale in both the configural invariant model and the partial invariant model. ~ indicates that the intercept was estimated freely because the loading for this indicator in this person was essentially 0 and was fixed at 0 in all models. Columns are the parameter estimates for each of five persons assessed for over 100 consecutive days.

method of scaling, the scaling constraint is placed on a loading. Having a loading constrained to be the same across groups for scaling purposes confounds any test of a nonconstrained loading or intercept when searching for the noninvariant parameters. Only the fixed factor method leads to unbiased detection of the noninvariant loading(s) or intercept(s).

The last five columns of Table 7.7 show the results of the final partial-invariance model. For the partial invariant model, the first participant is used as the reference "group" that provides the scale for all the other parameters of the model. A careful look at the first column of Table 7.7 reveals that the loadings for Participant 1 are all quite a bit lower than the loadings for the other participants. As a result, when Participant 1 is used as the reference group for scale-setting purposes, the estimated construct variances are accordingly larger in magnitude, with one nonsignificant exception.

When I evaluate factorial invariance constraints, I don't blindly rely on the heuristics of change in model fit. The impact of such constraints needs to be scrutinized carefully. When the loss in fit is evenly distributed across the set of constraints and the change in model fit is not too much, then the test of invariance would be acceptable. When the loss in fit is localized with a small number of parameter estimates, then prudence is needed before concluding invariance. I have mentioned before that partial measurement invariance is a tolerable outcome of invariance testing. There is no reason to panic if a small number of loadings or intercepts are not invariant. Three of these participants showed invariance for the loading of "peppy," and the other two showed invariance for the loading of "peppy" but at a higher magnitude than the first three participants. For the tests of the intercepts, again Participants 4 and 5 shared a pattern that was not shared by Participants 1–3. Here, the means of "lively" and "peppy" were invariant for Participants 4 and 5, but their invariant intercepts differed from those of Participants 1–3 (who had invariant intercepts for these two indicators). The latent mean of positive energy still has a common scale because the indicator "active" was invariant across all 5 of the participants.

These differences in loadings and intercepts across these 5 participants highlight the ideographic attraction of P-technique models. These kinds of models are consistent with Molenaar's (2004) call for modeling at the level of the individual in order to test the ergodicity assumptions of statistical models. In psychology, a model of dynamic change is ergodic if it is applicable at the level of a single individual, as well as across a group of individuals. In these 5 participants, I would conclude that the constructs' measurement properties are sufficiently ergodic (factorially invariant) to allow comparisons of the similarities and differences in the latent construct relationships.

Thus far I have been discussing standard P-technique analysis. These analyses are used primarily to understand the factorial structure among the set of six indicators and to determine whether the measurement characteristics are sufficiently factorially invariant to allow further assessments of the dynamic relationships in these two constructs. Dynamic P-technique is the next extension for modeling multivariate time-series data such as these. A key point of interest in data such as these is how a person's scores on one day influence or predict her scores on the next day. To examine these day-to-day or observation-to-observation associations, the data matrix needs to be lagged. Figure 7.7 is a representation of how a lagged dataset is created. Figure 7.7 shows two lags of the original dataset. The original dataset is sometimes labeled Lag 0, as it is not technically lagged. Lag 1 represents the immediate associations between an observation and the very next observations across each of the observational records. Lag 2 represents a separation of two observations.

For these data, observations were made on a daily basis. Observational record 1 contains the reported mood ratings on Day 1, observational record 2 has the reported mood ratings on Day 2, observational record 3 has the reported mood ratings on Day 3, and so on. When the data are transformed to create the Lag 1 information, the observational record at the second occasion is copied and placed on the same row as the first observational record. The third occasion is copied and placed on the same row as the second observation. And the last observational record is copied and placed on the row for the immediately preceding day. To create Lag 2, the observational records are copied and placed one row up to create the data structure that I have placed in Figure 7.7. The scores for Day 2 (3,3,3,0,1,1), for example, are in Row 2 under the Lag 0 set of columns, and they are in Row 1 under the Lag 1 set of columns. The scores for Day 3 (1,1,1,3,3,3) are in Row 3 under the Lag 0 columns, in Row 2 under the Lag 1 columns, and in Row 1 under the Lag 2 columns. Each

Participant 1	Day	Lag 0 A L P S T W	Lag 1 A L P S T W	Lag 2 A L P S T W
	-1	(missing data)	(missing data)	1 1 1 2 1 2
	0	(missing data)	1 1 1 2 1 2	3 3 3 0 1 1
Data from day 1	1	1 1 1 2 1 2	3 3 3 0 1 1	1 1 1 3 3 3
Data from day 2	2	3 3 3 0 1 1	1 1 1 3 3 3	3 3 3 0 1 1
Data from day 3	3	1 1 1 3 3 3	3 3 3 0 1 1	2 3 3 1 1 1
Data from day 4	4	3 3 3 0 1 1	2 3 3 1 1 1	3 3 3 1 1 1
Data from day 5	5	2 3 3 1 1 1	3 3 3 1 1 1	3 4 4 0 0 0
Data from day 6	6	3 3 3 1 1 1	3 4 4 0 0 0	2 2 2 1 1 1
Data from day 7	7	3 4 4 0 0 0	2 2 2 1 1 1	3 3 3 0 0 1
•••		•••	•••	
•••		•••	•••	
•••		•••	•••	
Data from day 100	100	3 4 3 1 1 1	3 3 4 1 1 1	1 1 0 3 4 3
Data from day 101	101	3 3 4 1 1 1	1 1 0 3 4 3	(missing data)
Data from day 102	102	1 1 0 3 4 3	(missing data)	(missing data)

FIGURE 7.7. Dynamic data setup for one person, two lags. A = Active, L = Lively, P = Peppy, S = Sluggish, T = Tired, W = Weary.

observational record follows this pattern: under the Lag 1 columns, the Lag 0 scores are shifted up one row, and under the Lag 2 columns the Lag 0 scores are shifted up two rows. These shifts also produce some very small amounts of missing data. Observational record 1, for example, does not have a preceded record to match, so the Lag 0 data at Day 0 is missing. Similarly, for Lag 2, the observations at day –1 do not have matching records at Lag 0 or Lag 1 resulting in missing data.

These missing values are easily imputed using modern approaches. After imputation, the 102 days of observation actually led to 105 days of analyzable information. After imputation, these 18 columns of information can be summarized as a set of sufficient statistics for the six variables across two lags (three assessment intervals). Figure 7.8 displays the block Toeplitz matrix that results from calculating the variance–covariance matrix of the 18 columns of information from lagging the

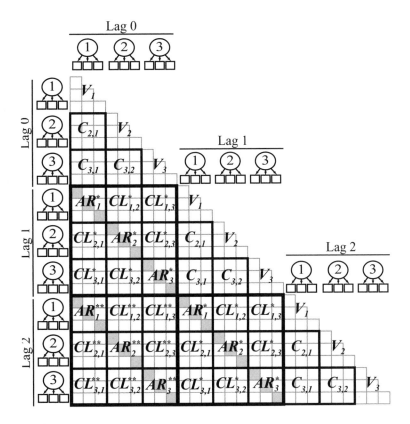

FIGURE 7.8. A dynamic P-technique data matrix or block Toeplitz matrix. This stylized representation has three constructs, each with three indicators. C refers to covariances, V refers to variances, CL refers to the cross-lagged associations, and AR refers to the autoregressive associations. The variances and covariances within a given lag are essentially identical values across the lags. The elements denoted with * are essentially identical values between lag 0 and lag 1 and between lag 1 and lag 2. The elements denoted with ** are unique associations between lag 0 and lag 2.

original data matrix two times. A block Toeplitz matrix is one that has repeated elements in specific parts of the matrix. The diagonal elements representing the associations among the variables at Lag 0 is repeated when the associations among the variables at Lag 1 and at Lag 2 are examined. The data at Lag 1 are the same data as at Lag 0, and so the within-lag associations will be essentially identical. There will be some noise due to the uncertainty of the few data points that were imputed, but from a statistical perspective the elements in these parts of the matrix are equivalent. Similarly, the quadrant that contains the associations between Lag 0 and Lag 1 and the quadrant that contains the associations between Lag 1 and Lag 2 will also be the same because these quadrants contain the same data information separated by a single measurement occasion. In this block Toeplitz matrix, the information contained in the lowest quadrant is the unique set of associations between Lag 0 and Lag 2. Only this one quadrant contains the separation of two measurement occasions.

Another feature to note in the stylized block Toeplitz matrix of Figure 7.8 is that I have labeled subquadrants with the kind of modelable information that is contained within it. Like any longitudinal data matrix, the association of a variable with itself is termed an autoregressive path (AR). The autoregressive correlations are located on the subdiagonals of the block Toeplitz matrix and are labeled AR_1–AR_3. The autoregressive associations are separated by one measurement occasion. In the lower left quadrant of Figure 7.8, the autoregressive associations are between Lag 0 and Lag 2. These autoregressive associations would be separated by two measurement occasions and are technically AR_2 associations. The cross-lagged associations among these hypothetical variables and constructs follow a similar block Toeplitz pattern. The cross-lagged associations between Lag 0 and Lag 1 are essentially identical to the cross-lagged associations contained between Lag 1 and Lag 2. The unique cross-lagged associations between Lag 1 and Lag 2 are shown in the lower right quadrant of the matrix.

When a dynamic SEM model is fit to this kind of data matrix, the parameter estimates for the constructs take on very specific constraints because of the essential equivalence found in the block Toeplitz quadrants. Because the within-lag information is essentially equivalent, all parameters associated with a given construct would be invariant in the CFA buildup to the structural model. In Figure 7.9, I have presented the basic CFA with parameter labels for the positive and negative energy constructs across Lag 0, Lag 1, and Lag 2.

Not only would the loadings (e.g., $\lambda_{1,1} = \lambda_{7,3} = \lambda_{13,5}$) and intercepts (e.g., $\tau_1 = \tau_3 = \tau_5$) be equal across the lags, but so too would the residuals (i.e., strict factorial invariance across lags would be enforced (e.g., $\theta_{1,1} = \theta_{7,7} = \theta_{13,13}$). Strict invariance would be enforced in lagged data because the information within lags is essentially equivalent and, statistically, should possess the same parameter estimates. Even the between-lag correlated residuals would be equal when they are separated by the same number of lags. Specifically, the correlated residuals between Lag 0 and Lag 1 would be equal to the corresponding correlated residuals between Lag 1 and Lag 2

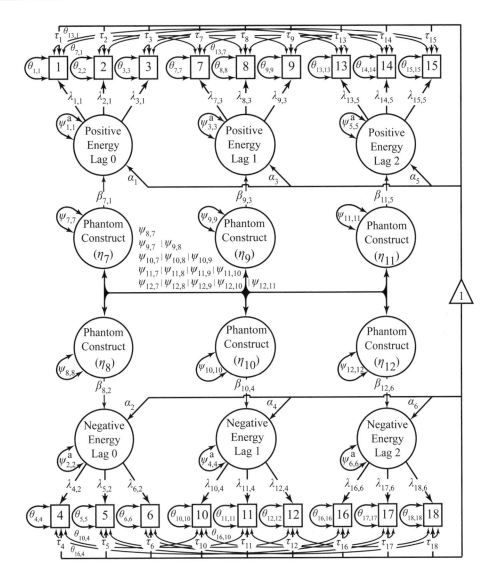

FIGURE 7.9. Parameter labels for a two-lag dynamic P-technique analysis with positive energy and negative energy. With the dynamic P-technique CFA all of the corresponding within-lag parameters are equated over lags. All corresponding between-lag parameters (i.e., between lag 0 and lag 1 and between lag 1 and lag 2) would also be equated because the information is essentially equivalent given the duplication of data to form the lagged data structure of the block Toeplitz matrix. ^{a} = parameter is fixed to 0.

(e.g., $\theta_{7,1} = \theta_{13,7}$). The correlated residuals between Lag 0 and Lag 2 (e.g., $\theta_{13,1}$), on the other hand, would be uniquely estimated because they are separated by two occasions of measurement.

In this version of a dynamic model, I used phantom constructs to estimate the associations among the constructs as correlations in each participant. Thus, the variances of the constructs are now estimated as standard deviations; that is, $\beta_{7,1}$ is the standard deviation of positive energy at Lag 0, and $\beta_{8,2}$ is the standard deviation of negative energy at Lag 0. The variances of the lower order constructs are fixed at 0 to force the common variance that is captured by the loadings to be transported directly to the phantom construct level. The phantom constructs have their scale set by fixing the variance parameter to 1.0 (e.g., $\psi_{7,7}$ and $\psi_{8,8}$ are fixed at 1).

In addition to equating all the measurement model parameters, a dynamic P-technique CFA would also have identical construct-level parameter estimates. Thus, with the phantom construct representation in Figure 7.9, the latent standard deviations would be the same at each lag (e.g., $\beta_{7,1} = \beta_{9,3} = \beta_{11,5}$), and the construct means would be the same at each lag (e.g., $\alpha_1 = \alpha_3 = \alpha_5$). The within-lag correlations among the constructs would be the same (i.e., $\psi_{8,7} = \psi_{10,9} = \psi_{12,11}$), and the between-lag correlations among the constructs would be identical between Lag 0 and Lag 1 and between Lag 1 and Lag 2 (i.e., $\psi_{9,7} = \psi_{11,9}$; $\psi_{10,7} = \psi_{12,9}$; $\psi_{9,8} = \psi_{11,10}$; $\psi_{10,8} = \psi_{12,10}$). Only the correlations between Lag 0 and Lag 2 would be uniquely estimated (i.e., $\psi_{5,1}$; $\psi_{5,2}$; $\psi_{6,1}$; $\psi_{6,2}$).

These essentially equivalent quadrants of a dynamic P-technique block Toeplitz matrix are predicated on the idea that observations are indistinguishable by other characteristics (e.g., day of the week). If observations have a distinguishable characteristic, then the essential equivalence is not likely to hold. In this case, the data would be lagged in such a way that the known characteristics determine the lag bin. For example, all Monday observations go in to a Monday-to-Monday bin, all Tuesday observations go in to a Tuesday-to-Tuesday bin, and so on for each day of the week. In such a setup, the lagged constructs represent mood ratings on a given day of the week. This more elaborate variation on dynamic P-technique is beyond the scope of what I want to discuss here, and, unfortunately, the dataset that I am using as an example does not have day of the week included to even allow such a data setup (see Lee & Little, 2012, for an example of a day-of-the-week data setup).

Table 7.8 reports the model fit information for the dynamic 2-lagged P-technique data with partial measurement invariance imposed. The partial invariance constraints stem directly from the nonlagged multiple-group test of invariance across

TABLE 7.8. Model fit statistics for tests across five participants with dynamic P-technique SEM models

Model tested	χ^2	df	p	$\Delta\chi^2$	Δdf	p	RMSEA	RMSEA 90% CI	CFI	ΔCFI	TLI/ NNFI	ΔTLI	Pass?
						SEM comparisons across three lags							
CFA weak/partial	722.21	705	= .32	---	---	---	.000	.000;.019	.999	---	.998	---	Yes
Equal variances	959.41	713	<.001	236.85	8	<.001	.023	.000;.038	.975	.024	.967	.031	No
Initial SEM	771.08	725	= .11	48.52	20	<.001	.000	.000;.027	.995	.004	.994	.004	No
Final SEM	776.27	746	= .21	53.71	41	= .09	.000	.000;.023	.997	.002	.996	.002	Yes

Note. The CFA weak/partial is based on the final SEM of the simple P-technique CFA, all parameters are significant and no further modifications indicated. In that model, the loading of "sluggish" was nonsignificant for Participant 5 and was fixed to 0. Two loadings showed evidence of significant differences and were adjusted (see discussion of the simple CFA).

the 5 participants. Again, because of the essential equivalence of the lagged data, the same pattern of partial invariance across participants would show up at each lag. Also, because of the redundant information, the model fit for the partial invariant CFA is outstanding. This model fit information is meant to provide the baseline of model fit in order to evaluate the structural model that will be fit to these data.

For the structural model, the cross-lag associations are now converted to directed regression paths. Lag 0, which I refer to as "yesterday," will predict the scores at Lag 1, which I refer to as "today," and Lag 1 will predict Lag 2, which I refer to as "tomorrow." These labels are convenient because they convey the essential idea of dynamic P-technique modeling—the day-to-day associations over the course of a large span of observed days. Because the information between yesterday and today is the same as between today and tomorrow (i.e., the lagged block Toeplitz structure), any associations found between Lag 0 (yesterday) and Lag 1 (today) will be essentially identical to those between Lag 1 (today) and Lag 2 (tomorrow). Only potential delayed effects from yesterday to tomorrow would be uniquely estimated in these structural models.

Table 7.8 also shows the fit of the initial structural model. Similar to some of the initial structural models of longitudinal data, I assumed that the dynamic relations over these three observation points would follow a simplex pattern of association: yesterday would affect today, which, in turn, would affect tomorrow. The impact of yesterday on tomorrow would be indirect via its effect on today's mood. I also had no a priori predictions for the cross-lagged influences that may be inherent in day-to-day mood processes. Therefore, the initial model specified autoregressive and cross-lagged effects between Lag 0 (yesterday) and Lag 1 (today) and between Lag 1 (today) and Lag 2 (tomorrow). Because the variances of Lag 1 and Lag 2 are now residual variance estimates, I no longer force these variances to be equal to the variances of their corresponding constructs at Lag 0. Similarly, the within-lag covariances at Lag 1 and Lag 2 are now residual covariances after controlling for the prior lag's influence. These covariance estimates would not be equated necessarily with the zero-order covariance of the two mood constructs at Lag 0. The zero-order covariance at Lag 0 and the residual covariances at Lag 1 and Lag 2 may turn out to be equal, but they would not necessarily be predicted to be equal.

The other feature of the dynamic structural model that I specified is the inclusion of phantom constructs for each lag to account for the dramatic differences in the variances of the mood ratings across the 5 participants. The formal test of the differences verified what a casual glance at the variances suggested. These 5 participants were quite different in daily ratings of their positive and negative energy. These differences are readily apparent in Table 7.6. In Figure 7.10 and Figure 7.11, each variance is estimated as a standard deviation, which means that the values in the figures are pretty close to the square roots of the values for the variances in Table 7.6. Had I not used phantom constructs to examine the cross-lagged relations in these two constructs across these 5 participants, the estimated beta paths would

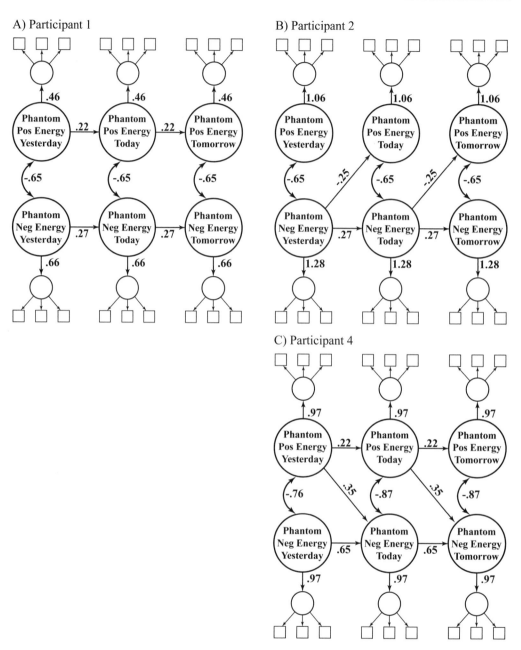

FIGURE 7.10. Final dynamic P-technique model for three of five participants. The measurement model is presented graphically to illustrate that the lower order factors are represented by multiple indicators. The loadings are invariant across the three lags and across all five of the participants, except for one loading that showed differences in a particular participant: the third indicators of positive affect in the fourth and fifth participants were equal to each other but different from those of the first three participants. The first indicator of negative affect in the fifth participant was fixed to 0. The results for Participants 3 and 5 are presented in Figure 7.11. Values that are identical were tested for differences and found to be nonsignificantly different at $p = .10$ or greater. They are equated to present the estimated values in the most parsimonious manner. Overall model fit is outstanding: $\chi^2_{(n=525,746)} = 776.3$, $p = .22$; RMSEA $= .000_{(.000; .024)}$; CFI $= .999$; TLI/NNFI $= .997$.

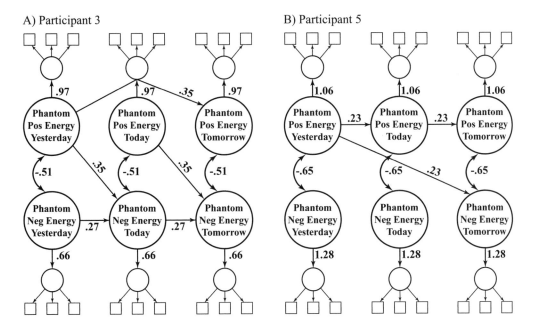

FIGURE 7.11. Final model for the remaining two participants (see Figure 7.10 for the other three). See Figure 7.10 caption for details of model fit and specification details.

have been on dramatically different metrics. The differences in metrics are apparent in Table 7.6. In the partial invariant model, where the estimates are made on a scale defined by Participant 1, the estimated covariances between positive and negative energy vary from –.660 to –2.536. When Participant 1 is used for the scale-defining constraint (Group 1 using the fixed factor method of identification), the estimated associations are no longer on a standardized or common metric; that is, –2.536 cannot be interpreted as a strength-of-association value that is comparable to the –.660 value. The –.660 is a correlation and has direct interpretation in terms of variance overlapping. The –2.536 is a covariance that needs to be transformed so that we can understand the strength of association in terms of the correlational metric. Using phantom constructs allows me to estimate the associations among the constructs in a standardized and comparable metric. This estimated standardized solution thereby allows me to test parameters for equality across the 5 participants and to eventually end up with the final SEM models that I have displayed in Figures 7.10 and 7.11.

The final SEM models for each of the 5 participants are striking in terms of the common associations that emerged across the 5 participants. For example, Participants 1, 4, and 5 each showed weak but positive stability in day-to-day fluctuations in positive energy (β = .23). Similarly, Participants 1, 2, and 3 showed weak but positive stability in the day-to-day fluctuations in negative energy. In terms of the within-lag correlations among the two mood constructs, three participants (1, 2, and

5) showed the same $-.65$ association at each lag. I mentioned that the Lag 1 and Lag 2 associations are residual correlations. If the cross-time effects are pronounced, then these residual correlations can change in magnitude—only Participant 4 showed this pattern of change in magnitude. The zero-order correlation was $-.76$ at Lag 0, but after the cross-time effects are accounted for, the residual correlations between the two constructs are $-.87$. This participant showed quite stable negative energy ($\beta = .65$); but when affect did change, it was predicted to a moderate degree ($\beta = .35$) by the prior day's level of positive energy. All the other participants showed effects that were generally weak or modest, and the resulting correlations between the two mood constructs were the same as the zero-order correlation at Lag 0.

In these dynamic models, Participants 3 and 5 showed a delayed effect of mood "yesterday" (Lag 0) influencing mood "tomorrow" (Lag 2). For Participant 3, there was a delayed effect in the autoregressive effect of positive energy at Lag 0, showing a modest positive impact on positive energy at Lag 2 of $\beta = .35$. A similar effect emerged for Participant 5, who had a cross-lagged effect of $\beta = .23$ between positive energy at Lag 0 and negative energy at Lag 2. These delayed effects can be interpreted as rebound effects.

Three of the participants showed a cross-lagged effect from positive energy to negative energy. Each of these effects was positive, meaning that the higher the positive energy was yesterday, the more negative energy was reported today (Participants 3 and 4) or tomorrow (Participant 5). One of the cross-lagged effects was negative; specifically, for Participant 2, higher negative energy consistently predicted lower positive energy the next day.

These dynamic P-technique models highlight both the ideographic and the nomothetic interpretations of fitting these kinds of multiple-group models to multivariate time-series data. The partial measurement invariance showed, for example, that one participant (5) would not endorse "sluggish," and it was, therefore, not an effective indicator of negative energy for that participant. At the construct level, this participant showed a similar level of stability in positive energy to two other participants but showed the only delayed effect of positive energy predicting negative energy ($\beta = .23$). More nomothetic conclusions could be drawn if a larger pool of participants were selected for such a study.

Variations on the dynamic P-technique models exist. For example, chained P-technique is useful when many individuals can each provide a shorter time series. Here, I might have access to 30 or so individuals who are able to provide data for a short period of time, such as 2 weeks. These data can be concatenated such that a single model can be fit to the resulting 30 persons by 2 weeks' worth of time-series data. If the data are combined into a single dataset, this approach must assume that the measurement model for the measures is factorially invariant across all participants and that the structural model that is fit to the data is also invariant across all participants. I might consider fitting such data as a 30-group model with factorial invariance examined. The power to detect noninvariance would be limited, but if invariance across participants is warranted, the model parameters would be grounded in the total set of observations. A multiple-group approach would have challenges and some power issues. Very little work on this approach has been conducted, so there is not much I can say in terms of guidance at this time. From what we do know about nested data structures, a chained P-technique model may be best fit as a multilevel model rather than a multiple-group model. In future editions of this book, I'll likely elaborate more on these kinds of models and their variations. For now, I hope this brief introduction will entice more researchers to utilize these kinds of data collection procedures and the SEM models that can be fit to them.

SUMMARY

In this chapter, I focused on the ins and outs of multiple-group comparisons. Using a traditional examination of a longitudinal structural model across genders, I detailed the numerous steps that are involved. The most significant benefit of all these steps is increased validity. Rather than my assuming factorial invariance or that some other factor, such as school context, does not have an impact on the results of the focal analyses, the multiple-group framework allows me to examine the veracity of these assumptions. Other benefits of the multiple-group framework are those associated with the latent-variable SEM approach in general (e.g., correcting for measurement error, establishing the content validity of indicators, informing the discriminant and convergent validity of the constructs).

I also demonstrated how this same multiple-group approach can be applied to the dynamic P-technique context. Here, the procedures for testing factorial invariance can be used to identify and highlight the ideographic response patterns of a given individual. They also can be used to establish the similarities and differences among the construct associations.

As I turn to Chapter 8, I focus on the new developments in modern statistical modeling for addressing the nested data structures: multilevel modeling. Although multilevel modeling has numerous advantages, it does have at least two significant limitations that are not limitations of the multiple-group framework. First, multilevel models assume factorial invariance and do not have the capability of allowing partial invariance across the lower units of a multilevel analysis. A multiple-group framework does not have a limit on the number of groups that can be examined; only computing power would be the limiting factor on the number of groups that could be included. The multiple-group approach, however, does not have the ability to model the associations among the constructs as random effects (see my detailed description of multilevel modeling in Chapter 8). The second limitation of multilevel approaches that are not problematic in the multiple-group framework is that the model for the associations among the constructs can vary dramatically across groups. The different models for the 5 participants in the dynamic P-technique exemplify this idea.

With multilevel models, the structural model is assumed to be the same across all groups, and only the parameter magnitudes vary across groups.

KEY TERMS AND CONCEPTS INTRODUCED IN THIS CHAPTER

Chained P-technique SEM. A way to leverage multiple time-series datasets and combine them into a single data matrix. This approach requires a number of assumptions, such as the invariance of both the measurement and structural models across the chained participants.

Dynamic P-technique SEM. The label for SEM models that are fit to lagged block Toeplitz matrices generated from multivariate time-series data obtained from a single individual.

Ergodicity. The generalizability of findings when the level of analysis is higher than the level at which generalizability is attempted. Models fit to a sample of individuals from a population of individuals are generalizable to the population of individuals; however, the results may not generalize to the level of a given individual or to a level of a small sample of individuals. The P-technique approach fits models that are at the level of an individual, and therefore the model results are generalizable to the person.

Fixed effects. With multiple-group models, comparisons across groups are conducted as fixed effects comparisons. A fixed effect is any parameter of a model that describes a characteristic of the data for a discrete group. The parameter for a given group could be its mean, variance, covariance, regression slope, loading, intercept, or indirect effect. When two or more groups share a common parameter estimate, the significance of the difference in this parameter is conducted as a fixed effect comparison. In multiple-group SEM, this comparison is typically conducted as a χ^2 difference test. Fixed effects can be contrasted with random effects.

Lagged block Toeplitz. A block Toeplitz matrix is one that has repeated elements in specific parts of the matrix. A lagged block Toeplitz matrix is one that results from intentionally duplicating a multivariate time-series data matrix and then aligning the observations so that observations in row n are aligned with the duplicated observations for all $n + 1$ observations. The sufficient statistics for the original dataset and the duplicated dataset are essentially identical. Only trivial differences occur due to imputation of unmatched observational records (e.g., the first observation and the last observation do not have matching records and the missing information is imputed).

Multiple-group SEM. When two or more samples of observations exist based on known, discrete, and mutually exclusive classifications, a multiple-group SEM model can be conducted. Multiple-group SEM involves fitting a formal SEM model simultaneously across the two or more groups.

P-technique factor analysis. P-technique involves variables-by-occasions data. P-technique factor analysis and SEM examine the covariation patterns among variables that are repeatedly sampled for a single individual or entity. It is a form of time-series analysis. Dynamic P-technique involves using a lagged P-technique dataset to examine the associations among the variances between the observations.

Q-technique factor analysis. Q-technique involves persons-by-variables data. Q-technique factor analysis and SEM examine the covariation patterns among persons to identify similarities or clusters of profiles of scores on a number of variables. Q-technique is a form of cluster analysis.

R-technique factor analysis. R-technique involves variables-by-persons data. R-technique factor analysis and SEM are the dominant modes of factor analysis and SEM. Longitudinal R-technique factor analysis is a form of the typical SEM model for panel data.

Random effects. Model-based estimates that can be defined as having a mean and a distribution of possible estimates. When a sufficiently large number of groups exist, a parameter of interest can be characterized as a mean estimate with a distribution. When groups are too small, each group's parameter estimates are treated as discrete fixed effects.

RECOMMENDED READINGS

The Data Box

Cattell, R. B. (1952). The three basic factor-analytic research designs: Their interrelations and derivatives. *Psychological Bulletin, 49*, 499–551.

> This is the classic work in which the idea of the data box is presented.

P-Technique and Dynamic P-Technique

Hawley, P. H., & Little, T. D. (2003). Modeling intraindividual variability and change in bio-behavioral developmental processes. In B. Pugesek, A. Tomer, & A. von Eye (Eds.), *Structural equation modeling: Applications in ecological and evolutionary biology research* (pp. 143–170). Cambridge, UK: Cambridge University Press.

Lee, I. A., & Little, T. D. (2012). P-technique factor analysis. In B. Laursen, T. D. Little, & N. A. Card (Eds.), *Handbook of developmental research methods* (pp. 350–363). New York: Guilford Press.

> In these two chapters colleagues and I have discussed P-technique exploratory factor analysis (EFA) and dynamic P-technique SEM in various contexts and provide different examples.

8

Multilevel Growth Curves and Multilevel SEM

Chapter 7 covered longitudinal panel models in the context of multiple groups. In this chapter, I focus on growth curve and multilevel SEM models. The reason that I am treating these two topics together in the same discussion is that they are both members of the same family of models. These models can be broadly referred to as random-coefficient multilevel models for nested data. In the case of growth curve models, the longitudinal observations are nested within each individual person. In addition, the specified constructs of the growth model can vary for each individual. In other words, growth curve models are multilevel models that estimate the changes within persons as slopes and intercepts and, at the same time, summarize the between-individual differences in these person-level slopes and intercepts.

For general multilevel SEM models, some clustering variable other than time (e.g., classrooms or schools) has individuals nested within it. A given model, when fit at the level of the individual, can vary across the clustering variable (i.e., just like the model for growth for an individual can vary across individuals, a model for persons in a given cluster can vary across the clusters). The parameters of these models can have a mean and a distribution across levels of the clustering variable. Because estimates can have a distribution of values, it also means that other variables can be used to predict the standing of the scores in the distribution. Multilevel models share the common goal of accounting for the dependency among the sampled observations that occurs when the observations are nested. In fact, the dependency is more than "accounted for"; it is explicitly represented as a predictable (randomly varying) parameter in the statistical model that is fit to the data. In the parlance of multilevel models, the equations used to model the nested observations are referred to as Level 1 equations, and the observations are referred to as Level 1 units. On the next level they are referred to as Level 2 equations and Level 2 units, respectively. The variability in the scores associated with each level is estimated. The intraclass correlation (ICC) quantifies the amount of variance at higher levels relative to the lower levels. Multilevel models can have any number of nested levels. A three-level model, for example, could involve observations (Level 1) nested within individuals (Level 2), and these individuals (Level 2) could be further nested in classrooms (Level 3). A four-level model could also occur, with classrooms (Level 3) nested within schools (Level 4). Individuals (Level 2) would still be nested in the classrooms (Level 3) and time (Level 1) would be nested within persons (Level 2).

As I mentioned in Chapter 7, multiple-group models are useful when the number of groups is relatively small (cohorts, ethnic groups, gender, schools) and the parameters that characterize a group are fixed effects (i.e., a parameter describes each group's overall value, and these values are compared across the groups). Multilevel models are useful when the number of groups (or clusters such as classrooms) is relatively large (e.g., around 30 or so distinct units) and the parameters that characterize the groups can be treated as random effects (i.e., the parameter has a mean and a distribution across the groups and can now be predicted by other variables or distributions of other parameters). In this chapter, I walk through examples of growth curve models, as well as more general multilevel models, and then address the basics of general multilevel SEM models in the context of other longitudinal models. This chapter is not meant to be comprehensive, but it is reasonably thorough.

LONGITUDINAL GROWTH CURVE MODEL

One of the most popular multilevel models for longitudinal data designs is the latent growth curve model. In fact, its popularity is so strong that when the term *longitudinal model* is used, many people now think "growth curve model." As I mentioned, growth curve models are multilevel models because the repeated observations are nested within individuals. That is, each measurement occasion is clustered within each person. This clustering of observations can be represented as a panel model in which the question being addressed is just about the Level 2 associations. When a panel model is fit, the Level 1 part of the model is a simple saturated model at each time point (i.e., the scores for all individuals are characterized as a mean and a variance at each time point). Growth curve models, on the other hand, attempt to fit a nonsaturated (more parsimonious) model to the cross-time observations for each individual. This model is often a simple regression model to characterize the intercept and slope of change for each person.

A key characteristic of growth curve models (and any multilevel model, for that matter) is that these intercepts and slopes are characterized by a set of Level 2 equations used to examine (i.e., model, predict) the information contained in the mean and variances of the Level 1 intercept and slope parameters. These relationships can be seen pretty clearly when represented using the standard multilevel regression framework shown in Equation 8.1. Note that the scores have an i subscript to represent individuals and an o subscript to represent the occasions of measurement. The parameters of the longitudinal model that is fit to each individual (as depicted by the i subscript) are used to represent the changes over time (as depicted by the o

Equation 8.1. Basic multilevel equations for a growth curve model

Level 1: $y_{io} = \pi_{0i} + \pi_{1i}(time) + \varepsilon_{io}$

a) without a Level 2 predictor

Level 2: $\pi_{0i} = \gamma_{00} + \zeta_{0i}$

and, $\pi_{1i} = \gamma_{01} + \zeta_{1i}$

b) with a Level 2 predictor:

Level 2: $\pi_{0i} = \gamma_{00} + \gamma_{10}(male) + \zeta_{0i}$

and, $\pi_{1i} = \gamma_{01} + \gamma_{11}(male) + \zeta_{1i}$

- i refers to the individual.
- o refers to the occasions of measurement.
- y_{io} are the scores for each individual i at each occasion o.
- π_{0i} is intercept (0) for each individual i.
- π_{1i} is the regression slope (1) for each individual i as a function of measurement occasion (labeled "time").
- ε_{io} is the error in prediction for each individual i at each occasion o.
- γ_{00} is the intercept (0) of the Level 2 equation predicting the Level 1 intercepts (0).
- γ_{01} is the regression slope (1) for the intercepts (0) estimated at Level 1 as a function of gender (labeled "male" because male = 1 and female = 0).
- ζ_{0i} is the variance in the intercepts (0) for each individual i in A and the unexplained variance in B.
- γ_{01} is the intercept (0) for the Level 2 equation predicting the Level 1 slopes (1).
- γ_{11} is the regression slope (1) for the slopes (1) estimated at Level 2 as a function of gender.
- ζ_{1i} is the variance in the slopes (1) for each individual i in A and the unexplained variance in B.

subscript). Then the Level 2 equations are used to characterize these estimates at the level of the individual.

Before I delve into growth curve models, I do want to point out that panel models for longitudinal data have many merits and are still developing (Little, Preacher, Selig, & Card, 2007). And given the number of chapters that I have devoted to them, it should be clear that they are still the foundations and fundamental building blocks of all longitudinal models. Moreover, panel models are still useful because they ask and answer very important questions about change at the level of persons. They address questions related to the direction of influence in a change process, whether a variable can serve as a mediator of a change process, and fundamental questions related to the variances and correlations among a set of constructs. In panel models, therefore, the focus is solely on the individual-differences (between-person) stand-ings in the scores across persons. Panel models still account for the nested aspect of observations within individuals. More specifically, at each time point, the scores of the individual on the measured indicators are reproduced as scores on the latent factor. In panel models, because the latent factor has an estimated mean and vari-ance at each time point, the Level 1 part of the multilevel model is, as I mentioned already, saturated (no degrees of freedom remain). Because Level 1 is accounted for, the "music" happens at the Level 2 part of the model, when between-person differ-ences are examined.

In comparison with panel models, growth curve models ask and answer very different questions about change. Here, the focus is on intraindividual (within-per-son) change; each person typically has an intercept and slope parameter that char-acterizes his or her growth trend over the course of a study. Growth curve models address questions about the rate of change and the shape of change that characterizes a sample of persons. As I already indicated, the growth curve model characterizes the set of intercepts and slopes for all participants into a mean intercept with a dis-tribution of intercept values and a mean slope with a distribution of slope values.

Equation 8.1 is a basic multilevel regression model; Figure 8.1 is a basic manifest-variable growth curve model. I walk through both of these in this section. This basic manifest-variable growth curve model, which can be fit in the SEM framework, and

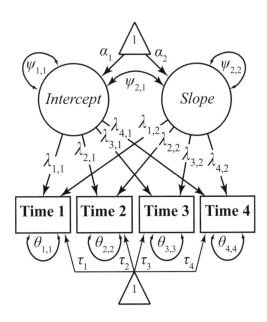

FIGURE 8.1. Parameters for a basic growth curve model in SEM. Many of these parameters must be fixed to set the scale for the other param-eters and to identify the model. The fixed values also define the meaning of the constructs.

the random-coefficient model, which can be fit in the multilevel regression framework, are identical models. The key differences between the two approaches are (1) how the data are organized and (2) the flexibility to add complexity to the overall model that is fit to the data. I want to distinguish between manifest-variable growth curve modeling and latent-variable growth curve modeling. At this point, I am referring to manifest-variable growth curve modeling. Later in this chapter, I discuss the latent-variable growth curve model, which is sometimes called the curve-of-factors model. The latent curve factors (i.e., the intercept and slope factors) are indicated by boxes or manifest variables in this current discussion, whereas in the curve-of-factors approach, the two latent curve factors are defined by latent factors, each of which has multiple indicators. Perhaps curve of boxes versus curve of circles would better clarify the two approaches. In the following, I mainly refer to the curve-of-boxes approach.

Regarding the data structure of the multilevel regression model versus the SEM curve-of-boxes approach, the growth curve model uses the "wide" format for organizing the data, whereas the multilevel regression approach utilizes the "tall" format. With the wide format, each variable at each occasion of measurement is represented as a separate column in the dataset. Variable names are uniquely specified to designate the variable and the time of measurement (e.g., Time 1, Time 2, Time 3). Conversely, in the tall format, each occasion of measurement is represented as a unique row in the dataset, and a variable is created to designate the occasion of measurement. Table 8.1 provides a visual of the differences in these two data formats using a hypothetical example of a single person measured on four occasions. As seen in the wide format of Table 8.1, each measurement occasion is a distinct variable and would be represented as a unique box in the SEM model that is fit to the data.

Continuing with a hypothetical four-time-point model in the SEM framework, Figure 8.1 depicts the possible parameters of a growth curve model. The possible parameters in Figure 8.1 are not yet identified, and many of them need to be fixed to specific values in order to ensure that the two constructs can be interpreted as an intercept and a slope. I rely on this figure throughout the discussion in order to clearly identify the specific parameter(s) to which I am referring.

TABLE 8.1. The tall format versus the wide format

Tall-formatted dataset				Wide-formatted dataset				
ID	Intercept	Time	y_{io}	ID	Time 1	Time 2	Time 3	Time 4
001	1	0	3.1	001	3.1	3.4	3.7	4.0
001	1	1	3.4					
001	1	2	3.7					
001	1	3	4.0					

Note. For the wide format, each observation (y_{io}) for a given person is in a separate column.

The graphic representation in Figure 8.1 does not yet map onto the Level 1 estimates that are depicted in Equation 8.1. In Figure 8.1, I labeled the first construct "intercept" and the second construct "slope." These two constructs will eventually reflect the estimated parameters π_{0i} and π_{1i}, once the loadings are properly specified. Importantly, the Level 1 equation of an SEM growth model is defined by how the loadings are specified. Unlike a common-factor model where the loadings are typically freely estimated parameters, the loadings in growth curve models are typically fixed at specific values so that the factors can be interpreted as an intercept and slope.

The key parameters of this model are the elements labeled α_1 and $\psi_{1,1}$ for the intercept construct and α_2 and $\psi_{2,2}$ for the slope construct. Here, α_1 is the mean intercept of the person-level regression; α_1 is the same as the γ_{00} parameter of the Level 2 equation depicted in Equation 8.1a; and $\psi_{1,1}$ is the variance around the mean intercept, which is the same as ζ_{0i} in Equation 8.1a. Figure 8.1 makes it explicit that the intercept factor covaries with the slope factor; this estimate is not explicitly shown in Equations 8.1a or 8.1b.

To help you understand the relationship between the loadings of the SEM growth model in Figure 8.1 and the Level 1 estimates depicted in Equation 8.1, I need to go into some detail about how the data are set up in a multilevel regression framework. The Level 1 model in Equation 8.1 contains a variable called "time." Time reflects the slope of change over the four measurement occasions in this example. In the tall formatted data file for this model, there are four rows of data for each individual (see Table 8.1). The variable time can be coded in many ways. One popular way to code the variable time is to set Occasion 1 to be 0, Occasion 2 to be 1, Occasion 3 to be 2, and Occasion 4 to be 3. This coding of time makes the interpretation of the parameters such that the intercept of the Level 1 equation is represented as the mean of the scores at Occasion 1, and the slope of the variable time is the change in y_{io} for each 1 unit change in time.

Following this coding convention, in row 1 for individual i in Table 8.1 the value of the intercept is a fixed value of 1.0 and the value of time (the variable that will index the slope of change) is 0, while the value of y_{io} is the observed score for individual i at Occasion 1. In Row 2 for this individual, the value of the intercept is again 1, but the value of time increments to 1 and the value of y_{io} is the observed score for individual i at Occasion 2. In Row 3, the value of the intercept is again 1, the time value increments to 2, and the value of y_{io} is the observed score for individual i at Occasion 3. In the fourth and final record for individual i, the value of the intercept is again 1, the time value increments to 3, and the value of y_{io} is the observed score for individual i at Occasion 4. When the scores of y_{io} are regressed onto the intercept constant and the time variable, the intercept does not vary and therefore captures the mean y_{io} score when the variable time is 0. This standard interpretation of the intercept from simple regression analysis applies to multilevel regression models and growth curve models equally. In simple and multilevel regression, the constant vector of 1 is contained in the intercept column of Table 8.1. This column of 1's is commonly implied (i.e., not explicitly shown) in the regression equation because it does not vary and always has the interpretation of being the mean of y when the predictor variable is 0.

In Figure 8.1, the intercept construct has four loadings labeled $\lambda_{1,1}$, $\lambda_{2,1}$, $\lambda_{3,1}$, and $\lambda_{4,1}$. In order to define the first construct as the intercept, the values for each of the lambdas must correspond to the values of the intercept when the data are in the tall format. Therefore, each of these four lambdas would receive a fixed value of 1.0. Similarly, the slope construct has four loadings labeled $\lambda_{1,2}$, $\lambda_{2,2}$, $\lambda_{3,2}$, and $\lambda_{4,2}$. In order to define this construct as the slope, the values for each of the lambdas must correspond to the values of the time variable when the data are in the tall format. Therefore, $\lambda_{1,2}$ would be fixed to 0, $\lambda_{2,2}$ would be fixed to 1, $\lambda_{3,2}$ would be fixed to 2, and $\lambda_{4,2}$ would be fixed to 3. With these loadings fixed in this way, the parameter estimates of the multilevel regression shown in Equation 8.1a and the parameter estimates of this SEM growth curve model would be identical. In Figure 8.1, I have also added the tau parameters (τ_1 through τ_4). These parameters would be interpreted as the means of the residual variance. Because the mean of a residual is necessarily 0, these four parameters are fixed at 0 and not involved in the equations that define the intercept and slope constructs.

In both multilevel regression modeling and growth curve modeling, the fit of this linear growth curve model is typically contrasted with the so-called unconditional model. The model is called unconditional because it does not force the slope of change across the measurement occasions to be a strict linear function. The shape of the growth curve over time is simply estimated as parameters of the model. In Figure 8.2, I have depicted the SEM version of two potential unconditional models. In the SEM growth curve modeling world, the unconditional growth model is often referred to as the *level and shape* model. Thus, I have renamed the constructs for the unconditional growth models in Figure 8.2 to be *level* and *shape*. In the unconditional model, one of the lambda parameters of the shape construct must be fixed to 0, and one of them must be fixed to a nonzero value. Usually, a value of 1 is used, because it has inherent meaning and simple mathematical properties that make it preferred over most other nonzero values.

To be consistent with the intercept and slope model I just described, I fixed $\lambda_{1,2}$ to be 0. Fixing this loading to 0 makes the interpretation of the intercept to be again the mean of the scores at the first measurement occasion. Now, using 1 as the scaling value, I fixed $\lambda_{4,2}$ to 1 in Figure 8.2A, and I fixed $\lambda_{2,2}$ to 1 in Figure 8.2B (technically speaking, I could also choose to fix $\lambda_{3,2}$ to 1). Variants A and B in Figure 8.2 are about equally common. At this point in the discussion, I assume that all participants are measured at the same time and thus the scores are balanced with regard to the measurement occasions. Later, I discuss a few options when the scores are gathered at different intervals for different persons.

To illustrate what I am describing, it's useful to pull up a data example. I return

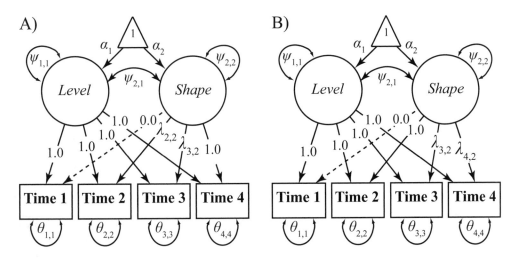

FIGURE 8.2. Two common specifications of an unconditional level and shape model. The numbers on the loadings are fixed parameters that define the meaning of the constructs, as well as set the scale, and allow identification of the estimated parameters. The Greek labels are the estimated parameters of a level and shape model. In A, the scale of the Shape factor is the total amount of change between Time 1 and Time 4; in B, the scale of the Shape factor is the amount of change between Time 1 and Time 2. The correlation between the level and shape constructs is not affected by the scale setting choice; however, means and variances of the shape construct will vary depending on how the scale is set.

to the concept of affect to illustrate these models. Table 8.2 contains data from four times of measurement for negative affect. These means clearly show a downward trend over the four occasions.

The results of fitting the two unconstrained growth curve models shown in Figure 8.2 are presented in Figure 8.3A and B. In Figure 8.3A, the interpretation of the parameters depends on the amount of change that has taken place between Time 1 and Time 4. In Figure 8.3B, the interpretation of the parameters depends on the amount of change that has taken place between Time 1 and Time 2. The parameters in Figure 8.3A are interpreted in terms of the total change across the four measurement occasions. In Figure 8.3B, the interpretation of the parameters is in terms of the amount of change from Time 1 to Time 2.

TABLE 8.2. Means and standard deviations for negative affect

	Time 1	Time 2	Time 3	Time 4
Mean	2.08	2.00	1.89	1.78
STD	0.79	0.72	0.65	0.63

Note. n = 1684.

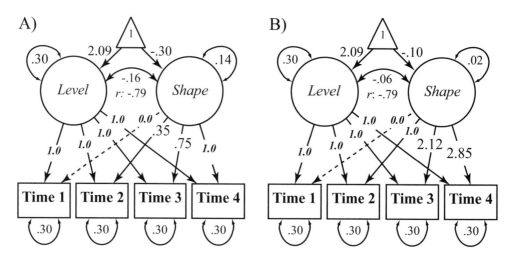

FIGURE 8.3. Results from fitting these models to the negative affect data. The italicized numbers are fixed values. Model fit for both models is identical and quite good, with $\chi^2_{(n=1684,\ 6)} = 29.60$, RMSEA = $.048_{(.031;\ .067)}$, TLI/NNFI = .980, CFI = .980.

Notice that the residual of each indicator at each time point is exactly the same value. I specified these models with equality constraints on these residuals. This constraint is sometimes described as enforcing the assumption of stationarity of the residuals. The need for and behavior of this constraint has not been examined in a detailed or systematic fashion (at least as far as I am aware at the time of this writing). I find that the constraint does help with model estimation and that the parameters of the model are more stable when I fit growth curves to manifest indicators, as I am doing here. I do find it somewhat dissatisfying because the constraint is rather strict in that it forces both the reliable unexplained variance in the indicators plus the degree of unreliability at each time point to be exactly equal over time. A little later in this chapter, I fit this same model to latent constructs of this negative affect variable at each time point. In a multivariate latent-variable growth curve model (the curve-of-circles or curve-of-factors idea), the constraint of stationarity for the variance in the constructs not explained by the level and shape constructs is more reasonable because error variance is disentangled from unexplained variance related to the growth curve representation.

Fundamentally, growth curve models are models for the mean structures; they are not particularly well suited to represent the covariance structures. I return to this idea later. For now I want to focus on how the means are reproduced. I presented the equation for the mean structures earlier. The equation was the tau estimate of the indicator plus its lambda loading multiplied by the latent-variable mean. Looking at the values shown in Figure 8.3, I can simply calculate the means that are estimated for each of the four times of measurement. Table 8.3 provides the side-by-side calculations for both Figures 8.3A and 8.3B. Both models reproduce the observed means

TABLE 8.3. How the means are reproduced: Unconstrained models

	From Model 8.3A						From Model 8.3B					
	Level		Shape				Level		Shape			
$\overline{X} \approx \tau_n +$	$\lambda_{n,1}$	A_1	$+ \lambda_{n,2}$	A_2	$=$	μ	$\overline{X} \approx \tau_n +$	$\lambda_{n,1}$ A_1		$+ \lambda_{n,2}$	A_2	$=$	μ
2.08 0	1	2.09	0	-.30		2.09	2.08 0	1	2.09	0	-.10	2.09
2.00 0	1	2.09	.35	-.30		1.99	2.00 0	1	2.09	1	-.10	1.99
1.89 0	1	2.09	.75	-.30		1.87	1.89 0	1	2.09	2.12	-.10	1.88
1.78 0	1	2.09	1	-.30		1.79	1.78 0	1	2.09	2.85	-.10	1.80

Note. n refers to the indicator numbers 1–4, respectively. Table values are based on two decimals. Calculations done with full precision give identical results.

with the same degree of fidelity, and both models give the exact same estimated value of the model-implied means. Both models are isomorphic in every respect with the exception of the scaling constraint. Note that in Table 8.3, the values are not exactly identical; this lack of precision occurs because I used the two decimals that are subject to rounding error in calculating the values. Using full precision (typically five or more significant digits), the values are exactly the same.

In Figure 8.3A, the constraint that sets the scale is the fixed 1.0 for $\lambda_{4,2}$, whereas in Figure 8.3B the constraint that sets the scale is the fixed 1.0 for $\lambda_{2,2}$ (see Figure 8.1 for the parameter labels). In the standardized metric, the implied correlation between the level and shape constructs is identical. Also, the model fit of both versions is identical, which supports the idea that the model-implied values from both models are identical when rounding error is not in play. In this example, scaling only influences the interpretation of the parameters. In Figure 8.3A, the .35 and .75 that were estimated for $\lambda_{2,2}$ and $\lambda_{3,2}$ are interpreted as the proportion of the total change between Time 1 and Time 4. In other words, at Time 2, 35% of the total change had occurred, and at Time 2, 75% of the total change had occurred. In Figure 8.3B, the 2.12 and 2.85 that were estimated for $\lambda_{3,2}$ and $\lambda_{4,2}$ are interpreted as a multiplicative of the amount of change from Time 1 to Time 2. In other words, at Time 3, the amount of change was 2.12 times more than the change from Time 1 to Time 2, and at Time 4 the amount of change was 2.85 times more than the change from Time 1 to Time 2. These loadings are also often referred to as the basis weights. In this regard, they form the basis by which the shape factor is determined and the means at the different time points are reproduced.

Typically, after fitting the unconstrained model, a model is then specified that tests the nature of the change function. For this example, I focus only on the test of a linear function and work through a number of different ways that the linear function can be estimated. These variations in how the linear function can be specified do *not* have implications for determining the adequacy of the linear trend (i.e., Is the linear trend significantly different from the unconstrained model?). Each model gives the exact same model fit; only the meaning and interpretation of the parameters are affected. In other words, the models are isomorphic with regard to model fit but divergent in terms of the story that many of the model parameters would tell.

A number of coding schemes for a linear trend can be used. The important feature to keep in mind is that *the intercept is defined by the location of the 0 in the specification of the slope factor*. This idea is exactly the same as a standard regression in that the intercept is the mean of the dependent variable when the predictor is 0. In SEM, many different coding schemes are possible. The most common, of course, is to follow the typical regression framework and choose Time 1 to be 0 for the slope construct so that the intercept is defined as the mean at Time 1. Some authors have advocated centering the predictor so that the intercept would be the standing of the individuals at the midpoint of the time span assessed. Centered orthogonal contrast codes from a standard ANOVA framework are often used in this context. In Table 8.4, I have listed two sets of contrast codes. I discuss the quadratic and cubic values, as well as "Time 1 as intercept contrast codes," later in this chapter when I discuss fitting some nonlinear trends. For this example, I can use the "$t = 4$" linear codes to center the slope and define the intercept as the midpoint of the time span covered.

All of the coding schemes that I discuss at this point assume that the measurement occasions are separated by the same amount of time (i.e., equal intervals between occasions). If the occasions of measurement are not equidistant, then the codes need to be modified and adapted to reflect the true time gap in the measurement occasions. For example, if a scheduled fourth measurement occasion were postponed for some reason and delayed by the same length of time that separated the earlier measurement occasions, I could use the five-time-point codes but omit the fourth time point. The linear slope could then be coded 0, 1, 2, and 4. Or if the missed occasion were delayed by 3 months but the other intervals were 6 months apart, I could code the change in units of months: 0, 6, 12, and 21. As mentioned, for these basic growth models to work properly, all participants need to be assessed at the same intervals. Mehta and West (2000) discuss the bias that occurs when different intervals for different individuals are used. More complex models, however, are

TABLE 8.4. Different contrast codes for slopes with 4–6 time points

Centered intercept contrast codes									Time 1 as intercept contrast codes								
$t = 4$			$t = 5$			$t = 6$			$t = 4$			$t = 5$			$t = 6$		
Ln	Qd	Cb	Ln	Qd	Cb	Ln	Qd	Cb	Ln	Qd	Cb	Ln	Qd	Cb	Ln	Qd	Cb
-3	1	3	-2	2	-1	-5	5	-5	0	1	3	0	2	-1.2	0	3.3	-3.0
-1	-1	-3	-1	-1	2	-3	-1	7	1	-1	-3	1	-1	2.4	1	-0.6	4.2
1	-1	3	0	-2	0	-1	-4	4	2	-1	3	2	-2	0	2	-2.6	2.4
3	1	-3	1	-1	-2	1	-4	-4	3	1	-3	3	-1	-2.4	3	-2.6	-2.4
			2	2	1	3	-1	-7				4	2	1.2	4	-0.6	-4.2
						5	5	5							5	3.3	3.0

Note. t = number of time points for the slope construct. Ln = linear trend, Qd = quadratic trend, Cb = cubic trend.

possible when individuals are measured at different intervals (see Mehta & West, 2000, for some examples).

Like the scaling constraint for the unconstrained model, how the linear trend is specified does not affect model fit. It only influences the interpretation of the parameters. In some circumstances, however, this impact on the interpretation of the model parameters can have a dramatic impact on the conclusions (see Biesanz, Deeb-Sossa, Papadakis, Bollen, & Curran, 2004). The potential for this dramatic impact can already be seen in the four different models that I present in Figure 8.4.

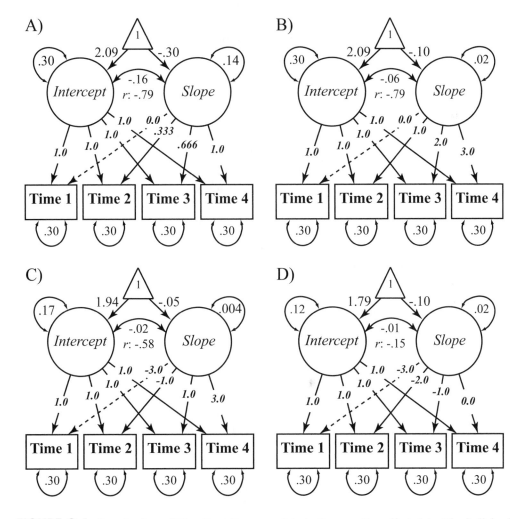

FIGURE 8.4. Results from fitting these linear models to the negative affect data. The italicized numbers are fixed values. Model fit for all four models is identical and quite good, with $\chi^2_{(n=1684, 8)}$ = 32.65, RMSEA = .043$_{(.028; .059)}$, TLI/NNFI = .984, CFI = .981. The correlation between the level and shape constructs changes depending on the definition of the intercept. In A and B, the intercept is the level at Time 1; in C, the intercept is the level at Time 2.5; and in D, the intercept is the level at Time 4.

The mean structures are reproduced by the decomposition from the two growth factors. Because there are an infinite number of codes that can be used to locate the 0 for a linear trend, there are an infinite number of equivalent fitting models that can be fit to a simple linear growth trend. The intercept will vary in each solution to be the mean and distribution of individual differences at the point at which the linear trend is 0. I can make 0 be outside the time frame of the data collection, but this placement of the intercept would usually be nonsensical from a theoretical standpoint. On the other hand, one might have a good reason to put the intercept at a developmentally meaningful reference age, even though no data are collected at that age. For example, data collected at 12, 18, 24, and 36 months on some measures of growth and development might want to locate the 0 at birth. Here, defining the slope basis values (loadings) as 12, 18, 24, and 36 would make the intercept be the implied individual-differences standings at birth.

Table 8.5 shows the identical values that emerge for the model-implied means regardless of how the parameters for the basis loadings are specified. Again, because of the two-decimal precision I am using, there's the potential that the values wouldn't be exactly equal due solely to rounding error. With appropriate precision the model-implied means are identical, and in this case they are identical to two decimal places. Even though the correlation between the two constructs shifts depending on where the distributions are located, the overall mean trend is reproduced to the same degree because the model-implied means are the combination of the means estimated for both constructs (i.e., the mean of the intercept plus the mean of the slope).

Regarding Figure 8.4 and the covariance decompositions, notice particularly that the implied correlation between the intercept and slope factor changes depending

TABLE 8.5. How the means are reproduced: Linear trend models

From Model 8.4A							From Model 8.4B						
		Intercept		Slope					Intercept		Slope		
$\overline{X}$	$\approx \tau_n +$	$\lambda_{n,1}$	A_1	$+ \lambda_{n,2}$	A_2	$= \mu$	$\overline{X}$	$\approx \tau_n +$	$\lambda_{n,1}$	A_1	$+ \lambda_{n,2}$	A_2	$= \mu$
2.08	0	1	2.09	0	-.30	2.09	2.08	0	1	2.09	0	-.10	2.09
2.00	0	1	2.09	.33	-.30	1.99	2.00	0	1	2.09	1	-.10	1.99
1.89	0	1	2.09	.66	-.30	1.89	1.89	0	1	2.09	2	-.10	1.89
1.78	0	1	2.09	1	-.30	1.79	1.78	0	1	2.09	3	-.10	1.79

From Model 8.4C							From Model 8.4D						
		Intercept		Slope					Intercept		Slope		
$\overline{X}$	$\approx \tau_n +$	$\lambda_{n,1}$	A_1	$+ \lambda_{n,2}$	A_2	$= \mu$	$\overline{X}$	$\approx \tau_n +$	$\lambda_{n,1}$	A_1	$+ \lambda_{n,2}$	A_2	$= \mu$
2.08	0	1	1.94	-3	-.05	2.09	2.08	0	1	1.79	-3	-.10	2.09
2.00	0	1	1.94	-1	-.05	1.99	2.00	0	1	1.79	-2	-.10	1.99
1.89	0	1	1.94	1	-.05	1.89	1.89	0	1	1.79	-1	-.10	1.89
1.78	0	1	1.94	3	-.05	1.79	1.78	0	1	1.79	0	-.10	1.79

Note. n refers to the indicator numbers 1–4, respectively. Table values are based on two decimals. Calculations done with full precision would give identical results for each model.

upon where in this dynamic change process the intercept is located. When the intercept is defined as Time 1 (as in Figure 8.4A and 8.4B), the implied correlation is –.79. When the orthogonal contrast codes are used to center the intercept at the midpoint of the change process, the implied correlation is –.57. If I desire to define the intercept as the last time point, then the implied correlation between the two constructs is –.15. In fact, for the sake of completeness, if I picked Time 2 as the location for the intercept, the correlation would be –.67, and if I used Time 3 for the intercept, the correlation would be –.46.

These differences in the slopes' coding change the magnitude of the correlation between the intercept and slope constructs, but they generally do not change the sign. I have not yet run across an example where the sign has changed; only the magnitudes have been affected. The susceptibility of the correlation between intercept and slope to change depending on how the parameters of the model are specified means that the distributions of the intercept and slope factor will also vary depending on how the parameters are specified. This type of moving target has direct implications for theories that try to predict the individual-differences standing in the intercept or the individual-differences standing in the slope. The theory must be well enough developed to state which intercept distribution and which slope distribution are directly relevant to the question at hand. An unscrupulous researcher could try all combinations until a desired outcome emerges. A scrupulous researcher would have a clear set of distributions in mind. Some researchers have argued that the parameters of the model should be set so that the correlation between intercept and slope is at its smallest value (e.g., Hancock & Choi, 2006). For more exploratory applications of these kinds of models, this advice is not problematic. Theory, however, should trump any one-size-fits-all advice on how to model data.

Regardless of the magnitude, the interpretation of a correlation between an intercept and a slope construct is particularly tricky to get used to. In most applications of statistics, the distribution of numbers is either centered at 0 or is a distribution of positive numbers. In these situations, we have a good idea of how to interpret a correlation. In growth curve models, the slope factor often will have a negative mean. When the mean of a distribution is negative, the interpretation of a correlation can get muddied. I created Figure 8.5 many years ago to help me and others understand this problem. I have a stylized distribution of the intercept with a positive mean of 1.5; I have also marked 1 standard deviation above the mean as 1.9 and 1 standard deviation below the mean as 1.1. I have put two slopes, one with a positive mean of 0.3 and lines reflecting 1 standard deviation above the mean (0.5) and 1 standard deviation below the mean (0.1). I also have a second slope distribution with a negative mean of –0.3 and two lines reflecting 1 standard deviation above the mean (–0.1) and 1 standard deviation below the mean (–0.5). A negative correlation between the intercept and slope in the current example with a decreasing trend for negative affect would be interpreted as magnitudes of a decreasing trend. That is, scores of persons higher in negative affect at the start of the period would decrease more in the

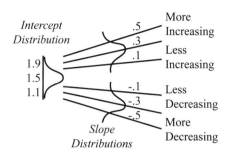

FIGURE 8.5. Interpreting a negative correlation in growth models. With a negative *r*, high scores go with low scores. With a positive slope, .1 is lower than .5, but, with a negative slope, –.5 is lower than –.1.

slope distribution; scores of persons lower in initial negative affect standing would decrease less in the change distribution.

A negative correlation between intercept and slope is very common when the scale of measurement is a closed-ended Likert-type scale and the items are worded in terms of characteristics, attitudes, behaviors, and so forth. For example, if a person reported a 4 on the 1–4 scale for negative affect at time 1, there'd be no option for this person to report greater negative affect at later time points. He or she could report only the same level of negative affect. Similarly, if a person reported a 1 on negative affect at Time 1, he or she would be unable to report a decrease in affect. A scale of this nature would be sensitive only to persons who had decreasing affect and who started in the upper portion of the distribution. Similarly, the scale would be sensitive to persons who showed increasing affect who started in the lower part of the distribution.

This negative correlation, which is an artifact of the scaling methods, can be remedied by developing change-sensitive measures. For example, if data are collected via computer, each person's Time 1 response can be displayed, and the question can then become "How much has your negative affect changed since this last recorded score?" Potential response options could be something like "down a lot," "down a little," "no change," "up a little," and "up a lot." At the next time point, the implied new level of affect can be displayed, and the questions about how much has changed could be asked again. Variables that have unlimited values or that are not readily bounded can easily lead to positive correlations between intercept and slope. For example, in a study of infant–youth language development, the number of words in a child's vocabulary at the beginning of a study may be positively associated with the rate at which his or her vocabulary increases over time—a "rich get richer" phenomenon with regard to vocabulary size.

MULTIVARIATE GROWTH CURVE MODELS

The previous discussion of growth curves focused on the very simple univariate manifest-variable approach—that is, a single variable measured with a single indicator at the different time points—the curve-of-boxes approach. Although these kinds of growth models are popular, they lose many of the advantages that a multiple-indicator latent-variable approach would provide. The manifest-variable approach still gives two latent constructs (i.e., the intercept and the slope) because the manifest indicators each have an estimated residual. Hence, many authors will describe this type of model as a latent-variable growth curve model. The curve-of-circles approach, on the other hand, involves specifying a traditional longitudinal panel model with multiple indicators of the constructs at each time point. With this starting point, key assumptions can be tested as part of the modeling process. For instance, the curve-of-boxes approach assumes factorial invariance. The curve-of-circles approach tests the assumption of invariance. If strong invariance holds, then the growth curve model can be specified on top of the panel model data. In addition, the residual variances of the boxes in the curve-of-boxes approach are the sum of two sources of information: the truly random noise and the reliable but unexplained portions that are specific to each time point. In the curve-of-circles approach, the unexplained variance can be decomposed more cleanly into variance that is unexplained by the intercept and slope factors and variance in the indicators that is unexplained by the lower order constructs at each time point.

Figure 8.6 provides a full graphical representation of a curve-of-circles growth curve model. Each lower order construct is indicated by three parceled indicators of negative affect. To fit the growth curve constructs, strong factorial invariance must be specified (and supported based on model fit). In addition, the residuals of each indicator are allowed to be freely estimated at each time point, and the residual correlations among the corresponding indicators are allowed to be estimated (as is typical of a panel model). The lower order constructs thereby represent the reliable variance among the indictors. The "trick" to fitting this kind of growth model is to use the effects coded method of identification. This method (and only this method) provides a nonarbitrary metric for the constructs. This nonarbitrary metric allows the growth curve parameters to be estimated in exactly the same metric as the manifest-variable growth curve approach.

In looking at these results, there are a few notable features. First, the parameter estimates that define the intercept and slope factors are nearly identical to the curve-of-boxes version that I presented in Figure 8.4B. This outcome is solely a feature (and a nice one at that) of the effects coded method of identification. Only this identification method keeps the integrity of the scale of the mean-level information intact such that the latent mean of the intercept remains 2.08 and the mean of the slope remains −0.10. Also notice that the correlation between the two factors remains -.79.

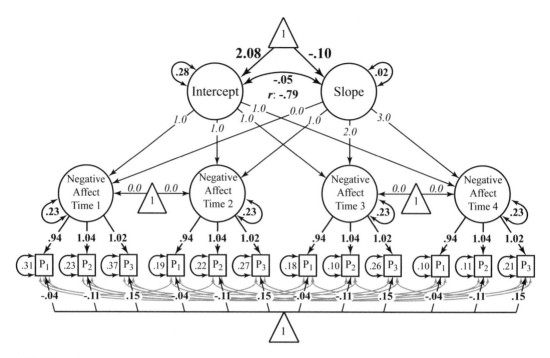

FIGURE 8.6. A multivariate growth model: The curve-of-factors model. Values in italics are fixed parameters (e.g., the means of the lower order constructs are fixed at 0). Strong factorial invariance is specified using the effects coded method of identification, which allows the same metric for the manifest-variable growth curve models. The residual variances among the corresponding indicators over time are allowed to associate. $\chi^2_{(n=1684, 50)} = 391.76$, RMSEA = .063$_{(.057;\ .069)}$, TLI/NNFI = .970, CFI = .950.

The fact that the correlation remains the same is not related to the method of scale setting. Any method of setting the lower order constructs would produce the same correlation among the growth constructs (as long as the 0 point of the slope is in the same location).

One of the reasons that the curve-of-circles/factors and the curve-of-boxes models produced essentially the same results for the intercept and slope factors has to do with the nature of this particular dataset (and the method of scale setting). The consistency in these data is related to the fact that the parceled indicators used in this model are essentially tau-equivalent. Congeneric indicators could produce slightly different results, and only the curve-of-circles/factors approach would yield a correct solution in the congeneric case. The reason for this potential difference in results is that, in addition to assuming factorial invariance over time, the curve-of-boxes approach assumes essential tau-equivalence of the indicators that are averaged to represent the observed scores at each time point. If the indicators are congeneric, taking their average is not easily justified.

The model presented in Figure 8.6 does not make these assumptions. Factorial invariance is explicitly tested (and a minimum of partial strong invariance is required to proceed with the growth modeling). The indicators of the lower order constructs can also be essentially congeneric and still provide meaningful mean-level information to inform the interpretation of the growth factors. Another feature of the model in Figure 8.6 is that it explicitly disentangles the measurement error from the reliable construct variance. The constraint of stationarity on the latent construct residual variances is now reasonable to assess and can be explicitly tested as a χ^2 difference test. Because this model has (1) many degrees of freedom and (2) a well-defined measurement model, the constraint of stationarity is not typically needed to ensure that the growth curve constructs' parameters can be estimated. With manifest variables, the estimation process is sometimes not as stable, and the stationarity constraint is often needed just to get the model to converge and provide estimates that are not out of bounds.

The last notable feature of Figure 8.6 is that the means of the lower order constructs are fixed at 0. The effects coding constraints on the indicators' intercepts transfer the mean-level information about the constructs to the first-order level. Fixing the means of the first-order constructs to 0 results in the transfer of the mean-level information about the constructs to the intercept and slope constructs. Recall that growth curve models are fundamentally models about the means structures. They use the covariance structures information to determine the variance of the intercept, the variance of the slope, and the covariance between the two constructs. All the other types of models that I have presented are models that are explicitly about the covariance structures. In this regard, model fit with growth curve models is a bit of a hit-or-miss proposition. After the CFA model is fit to the data and one is confident in the fit of the model as a covariance structures panel model, converting the parameters to a growth curve model can lead to a significant drop in model fit (see Table 8.6 and, later, Table 8.8). Unfortunately, the necessary and allowable parameters of a traditional growth curve model are highly circumscribed. Thus, there typically aren't additional parameter estimates that can be added to improve model fit if the unconditional model yields poor model fit.

Table 8.6 provides the complete picture of what is gained using a curve-of-circles/factors approach. First, the tests for configural invariance through strong factorial invariance are shown as explicit steps, and the results clearly support strong invariance. Then the unconditional growth model is specified. Note that I have put *n/a* (*not applicable*) under the "pass" column. The unconditional growth model is what it is—it is the best fitting and least parsimonious growth model. It provides the baseline model fit information for evaluating other questions, such as the question of stationarity of the unexplained variance in the first-order constructs. The results in Table 8.6 indicate that stationarity is tenable. From this model, I can now test whether the trend is linear by fixing the basis loadings to 0, 1, 2, or 3 (or some other linear function). As shown in Table 8.6, the test of the linear trend demonstrates that the growth trend is optimally characterized as a linear function.

The curve-of-circles/factors model can be further expanded to examine the

TABLE 8.6. Fit information for the multivariate latent growth curve model (Figure 8.6)

Model tested	χ^2	df	$\Delta\chi^2$	Δdf	p	RMSEA	RMSEA 90% CI	CFI	ΔCFI	Pass?
Null model	11608.8	84				---	---			---
Configural invariance	168.38	30				.052	.044;.060	.988		Yes
Weak invariance	202.65	36				.052	.045;.059	.986	.002	Yes
Strong invariance	324.06	42				.067	.061;.074	.976	.010	Yes
Unconditional LGC	386.34	45	62.27	3	<.001	.066	.060;.072	.970	.006	n/a
+ stationarity	389.98	48	3.64	3	.30	.064	.058;.070	.970	.000	Yes
Linear LGC	391.76	50	1.78	2	.41	.063	.057;.069	.970	.000	Yes

Note. For the measurement model tests of invariance, a change in CFI of .01 or less is used. The criterion for determining too much loss in fit in the latent space, given the power of the sample size, would normally be a *p*-value less than .001 or a change in CFI greater than .002. In the case of the unconditional latent growth curve model (LGC), no other changes can be made to achieve better model fit; thus, the loss in fit idea is not applicable when going from the strong invariance model to the unconditional LGC model.

growth relationships between two constructs. Recall from Chapter 6 that I introduced Espelage's data on the associations among bullying and homophobic teasing. In Figure 8.7, I display the unconditional level and shape representations among these two constructs. In Chapter 6, I demonstrated that the constructs are strong factorially invariant across the five time points. Because strong invariance holds, fitting a level and shape model on top of each set of lower order constructs is fully warranted. In Figure 8.7, the lower order constructs are labeled B_1–B_5 for bullying measured at Time 1–Time 5, respectively. Homophobic teasing lower order constructs are labeled H_1–H_5.

Recall that to scale the growth constructs so that they are in the metric of the observed variables, the effects coded method of identification needs to be employed. I have used this method for the estimates in Figure 8.7. The loadings, residuals, and intercepts of the measurement model are not shown in Figure 8.7 because the figure would become unwieldy. This information is displayed in Table 8.7 in the form of the common (invariant) set of unstandardized loadings, the common (invariant) set of unstandardized intercepts, and the total explained variance in each of the indicators at each of the five measurement occasions. Notice that because of the effects coding scaling constraint, the unstandardized loadings average 1.0 and the intercepts average 0. Also notice that the amount of variance explained in the indicators at all times of measurement are quite good and consistent across each occasion.

For the model in Figure 8.7, I also added a set of phantom constructs so that I could represent the variance–covariance information among the level and shape constructs as latent standard deviations and latent correlations. These estimated correlations are the same as one would get from requesting the standardized solution. Recall that the standardized solution is a postestimation transformation of the parameter estimates. Fitting the model with phantom constructs allows me to estimate the correlations as parameters of the model and to obtain correct standard

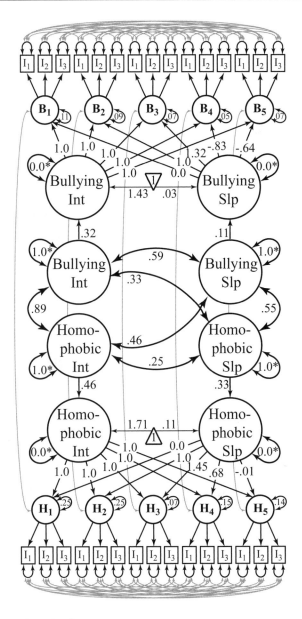

FIGURE 8.7. A multivariate growth model: Two curves of factors. The within-time cross-construct covariance estimates are: .11, .06, .03, .03, and .05 for Times 1–5, respectively. Model fit is: $\chi^2_{(n=1132,\ 362)} = 1330.80$, RMSEA = $.048_{(.045;\ .051)}$, CFI = .967, TLI/NNFI = .955.

TABLE 8.7. Unstandardized loadings and intercepts and communality for the indicators in the dual curves-of-factors model in Figure 8.7

	λ	τ	Communality (variance explained)				
			Time 1	Time 2	Time 3	Time 4	Time 5
Bullying 1	.865	.147	.718	.712	.751	.667	.735
Bullying 2	1.122	-.111	.833	.794	.796	.821	.782
Bullying 3	1.013	-.036	.809	.757	.777	.739	.809
HmPhTs 1	1.033	-.064	.769	.711	.738	.794	.757
HmPhTs 2	.942	-.005	.849	.747	.778	.766	.728
HmPhTs 3	1.026	.069	.591	.559	.537	.567	.470

Note. HmPhTs = Homophobic teasing. Indicators of the constructs are parceled items. λ = the unstandardized loading and τ = the unstandardized intercept from the strong invariant model.

errors for these parameter estimates. It will also allow me to do some dependent-samples tests of the differences between sets of correlations, which I demonstrate shortly.

As noted in Figure 8.7, the model fit for this particular dual growth model is quite good, with an RMSEA of .048, a CFI of 0.990, and a TLI/NNFI of 0.998. A number of features of this model warrant discussion. First, and quite commonly, when you're fitting a model with two or more constructs, the corresponding constructs at each occasion of measurement will have some residual correlation. The variance in bullying at Time 1 that is not explained by the intercept and slope factors covaries with the variance in homophobic teasing at Time 1 that is not explained by its intercept and slope factors. A significant residual correlation emerged at each corresponding time point. The estimated covariances were .11, .06, .03, .03, and .05, respectively. These correlated residuals were critical for this model because when they were not estimated their omission produced biased estimates of the correlations among the intercept and slope constructs. The two intercept constructs had an out-of-bounds correlation of over 1.0, as did the two constructs representing the slopes. The model was attempting to reproduce these time-specific correlations by inflating the correlations between the respective growth curve constructs. In addition, inspection of the modification indices strongly suggested that time-specific residual correlations were warranted. The difference in model fit between not estimating these time-specific associations and including them was pronounced, $\Delta\chi^2_{(n=1132, 5)} = 613.40$ (see Table 8.8).

I also tested the stationarity of the residuals for these two growth curves. As noted in Table 8.8, the stationarity assumption did not hold for these data, which is fine. It just means that the unexplained variances in the constructs at the various time points are not equal. Unequal variances suggest that other time-varying factors (e.g., context influences) are affecting the constructs.

TABLE 8.8. Fit information for the dual multivariate latent growth curve models (i.e., Figure 8.7, Figure 8.8, Table 8.9)

Model tested	χ^2	df	$\Delta\chi^2$	Δdf	p	RMSEA	RMSEA 90% CI	CFI	ΔCFI	Pass?
Null model	29518.2	483				---	---			---
Configural invariance	886.50	300				.052	.044;.060	.980		Yes
Weak invariance	1023.22	316				.043	.040;.046	.976	.004	Yes
Strong invariance	1145.83	332				.045	.042;.048	.972	.004	Yes
Unconditional LGC	1330.80	362			<.001	.048	.045;.051	.967	.005	n/a
+ correlated resids?	1944.20	367	613.4	5	<.001	.062	.059;.064	.946	.021	No
+ stationarity?	1465.10	370	134.3	8	<.001	.051	.048;.054	.962	.004	No
Linear	2263.51	381	1117.1	49	<.001	.067	.065;.070	.935	.037	No
Quadratic	1596.71	360	450.9	28	<.001	.054	.051;.057	.957	.015	No
Cubic	1184.94	338	39.1	6	<.001	.045	.042;.048	.971	.001	No
Final polynomial	1352.01	355	206.2	23	<.001	.048	.045;.051	.966	.006	Yes
ALT model	1228.65	355	82.8	23	<.001	.046	.043;.048	.970	.002	Yes

Note. For the measurement model tests of invariance, a change in CFI of .01 or less is used. The criterion for determining too much loss in fit in the latent space, given the power of the sample size, would normally be a *p*-value less than .001 or a change in CFI greater than .002. In the case of the unconditional LGC model, no other changes can be made to achieve better model fit; thus, the loss in fit idea is not applicable when going from the strong invariance model to the unconditional LGC model.

The model-implied growth trends from these dual level and shape models are plotted in Figure 8.8. I have also plotted the upper and lower 95% interval for the distribution of individual differences around this mean-level trend. To plot the 95% interval, I multiplied the estimated latent standard deviations from the phantom constructs by 1.96 and added this to the mean to get the upper trend line, then I subtracted this value from the mean to get the lower trend line. When phantom constructs are used, the variance and covariances of the lower order constructs are decomposed into their respective standard deviations and correlations, so these values are easy to obtain.

The correlations among the level and shape constructs tell a dynamic story. First, at the start of the study, where I have located the intercept, bullying and homophobic teasing are strongly linked, with nearly 80% of the reliable variance overlapping. The two intercepts are both positively correlated with their respective slope factors. These positive correlations indicate that those higher in bullying and homophobic teasing increased more in their behaviors than those who were lower in bullying and homophobic teasing. Finally, the individual differences in the slope of bullying are dynamically linked with individual differences in the changes over time for homophobic teasing, with a positive correlation of .55. This positive correlation between the respective slopes shows that over the span of the study, the changes in these two constructs are linked. What the growth curve model cannot address, however, is whether there is a lead-lag relationship among the two constructs. From the panel model of Figure 6.7 (see Chapter 6), the data clearly indicate that prior levels of bullying positively influence changes in homophobic teasing, but the converse is not

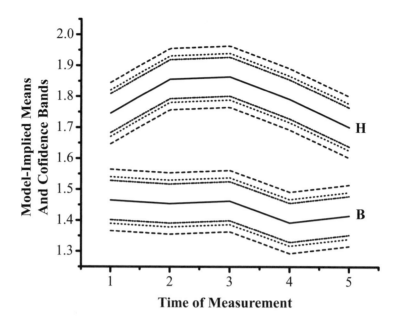

FIGURE 8.8. Plot of model-implied means for bullying (bottom) and homophobic teasing (top). B = mean of bullying, H = mean of homophobic teasing. The solid lines are means, the short dotted lines are the 90% confidence bands, the regular dotted lines are the 95% confidence bands, and the dashed lines are the 99% confidence bands.

the case. Bullying leads to changes in homophobic teasing (and not the other way around) in this sample of adolescents.

The plot of the trends in Figure 8.8 indicates that the trajectories of these two constructs are nonlinear in nature. Although it is not well justified in all instances, a common approach to modeling nonlinear trends in growth curve models is to use the polynomial contrast codes that are depicted in Table 8.4. The model fit information for testing the nature of these slopes is presented in Table 8.8. Imposing linearity on both trends leads to a dramatic loss in fit. The difference tests listed in Table 8.8 are relative to the strong invariance model. The linear trend is nested within the unconditional latent growth model. The difference between these two models is still pronounced: $\Delta\chi^2_{(n= 132,\ 19)} = 932.7$. Given that the trends are not approximated as linear functions, I then introduced two additional constructs to represent a quadratic bend. These two additional constructs have fixed loadings, following Table 8.4. When building nonlinear models with contrast polynomials, the steps involve adding the higher order terms (e.g., quadratic) while keeping the lower order terms (e.g., intercept, linear) in place. In this case, the intercepts and linear trend constructs are kept in the model. The quadratic trends are added as two additional constructs. The two new constructs are allowed to correlate with each of the intercept and linear trend constructs (for both bullying and homophobic teasing) and with each other. As seen in Table 8.8, this model leads to a significant increase in model fit. Compared with the linear trend, the difference is pronounced: $\Delta\chi^2_{(n=1132,\ 21)} = 666.8$.

The next higher level polynomial for nonlinear functions is the cubic trend. As with the quadratic trend, the cubic factors are added to the existing trends and evaluated. This model also showed a significant improvement in model fit: $\Delta\chi^2_{(n=1132,\ 22)} = 411.8$. You may be wondering why I'm reporting the χ^2 difference test for comparing these trends instead of using a non-nested comparison approach. I am using the nested model χ^2 difference test because the lower order trends are nested within the higher order trends. That is, I can derive the quadratic model from the cubic model simply by fixing the means, variances, and covariances of the cubic trends to be 0. The change in χ^2 of 411.8 is the significance of the difference between the two trend models. This difference suggests that a quadratic trend is not sufficient to capture the nonlinearity of the mean trends.

The next important step in the process of evaluating the adequacy of any model is to examine the parameter estimates of the model. Are the estimates admissible? Are they significant? Are they properly estimated? Do the directions and magnitudes make sense theoretically? Depending on the answers to these questions, the model may need to be modified. With these data, a number of parameter estimates were out of bounds. For the homophobic teasing constructs, the cubic trend had a number of correlations with other trend constructs that were greater than 1.0. For bullying, the quadratic trend had a 0 mean, a 0 variance, and no relations with other constructs. With the quadratic trend in the model, a number of parameters were also out of bounds. I removed this trend and made sure that it did not affect the estimates for the cubic factor, which it did not.

Table 8.9 contains the estimated correlations among the constructs, the variances, and the means. Notice that the cubic trend for bullying has a variance of 0 and no covariances with the other constructs. I kept the cubic trend in the model because the mean structure information that it represented was needed to accurately reproduce the means. There was no variability in this construct. In fact, it was a negative value in the sixth decimal place. I did not fix it to be 0 because that would put too much influence on the other parameters of the model and would adversely influence the model fit. I am not reporting the estimates associated with this construct because they are noninterpretable (they were all around .01 or −.01).

With the intercept defined as the standing at Time 1, the correlation between the two intercepts is quite high (a bit higher than the panel model estimate of .70 in Figure 6.7 but about the same as the level and shape model in Figure 8.7). Both linear trends were positive in terms of their mean levels but were negatively correlated with the intercepts. Youths who were higher in bullying and homophobic teasing at the beginning of the measurement window were lower in the distributions of the linear trends (less increasing). The quadratic trend for homophobic teasing was a positive value, meaning that the trend has an accelerating aspect to

TABLE 8.9. Correlations, variances, and means for the polynomial contrast codes applied to the nonlinear trends in the bullying and homophobic teasing data

	Bullying			Homophobic teasing		
	Int	Lin	Cube	Int	Lin	Quad
Bullying intercept	1.00					
Bullying linear	-.558	1.00				
Bullying cubic	--	--	-0.00			
HmPhTs intercept	.886	-.657	.--	1.00		
HmPhTs linear	-.301	.875	.--	-.458	1.00	
HmPhTs quadratic	-.252	.266	.--	-.413	.018	1.00
Variances	.143	.003	-.000	.373	.013	.010
Means	1.472	-.017	-.006	1.814	-.014	-.033

Note. HmPhTs = Homophobic teasing. The variance of the cubic trend for bullying was negative in the sixth decimal place and, therefore, was not standardized. The covariances with this factor are not presented because a negative variance is meaningless.

it. The distribution around this rate of acceleration was negatively correlated with the intercepts. This negative correlation suggests that higher rates of bullying or homophobic teasing accelerate less than lower rates at the beginning of the measurement window.

I report these polynomial models for the sake of thoroughness. I'm not a big fan of them. As Grimm (2007) and others have argued, there are many possible functional forms that a nonlinear trend can take. The quadratic is a smooth bowl-like trend that sits on top of the linear trend. This trend has been described as the trajectory of a missile; I am not sure how many behavioral science trends would have this trajectory. In addition, the polynomial approach attempts to decompose the variance–covariance information into relatively arbitrary approximations of the possible trend. If these approximations don't map onto the true elements very well, they will likely provide a biased view of the associations.

My general bias for fitting nonlinear trends is to simply use the level and shape model. The basis weights optimally track the nonlinear trend line in the data and produce a single distribution around that trajectory. The associations among the shape constructs displayed in Figure 8.7, for example, tell a different story from the odd story depicted in the correlations among the polynomials (see Table 8.9). Persons who are high in bullying or homophobic teasing at the beginning of the study are higher in the distributions of the shape factors than those who are lower in these characteristics at the beginning of the measurement window. Figure 8.8 shows the shape trend. Most research areas in the social and behavioral sciences lack sufficient theory to predict the specific elements of a nonlinear trend. The level and shape model allows me to optimally fit the growth trend and evaluate the individual differences in this trend, regardless of its specific functional form. Of course, if I have strong theory, then I would not recommend the level and shape model but instead would recommend fitting a nonlinear model that optimally approximates the theoretical model.

Recently Ken Bollen and Patrick Curran (2004) have introduced a hybrid between a standard panel model and a growth curve model. They call this model autoregressive latent trajectory (ALT). This model is often touted as containing the best of both worlds. Figure 8.9 displays an application of the ALT model to the same data that I presented in Figure 8.7. The ALT model involves estimating the autoregressive relationships among the constructs, as well as any potential cross-lagged effects. In these data, only the homophobic teasing constructs showed a consistent and significant autoregressive effect between each of the time points. Unlike the consistent cross-lagged effects of the pure panel model in Figure 6.7, the only cross-lagged effect that was significant was from bullying at Time 2 to homophobic teasing at Time 4. Bullying had two significant autoregressive paths, which were negative. These patterns are quite different from the panel results I reported in Figure 6.7.

As with polynomial models, I'm not a fan of the ALT model. The panel part of the ALT model is a conditional panel model based on the residual variances of the constructs that are not explained by the growth curve constructs. The variance–covariance information is needed to define the distributions of the intercepts and the slopes. To also model the residual variance–covariance information as a panel model makes little sense to me. To me, the ALT model is conflating two very different kinds of questions that can't be answered in the same model. The consequences of this conflating are seen in the models that I have estimated. With the panel component estimated in the ALT model, the relationships among the level and shape constructs have changed dramatically. The correlation between the slope and the intercept of homophobic teasing was .25, but with the autoregressive associations estimated, the correlation becomes −.34, which is a significant change: $\Delta\chi^2_{(n=1132,\ 1)}$ = 411.8, $p < .001$. The correlation between the two slope factors has dropped from .55 to .25, which is a significant decrease: $\Delta\chi^2_{(n=1132,\ 1)} = 411.8$, $p < .001$. The third correlation to show a significant change is the association between the intercept of bullying and the slope of homophobic teasing, $r = .33$ versus $r = -.16$, $\Delta\chi^2_{(n=1132,\ 1)} =$ 411.8, $p < .001$. The other notable change is the value of the slope's mean level. The slope trend is now a −.55, and the basis weights have shifted.

In terms of the bullying constructs, the only autoregressive paths that were significant were between Time 1 and Time 2, and these "stability" coefficients were negative. The panel model from Figure 6.7 indicates autoregressive stabilities in the .5 region for both constructs. The correlations among the constructs inform the distributions of the intercept and slope constructs. When the lower order information is conditioned on the two growth curve constructs, there is no longer a positive stability manifold for the bullying constructs. In my view, these changes between a traditional level and shape growth curve model (Figure 8.7) and the recently introduced ALT model are unsatisfying as they do not shed light on the dynamic

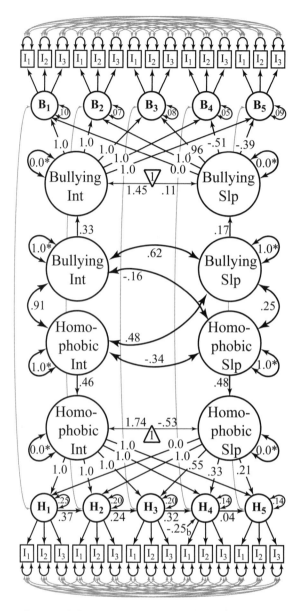

FIGURE 8.9. Results after implementing the Bollen and Curran ALT model. The within-time cross-construct covariance estimates are: .10, .05, .05, .03, and .05 for Times 1–5, respectively. Model fit is: $\chi^2_{(n=1132, 355)}$ = 1228.65, RMSEA = .046$_{(.043; .048)}$, TLI/NNFI = .988, CFI = .990. b = path from B2.

intraindividual-difference associations of the growth curve model or the more static interindividual-difference associations of the panel model.

You'll notice that I reported change in χ^2 values to reflect the significance of the differences in the correlations. These are dependent-sample tests of the correlations. To get these values, I set up the model in Figure 8.7 and the model in Figure 8.9 as a two-group model, with each group using the same data but with the two different models applied to the data. Using the χ^2 value from this two-group model as the baseline value, I simply constrained the corresponding correlations among the intercept and slope constructs to be equal. The difference in χ^2 between (1) the two-group model in which the correlations are freely estimated in both groups and (2) the two-group model in which one of the correlations is constrained to be equal is the difference in χ^2 that I reported before. To determine the p-value for this χ^2 difference, a simple lookup in a χ^2 table or a simple function call in Excel or any other statistics calculator would suffice.

Another latent growth curve model that has been discussed in the literature is the factor-of-curves model. This model is predicated on the idea that growth curve models can be fit to a set of constructs that represent a common domain. For example, I have been using the I FEEL questionnaire for illustration purposes. This questionnaire contains multiple dimensions of affect. It has a scale for energy, a scale for self-evaluation, a scale for "pure" affect, and a scale for interpersonal relationships. These four subscales have a positive mood dimension and a negative mood dimension. Figure 8.10 provides a graphical representation of what this model would look like for a full treatment of fitting latent constructs for each subscale at each time point, adding an intercept and slope construct to represent the change over time in each subscale, and then adding, at the tertiary level, factors to represent the communality among the intercepts and slopes for each of the subscales as higher order intercept and slope factors for positive and negative affect. Unfortunately, at the time of this writing, the data that I do have are giving me fits (nonconvergence issues), and I would need to collect new data that are better conditioned to get this model to converge. Maybe I'll have the data by the second edition.

MULTILEVEL LONGITUDINAL MODEL

Multilevel regression modeling has been around for some time. Multilevel SEM, however, is a relatively new development in the field. The basic idea with a multilevel model is that observations at one level are nested in a superordinate level. The classic example is that of students nested in classrooms. Why is this nested data structure a potential issue? The answer is twofold. First, nested observations are not independent observations. Imagine that I want to measure positive affect in a group of school-age youths. A child from a classroom that has a large proportion of children with high positive affect and a teacher who is very upbeat and enthusiastic is

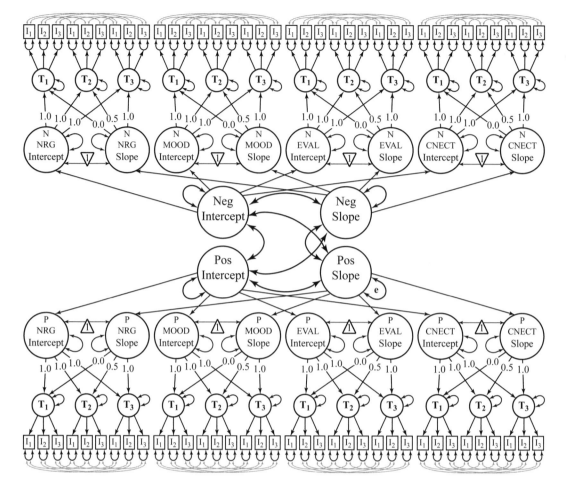

FIGURE 8.10. A multivariate growth model: A factor-of-curves-of-factors model. P and Pos = Positive, N and Neg = Negative. NRG = Energy, EVAL = Self-Evaluation, CNECT = Connectedness. This model is a possible model that could be fit to the I FEEL. Each of the subdomains of affect would be expected to start and change in similar ways such that a set of common factors could account for the covariation patterns in the lower order growth constructs. Data for this model have not yet been collected.

likely to have a higher positive affect score than is a child who is in a classroom that has a large proportion of children with low positive affect and a teacher who is dour and uninterested. This influence of classroom-level characteristics would bias any relationships that would otherwise emerge at the individual level. For example, if the nested data structure were ignored, a researcher might find a strong positive correlation between positive affect and school performance. This finding would be a spurious finding, because the effect is due to the vibrant nature of the teachers, which leads me to discuss the second reason that it is important to correctly model nested data: the nature of the dependency can be examined as a predictable source of variance. In this example, I can examine the reasons that affect and school performance are strongly related at the classroom level but not at the individual level. Teacher characteristics can be included to model or predict the amount of the classroom-level affect.

A standard multilevel regression equation for this type of scenario is presented in Equation 8.2. A key to understanding a multilevel model is in the subscripts. The variable being predicted is y_{ic}. The i subscript designates the score belonging to an individual, and the c indicates that the score also belongs to a cluster, such as the classroom in which the individuals are nested. On the predictor side, there are equations to reflect predictors at the individual level and predictors at the cluster level. In this hypothetical example, I can predict the dependent variable with variables such as gender (male), some ethnicity dummy codes (black, Hispanic), and possible continuous variables such as achievement scores, attitude measures, or personality

---

Equation 8.2. Multilevel equations for clusters

Level 1: $y_{ic} = \pi_{0c} + \pi_{1c}(male) + \varepsilon_{ic}$

a) without a Level 2 predictor:

$$\text{Level 2: } \pi_{0c} = \gamma_{00} + \zeta_{0c}$$
$$\text{and, } \pi_{1c} = \gamma_{01} + \zeta_{1c}$$

b) with a Level 2 predictor:

$$\text{Level 2: } \pi_{0c} = \gamma_{00} + \gamma_{10}(tenure) + \zeta_{0c}$$
$$\text{and, } \pi_{1c} = \gamma_{01} + \gamma_{11}(tenure) + \zeta_{1c}$$

- i refers to a person's individual score.
- c refers to the cluster membership.
- y are the scores on the indicators.
- π_{0c} is intercept (0) for each cluster c.
- π_{1c} is the regression slope (1) for each cluster c as a function of child gender (labeled "male").
- ε_{ic} is the error in prediction for each individual i within each cluster, c.
- γ_{00} is the intercept (0) of the Level 2 equation predicting the Level 1 intercepts (0).
- γ_{10} is the regression slope (1) for the intercepts (0) estimated at Level 1 as a function of teacher tenure (labeled "tenure").
- ζ_{0c} is the variance in the intercepts (0) for each cluster c in A, or it is the unexplained variance, as in version B.
- γ_{01} is the intercept (0) for the Level 2 equation predicting the Level 1 slopes (1).
- γ_{11} is the regression slope (1) for the slopes (1) estimated at Level 2 as a function of tenure.
- ζ_{1c} is the variance in the slopes (1) for each cluster c in A and the unexplained variance in B.

factors. Each predictor would have a regression coefficient associated with it. In a multilevel context, these regression coefficients can become a "variable" that is predicted by the Level 2 predictors. In this hypothetical example, I could have teacher tenure, teacher gender, and/or teacher vibrancy as possible predictors of classroom differences in overall classroom-level affect.

In Equation 8.2, I have used *male* as the Level 1 predictor and *tenure* as the Level 2 predictor. At Level 1, the scores within each cluster can be represented as an intercept and a slope to reflect the amount that males differ from the cluster mean. With *male* coded as 1 versus 0, the two scores simplify to the intercept (π_{0c}), which is equal to the mean score of the females in each cluster, and the slope (π_{1c}), which is the mean difference of the males. That is, the scores within each cluster are divided into the mean for girls and the mean difference for boys. These means, however, vary across the Level 2 clusters (in this case, classrooms). At Level 2, the predictor variable of teacher *tenure* is entered into the model to account for any potential differences in the scores for females, γ_{10}, or the scores for males, γ_{11}, as a function of how long the teacher has been teaching (i.e., tenure).

Equation 8.3 extends the multilevel regression equations (see Equations 8.1 and 8.2) to multilevel SEM equations for longitudinal data. As I mentioned, with longitudinal data, observations are nested within individuals; individuals in turn are nested within higher units such as classrooms. I have reproduced the foundational

---

Equation 8.3. Multilevel equations for SEM

a) $y_{ioc} = \mathbf{T}_{oc} + \mathbf{\Lambda}_{oc}\eta_{ioc} + \mathbf{\Theta}_{ioc}$

b) $E(y_{ioc}) = \mu_{y_{oc}} = \mathbf{T}_{oc} + \mathbf{\Lambda}_{oc}\mathbf{A}_{oc}$

c) $\mathbf{\Sigma}_{oc} = \mathbf{\Lambda}_{oc}\mathbf{\Psi}_{oc}\mathbf{\Lambda}'_{oc}\mathbf{\Theta}_{ioc}$

- *i* refers to a person's individual score.
- *o* refers to the occasions of measurement.
- *c* refers to the cluster membership.
- *y* are the scores on the indicators.
- $E()$ is the expectation operator.
- μ_y is the vector of means.
- **T** is the column vector of indicator means.
- **A** is the column vector of latent construct means.
- **Σ** is the model-implied variance–covariance matrix.
- η is the latent construct scores.
- **Λ** is the matrix of loadings or estimates of the indicator to construct relations.
- **Ψ** is the matrix of variances and covariances among the constructs.
- **Θ** is the matrix of residual variances or unique factors and residual covariances among the indicators.
- **Λ′** is the transpose of the **Λ** matrix.

equations of SEM but added the multilevel subscripts to designate the various levels of nested information that are modeled in a multilevel SEM. In Equation 8.3, y_{ioc} is the score for person i at occasion o within cluster c. The means of the indicators are represented in the mean vector $\mathbf{T}$, which has the oc subscripts, meaning that each indicator has a mean within each occasion and each cluster. The matrix Λ contains the slopes of the individuals' scores for each indicator onto the latent construct. The slopes have the oc subscripts because they can vary across occasions and clusters. The scores on the latent factors (η) can vary across individuals, occasions, and clusters and, hence, have the subscripts ioc. The deviation of each person's score from the intercept (τ) and slope (λ) that links the indicators' scores to the latent factor's scores, η, are represented in the residual matrix (Θ) which also has the ioc subscripts because a residual varies across individuals, occasions, and clusters. From this information, the equations for the mean structures (Eq. 8.3b) and the covariance structures (Eq. 8.3c) all have parameter matrices that vary across occasions and clusters (they have the oc subscripts) with the exception of adding the unexplained variance represented in the residual matrix Θ_{ioc}.

Equations can be mind-numbing at times. I find it helpful to take a deep breath before I dive into an equation; I also find it helpful to "see" the equation as a diagram. Figure 8.11 is a graphical representation of the same ideas contained in Equations 8.3a–c. In Figure 8.11, I have left out the mean structures information because the figure would be too busy to follow. The parallels between the intercepts and the loadings are straightforward. I have six boxes to reflect three indicators of a given construct that is measured at two time points. Each box is decomposed into three sources of variance; namely, each box has a λ^w, a λ^b, and a residual variance, θ. The six estimated λ^w parameters are the amounts of variance that are explained by the construct *within* each cluster. The six λ^b parameters are the amounts of variance that are explained by the construct *between* each cluster. The dashed line that separates the within versus the between parts of the model is a simple figural convention to show that the variances are being partitioned into their respective within-cluster and between-cluster components.

I also used the superscripted letters e, f, and g to designate that the corresponding loadings are set to be equal over time (factorial invariance is tested and specified) for the within-cluster estimates. In Figure 8.11, I used i, j, and k to designate that the corresponding loadings are also set to be equal over time for the between-cluster estimates. The construct parameters of ψ and β are estimated within each cluster, and they are estimated as a between-cluster parameter. That is, between clusters the ψ and β represent the mean and the distribution of the ψ and β estimates that are made within each cluster. In these models, one could include a within-cluster variable to predict within-cluster variability in these estimates (e.g., use gender as a predictor of within-cluster differences in victimization).

At the between-cluster level, predictors can also be added. In Figure 8.11, I have depicted a simple dummy-code predictor for intervention versus control. This

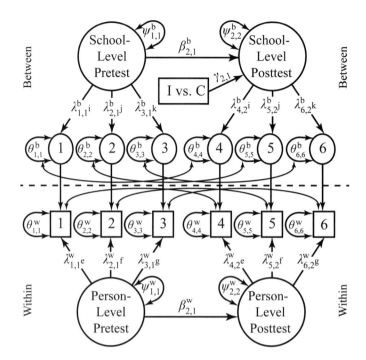

FIGURE 8.11. Example diagram of a multilevel SEM. Variables labeled 1, 2, and 3 are measured indicators of an underlying construct. The same variables are measured at posttest, but they are now labeled 4, 5, and 6, respectively. Factorial invariance is tested and specified over time, and the residuals are allowed to correlate over time at the within-person level. The loadings at the between level are also factorially invariant. The intervention is tested by the significance of the path $\gamma_{2,1}$ controlling for between-school differences in the pretest scores. Only one construct is shown for simplicity, but many constructs can be tested simultaneously in this multilevel SEM framework.

variation of a multilevel SEM model depicts the kind of model I would fit for a pre–post study of an intervention where the level of assignment to the intervention versus the control condition is at the cluster level (e.g., schools are randomly assigned to intervention vs. control). A dummy-coded variable representing intervention versus control would be entered in the between part of the model, and the construct at Time 2 would be regressed onto the dummy-coded variable. The parameter estimate labeled $\gamma_{2,1}$ would represent the mean-level change in the construct at Time 2 that is due to the intervention effect after controlling for the prior between-cluster differences in the construct at Time 1, which is represented in the parameter labeled $\beta_{2,1}$.

As an example of a longitudinal multilevel SEM, the model depicted in Figure 8.11 was fit to the KiVa dataset. KiVa is an antibullying intervention developed by Christina Salmivalli in Finland. Figure 8.12 shows the results of fitting a simple multilevel SEM to the peer-reported victimization construct from the KiVa dataset. In KiVa, 295 classrooms and a total of 5,422 students were randomly assigned to the KiVa intervention or to a business-as-usual control condition. Assessments were conducted as a pretest in the spring of the school year and as a posttest in the spring of the following school year (for more details of the intervention and the tests of its efficacy, see Kärnä, Voeten, Little, Poskiparta, Alanen, & Salmivalli, 2011; Kärnä, Voeten, Little, Poskiparta, Kaljonen, & Salmivalli, 2011).

As shown in Figure 8.12, the regression slope for the dummy-coded variable representing intervention versus control is –.19, which indicates that schools in the intervention condition were –.19 between-school standard units lower in peer victimization than were the schools in the control condition. This effect accounts for 17% of the variance in peer-reported victimization, which, for bullying intervention work, is a very large decrease in victimization. The correlation between Time 1 victimization on intervention versus control is a –.12, which indicates that the intervention schools started off with lower rates of victimization than the control conditions. This pretest difference, however, is controlled for by the .63 between-school

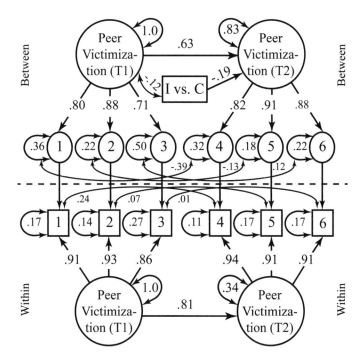

FIGURE 8.12. Results from the KiVa intervention. Strong factorial invariance is specified over time. The fixed factor method of identification is used for both the within and the between model specifications. The standardized parameter estimates are reported. Because the standardization occurs within each time of measurement, the standardized parameter estimates will no longer be equal across time (i.e., the unstandardized loadings are equal across time).

autoregressive effect. At the student level, the autoregressive effect is even more stable, with an estimate of .81. Also, notice that the loading of the indicators onto the constructs at the within and the between levels are quite strong, indicating that these constructs are measured quite reliably at both levels of analysis. It is not uncommon for the between-level loadings to be noticeably smaller than the within-level loadings. Larger loadings suggest more between-cluster variance than lower loadings. The key here is that the loadings should have a significant amount of variance in order to evaluate the between-level effects. Also, for this model, the intercepts were estimated and evaluated, but they are not reported here because the figure would be hard to read and because the primary effect of interest is in the covariance-structures parts of this particular model.

In terms of model fit, the estimated model in Figure 8.12 provides a reasonable approximation of the data at both the within and the between parts of the model. In Table 8.10 I have listed the model fit information. This information is based on a couple of different approaches to estimating model fit that have been offered in the literature. At this point in time, however, we do not yet have clear guidance on how best to evaluate model fit for multilevel SEM models. The simultaneous method relies on the model fit information that comes automatically from the software packages. This approach is undesirable for a number of reasons. First, the fit information is the sum of the within and between parts of the model. Any misspecifications may either be masked (e.g., between-level units are often small relative to within-level units, and misspecification can be glossed over) or confounded (i.e., misspecification at one level can't be differentiated from misspecification at another level).

Recently two methods to determine model fit based on level-specific evaluations have been proposed. One method is called the segregating approach (Yuan & Bentler, 2007). This approach involves estimating two matrices based on the raw data: a within-cluster covariance matrix and a between-cluster covariance matrix. These segregated covariance matrices are then used as the sufficient statistics for a single-level SEM model. One model is run on the within-clusters matrix to evaluate model fit at that level, and a second model is run on the between-clusters matrix to evaluate model fit at that level.

A second method is to fit a model where one level is saturated (i.e., all possible parameters are estimated and no degrees of freedom are associated with the saturated level; Ryu & West, 2009). When one of the levels of the model is saturated, that part of the model will only trivially contribute to model misfit; any meaningful misfit must be due to the other parts of a given multilevel model. Specifically, with one level saturated, model fit is evaluated for the level in which a restricted and parsimonious set of estimates are made. This approach is done once for Level 1, or the within-cluster part of the model, and once at Level 2, or the between-cluster part of the model. One feature of the partially saturated approach is that to get model fit information, a null model must be specified and estimated to get information on how much information is contained at each level. This feature of the partially saturated approach is nice because it forces users to consider the null model and to specify the one that is most appropriate for the data at hand. With the segregating approach (and the simultaneous approach), a user could resort to using the default null model that is built into the software and used in calculating various model fit indices, which, as I have emphasized, is an unwarranted idea.

In Table 8.10, the model fit using the partially saturated approach shows that the within-cluster part of the model is a reasonable approximation of the data with an RMSEA of .051 and a CFI of .997. The segregating approach gives about the same guidance in terms of the within-clusters part of the model. For the between-clusters part of the model, the partially saturated approach shows model fit information that appears not to be too promising when evaluated using the heuristics that have been developed for single-level SEM models. Here, the RMSEA is .123 and the CFI is .711, but the standardized root mean residual for the between part of the model (SRMR-B) value is .073. The SRMR-B is in the range of acceptable model fit, but the other two indices are not. Unfortunately, we don't have enough simulation work done at this point to know if these values for the RMSEA and the CFI are good or bad values. Until further guidance can be provided, I recommend that these values be reported. If the values are low, such as the ones in this example, I would argue for the quality of the model based on other features, such as evaluation of the residuals and modification indices, as well as the parameter estimates and their standard errors. In the KiVa data example here, the residual information is within tolerances and there's no other indication of misspecification. Instead, the low amount of information for the between-cluster part of the model (see Null model between in Table 8.10) suggests that there is low power to determine the adequacy of the model's ability to reproduce the data at Level 2.

A work group at the University of Kansas and other researchers are currently conducting some large-scale simulation studies to evaluate the tenability of these approaches and will provide guidance as to the cutoffs that may be most useful for

TABLE 8.10. Fit information for the multilevel SEM model (Figure 8.12)

Model tested	χ^2	df	SRMR-W	SRMR-B	RMSEA	RMSEA 90% CI	CFI
Simultaneous	198.01	24	.007	.074	.037	.030;.044	
Null model within	31801.4	18	n/a	n/a	n/a	n/a	n/a
Null model between	288.14	27	n/a	n/a	n/a	n/a	n/a
Partially saturated W	103.95	7	.008	.013	.051	.043;.064	.997
Partially saturated B	92.55	17	.001	.073	.123	.093;.142	.711
Segregated within	110.43	7	.025	n/a	.064	.058;.070	.997
Segregated between	n/c	17	n/a	n/c	n/c	n/c	n/c

Note. The simultaneous approach does not disentangle level-specific fit other than the SRMR. n/c = nonconvergence (the segregated between model would not converge for this example). n/a = not applicable.

evaluating model fit at both the within and between levels of analysis. Keep an eye out for the publication of this work (see *www.guilford.com/little-materials* for updates). I'll be sure to expand and update this material in future editions of this book.

SUMMARY

This chapter provides an introduction to multilevel models as a feature of longitudinal SEMs. All longitudinal models are multilevel models to a degree in that the dependent observations that occur from repeated observations of the same person are explicitly modeled. For panel models, the Level 1 nested nature of the data is a saturated model in that the scores for each person are fully represented as the mean and variance of the scores within a time point and the dependency is the cross-time covariance. For growth curve models the cross-time observations are represented as more parsimonious models of the growth process for each individual, and the parameters of these models are characterized as between-person differences in growth. Other levels of nestedness can co-occur with longitudinal data. In these situations a multilevel model of three, four, or more levels must be specified. The recent advances in SEM models now allow at least three-level SEM (when time is modeled in a traditional longitudinal manner). The developments in this area of statistics are likely to be pronounced in the coming years, and I'll have lots to offer in terms of expansions to this chapter.

KEY TERMS AND CONCEPTS INTRODUCED IN THIS CHAPTER

Basis weights. The loadings of the shape factor in a level and shape growth curve model. These loadings determine the basis by which the functional form of the estimated trajectory is calculated. These weights can also be fixed to specific values to define a functional form that can then be tested against the data to determine its adequacy.

Dependency or dependent versus independent observations (see Nested data). A given observation or line of data is typically a random sample from a clearly defined population. If the observations are a truly random selection from this population, the observations would have nothing in common. One observation would be no more likely to occur than a second observation. In this case, the observations would be truly independent, which is a core assumption of statistical inference methods. On the other hand, when observations are selected where some have a higher likelihood of looking like or correlating with some subset of the observations, a dependency in the data is said to exist. This dependency will occur when observations are nested in a circumscribed context. Repeated observations for an individual are nested within a given person because the second observation of that person is likely to be correlated with the first observation of that person. This dependency must be accounted for in a statistical model if the parameters of the model are to be properly estimated and the standard errors of the parameters are to be as accurate as they should be. Longitudinal models, by their nature, account for and, in fact, focus on the dependency in the data resulting from repeated observations. This dependency is characterized as growth and change across individuals. When the dependency occurs because of a clustering influence, such as students nested in classrooms or schools, a multilevel model that accounts for and that may even focus on the dependency due to clustering is required.

ICC. Intraclass correlation. It is a measure of how much of the total variability in a set of scores is due to the class or cluster variability.

Level 1 units or parameters. Observations or measurements that are at the lowest level of the nested data structure are referred to as Level 1 units, and model estimates at this level are referred to as Level 1 parameters.

Level 2+ units or parameters. Observations or measurements that are at the next highest level of the nested data structure are referred to as Level 2 units, and model estimates at this level are referred to as Level 2 parameters.

Nested data (see Dependency). When two observations or measurements are more likely to be similar than a truly random selection of observations, the assumption of independence is violated. The source of the dependency is typically viewed as a higher level influence that affects two or more observations. These dependent observations are "nested" in the higher level influence. Two or more observations from the same person are not random because the person from whom the observation is taken is determined. Two or more observations from the same classroom are not random because the students share the classroom environment, the influence of the same teacher(s), and perhaps were assigned to the classroom on the basis of a shared characteristic (e.g., based on street address, birth month). They also share personal interactions and within-classroom events. Two persons who are best friends are not random because they share enough common interests, common experience, and/ or common environment to become best friends. Mutual antipathies are similarly not random samples from a population of individuals. Multilevel models explicitly model the nested data structures for all levels of nestedness.

Unconditional/level and shape model. In multilevel growth models, the unconditional model typically provides the baseline model against which specific trends of change are tested. In some literatures, this model is also referred to as the level and shape model. The shape of change is determined by the data and is not constrained to take on any particular functional form. The shape of change is reflected in the loadings or basis weights.

RECOMMENDED READINGS

Growth Curve Modeling

Bollen, K. A., & Curran, P. J. (2006). *Latent curve models: A structural equation perspective*. Hoboken, NJ: Wiley.

Hancock, G. R., & Lawrence, F. R. (2006). Using latent growth models to evaluate longitudinal change. In G. R. Hancock & R. O. Mueller (Eds.), *Structural equation modeling: A second course*. Greenwich, CT: Information Age.

Hedeker, D., & Gibbons, R. D. (2006). *Longitudinal data analysis*. Hoboken, NJ: Wiley.

Preacher, K. J., Wichman, A. L., MacCallum, R. C., & Briggs, N. E. (2008). *Latent growth curve modeling*. Thousand Oaks, CA: Sage.

> These readings will give you a very good review of growth curve modeling and the multilevel approaches to modeling longitudinal change. These kinds of models ask and answer very different kinds of questions than are addressed by the longitudinal panel models that I focus on in this book.

The Importance of Coding Time Properly

Biesanz, J. C., Deeb-Sossa, N., Papadakis, A. A., Bollen, K. A., & Curran, P. J. (2004). The role of coding time in estimating and interpreting growth curve models. *Psychological Methods, 9*, 30–52.

Mehta, P. D., & West, S. G. (2000). Putting the individual back into individual growth curves. *Psychological Methods, 5*, 23–43.

> These two papers provide a thorough explanation of why and how coding time affects interpretations of growth models. Biesanz et al. address issues of power and precision in the estimates and provide compelling arguments for graphing the trends of a growth model (with a number of nice examples for such graphs).

The ALT Model

Bollen, K. A., & Curran, P. J. (2004). Autoregressive latent trajectory (ALT) models: A synthesis of two traditions. *Sociological Methods and Research, 32*, 336–383.

Curran, P. J., & Bollen, K. A. (2001). The best of both worlds: Combining autoregressive and latent curve models. In L. M. Collins & A. G. Sayer (Eds.), *New methods for the analysis of change* (pp. 107–135). Washington, DC: American Psychological Association.

> These two contributions introduce the ALT model, which, as I have pointed out here, has some troublesome properties that need to be explored further.

Hamaker, E. L. (2005). Conditions for the equivalence of the autoregressive latent trajectory model and a latent growth curve model with autoregressive disturbances. *Sociological Methods and Research, 33*(3), 404–418.

Voelkle, M. (2008). Reconsidering the use of autoregressive latent trajectory (ALT) models. *Multivariate Behavioral Research, 43*, 564–591.

> These are a few recent contributions that are critical of the ALT approach. I think more work needs to be done to understand under what conditions the ALT model is appropriate.

The KiVa Intervention

Kärnä, A., Voeten, M., Little, T. D., Poskiparta, E., Alanen, E., & Salmivalli, C. (2011). Going to scale: A nonrandomized nationwide trial of the KiVa antibullying program for grades 1–9. *Journal of Consulting and Clinical Psychology, 79*, 796–805.

Kärnä, A., Voeten, M., Little, T. D., Poskiparta, E., Kaljonen, A., & Salmivalli, C. (2011).

A large-scale evaluation of the KiVa anti-bullying program. *Child Development, 82,* 311–330.

> These two papers are the first to evaluate the efficacy of the KiVa antibullying program and provide good examples of multilevel SEM models in the applied developmental literature.

Multilevel SEM Fit Evaluation

Ryu, E., & West, S. G. (2009). Level-specific evaluation of model fit in multilevel structural equation modeling. *Structural Equation Modeling, 16,* 583–601.

Yuan, K.-H., & Bentler, P. M. (2007). Multilevel covariance structure analysis by fitting multiple single-level models. *Sociological Methodology, 37,* 53–82.

> These two papers describe the two methods for determining level-specific model fit in a multilevel SEM framework.

9

Mediation and Moderation

The distinctions between mediation and moderation are still confusing to many practitioners. Yet hypotheses about mediation and moderation abound in most literatures across the social and behavioral sciences. Mediation and moderation are but a few of the many statistical models that can be estimated on data. In Figure 9.1, I have listed a number of schematic drawings of various statistical models that can be fit in either cross-sectional or longitudinal designs (see Wu & Little, 2011). The statistical models in Figure 9.1 are represented as manifest-variable models for simplicity. Each of these general statistical models, however, can be represented as latent-variable models (create a measurement model for each variable and use circles to represent the fact that the variables are latent instead of manifest). Each of these models can also be fit and tested for differences in a multiple-group framework to examine group differences on any of the model's parameters. They can also be estimated in a multilevel framework to examine how much variation is related to the within-cluster differences versus the between-cluster differences (and of course, mixture distributions can also be applied). Although this list is not exhaustive, it is generally comprehensive in terms of the basic kinds of models that can be fit to data. Many hybrid versions, for example, can be assembled from the parts and pieces of these basic models.

In Figure 9.1, I have started with a bivariate correlation, which can be extended to the multivariate case quite easily. This statistical model is the most basic and least informative with regard to unique relations among a set of variables. In Panel B, the basic multiple regression equation is presented, and it, too, can be expanded easily in terms of the number of predictors and the nature of the different outcome variables (e.g., using link functions to represent count or categorical variables as dependent variables; see Coxe, West, & Aiken, 2012). The key aspect of the multiple-regression model is that the bivariate associations are now converted into unique influences. When the predictor variables are correlated to a nontrivial degree, the unique effects can often be quite different from what the bivariate association implies. It is also the case that when the predictor variables are correlated, the "common" variance among the predictors is allocated to the variable that has the larger unique influence on a given outcome variable. That is, the variable with the larger unique influence gets credit for the common information that the predictors share.

Panel C of Figure 9.1 is the basic cross-lagged model that I covered in Chapter 6. Panels E through M depict variations on mediation and moderation, including moderated mediation of the various parts of the mediation puzzle and an example of mediated moderation (Panel I; i.e., Z predicts M, which in turn moderates the X-to-Y association). Also note that the various moderating influences can also be applied to the half-longitudinal and full longitudinal mediation models. Panels N and O are meant to show the statistically illogical idea of a bidirectional relationship when the data are assessed at the same time. The model in Panel N simplifies to the model in Panel O, which is the bidirectional association that is represented as a statistically meaningful covariance or correlation. The model in Panel N is not identified. To make it identified requires constraints on the two parameters that connect the two variables. The most reasonable constraint is one of equality of the two pathways, which is tantamount to the model in Panel O. When the two directional paths are constrained to be equal, the result is a bidirectional relationship. To correctly test for a bidirectional relationship, the variables must be assessed on multiple occasions, and their prior levels must be controlled. When done properly, then, a test of bidirectionality becomes the cross-lagged panel regression in Panel C of Figure 9.1.

MAKING THE DISTINCTION BETWEEN MEDIATORS AND MODERATORS

Clearly the details surrounding the concepts of mediation and moderation are broad enough in scope to warrant book-length treatments of them (see Hayes, 2013; MacKinnon, 2008). This chapter is my attempt at providing a summary of the key issues that underlie these concepts as they are related to panel models of longitudinal data and to highlight issues that are particular to SEM or longitudinal models for testing mediation and/or moderation.

Fundamentally speaking, mediation describes the intermediary mechanism by which one variable exerts its causal influence on another variable. An expectation about mediation is undisputedly a strict causal hypothesis. It is an expectation about the way in which (or the "how" by which) one variable causes *changes* in another variable, which in turn causes *changes* in an outcome variable. I emphasize changes because change is a core piece that must be demonstrated in order to claim mediation; without evidence of *change*, the only effects that can be shown are simple indirect effects (not mediation). An indirect effect is a necessary characteristic of mediation, but it alone is not sufficient to claim mediation. In other words, all mediation effects are indirect effects, but not all indirect effects are mediation effects. Only when the indirect effects involve changes in the relations among a set of variables can the indirect effect then be considered a mediating pathway. The nonlongitudinal simplex models for continuum theories that I presented in Chapter 6 are good

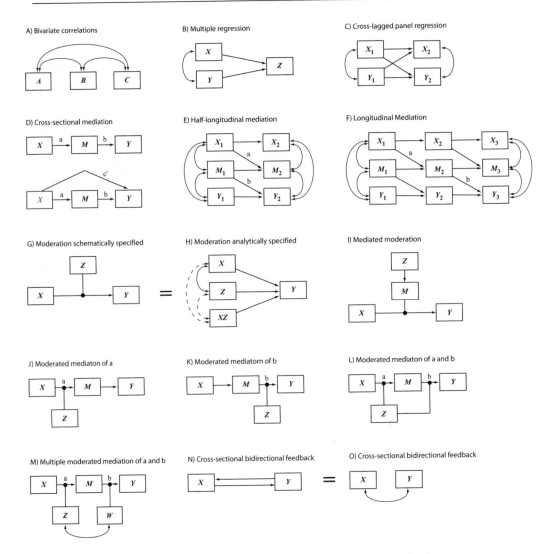

FIGURE 9.1. A simple taxonomy of statistical analysis models and names for them.

examples of indirect effects that do not involve change. Also, in cross-sectional tests of mediation, indirect effects are used as a proxy for mediation but without the evidence of causing change in the mediator or outcome variables.

A mediating variable is the "go between," the "letter carrier," or the "transmitter" to a causal system. A mediator takes the handoff and, in turn, gives it away—and in this way it becomes a causal mechanism by which information is communicated from a source through a conduit to an outcome recipient (think of tumbling dominos—the last one falls because of the preceding ones, which were caused to fall by the ones preceding them). A mediator is also like the medicine that a doctor prescribes, which, if the doctor has made the correct diagnosis and written the correct prescription, causes our illness to improve. A mediator is a "med" in this case (note: *med*iator, *med*ication). The doctor diagnoses the problem and, through the act of prescribing (causing the delivery and amount of delivery), the med (mediator) is delivered and causes changes in our illness state, and we get better (go from illness to wellness). In this regard, a mediating variable must be something that can change states as a result of another variable's influence upon it. In the "med" example, the doctor's act of accurately diagnosing and prescribing causes a change from no medicine to some amount of the correct medicine, which is the causal mechanism by which the doctor's actions lead to improved health, via the pharmacological agents in the prescribed medication.

A moderating variable, on the other hand, is one that is a filter or catalyst for the relations between two or more variables. Depending on how it exerts its influence, a moderating variable creates a context that either dampens or enhances the *strength of an effect* of one variable on another variable. It is a variable that changes the strength of an association between two variables. A moderating variable is the answer to an "it depends" kind of theoretical question about the strength of the association between two variables. For example, personal agency predicts actual school performance. If you ask the question, "Does the strength of that association depend on anything?" and the answer is "yes," then a moderator is likely involved.

A moderating influence can be represented as a continuous variable, as I have depicted moderation in Figure 9.1, or it can be a nominal variable (e.g., gender, ethnic group, school). Regardless of the metrical quality of a moderator, it reflects a context or mode in which two or more variables are associated. The context of gender, for example, is often a moderator of the linkage between personal agency and academic performance. Even this moderated relationship is also often further moderated by the context of age and culture. The filtering or catalyzing context of a moderator can be external to the individual, such as growing up in a nurturing parental environment, or it can be internal to the individual, such as having a cognitive schema about how school performance actually happens.

Mediators and moderators are both "third" variable influences. A moderator is a "third" variable that changes how one variable influences another. In this regard, it is an interaction variable. As mentioned, moderators can be single variables or sets of variables that work in concert or in a nested manner. Regardless of the complexity of variables, a moderator describes the mode in which two variables exert their influence (note: *mod*erator, *mod*e). For example, the relationship between the RPMs of the engine and the speed of the automobile is moderated by the mode that the transmission is in. In first gear the speed varies from 0 to about 20 or so, in second gear the speed varies from 20 to 40 or so, in third gear the speed varies from 40 to 60 or so, and so on. A moderator is the mode (or context, or modulator) that dictates how two (or more) variables are associated. In this case, the relationship between an engine's RPMs and the speed of a car depends on what gear it is in.

A moderator is a "third" variable influence that modulates the link between two or more variables, whereas a mediator is a "third" variable influence that is the ultimate proximal link that carries a distal influence to the outcome variable. Of course, other "third" variables exist that are neither mediators nor moderators but, instead, operate as direct effects or as unmeasured effects. When they are unmeasured effects, they are potentially confounding variables.

Whether or not "med" and "mode" help in distinguishing these two concepts, it should be clear that they are two very different concepts and represent very different kinds of "third" variable circumstances. And, although mediators and moderators are lumped into the category of "third" variables, they are "third" variables only in the simplest of situations. In this regard, they are the extraneous variables that can affect a system of relations among two or more variables.

Mediation processes can be far more complex than a simple three-variable scenario. I describe some of these more complex processes later. The most important point that I need to make here is that, except for very rare situations, a true test of mediation must be longitudinal in nature (Cole & Maxwell, 2003; Maxwell & Cole, 2007). Although I present an example shortly in which a cross-sectional test of the mediating relationship could be justified, such situations are quite rare. Usually researchers have in mind sets of variables that ebb and flow quite fluidly and are, therefore, not amenable to a cross-sectional analysis. Despite its popularity, the cross-sectional approach is feasible only under very limiting conditions (Maxwell & Cole, 2007).

Cross-Sectional Mediation

Figure 9.2 presents the simplest of cross-sectional examples for considering mediation. In this model, the parameter pathways are labeled a, b, and c (as well as c'). These path labels are the traditional labels used to discuss mediation. In this example, I rely on data from Gallagher and Johnson (2008), who examined the mediating effect of neuroticism on age-related changes in negative affect. That is, to what degree does neuroticism as a personality trait mediate the effect of age on negative affect? In Figure 9.2 I have listed the conceptual relationships with their labels, and in Figure 9.3 I have listed the parameter values from a cross-sectional test of the mediation hypothesis. In Figure 9.2, the a path is the effect of the predictor variable on the mediator, and the b path is the effect of the mediator on the outcome variable. In Panel A, the path that connects the predictor and the outcome is labeled c. This path represents the direct effect of the predictor on the outcome. In Panel B, the path that connects the predictor and the outcome is labeled c'. This path is the unique effect of the predictor on the outcome after controlling for the effect of the mediator.

In Panel B, the predictor has one indirect pathway by which it influences the outcome variable. Specifically, I can trace the indirect effect of the predictor by following the path labeled b and then the path labeled a. This tracing leads to a value of the magnitude of the indirect effect, which is simply the product of b and a. The

A) Direct effect model without mediator

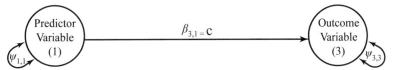

B) Direct and indirect effects model with mediator

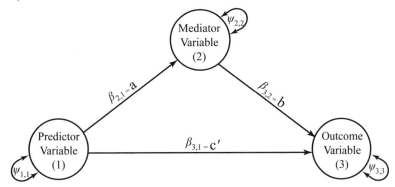

FIGURE 9.2. The key elements of cross-sectional mediation. For simplicity, I have eliminated the representation of the measurement model from the diagram. A measurement model similar to that found in Figure 6.1 is assumed for all of the path diagrams wherein I have removed the graphical representation of the measurement model.

ab product term is the only effect that pertains to mediation. In this simple three-variable example, mediation exists if the *ab* product term is significant, regardless of whether the *c'* path is significant. In other words, mediation exists or does not exist, regardless of the magnitude of any direct effect; when the indirect effect of the predictor on the outcome through the mediator is significant, mediation is supported (in this cross-sectional example, however, the lack of control for prior levels is problematic).

The results reported in Figure 9.3 are from Gallagher and Johnson (2008), who analyzed the data from the Midlife in the United States survey (MIDUS 1 and MIDUS 2). The results in Figure 9.3 are for both the Time 1 (1995) and Time 2 (2004) occasions of measurement. These models fit the data well but did require a dual loading of one neuroticism indicator on age and a dual loading of one indicator of negative affect on neuroticism. These dual loadings emerged even though the items were parceled. This example serves well to show that parcels don't magically fix things. When I fit this model at the item level, the one neuroticism item and the one negative affect item had the dual loadings, but the values were much larger than in the parcel model. In the item-level solution, the negative affect items required two residual correlations. Parceling did eliminate the need for the two residual

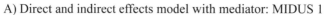

A) Direct and indirect effects model with mediator: MIDUS 1

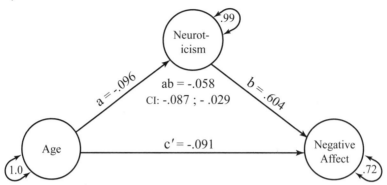

B) Direct and indirect effects model with mediator: MIDUS 2

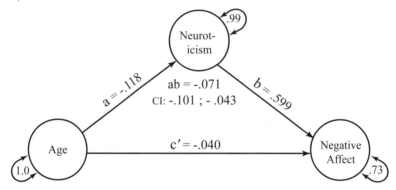

FIGURE 9.3. Results of two cross-sectional mediation models. These data are from a project by Gallagher and Johnson (2008). Neuroticism has four indicators, Negative affect has three indicators; age would only have a single indicator and thus would actually be a manifest variable at the latent variable level (see Chapter 3). The data are from MIDUS 1 and 2. CI is the 95% confidence interval for determining significance of the *ab* parameter.

correlations. The parameter estimates and the conclusion regarding mediation were the same in both the item-level and the parcel-level solutions. Model fit was better in the parcel solution. For the MIDUS 1 model, RMSEA = $.072_{(.064;\ .080)}$, CFI = .986, and TLI/NNFI = .970. For the MIDUS 2 model, RMSEA = $.074_{(.065;\ .082)}$, CFI = .977, and TLI/NNFI = .952.

In terms of the parameters, although the age effects are small, they are significant and they are consistent, not only across the two waves of the MIDUS assessments but also across other samples that have examined the relations among these variables. The viability of this model as a cross-sectional test of mediation, is, perhaps, more reasonable than for other models, but it still has some interpretational conundrums that must be dealt with. First, age is rarely a true independent variable. It is more often a proxy for age-related effects, cohort-related influences, and impacts from the particular time of measurement. In the MIDUS studies, these fundamental confounds with age are still present.

Because everyone was assessed at the same time, the impact of time of measurement as a main effect is minimal, but a time of measurement by age or cohort influence is also a possibility. Replicating the results across a 10-year span also helps the interpretation that these effects are related to age and not time of measurement or strongly influenced by cohort. In addition, other studies have supported the age-related association with negative affect, so thinking of what the mediating mechanism might be is warranted. Again, in this study, focusing on neuroticism as a mediating characteristic of personality seems reasonable. Neuroticism as a personality trait functions as a filter of the age-cohort-related experiences and the declines in an individual's experiences and thereby affects the person's feelings of negative affect. In other words, neuroticism is a fairly stable personality characteristic, and it is hypothesized to be a characteristic that shapes how one views the world and personal events within it. One drawback to the cross-sectional test of this hypothesis is that I cannot disentangle the stable features of neuroticism that are linked to feelings of negative affect. That is, I know that persons who are higher on neuroticism are also higher on negative affect. The indirect effect shown in Figure 9.3 is consistent with a mediating pathway, but the effect is perfectly confounded with the stable characteristics that lead neuroticism and negative affect to be correlated with the change characteristics. With cross-sectional data I cannot be certain that it is the *changes* in neuroticism that are associated with age cohort that predict *changes* in negative affect. To examine change, the prior levels of a variable must be measured and controlled for (i.e., longitudinal data are required to examine *change*).

Half-Longitudinal Mediation

As I have mentioned, the best way to address a question of mediation is to pose the question using a longitudinal design. Given that mediation is a statement of change, the change information should be an explicit part of the model. In this example, the variables of interest have been measured at two measurement occasions. With at least two occasions, it is now possible to model the prior levels of a given variable in order to isolate the change variance. Cole and Maxwell (2003) describe a mediation model with just two time points as a half-longitudinal design. The basic setup for a model to test mediation with just two occasions is depicted in Figure 9.4. The path labeled $\beta_{4,1}$ is the *a* path of a mediation model. It is the strength of the association between a predictor variable and a mediating variable, controlling for prior levels of the mediating variable (i.e., the path labeled $\beta_{4,2}$). The path labeled $\beta_{4,1}$ is, therefore, the predictive strength of the change variance in the mediator by the predictor variable. The path labeled $\beta_{5,3}$ is the strength of the association between the mediating variable and the outcome variable when prior levels of the outcome variable are controlled (i.e., the path labeled $\beta_{5,2}$). This path is the *b* path of a mediation model.

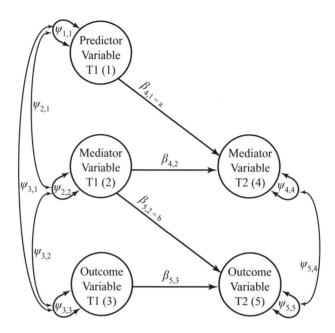

FIGURE 9.4. The half-longitudinal design for testing mediation. The representation of the measurement model is removed from the diagram. This design is the minimum required in order to empirically demonstrate mediation as a causal hypothesis.

Before I delve into the specifics of the half-longitudinal model, I need to define some key terms and concepts related to longitudinal mediation testing. The first term is *stationarity*. In the context of longitudinal mediation with panel data, stationarity refers to the unchanging causal structure among the measured constructs. That is, all predictive paths from occasion to occasion are at the same magnitude between each of the measurement occasions. When thinking about mediation in the social and behavioral sciences, the assumption of stationarity is a weak assumption. By weak, I mean that it is not the kind of assumption that invalidates the pattern of observed relations. If stationarity holds, great; however, nonstationarity is not a problem for inferring mediation. In longitudinal research in the social sciences, the causal pathways that are observed over time more often than not are also undergoing change, particularly from a lifespan perspective. From this perspective, stationarity is almost always violated to some degree in the various social and behavioral science literatures. Similarly, with intervention studies, the stationarity assumption is typically violated if the intervention has an effect, because the effect of the intervention will change over time (I discuss this idea more when I introduce a multiwave test of mediation).

Another related assumption that is discussed in this modeling context is the assumption of equilibrium. Equilibrium occurs when the variances and covariances among the measured constructs are unchanging over time. I have already described this idea as the homogeneity of the variance–covariance patterns within each wave. Given the change processes that govern the development of humans, this assumption is also rarely supported. Like stationarity, I see this assumption as a weak one that is seldom obtained in longitudinal data. Both of these assumptions are based on closed-systems models that have a teleological end state on which the measured processes will eventually converge. From my perspective, the assumption of equilibrium is hardly tenable at any given age and especially not across the lifespan, particularly in the social and behavioral sciences. My suggestion is to test these assumptions, and, if they hold, you have a strong basis from which to discuss a mediating process. If they do not hold, you still have a basis to discuss mediation, but the system is not stable. An unstable system also means that other unmeasured variables may be affecting the system and that these impacts may be attenuating or confounding the mediation effects that are being examined. In this regard, the discussion of mediation needs to acknowledge the limitations that are present.

Back to the half-longitudinal model: it requires certain assumptions to be met, like any model. In this case, stationarity is assumed. Here, the assumption is that the causal effects observed between the two measurement occasions would also emerge again if a third wave of data were collected. This half-longitudinal model also assumes that the selected interval of measurement is optimal for revealing both the $X \rightarrow M$ relation (controlling for prior levels of M) and the $M \rightarrow Y$ relation (controlling for prior levels of Y). Although stationarity is assumed with the half-longitudinal model, it is also the case that this model might be well suited to model a hypothesized mediation effect that is not expected to be stationary. For example, if I had a hypothesis about how personal agency mediates the effect of coping strategy on adjustment, such a hypothesis would be expected to reveal itself when the individual is under duress or in a period of transition. It may not be manageable to effectively obtain three waves of data during the period of transition. In this situation, the half-longitudinal model may be well suited to the task. That is, all the relevant measures can be taken at the start of the transition and again toward the end of the transition. The half-longitudinal design could then be used to test the mediation hypothesis. In a situation like this, a third measurement occasion would not be expected to show the effects again, because the measurements would be outside the "window" of the adjustment episode.

The half-longitudinal model is a significant improvement in inferential power over a cross-sectional test of mediation. In fact, when I work within the context of a cross-sectional model, I try to avoid using the word *mediation*. Instead, I simply talk about the significance (or lack thereof) of the indirect pathway, because cross-sectional data has such limited utility for inferring mediation. In the half-longitudinal design, on the other hand, I am now able to control for prior levels and examine the significance of the influences on the *change* variance of the mediator and the outcome.

Unfortunately, in the half-longitudinal model, a number of key assumptions are still made about the nature of the mediation process. Clearly, one key assumption is that the path *a* and the path *b*, which are estimated at the same time, would have a time-ordered relationship if more than two occasions of measurement were possible to obtain. In other words, the effect of the predictor on the mediator from Time 1 to Time 2 would then be followed at a later time point by the effect of the mediator on the change in the outcome variable from Time 2 to Time 3. In the half-longitudinal design, the assumption is that this time-ordered relationship would be the case.

The test of mediation in the half-longitudinal design relies upon using some modern features of SEM packages to create an additional phantom variable or alternative parameter that can estimate the product *ab* as part of the model and test it for significance. Cole and Maxwell (2003) note that if the *a* path and the *b* path are both significant, then the product of the two paths is also significant; however, this statement has been debated, and I would still suggest properly testing the product of *ab* for significance. Another problem with the joint null test of the *ab* product is that it is not a very powerful test. If either the *a* or the *b* path is not significant in this circumstance, then you need to test the *ab* path using a more powerful approach.

A number of tests of indirect effects exist, but only a couple of them are reasonable. Only two of the tests of the significance of a mediation effect do not make assumptions about the distribution of the *ab* product term. Most of the older methods (e.g., Baron & Kenny, 1986; Sobel, 1982) assume that the *ab* product term is normally distributed. Unfortunately, the product of two parameters is not normally distributed. In this case, a more precise method for conducting the significance of the *ab* pathway is needed. Two approaches that I recommend are the Monte Carlo simulation approach developed by MacKinnon and colleagues (2004; see also Preacher & Selig, 2012) and bootstrap estimation (Preacher & Hayes, 2008a; Shrout & Bolger, 2002). Either of these methods is reasonable for testing the significance of the *ab* pathway.

With the Monte Carlo approach, the *a* parameter and its distribution (as indicated by its standard error) and the *b* parameter and its distribution (as indicated by its standard error) are used to make numerous samples of *a* times *b* from the possible parameter space defined by the two distributions. A confidence interval is then calculated from the Monte Carlo distribution to determine significance. Similarly, bootstrap estimation uses resampling from the original sample to approximate the empirical standard error of the *ab* product term. Here, *ab* is calculated on the repeated bootstrap samples, and a distribution of these *ab* product values is generated. As with the Monte Carlo approach, the confidence interval of the parameters is used to determine the significance of the *ab* product. If the value of the null hypothesis is not within the confidence interval, then the null hypothesis would be rejected at an alpha level equal to 1– the confidence interval percentage. In all of my examples, I report the 95% confidence interval, which corresponds to the $p < .05$ alpha level.

In Figure 9.5, I have presented the results of the half-longitudinal analysis of the

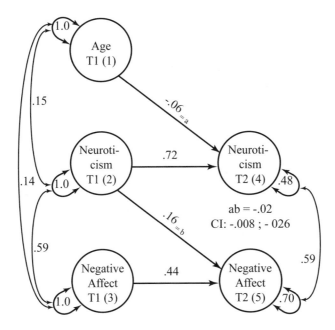

FIGURE 9.5. Gallagher and Johnson's test of neuroticism as a mediator of age effects on negative affect. The representation of the measurement model is removed from the diagram.

mediation model that Gallagher and Johnson (2008) tested. As mentioned, they had two time points separated by 10 years. But given the pace of change in the variables assessed, a 10-year interval is not unreasonable. Personality, for example, is a rather slow-changing trait (in fact, some work suggests that it remains remarkably stable in adulthood). In order to detect changes in neuroticism and its effect on trait levels of negative affect across the lifespan, allowing a long interval would be prudent.

As can be seen in the model (Figure 9.5), the personality trait of neuroticism is reasonably stable, with a .72 stability coefficient. Age reliably predicts the change variance in neuroticism with a cross-time effect of –.06. The magnitude of this effect is slightly larger than the cross-sectional effect (–.002), but this difference in magnitude is probably not significant. The size of the effect of neuroticism on negative affect (.16), on the other hand, is quite a bit lower than the estimate that was derived from the cross-sectional data (.48). The change in the magnitude of this effect highlights a key difference/confound between a cross-sectional approach and a longitudinal approach. In the cross-sectional approach, the association between neuroticism and negative affect is inflated by the stable trait-like characteristics of the association between these two constructs. In Figure 9.5, I show that the product of *ab* is estimated as –0.02, and the Monte Carlo confidence interval indicates that this parameter is clearly outside the 0 estimate (–0.008 is the upper confidence interval for this negative point estimate, whereas –0.026 is the lower estimate).

Full Longitudinal Mediation

Figure 9.6 depicts a full longitudinal model of mediation. As can be seen in the figure, at least three time points are required to estimate a true indirect pathway across the two time spans. Path *a*, which is seen in parameters $\beta_{5,1}$ and $\beta_{8,4}$, and path *b*, which is seen in parameters $\beta_{6,2}$ and $\beta_{9,5}$ has only one contiguous indirect pathway by which the predictor variable can indirectly influence the outcome variable. Namely, the *ab* product can be estimated and defined by the product of the path $\beta_{5,1}$ and $\beta_{9,5}$.

The full longitudinal model, like the half-longitudinal model, relies on the assumption that the intervals between measurement occasions are optimal to detect the effects of interest. As Cole and Maxwell (2003) point out, most measurement occasions in the social and behavioral sciences are chosen based on convenience or tradition, and not on any theoretically or empirically supported measurement schedule. When using fixed time intervals for assessing longitudinal mediation, timing is everything! How much time must pass before the causal effect of *X* on the mediator (*M*) will be optimally detected? How much time must pass before the causal effect of *M* on the outcome (*Y*) will be optimally detected? The answer to these two questions may be different. To answer these questions would likely require pilot data. A pilot study might use a randomly assigned lag interval in order to model the change effect as a function of time. This distributed lag study could show when an effect begins and when it ends, as well as when it peaks. I could also use a lag as moderator

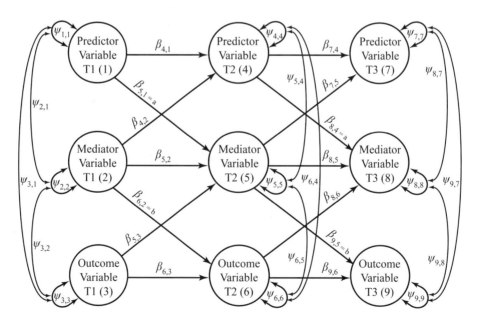

FIGURE 9.6. The key elements of a full longitudinal mediation model. For simplicity, I have eliminated the representation of measurement model from the diagram.

analysis to potentially identify whether an effect changes in its magnitude over time (see Chapter 2; see also Selig, Preacher, & Little, 2012). Regardless of what methods are used, determining the optimal lags for the measurement occasions is extremely important.

A related "timing" issue is selecting the developmental epoch during which the mediating process takes place. This developmental period should be represented in its entirety. For example, if the mediation is restricted to the period of adolescence, the full range of the adolescent period should be sampled. If the full period of time is not represented, the evidence of mediation is not as compelling as it could be. Particularly for more mature areas of research, a thorough examination of the full period would further scientific understanding. In less mature areas of research, perhaps a sample of the interval would be sufficient to spur further discovery. To sample from a full developmental period, utilizing the power and efficiency of planned missing data designs would allow coverage of the period of interest.

Cole and Maxwell (2003) outlined a series of five steps for testing mediation in a longitudinal model. They discussed a number of steps within the context of their Steps 1 and 2 that I think are somewhat out of order. In Table 9.1, I have outlined the steps, with some of the implicit tests made explicit, and reordered a couple of

TABLE 9.1. Steps in the process of testing of mediation

Steps for testing mediation	Needed outcome to continue
Step 1: Establish factorial invariance. 　　Step 1a: Configural invariance 　　Step 1b: Weak invariance 　　Step 1c: Strong invariance	At least partial strong invariance is essential to proceed with testing mediation.
Step 2: Test the homogeneity of the within-time variance-covariance matrix.	Equilibrium is nonessential, but should be tested.
Step 3: Test the stability of the mean structures over time.	Mean-level stability is nonessential but testable.
Step 4: Test the endogenous constructs for nonzero residual correlations.	No omitted variables is nonessential but testable.
Step 5: Test the need for other cross-time paths (i.e., fit only mediation paths).	Omitting paths that are significant produces bias.
Step 6: Calculate magnitudes of indirect, total, and direct effects.	The total indirect effect is key mediation parameter.
Step 7: Test all the effects for significance using bootstrap or Monte Carlo.	The total indirect effect should be significant.
Step 8: Estimate final model with all significant paths estimated.	Is mediation still evident when the other paths are included?

Note. These steps are based on Cole and Maxwell (2003) but reflect my view on the order and the importance of some of the steps involved.

things (e.g., test for strong factorial invariance before testing the homogeneity of the variance–covariance matrix within time points). Table 9.1 has eight basic steps. The first step, from my perspective, is to establish strong factorial invariance. I outlined the sequence of steps in making this determination in Chapter 5. In Table 9.1, I have labeled these as steps 1a, configural invariance; 1b, weak factorial invariance; and 1c, strong factorial invariance. As I see it, factorial invariance is a necessary precondition for testing any questions in the context of a panel model. I also outlined a number of questions that can be addressed about the construct relations in the longitudinal CFA model. The second step, therefore, is the test of the homogeneity of the variance–covariance relations among the constructs. In the table, I have also listed the degree to which the tested assumption is necessary to infer whether a mediated process is evident. You'll see that I have listed equilibrium as nonessential, whereas factorial invariance (or at least partial strong invariance) is essential. Step 3 involves testing the stationarity of the mean structures over time. This step, like equilibrium, is a nonessential element of mediation testing.

Steps 4 and 5 are tests that Cole and Maxwell (2003) recommend to evaluate whether there is evidence of any omitted variables or whether there is evidence of causal processes that were not anticipated in the initial structural model. Steps 4 and 5 are informative exercises for evaluating the relations among the constructs, but as Cole and Maxwell also note, these tests are not necessarily ones that would contraindicate mediation if they were to fail. If they pass, on the other hand, then there is very strong evidence in favor of the mediation model being tested.

Step 4, for example, involves specifying a saturated regression model including any covariate influences and testing whether the residual variances of the constructs measured at the second time point onward are uncorrelated. This test is based on the assumption that if all relevant variables are included in a model, then all the meaningful variance in the constructs would be adequately explained. In other words, are the residual correlations among the constructs at a given measurement occasion statistically 0? A corollary of this test is that the residual variances of the constructs should approach 0. Having a model in which all the variance of all the constructs at later time points is fully explained is not common in the social and behavioral sciences. The logic of this idea is sound, and it is an ideal to which we can aspire, but we may not be likely to achieve it.

Step 5 involves testing the need for any other directed paths (either autoregressive paths of more than one lag or cross-lagged effects that are either direct effects on the outcome or reciprocal effects going in the other direction) above and beyond the mediation paths that are hypothesized. For example, the model in Figure 9.6 would be fit to the data, and the significance of the change in model fit from the baseline CFA model to this one would be evaluated. If the change in fit is trivial, then no other causal paths are needed above and beyond the mediation paths. This finding would be strong evidence in support of the hypothesized mediation model, and it would indicate that no other causal influences are lurking around and potentially affecting the mediation process. That is, if other direct or indirect pathways are needed, they may change the magnitude and significance of the mediated pathway (i.e., the total indirect effect). If covariates are included in the model, I would have the covariates just correlate with the focal constructs, but I could specify this model with the covariates included. If I just correlate the covariates, it is a clearer test of other causal processes. If the covariates are included, the test may be nonsignificant because the covariates represent the other causal processes that may be involved. This finding would make things a bit muddy.

Step 6 involves a direct test of the longitudinal mediation hypothesis. In this test, only the cross-lagged paths that are consistent with mediation are estimated, and the total indirect mediation effect is calculated. Cole and Maxwell (2003) also recommend that the total direct effect be calculated. With this model, the focus is solely on whether there is evidence for mediation in the absence of other parameter estimates, and overall model fit is not a key consideration. The focus is on calculating the mediation pathway. Unlike Step 5, however, in which all the other causal paths are fixed at 0, I recommend that all paths unrelated to mediation be specified as correlations among the constructs. This test would be an unbiased test of whether mediation is evident in the set of constructs being evaluated.

Step 7 involves evaluating the calculated quantities from Step 6 for significance. This step would be accomplished by using bootstrap estimation with alternative parameters in LISREL or using the model constraint command in Mplus. If bootstrap estimation is not feasible, then the Monte Carlo approach that Preacher and Selig (2012) elaborated on would be used (a more elaborate R function for using the Monte Carlo approach is available in the semTools package). I'm writing this up as a separate step to reinforce the idea that the appropriate test of significance for the indirect effects is either bootstrap estimation or the Monte Carlo approach.

Step 8 involves specifying all the theoretically meaningful elements of the structural relationships over time. Here, not only are the pathways that are consistent with mediation specified but so too are any reciprocal relations of the influences of Y and/or M on later instantiations of these constructs. This model must fit the data as well as the CFA model does. All directed regression relations that are significant are going to be estimated, and nonsignificant paths would be removed (pruned).

With a full longitudinal model, some of the assumptions of the half-longitudinal model no longer are invoked to infer mediation. An interesting feature of the full longitudinal model is that two half-longitudinal model replications are evident. That is, paths $\beta_{5,1}$ and $\beta_{6,2}$ can be multiplied as a proxy of the ab pathway. Similarly $\beta_{8,4}$ and $\beta_{9,5}$ can be multiplied as a proxy of the ab pathway. The only true indirect pathway that reflects the proper mediation effect is the product of pathways $\beta_{5,1}$ and $\beta_{9,5}$. The pathway by which X exerts its effect on Y is confined to this single pathway in a three-wave longitudinal study. When more waves of data are collected, the influence of X on Y during the period of interest increases considerably. I discuss this idea when I introduce Figure 9.7.

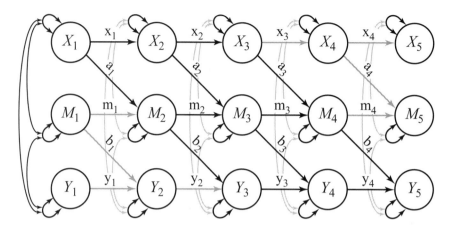

FIGURE 9.7. A full longitudinal mediation diagram of five waves, illustrating the various indirect effects whereby X_1 influences Y_5. The circles denote latent variables measured at five time points. The subscripts within the circles denote the time of measurement. The parameter labels also have a subscript to denote the occurrence of the effect. Modeled after Cole and Maxwell (2003).

In Figure 9.6, stationarity would be evident if the corresponding predictive paths between measurements were equal. Stationarity would be tested in this case as a straightforward χ^2 difference test with 7 degrees of freedom. That is, (1) $\beta_{7,4}$ would equal $\beta_{4,1}$, (2) $\beta_{8,4}$ would equal $\beta_{5,1}$, (3) $\beta_{7,5}$ would equal $\beta_{4,2}$, (4) $\beta_{8,5}$ would equal $\beta_{5,2}$, (5) $\beta_{8,6}$ would equal $\beta_{5,3}$, (6) $\beta_{9,5}$ would equal $\beta_{6,2}$, and (7) $\beta_{9,6}$ would equal $\beta_{6,3}$.

Figure 9.7 is a five-wave depiction of mediation that examines all possible pathways by which X at Time 1, the beginning of the expected period of mediation, influences Y at Time 5, the end of the expected period of mediation. I have omitted the measurement model for this figure. The subscripts of the latent factors X, M, and Y refer to the wave of measurement. The subscripts on the parameter labels refer to the linkages between waves of measurement. For example a_1 is the link between the predictor X at Time 1 and the mediator M at Time 2. Cole and Maxwell (2003) have argued that mediation should be assessed as the significance of the total indirect effect from the predictor at Time 1 to the outcome variable Y at the final wave of assessment. With five waves of data, as shown in Figure 9.7, the number of indirect pathways is six:

1. $a_1 \cdot b_2 \cdot y_3 \cdot y_4 +$
2. $a_1 \cdot m_2 \cdot b_3 \cdot y_4 +$
3. $a_1 \cdot m_2 \cdot m_3 \cdot b_4 +$
4. $x_1 \cdot a_2 \cdot b_3 \cdot y_4 +$

5. $x_1 \cdot a_2 \cdot m_3 \cdot b_4 +$

6. $x_1 \cdot x_2 \cdot a_3 \cdot b_4$

The total indirect effect would simply be the sum of these six indirect pathways by which X at Time 1 exerts its influence on Y at Time 5 via an indirect pathway through the mediator (M). Note that prior levels of all three variables are included as autoregressive paths so that all interpretations at later time points are in terms of changes in the individual-differences standings. Time-specific mediated pathways could be tested separately from the total indirect effect, but only when strong theory suggests that the effect should occur in a circumscribed span of time.

Figure 9.8 shows the results of fitting a longitudinal mediation model to four waves of data using the Espelage dataset. In this model, family conflict is expected to predict increases in substance use over time, which in turn is expected to lead to increases in victimization over time. This dataset has four waves of data that allow a full longitudinal mediation model to be estimated. The model fit information for these data is presented in Table 9.2.

In Table 9.2, the first step in establishing measurement invariance is very acceptably accomplished. Table 9.3 shows the resulting measurement model for the strong invariant model with these data. Table 9.3 is a nice format to use to show how the constructs have invariant loadings and intercepts across time, but when standardized the loading information changes somewhat at each time point, and the

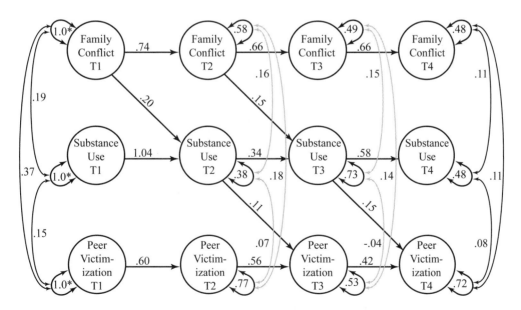

FIGURE 9.8. The full longitudinal mediation model of substance use mediating the effect of family conflict on victimization. The data for this example come from Dorothy Espelage's longitudinal dataset.

TABLE 9.2. Tests related to the mediation model presented in Figures 9.8 and 9.9

Model tested	χ^2	df	$\Delta\chi^2$	Δdf	p	RMSEA	RMSEA 90% CI	CFI	ΔCFI	Pass?
Null model	33015.4	957				---	---			---
Configural invariance	2682.9	642				.051	.049;.054	.936		Yes
Weak invariance	2935.7	660				.054	.052;.056	.929	.007	Yes
Strong invariance	3203.9	678				.056	.055;.058	.921	.008	Yes
Homogeneity var/cov	3758.6	696	554.7	12	<.001	.062	.060;.064	.904	.021	No
Mean stability	3336.8	687	132.8	9	<.001	.057	.055;.059	.917	.039	No
Omitted variables	3659.0	690	455.1	12	<.001	.061	.059;.063	.907	.014	No
Other causal effects	3503.6	719	299.7	41	<.001	.057	.055;.059	.913	.008	No
Final model	3379.1	778	175.2	100	<.001	.053	.052;.054	.919	.002	Yes

Note. For the measurement model tests of invariance, a change in CFI of .01 or less is used. The criterion for determining too much loss in fit in the latent space, given the power of the sample size, is a p-value less than .001 or a change in CFI greater than .002. The tests of the latent parameters includes covariate controls.

residual information is also time-specific. The column labeled h^2 is the communality estimate. The communality estimate is the amount of reliable variance in the indicator that is predicted by the latent factor at each time point. As seen in the table, the indicators of family conflict and peer victimization are congeneric in nature but still factorially invariant. In other words, the measurement model information also looks acceptable, and tests of mediation can proceed.

Referring back to Table 9.2, the results of Step 2, which tests the homogeneity

TABLE 9.3. Measurement model estimates for mediation example

	Equated estimates				Standardized loadings and time-specific residuals											
					Time 1			Time 2			Time 3			Time 4		
Indicator	λ	se	τ	se	λ	θ	h^2	λ	θ	h^2	λ	θ	h^2	λ	θ	h^2
Family conflict																
Parcel 1	1.12 (.02)		-.44 (.03)		.81	.35	.65	.79	.38	.62	.80	.36	.64	.82	.32	.68
Parcel 2	1.27 (.02)		-.51 (.04)		.90	.19	.81	.89	.20	.80	.85	.27	.73	.89	.21	.79
Parcel 3	0.61 (.02)		.95 (.04)		.45	.83	.17	.45	.81	.20	.44	.81	.19	.46	.79	.21
Peer victimization																
Parcel 1	1.05 (.01)		-.02 (.02)		.77	.41	.59	.80	.38	.62	.76	.43	.57	.78	.39	.61
Parcel 2	1.24 (.01)		-.25 (.02)		.86	.25	.75	.87	.24	.76	.84	.29	.71	.87	.24	.76
Parcel 3	0.72 (.01)		.27 (.02)		.75	.46	.56	.74	.46	.54	.70	.51	.49	.78	.40	.60
Substance use																
Parcel 1	0.99 (.01)		.08 (.01)		.77	.41	.59	.83	.31	.69	.82	.32	.68	.83	.32	.68
Parcel 2	1.05 (.01)		-.09 (.01)		.94	.11	.89	.94	.11	.89	.91	.18	.82	.92	.15	.85
Parcel 3	0.97 (.01)		.01 (.01)		.84	.30	.70	.88	.22	.78	.88	.23	.77	.76	.42	.58

Note. n = 1132. Results of the strong invariance test of the three constructs examining mediation. Standardized loadings are from the common metric completely standardized solution. λ = the loading, τ = the intercept, θ = the residual, se = the standard error, h^2 = the communality estimate/amount of reliable variance explained.

of the variance–covariance matrix, do not pass; but as I indicated earlier, this step is not crucial for determining mediation. The test of the stability of the mean structures was also not satisfactory, indicating that the constructs are changing in terms of their mean levels during this period of time. This step, too, is not crucial for testing mediation. The results of Step 4 also did not pass, suggesting that some other omitted variables may be lying in wait to undermine the observed mediating pathways.

In Table 9.4, I have entered the correlations, means, and variances from the strong factorial invariant model. As seen in the table, the correlations and variances do change some across time (although not dramatically and not systematically), and the mean levels of the constructs also change over time (again, not dramatically or systematically). Such a variable pattern of change is consistent with patterns I see when constructs such as these are measured in quasi-experimental settings. Extraneous stuff is happening all around, and this stuff produces variability in patterns of correlations, mean-level differences, and changes in the constructs' variances. This extraneous stuff is happening above and beyond the change processes that are at the heart of a given study. This extraneous stuff may be important, or it may not be. The failure of the various tests in Table 9.4 may reflect unimportant extraneous stuff or important confounding variables. Only theory and future research can determine what might be going on when these tests do not pass.

With four waves of data, there are three mediated pathways by which family conflict at Time 1 can exert its effect on peer victimization at Time 4 via the substance use mediator at the intervening times of measurement. The first route is from family conflict at Time 1 to substance use at Time 2 (.20) to peer victimization at Time 3 (.11) and through the autoregressive path of peer victimization predicting itself between Time 3 and Time 4 (.42). The second route goes from family conflict

TABLE 9.4. Correlations among the constructs in the mediation example: Zero-order estimates from the strong invariant model and residual estimates from the final model

	FC1	SU1	PV1	FC2	SU2	PV2	FC3	SU3	PV3	FC4	SU4	PV4
FC1	--	.182	.352									
SU1	.185	--	.041									
PV1	.335	.143	--									
FC2	.654	.189	.275	--	.427	.374						
SU2	.336	.766	.228	.421	--	.203						
PV2	.294	.040	.469	.378	.179	--						
FC3	.498	.215	.198	.705	.367	.282	--	.448	.343			
SU3	.284	.362	.244	.376	.508	.186	.442	--	.140			
PV3	.252	.114	.441	.313	.220	.662	.361	.176	--			
FC4	.545	.177	.272	.596	.340	.370	.706	.332	.337	--	.353	.355
SU4	.167	.310	.116	.232	.378	.143	.293	.726	.078	.332	--	.216
PV4	.316	.128	.330	.319	.240	.493	.349	.204	.498	.392	.210	--
Means	1.897	1.237	1.616	1.898	1.253	1.704	1.864	1.245	1.635	1.826	1.231	1.519
Vars	.294	.130	.350	.395	.277	.549	.339	.192	.396	.275	.124	.278

Note. Correlations below the diagonal are from the standardized solution of the strong invariant model. Correlations above the diagonal are from the standardized solution of the final structural mediation model. FC = family conflict, SU = substance use, PV = peer victimization at Times 1, 2, 3, and 4.

at Time 1 to substance use at Time 2 (.20) but then through the autoregressive path of substance use at Time 2 to substance use at Time 3 (.34) before going from substance use at Time 3 to peer victimization at Time 4 (.15). The final route starts with the autoregressive effect of family conflict at Time 1 to itself at Time 2 (.74), then goes from family conflict at Time 2 to the mediator, substance use, at Time 3 (.15) and further on to predict peer victimization at Time 4 (.15). The total mediated effect of family conflict at Time 1 on peer victimization at Time 4 would be the sum of these three routes of indirect influence. The significance of the sum of these values can be determined by using the Monte Carlo estimation method, which we have modified for larger and more complex expressions such as these multiple pathways (information is at *www.guilford.com/little-materials*, including how to use the semTools R package for this expression).

Figure 9.8 contains the estimates of the full mediation model, with all other causal pathways estimated as nondirectional covariance estimates. This model is used to calculate the overall indirect effects. The overall indirect effect of mediation for this example was 0.020. This estimate was tested for significance using the Monte Carlo method (as implemented in the semTools package of R). The confidence interval for this effect was 0.008–0.034, indicating that the overall indirect effect is significant. If the estimated indirect effects were based on the model from Step 5, where the test is whether other causal pathways are needed, the estimate of the size and significance of the total indirect effect would potentially be inflated. If other causal paths are not estimated in the model, the parameter bias of the ones that are estimated can become quite pronounced. For this example, the estimated total indirect effect of family conflict at Time 1 on peer victimization at Time 4 was 0.035, and the confidence interval for this effect was 0.023–0.047. This incorrectly estimated value is even significantly greater than the correctly estimated value of 0.020.

In Figure 9.9, I present the full final model with the significant cross-lagged effects and the additional autoregressive effects included in the model. This final model fits the data as well as the best fitting measurement model based on the change in CFI and the RMSEA fit measures. The χ^2 significance test was significant, but with 100 degrees of freedom involved in this test and a sample size of 1,132, the net effect of these trivial disturbances is significant. In the final SEM model, the mediation pathways remain significant even when the other cross-lagged and autoregressive parameters are entered into the model. The overall indirect effect in the final model is 0.019 with a confidence interval of 0.009–0.030. This effect is slightly reduced compared with the full test presented in Figure 9.8, primarily because family conflict has a direct effect on peer victimization at Time 4 and peer victimization had two additional autoregressive pathways that emerged and explained some of the variance in peer victimization at Time 4.

The preceding discussion of mediation is meant to provide a broad overview of how to test for mediation in longitudinal data. It contained my recommendations, which are based on the work of Cole and Maxwell (2003) and others. In the second

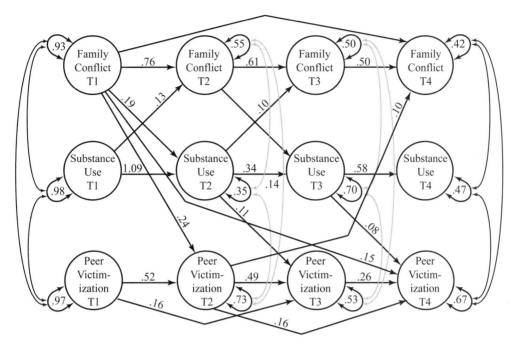

FIGURE 9.9. The final longitudinal model with the mediating effects among family conflict, substance use, and victimization. The data for this example come from Dorothy Espelage's longitudinal project. The total indirect effect of family conflict on peer victimization via substance use is still significant (95% CI: .009–.030) when all significant direct effects are included. The regression estimates are unstandardized. The variance terms are standardized to reflect the amount of variance that is unexplained. The amount explained would be 1 minus these values. In addition to the cross-time paths, significant effects of gender, grade, black, white, and three dummy codes for school are included.

half of this chapter, I turn the discussion to moderation. My focus here is on continuous variable moderation. I already showed an example of a discrete moderator when I examined gender differences in the pathways associated with the linkages between bullying and homophobic teasing. A discrete moderator is any variable that can be used as a grouping variable in a multiple-group context, and any pathway of such a model that is not statistically equal is thereby moderated by the grouping variable.

MODERATION

The idea of an interaction is one of the core second-step ideas conveyed in most introductions to statistics. An interaction is moderation—moderation is evinced when an interaction term is deemed significant. So moderation is just a simple interaction. Depicting a simple interaction in latent-variable modeling frameworks is not necessarily simple, but it is straightforward. In this section, I cover the basics of three different methods for representing an interaction in latent-variable models. I then discuss the tricky details that are involved in testing latent-variable interactions in a longitudinal modeling framework.

Quite often during my consultations with researchers, confusion arises between a moderated influence versus a profile of an individual on a set of variables that might, for example, reflect a set of risk and protective factors. Often in this case, a researcher may see a protective factor as moderating a risk factor when, in fact, it is canceling out the effect of the risk factor. Straightforward multivariate equations, in which some effects are positive (e.g., a protective factor if the outcome is scaled in the "good" direction) and some effects are negative (e.g., a risk factor if it is scaled in the "risk" direction), are not moderating effects but rather are balancing equations. For a person who is high on a risk factor, the fact that he or she is also high on a protective factor may reduce the potential risk. This person's profile on the set of variables would predict a neutral outcome. A person who is high on a risk factor but who is also low on the protective factor would have a predicted poor outcome. The choice of words to describe how one variable counteracts the effect of another variable is at the discretion of the investigator, with the exception of the word *moderation*. I refer to these kinds of relationships generically as additive effects. The model is a linear combination of multiple predictors. The regression weights, which indicate the direction of the effect as well as the relative strength of the effect, are added together to calculate a predicted outcome given the set of predictors that are in a given model.

When one effect is positive while another is negative, the effects can "cancel out," "counteract each other," "balance," "differentially contribute," "oppositely predict," "go in opposing directions," "countermand one another," or "provide predictive profiles," but they do not moderate one another. For example, the use of prosocial coping strategies has a positive influence on adjustment. The use of antisocial coping strategies has a negative influence on adjustment. These effects are unique effects that each control for the other. Moreover, the coping strategies are relatively unrelated. This lack of association between the strategies means that a person high on prosocial coping is just as likely to be high, medium, or low on antisocial coping. For those who are high on both prosocial and antisocial coping, the benefits of using prosocial coping are offset by the costs of also employing antisocial coping. For those who are low on antisocial coping, the benefits of positive coping are not offset, because the net predicted effect is a high adjustment value. A person's relative standing on each of these constructs provides the predicted level on the outcome. Each person has a profile that gives rise to the predicted value. Here, the individual rank, level, or standing on an outcome measure depends on the risk and protective profile of each person on the set of predictor variables. Although I emphasize this distinction between a profile and a moderator, it is possible for a variable to be either a risk or a protective factor and also to function as a moderating influence. In the empirical example that follows, I show how the construct of family closeness functions both as a protective factor and as a moderating buffering factor. My point here is that researchers need to be very clear about the difference between additive effects that lead to the same outcome via different standings on a set of variables and the concept of moderation.

Testing moderation in a cross-sectional framework is very straightforward and relatively easy to accomplish these days. Testing moderation in a latent-variable framework and testing it longitudinally is, as I have mentioned, more challenging. In Figure 9.10, I show how moderation is often depicted diagrammatically (see Panel A), but analytically the analysis model is quite a bit different (see Panel B). This feature of the diagramming system for representing statistical models is somewhat unsatisfying. I depict moderation as a full path diagram as I review the various techniques for testing latent-variable interactions. As mentioned, moderators can be either discrete variables or continuous variables. Discrete moderators are abundant insofar as we find gender differences, group (intervention vs. control) differences,

A) How a moderator is sometimes portrayed in SEM

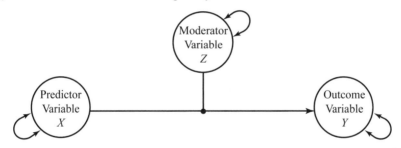

B) How a moderator is actually analyzed using SEM diagrams

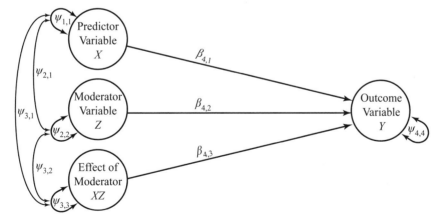

FIGURE 9.10. The key elements of cross-sectional moderation. For simplicity, I have eliminated the representation of the measurement model from this diagram. The moderator effect can be created in a number of ways. I review them below. Panel B contains all the key parameters of cross-sectional moderation.

ethnic differences, cultural differences, and the like in the association between any two variables. Moderation in this regard is not a question about mean-level differences but about the strength of an association between a set of variables that are the focus of a given study.

Moderation can be tested in latent-variable frameworks using one of two general approaches. The first approach is a model-estimation-based approach developed by Klein and Moosbrugger (2000) and subsequently implemented in Mplus (Muthén & Asparouhov, 2003). It is currently available only in the software package Mplus. The mathematical details of how this approach works are beyond the scope of my discussion here. Suffice it to say that if you own the software package Mplus, you would simply use the `XWITH` command to estimate a latent-variable interaction between two continuous latent variables. Although the `XWITH` command does have a number of features that make it relatively easy to specify, it is computationally demanding, especially in cases with multiple moderator variables, such as longitudinal models. I still generally prefer to create latent-variable interactions that use indicators based on manifest variables.

In this regard, Herb Marsh and his colleagues (2004), as well as our own research group (see Recommended Readings), have introduced a set of simple indicator-based methods for including latent-variable interactions in an SEM model. These indicator-based approaches build on ideas by David Kenny and follow simple regression-based logic. In regression modeling, an interaction term can be represented by creating a product variable by multiplying the scores on the two variables that are thought to interact with one another. One problem with this approach is the fact that the product variable will be highly correlated with the two variables from which it is calculated. One way to fix this collinearity problem is to mean-center the variables of interest before taking the product of the two. Mean centering simply involves subtracting the mean of the group from each score. The result is that the new set of scores contains some negative scores and some positive scores; in addition, these scores have a mean of 0. Mean centering is *not* the same thing as standardizing the variables. Standardizing would have the undesired effect of eliminating the covariance metric of the variable and would result in models in which the correlation metric would be estimated. Moreover, mean centering gives the illusion of fixing the collinearity problem, but all it does is shift the intercept to a new location.

A second, similar approach to fixing the collinearity problem with product terms is to orthogonalize the product variable with respect to the variables from which it is derived. Orthogonalizing is a simple regression approach to creating a new variable that is linearly independent of a set of predictors. Unlike mean centering, this approach does, in fact, create a truly uncorrelated interaction construct. Here, the product variable is regressed onto the constituent variables, and the unstandardized residuals are stored for later use. These stored unstandardized residuals reflect the information in the product variable that is the interaction. The orthogonalized residual and the mean-centered product variable both carry the same nonlinear information that is needed to test for a moderating effect of one variable on another.

To briefly summarize thus far, for creating indicator-based latent variables to represent an interaction, two data-based approaches and one model-based approach have been discussed. The model-based approach is specific to the Mplus software and is beyond the scope of this discussion. Of the data-based approaches, one is to double-mean-center the indicators of the interaction, and the other is to orthogonalize the indicators of the interaction with respect to the main-effect indicators. In the paper where my colleagues and I introduced the orthogonalizing approach (Little, Bovaird, & Widaman, 2006), we also recommended that the indicators of the latent-variable interaction term should consist of all possible product variables. Marsh and colleagues (2004) have argued that one can use a matched-pair approach. Assuming that each main-effect construct has three indicators, the matched-pair approach would take the first indicator of main-effect construct A and match it with the first indicator of main-effect construct B. The second indicator of A would be matched with the second indicator of B, as would the third indicator of A with the third indicator of B. The matched-pair approach is a bit subjective in that the indicators may not be optimally matched. If the indicators are tau-equivalent, this approach is a reasonably efficient way to produce indicators of an interaction. If the indicators are congeneric, however, then the matching process becomes critical for the matched-pair approach to work.

If all possible combinations of the main-effect indicators are used to create the indicators of the latent-variable interaction, then the information about the interaction is fully captured by the indicators. The drawback to the all-possible-combinations approach is that the residual covariances among these possible combinations will contain known associations that must be estimated in order to unbias the regression slope onto the latent-variable interaction construct. Figure 9.11 is a path diagram of a cross-sectional model to test moderation by Z of the regression between Y and X. In the figure, I have labeled the residuals of the interaction indicators because they are of critical focus in estimating latent interaction constructs. The product of X_1 and Z_1, for example, contains the product of the uniqueness of X_1 and the uniqueness of Z_1. The product of X_1 and Z_2 also contains the product of the uniqueness of X_1, but this time it is with the uniqueness of Z_2. Similarly, the product of X_1 and Z_3 also contains the product of the uniqueness of X_1, but this time it is with the uniqueness of Z_2. Thus, the indicators that are labeled X_1Z_1, X_1Z_2, and X_1Z_3 each contain the unique product information of X_1. This unique product information in each indicator will correlate with itself. Hence the three indicators involving X_1 have residual correlations specified. To ease estimation demands and because it is a reasonable assumption to make, I usually will place equality constraints on the set of corresponding correlated residuals. In Figure 9.11, I have labeled the corresponding sets of correlated residuals with the letters a–f.

With moderating relationships, one very important issue to keep in mind is

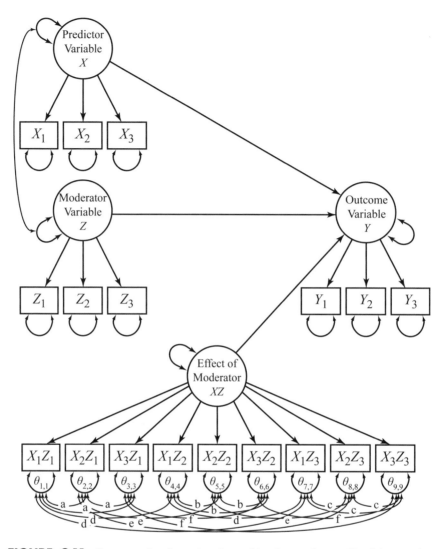

FIGURE 9.11. Cross-sectional moderation with nine orthogonalized interaction terms. The corresponding letters for the correlated residuals indicate residuals that can, and probably should, be set to equality. a = the residuals involving the uniqueness of Z_1; b = the residuals involving the uniqueness of Z_2; c = the residuals involving the uniqueness of Z_3; d = the residuals involving the uniqueness of X_1; e = the residuals involving the uniqueness of X_2; f = the residuals involving the uniqueness of X_3.

that the product term or interaction construct cannot address the question of which variable is moderating which variable. The interaction variable contains only the nonlinear information that is used to detect evidence of whether a moderating effect is present or not. The interpretation of moderation, therefore, depends on other considerations—most notably among these are the theoretical considerations. In many situations the distinction as to which variable is the moderator and which variable is the moderatee is very tenuous. An interaction variable can reveal only whether there is statistical evidence of moderation. It cannot reveal which variable is moderating which variable. To return to the car metaphor, the statistical model can't reveal whether the accelerator is changing the gear ratio or the gear ratio is changing the accelerator. I can use theory to rely on making a reasonable determination that the gear ratio is the moderator of the relation between the accelerator and the speed at which my car is traveling.

A moderator variable is purely a mathematical/statistical device to determine whether one variable has a moderating influence on another variable. Because of this quality of such a variable, model fit information is typically not a concern when the moderator variable is entered into a given model. I recommend that model fit be examined in the basic CFA model of the indicators of the assessed constructs, and once model fit is determined to be acceptable, then the moderator construct can be added into a model to examine the hypothesis of moderation. Testing the significance of the drop in fit between a final model and the best fitting CFA would require that the interaction constructs be included. Here, the overall model fit is not the focus; instead, the relative change in model fit when the structural paths are estimated becomes the focus. In the empirical example that follows, I walk through how this examination would be conducted.

My first example of moderation will be a simple cross-sectional moderation. Here, I have data from some work on personal agency, looking at its association with positive affect. On its own, personal agency has a positive correlation with positive affect: the more I believe that I possess the ability and wherewithal to accomplish my goals, the happier I am. If I have a belief system about whether ability and wherewithal are, in fact, means by which an outcome can be achieved, then my personal agency is useful. I would achieve my desired outcomes and I would be happy. On the other hand, if I think that ability and wherewithal are noncontingent for a given circumstance, then this noncontingency would undermine my personal agency beliefs. In other words, if I think the reason that good performance comes about is unknowable (i.e., a noncontingent environment), then my personal agency beliefs are undermined. I would not be able to be effective in this context, and it would undermine the relationship between having personal agency and having positive affect.

Table 9.5 presents the simple ordinary least squares (OLS) regression results predicting positive affect with two variables, personal agency (degree of effort and possession of ability) and unknown causes, the degree to which the context of performance is contingent upon one's actions (a causality belief). For more information on the theory and these variables, see Little (1998). In Table 9.5, I show three different ways of representing the interaction of personal agency and unknown causes. In the first column, I did nothing to the variables. They are uncentered, and I simply created the product of the two variables. This product variable is extremely highly correlated with the two main effects ($r = .92$). The second set of labeled columns represent the results when the two variables of personal agency and unknown causes

TABLE 9.5. Contrast of three different ways of testing an interaction effect

Model tested	Predictor	r_{xx}	Uncentered Beta	t	Mean centered Beta	t	Orthogonalized Beta	t
1) Main effects	Personal agency	.66	0.23	8.79	0.23	8.79	0.23	8.79
only	Unknown causes	.74	0.05	1.76	0.05	1.76	0.05	1.76
2) With	Personal agency	.66	0.59	6.81	0.23	9.01	0.23	8.84
multiplicative	Unknown causes	.74	0.62	4.63	0.04	1.56	0.05	1.77
interaction term	Interaction term	.62	-0.63	-4.37	-0.11	-4.37	-0.11	-4.37

Note. These are the results of a standard OLS regression analysis to examine the significance of an interaction between the two main-effect predictors "personal agency" and "unknown causes."

are mean centered. Mean centering is simply calculating the mean of a given variable and subtracting this value from every single observation. The resulting variable would now have a mean of 0, but the variance and rank order of the scores would be unchanged by the transformation. Such a transformation is called a *monotonic* transformation because it does not change the distributional characteristics or the associations among the distribution and any other distribution. The third set of columns represents the results based on orthogonalizing. Here, the beta weights when no interaction is included versus the beta weights when the interaction term is included are exactly the same. In fact, the interaction variable can be entered into the regression model without the main effects, and the estimate for the interaction construct would be exactly the same. Only orthogonalizing carries these characteristics. Also note that the significance of the interaction term is exactly the same when OLS regression analysis is used as the analysis method. In latent-variable SEM, things are less straightforward.

With longitudinal moderation, the interaction constructs should be entered into the model as saturated correlates of all constructs at all the time points except for the directed regression arrow where the moderator predicts the outcome at a later time point to determine whether moderation is significant. The other small exception to the saturated-correlates idea occurs when the moderator construct is created using the orthogonalizing technique. In this case the moderator construct would be perfectly uncorrelated with the two main effect indicators that were used to create the moderator construct. Remember that the moderator construct is a mathematical convention used to see whether a regression path between a predictor and an outcome is changed depending on the level of another predictor variable. The construct has no other substantive interpretation, so doing things like including the autoregressive path from prior time points or having other variables predict it or having it predict any other construct besides the outcome of interest is nonsensical. This general correlational pattern and predictive pattern for the moderator constructs of a longitudinal model is shown in Figure 9.12.

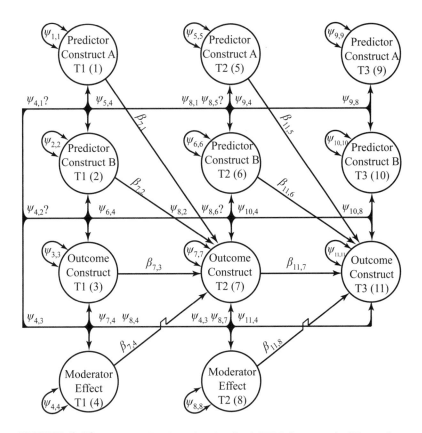

FIGURE 9.12. Moderation in a longitudinal SEM framework. The stylized covariance links among all the constructs represent the fact that each moderator construct correlates with each of the other constructs. The only exceptions are the directed path of a moderator construct on the outcome construct at the next time of measurement. All nonmoderator constructs correlate with each other within each time of measurement. Any additional autoregressive and cross-lagged paths between time points would be specified according to theory or else would be estimated as a covariance. The residual variances among the corresponding indicators would associate over time. The ? indicates that this covariation may be fixed at 0 if orthogonalizing is used to create the interaction construct.

In Figure 9.12, the correlation links are given for the moderator variables. All the linkages related to the moderating variables are labeled in the figure. As mentioned, the moderator construct will be correlated with every other construct in a model, with one definite exception and one possible exception. The definite exception is the path that links a moderator to the outcome variable at the subsequent time point. The outcome construct has one or more of the predictor constructs influencing it, and prior levels of the outcome construct are controlled for via the autoregressive path. The paths labeled $\beta_{7,4}$ and $\beta_{11,8}$ must be estimated as a regression path to test the potential change in the association between the moderated predictor and the outcome. For example, in Figure 9.12, I designate predictor construct A as the moderated predictor, and construct B is the moderating filter variable. All the correlations that should be estimated are labeled with ψ, and the parameter labels with a question mark ("?") beside them are the ones that might be fixed at 0 if orthogonalizing is the method of creating the moderation constructs.

To test moderation between Time 1 and Time 2, four regression paths would be estimated and evaluated for significance. All other relationships among the constructs would be represented as nondirectional covariances. The four paths are $\beta_{7,1}$, $\beta_{7,2}$, $\beta_{7,3}$, and $\beta_{7,4}$. The path $\beta_{7,3}$ is the autoregressive path. Longitudinal moderation is typically a question about change in the outcome and whether the influence of the focal predictor on the change in the outcome is moderated. Therefore, the autoregressive path is usually a required element. The key question of moderation might just be about the standing on a variable at a later time point, in which case the autoregressive path would be converted to a simple cross-time covariance estimate. The focal predictor variable's influence is represented in the path $\beta_{7,1}$. This path may or may not be significant. It is possible to have a moderating influence where the effect of the predictor on the outcome is nonsignificant when the interaction construct is 0, but it can become significant as the interaction construct changes. The path labeled $\beta_{7,2}$ runs from the moderator variable to the outcome. It must be entered as a directed regression relationship in order to estimate an unbiased evaluation of the moderating effect, unless the orthogonalizing approach is used. If orthogonalizing is used to create the latent-variable interaction construct, the effect is 100% uncorrelated with the predictors and would not be biased in terms of its significance if the path were not estimated. With mean centering, this path is required.

To test for moderation between Time 2 and Time 3, the four paths that were tested from Time 1 to Time 2 would be respecified as covariance relationships, and the four regression paths relating Time 2 to Time 3 would be specified as directed regression effects. These paths are labeled $\beta_{11,5}$, $\beta_{11,6}$, $\beta_{11,7}$, and $\beta_{11,8}$. As with the test of Time 1 to Time 2, these paths would be estimated and evaluated for significance to determine whether moderation is evident again, this time between Time 2 and Time 3. This process would repeat for each wave of data collection to determine whether the time-specific moderation effect is significant or not. These tests would be viewed as replications of the moderating influence at each subsequent point in time. Again, usually the autoregressive path of the outcome construct is estimated to control for prior levels and to examine moderation of the change relations, but, if theory dictated, this path could be omitted.

The final SEM model, on the other hand, would allow all significant directed regression relationships among the focal constructs that go forward in time. Here, the moderation tests would become tests of moderation on the residual variance information, controlling for all other directed regression influences. If moderation still holds in this final model, then the moderating influence would appear to be robust given the context of the other constructs in the model. Of course, other unmeasured variables might be lurking that could render the moderating effect nonsignificant.

As an empirical example of moderation, I again rely on the data from Dorothy Espelage's longitudinal study. In this model, I show the results of the moderating effect of family closeness on the association between peer victimization and substance use. The overall test of the model fit and tests of factorial invariance for these data is presented in Table 9.6. As can be seen in this table, strong factorial invariance is again easily achieved. Note that the moderator variable is not represented in these tests of invariance. The moderator variable is simply a mathematical device to determine whether one variable has an effect on the strength of the association between a predictor and an outcome. Thus, the tests of invariance (which is the basis for determining whether the model fit is acceptable) would be conducted on the measured constructs without the moderator constructs being present in the model. Besides the fact that the moderator constructs are mathematical devices, their influence on model fit creates bias.

Table 9.7 presents the correlations, means, and variances of the constructs used in the example of longitudinal moderation. Note that my colleagues and I are now focusing on family closeness in the moderation example, whereas we looked at family conflict in the example of longitudinal mediation (see prologue for information on these variables).

To evaluate the change in fit for the final SEM model with moderator constructs, the model χ^2 value for a baseline model with the moderator constructs must be estimated. This χ^2 value is not used to evaluate the adequacy of the model fit per se, but it is used as the reference point χ^2 to evaluate the adequacy of the final SEM model. Here, the final SEM model with the interaction constructs present should not differ meaningfully from the baseline model with the interaction constructs included. The baseline model with interaction terms included is either the strong invariant model or the weak invariant model, depending on whether the mean structures are included in the final SEM model. To evaluate the loss in fit from the baseline model to the

TABLE 9.6. Model fit statistics for the tests of invariance for the moderation example

Model tested	χ^2	df	p	RMSEA	RMSEA 90% CI	CFI	ΔCFI	TLI/ NNFI	ΔTLI	Pass?
Null model	33056.31	957	<.001	---	---	---	---	---	---	---
Configural invariance	1868.6	642	<.001	.040	.038;.142	.962	---	.943	---	Yes
Weak invariance	2170.7	660	<.001	.044	.042;.046	.953	.009	.932	.011	Yes
Strong invariance	2304.3	678	<.001	.045	.043;.047	.949	.004	.928	.004	Yes

Note. These tests of invariance are conducted to evaluate model fit and the tenability of the invariance constraints with only the focal constructs. The interaction constructs are not included in these models because they would introduce bias in the overall model fit information. Tests of relative differences, however, would have the interaction constructs included. These tests are shown in Table 9.8.

TABLE 9.7. Correlations among the constructs in the moderation example: Zero-order estimates from the strong invariant model and residual estimates from the final model

	SU1	PV1	FC1	SU2	PV2	FC2	SU3	PV3	FC3	SU4	PV4	FC4
SU1	--	.155	-.345									
PV1	.145	--	-.337									
FC1	-.347	-.076	--									
SU2	.768	.229	-.303	--	-.427	-.752						
PV2	.042	.467	-.092	.180	--	.621						
FC2	-.323	-.083	.645	-.332	.001	--						
SU3	.364	.243	-.273	.510	.185	-.283	--	-.166	-.741			
PV3	.116	.440	-.106	.222	.661	-.039	.174	--	.299			
FC3	-.218	.003	.547	-.264	-.027	.638	-.334	-.019	--			
SU4	.311	.116	-.233	.381	.143	-.246	.728	.078	-.298	--	-.035	-.689
PV4	.128	.328	-.102	.206	.491	-.050	.201	.497	-.037	-.210	--	.215
FC4	-.188	.002	.472	-.225	-.012	.522	-.255	.004	.733	-.335	-.003	--
Means	1.237	1.617	3.054	1.225	1.704	3.083	1.246	1.635	3.049	1.231	1.519	3.030
Vars	.129	.349	.179	.277	.547	.237	.193	.398	.228	.124	.279	.199

Note. Correlations below the diagonal are from the standardized solution of the strong invariant model. Correlations above the diagonal are from the standardized solution of the final structural moderation model. FC = family closeness, SU = substance use, PV = peer victimization at Times 1, 2, 3, and 4.

final SEM model in a very large model such as this, I suggest using the change in CFI of 0.002 as the criterion for too much change.

To calculate the CFI in the context of interaction constructs, I need to specify a null model for the data that includes the interaction indicators. The same longitudinal null model I introduced in Chapter 4 would be used, but with a couple of exceptions. First, the corresponding indicators of the interaction constructs would not be equated over time. As mathematical devices that aren't tested for invariance, equating the variances to be equal over time for the null model would not be valid. Second, the means of the indicators of the interaction construct are forced to be 0 by the way in which they are calculated. With double mean centering, the means are guaranteed to be 0. With orthogonalizing, the means are guaranteed to be 0. Therefore, the means of the indicators of the interaction construct would be fixed at 0 in the null model. In this model, fixing of these parameters would result in 27 degrees of freedom too many for the null model, and the null model degrees of freedom would need to be adjusted (27 would be subtracted). Each subsequent model fit to these data would also have these means fixed at 0 and would have 27 degrees of freedom too many. The null model, the baseline model, and the final SEM model would therefore have these degrees of freedom subtracted.

If the interaction indicators are created using orthogonalization, an additional number of degrees of freedom need to be subtracted from the null model, the baseline model, and the final SEM model. The reason for this adjustment is that the input matrix to be analyzed has known elements that are 0 by necessity. With orthogonalizing, each product indicator is regressed onto the indicators of the focal predictor constructs, creating known and of necessity 0 correlations between the interaction indicator and each indicator of the focal predictor constructs. In this example, family closeness and peer victimization each have three indicators, and I created nine inter-action indicators by multiplying all possible pairs of indicators. Thus, each interaction construct has nine indicators. At the first three time points when the interaction construct is included in the data, there are 54 (6 times 9) known and of necessity fixed 0's in the input covariance matrix. With the interaction construct represented three times, the model degrees of freedom will have 162 degrees of freedom too many. Table 9.8 provides the fit information for this adjusted null model, the baseline model, and the final SEM model. For this example, I excluded the mean structures from the final SEM model analysis, so the baseline model that was fit to these data was the weak invariant model with the moderation constructs included.

As I mentioned before, prior to building a final model, each time-specific moderation test would be conducted, with all other pathways estimated as covariance relationships. That is, the hypothesis of moderation would be tested for each measurement occasion without complicating the test by estimating all significant directed regression relationships. For the empirical example here, the moderation question was about the change in substance use. With four time points, the moderating influence of family closeness on peer victimization can be examined three times. In this example, the moderating effect of family closeness was significant at each measurement occasion. With no other directed regression relations estimated in the model, these moderating influences received an unbiased test of their significance. These pure tests of moderation can also be tested for differences across the successive time points. To do so would require a couple of additional steps. With these data, I created a three-group model with phantom constructs to test the equality of the moderating pathways across the successive time points. Group 1 consisted of the Time 1 and Time 2 data, Group 2 consisted of the Time 2 and Time 3 data, and Group 3 consisted of the Time 3 and Time 4 data. With invariance of the loading across groups and time in place, the comparison of the moderating pathways would be done as a χ^2 difference test. The baseline χ^2 value would not be interpreted—only the difference in χ^2 value would (see *www.guilford.com/little-materials* for the syntax files to do these tests). For these tests the questions are whether evidence of moderation exists at each time point and whether the standardized effects are the same or different across the time points. In the final SEM model, on the other hand, the question would

TABLE 9.8. Tests related to the moderation model in Figure 9.13

Model tested	χ^2	df	$\Delta\chi^2$	Δdf	p	CFI	ΔCFI	Pass?
Null model	61397.2	2307						n/a
Baseline CFA model	13203.4	1810				.807		n/a
Final model	13476.3	1939	272.9	129	<.001	.805	.002	Yes

Note. For the test of the adequacy of the final model, a change in CFI greater than .002 from the baseline model was used. The degrees of freedom for these models were adjusted by subtracting 152, the number of known and of necessity 0 elements in the analyzed sufficient statistics.

be whether these moderating effects remain significant when all other significant directed regression estimates are allowed and the covariate effects of gender, grade, black, white, and three dummy codes for school are controlled for in the analysis.

In Figure 9.13, I show the final model with the moderator constructs at each time point. I did not list the bidirectional covariances in the figure because the nature of these is detailed in Figure 9.12. The estimated residual correlations at each time point are in the upper triangle of Table 9.7 (note that the moderator constructs are not included in this table because the residual associations with them are not of substantive interest). The moderator construct is the product of peer victimization and family closeness. It predicts the outcome construct of substance use at each subsequent time point. In this example, family closeness is conceptualized as the moderator, and

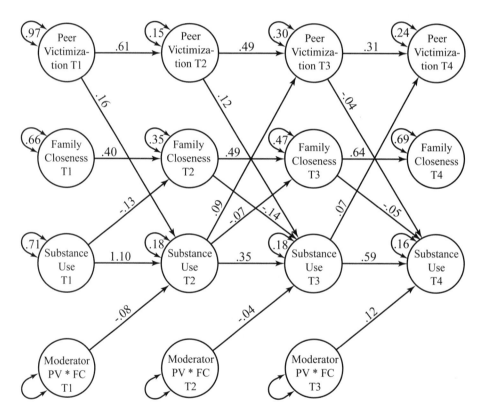

FIGURE 9.13. Moderation of the influence of peer victimization and family closeness on youth substance use. The data for this example come from Dorothy Espelage's longitudinal project. The covariance links among the constructs are omitted. The residual correlations are shown in Table 9.7. The moderator variables correlate with all other variables except where the directed regression is specified and when it has been made to be orthogonal to the main effect constructs within a time point. The regression estimates are unstandardized. The variance terms are standardized to reflect the amount of variance that is unexplained. The amount explained would be 1 minus these values. In addition to the cross-time paths, significant effects of gender, grade, black, white, and three dummy codes for school are included.

it is the contextual filter that changes the strength of the relationship between peer victimization and changes in subsequent substance abuse. Between Times 1, 2, and 3, higher scores on peer victimization are associated with increases in subsequent substance use. Family closeness has two effects on substance use. As a direct effect, youths with greater family closeness scores show a reduction in substance use at later measurement occasions. In this regard, family closeness is a protective factor for changes in substance use during this age range. Family closeness also functions as a buffering moderator in that the risk effect of peer victimization on changes in substance use is lower when family closeness is higher. Between Time 3 and Time 4 some interesting changes occur. First, the effect of peer victimization on changes in substance use changes sign. In this later adolescent time frame, the effect of peer victimization on substance use becomes negative, suggesting that greater peer victimization at Time 3 of this study is associated with reductions in substance use at Time 4. The protective effect and moderating buffer effect of family closeness, however, is still evident. That is, family closeness has a direct effect, indicating that higher family closeness leads to reductions in substance use. In addition, the moderator effect changes signs, indicating that the reduction in substance use by youths who were victimized was greater for youths with higher family closeness.

As with any test of moderation, these interactions can be probed. With orthogonalizing, the process of probing the full spectrum of the interaction is somewhat complicated. Geldhof, Pornprasertmanit, Schoemann, and Little (2013) provide the details on how to probe an interaction with orthogonalizing.

SUMMARY

This chapter presented an overview of two critical statistical concepts, mediation and moderation. These concepts are still often conflated ideas in the research literature. I have attempted to provide clear guidelines as to how to think about both these concepts, as well as how to statistically model them in the context of a longitudinal panel model. Many variations of mediation, such as multiple mediation, are possible. Similarly, many different ways of thinking about moderation are possible, including mediated moderation or moderated mediation, as well as multiple moderation. In the multiple mediation and multiple moderation scenarios, I generally recommend testing each mediator and each moderator separately first to determine whether there is evidence that the variable can function as a mediator or a moderator. Then I recommend fitting a model in which the multiple contextual constructs are pitted against each other to see whether there is still evidence of mediation when other mediators or other moderators are in a given model. That is, are there still unique effects of the mediators or moderators when the other constructs are controlled for? As a reminder, be sure to clarify in your own mind what you expect in terms of the contextual mechanism at play. The three alternatives are additive effects, mediation, and moderation. Many times the research question is simply an additive-effects hypothesis; this kind of hypothesis is still perfectly reasonable and valid. Not all research projects have to be driven by a desire to identify mediators and moderators. Determining the simple additive effects that different constructs contribute to an outcome is still an important scientific contribution.

KEY TERMS AND CONCEPTS INTRODUCED IN THIS CHAPTER

Additive effects. Additive-effects models are not causal hypotheses per se but are regression models in which two or more variables predict one's standing on an outcome variable. The predictor variables linearly predict the outcome, and the effects are linearly additive, weighted by the magnitude of the regression coefficients.

Conditional probability. The probability that some event (e.g., A) will occur when another event (B) is present. When the condition B is present, what is the probability of A occurring (as opposed to when B is not present)? A conditional probability is a moderating circumstance.

Equilibrium. Like stationarity, equilibrium refers to the unchanging relations among the variables in terms of their variances and covariances (and means, in some circles). With lifespan development unfolding from birth and stopping only in death, the assumption of equilibrium for most social and behavioral science constructs will not be supported. As with stationarity, violating this assumption does not necessarily invalidate evidence of mediation if the indirect pathway is significant.

Mediation. A causal hypothesis about the mechanism(s) by which one variable exerts its influence on another variable. A mediator variable, therefore, is one that functions as the carrier or conduit through which the causal effect is transmitted to an eventual outcome variable.

Moderation. A causal hypothesis about the conditions that change or influence the effect of one variable on another variable. A moderator variable, therefore, is one that functions as a changer or contextual filter that either dampens or enhances the effect of one variable on another variable.

Stationarity. The idea that the causal processes that underlie a set of measured variables are unchanging over time. That is, when the autoregressive paths and the cross-lagged paths achieve a state in which they are the same magnitude from wave to wave, stationarity is observed. This assumption of mediation testing is not a critical assumption because it does not invalidate finding a significant indirect path.

RECOMMENDED READINGS

The Coffin and the Nail in the Lid

Cole, D. A., & Maxwell, S. E. (2003). Testing mediational models with longitudinal data: Questions and tips in the use of structural equation modeling. *Journal of Abnormal Psychology, 112,* 558–577.

This paper pretty much built the coffin for those who would like to test mediation using cross-sectional designs.

Maxwell, S. E., & Cole, D. A. (2007). Bias in cross sectional analysis of longitudinal mediation. *Psychological Methods, 12,* 23–44.

This paper pretty much put the nail in the lid of the coffin for those who would like to test mediation using cross-sectional designs.

Monte Carlo Approach to Testing Indirect Effects

MacKinnon, D. P., Lockwood, C. M., & Williams, J. (2004). Confidence limits for the indirect effect: Distribution of the product and resampling methods. *Multivariate Behavioral Research, 39,* 99–128.

Preacher, K. J., & Selig, J. P. (2012). Advantages of Monte Carlo confidence intervals for indirect effects. *Communication Methods and Measures, 6,* 77–98.

These two papers give details of how to estimate indirect effects using the Monte Carlo approach, and an R-based calculator is available to test complex indirect pathways at *www.guilford.com/little-materials*. This calculator is based on the preceding work.

The Bootstrap Approach for Testing Indirect Effects

Preacher, K. J., & Hayes, A. F. (2008). Contemporary approaches to assessing mediation in communication research. In A. F. Hayes, M. D. Slater, & L. B. Snyder (Eds.), *Sage sourcebook of advanced data analysis methods for communication research* (pp. 13–54). Thousand Oaks, CA: Sage.

Shrout, P. E., & Bolger, N. (2002). Mediation in experimental and nonexperimental studies: New procedures and recommendations. *Psychological Methods, 7*(4), 422–445.

These two papers provide details of using bootstrapping. The Shrout and Bolger paper is the core source because they really drive home the need for bootstrapping.

Including Contextual Variables

Little, T. D., Card, N. A., Bovaird, J. A., Preacher, K., & Crandall, C. S. (2007). Structural equation modeling of mediation and moderation with contextual factors. In T. D. Little, J. A. Bovaird, & N. A. Card (Eds.), *Modeling contextual effects in longitudinal studies* (pp. 207–230). Mahwah, NJ: Erlbaum.

We offer an overview of how contextual variables can be included in longitudinal SEM as mediators or as moderators.

Ways to Create Interaction Constructs

Little, T. D., Bovaird, J. A., & Widaman, K. F. (2006). On the merits of orthogonalizing powered and product terms: Implications for modeling interactions among latent variables. *Structural Equation Modeling, 13,* 497–519.

This paper introduces the orthogonalizing approach for creating latent-variable interaction indicators in SEM models. It is in contrast to Marsh et al. (2004), who argue for mean centering and now are recommending double mean centering as a general approach, which does work well. You can use either approach if your data are relatively normally distributed.

Lin, G. C., Wen, Z., Marsh, H. W., & Lin, H. S. (2010). Structural equation models of latent interactions: Clarification of orthogonalizing and double-mean-centering strategies. *Structural Equation Modeling, 17,* 374–391.

Marsh, H. W., Wen, Z., Hau, K.-T., Little, T. D., Bovaird, J. A., & Widaman, K. F. (2007). Unconstrained structural equation models of latent interactions: Contrasting residual- and mean-centered approaches. *Structural Equation Modeling, 14,* 570–580.

These papers followed up with a comparison of the two approaches and introduced double mean centering as an effective way to create product indicators and their constituent main-effect indicators as well as to remove the mean-structures requirement for estimating the models.

10

Jambalaya

Complex Construct Representations and Decompositions

This final chapter is a jambalaya of various complex construct representations. All of these complex construct representations are applicable to longitudinal data. In the following, I discuss multitrait–multimethod construct decompositions, pseudo-multitrait decompositions, and higher order and bifactor decompositions. With proper seasoning, these spicy construct representations can prove very satisfying for your intellectual appetite and theoretical needs.

MULTITRAIT–MULTIMETHOD MODELS

Campbell and Fiske (1959) explicitly recognized that "Each test or task employed for measurement purposes is a *trait-method unit*" (italics mine, p. 81). With this recognition in mind, they also formalized key ideas that fit under the general framework called multitrait–multimethod (MTMM) models. The initial conceptualizations of MTMM models were heuristic-based and involved judging the adequacy of an MTMM approach by simply evaluating the correlation patterns of an MTMM matrix to see whether the correlation pattern generally conformed to an MTMM expectation. With the advent of SEM, MTMM models are now explicit statistical decompositions. Before I discuss MTMM models in the context of longitudinal data, I provide some basic background and define some terminology related to MTMM. I also give an example of a pseudo-MTMM model that allowed my colleagues and me to uncover a very important set of relationships among some key constructs of aggressive behavior. The term *trait* can be misleading in the MTMM framework, because it does not universally mean "trait" in the sense of, say, a personality trait or a trait–state distinction. In the MTMM framework, "trait" refers to any construct (affective, behavioral, or cognitive) that is measured by two or more different methods of assessment. The different methods can be different types of reports, such as self-reports, or friend, parent, or teacher reports of aggressive behavior, for example, or different tools, such as questionnaire versus blood sample to assess smoking behavior. As an aside, the two-method planned missing data design is predicated on MTMM concepts—here, the distinction between methods is cheap versus expensive and biased versus gold standard, with a method factor being estimated only for the cheap/biased measure.

With MTMM frameworks, the focus is on the pattern of convergent and discriminant validity among the constructs. When different methods of measuring a construct converge on a trait, it means that the different methods will correlate highly when they are measuring the same trait. Discriminant validity refers to how clearly distinguishable the different traits are. Traits that correlate too highly with other traits don't discriminate effectively as unique and distinct constructs. For example, when parents and teachers report on a child's personal agency and self-efficacy, the traits of agency and efficacy are likely to be so highly related that keeping them as two distinct traits or characteristics isn't feasible or warranted. In traditional MTMM frameworks, discriminant traits would need to show .7 or lower correlations. In SEM frameworks and in the presence of strong theory, correlations among traits in the upper .8's are not uncommon.

The lingo of MTMM is older than I am. These terms aren't necessarily intuitive. Having been around for as long as they have, however, it's hard to not talk MTMM without a brief overview of key terms. Four core sources of information are the focus of the MTMM framework: (1) monotrait, monomethod, (2) monotrait, heteromethod, (3) heterotrait, monomethod, and (4) heterotrait, heteromethod. *Mono-* is a prefix of Greek origin to indicate "one" or "single" (i.e., "same"). *Hetero-* is a prefix of Greek origin to indicate "other" or "another" (i.e., "different").

Monotrait, monomethod refers to a given (same) trait being measured by a given (same) method. The information contained in the monotrait, monomethod parts of an MTMM matrix is the reliability information of each trait measured by each method. In an SEM framework, the information of interest in the monotrait, monomethod parts would be the loadings of the indicators. The loadings of the indicators are the amounts of reliable variance that each indicator contributes to the construct, and they can be used to estimate reliability by means of the coefficient omega when multiple indicators are available for each trait–method combination. The degree to which the indicators converge and discriminate among constructs is also a piece of information that is valuable in establishing the convergent and discriminant validity among the constructs.

Monotrait, heteromethod is the part of the MTMM matrix that defines convergent validity of a given construct as measured by different methods. The general idea here is that different methods that measure the same underlying trait should show convergent correlations that are "sufficiently large to encourage further examination of validity" (Campbell & Fiske, 1959). It is difficult to say what magnitudes of the correlations between different methods would be considered sufficiently large with modern SEM approaches to MTMM analyses. Before SEM decompositions of MTMM relationships were developed, however, the general criterion was around .6.

In Campbell and Fiske's original discussion, they presented a hypothetical matrix that they created to reflect typical levels of correlation among MTMM measures in the literature around that era. Figure 10.1 is a reproduction of the matrix. Figure 10.2 is the same matrix containing different MTMM labels in the different quadrants. The quadrants labeled "validity diagonal" in Figure 10.2 have values that are in the .5 to .6 range, which are clearly seen in Figure 10.1. The values in Figure 10.1 would not be latent correlations (SEM was not available until the 1970s) but rather manifest correlations, so they would always be attenuated by the unreliability of measurement. The reliabilities along the diagonals of the MTMM matrix

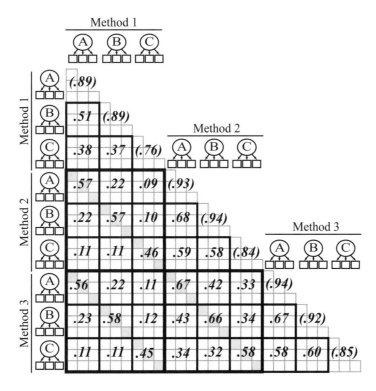

FIGURE 10.1. The multitrait multimethod matrix from Campbell and Fiske (1959). This stylized representation has three constructs or traits, each measured with three methods. The constructs and methods could have multiple indicators, as the light cells behind the Campbell and Fiske (1959) hypothetical correlations and the marginal diagrams are meant to suggest.

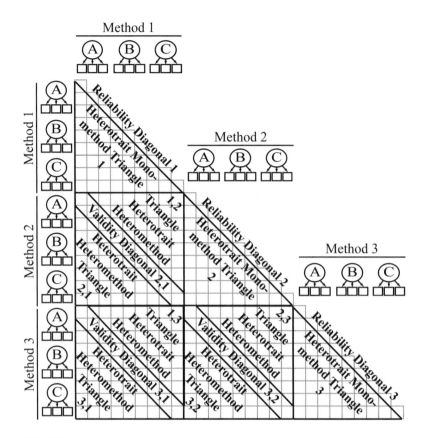

FIGURE 10.2. The lingo and labels for a multitrait multimethod matrix. *Mono-* is a prefix of Greek origin that means "same," and *hetero-* is a prefix of Greek origin that means "different." In the MTMM literature, *trait* is a generic term to refer to any construct that is assessed using multiple methods. Methods of assessment can be different reporters, different scales, different tools, or any other measurement means.

are respectable for the most part. When corrected for attenuation, the validity coefficients approach .6, which would be sufficiently encouraging.

In the MTMM literature, however, the convergent validity correlations are often much lower than this. In the peer relations literature, for example, correlations between different reporters are often only in the .3 range, even after correcting for unreliability. Peers and teachers can have higher agreement when they report on behaviors because both reporters see the behavior in the same context (i.e., the school context). When correlations among different methods fall below the sufficiently encouraging levels, then other encouragement is needed. Strong theory and a set of criterion-related predictions would need to be outlined and tested to demonstrate that the small amount of shared variance across the different methods is in fact still tapping into a meaningful trait.

Another criterion of traditional MTMM is that the validity diagonals should have higher correlations in them than in their off-diagonal counterparts (heterotrait–heteromethod). Here, the hope is that the shared trait variance (same trait) is greater than the shared method variance when the different methods involve different traits. In Figure 10.1, Method 1 and Method 2 have low levels of shared method variance for a given trait, but Method 2 and Method 3 have relatively high levels of shared method variance. The shared method variance among the three methods is still lower in the heterotrait–heteromethod triangles than along the validity diagonals. For example, the correlations for Trait A as measured by Method 2 and Method 3 is .67. Traits A and B as measured by Method 2 and Method 3 correlate .43 (Method 3, Trait B with Method 2, Trait A) and .42 (Method 2, Trait B with Method 3, Trait A), respectively.

A third feature of the MTMM logic is that the corresponding trait measures should correlate more highly with each other than with corresponding method measures. In other words, there should be higher correlations with other attempts to measure the same trait than with other traits that may use the same method. For example, the correlations among the traits measured by Method 1 are generally smaller than the correlations along the validity diagonals that involve Method 1. Methods 2 and 3, on the other hand, generally have larger within-method correlations among the traits compared with the validity correlations, particularly those involving Trait B. Before the advent of SEM, these patterns of correlations would be somewhat problematic, as they indicate the influence of an overpowering method variance. The signature advantage of an SEM decomposition of this matrix is that the variance due to method can be separated from the variance due to trait.

The fourth and final feature of MTMM logic is that the pattern of relative magnitudes of the correlations should be mirrored within each of the subtriangles. For example, the correlation between Trait A and Trait B is consistently the highest correlation in each of the subtriangles. The correlations between Trait C and Trait B and between Trait C and Trait A have essentially the same magnitude within a given triangle.

Figure 10.3 is a diagram of the multitrait–multimethod decomposition using the so-called correlated traits–correlated methods (CTCM) decomposition. In MTMM models, various options are possible for how the method–trait information is represented and controlled (I show some examples and their consequences later). In Figure 10.3, I have labeled the first indicator as T_aM_1 to reflect the scores for Trait A, Method 1. The last indicator is labeled T_cM_3 to reflect the scores for Trait C, Method 3. These indicators could also be constructs where Trait A, Method 1 would be represented by multiple indicators or scores at a lower level. To be consistent with the MTMM matrix in Figure 10.1, I am representing Campbell and Fiske's (1959) correlations as manifest indicators.

MTMM models are forms of a bifactor model in that each indicator loads on two different constructs. Like bifactor models, a key assumption that allows these

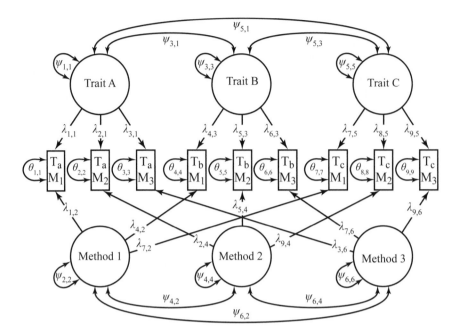

FIGURE 10.3. Parameter labels for a correlated traits–correlated methods multitrait–multimethod decomposition. All labeled parameters are estimated parameters of this model, except for the fixed scaling parameter. Using the fixed factor method makes good sense for scaling the factors in MTMM models such as this. The trait constructs are uncorrelated with the method factors by assumption and necessity (i.e., trait–method correlations are not identified and rarely make theoretical sense).

models to work is that the two factors that influence a given indicator are uncorrelated. For MTMM models, this assumption is perfectly defensible and is rarely even a point of discussion. Method variance is produced by a process of measurement that is independent of the trait being measured. In other words, the variance due to the method of assessment is independent of (uncorrelated with) the variance due to the trait that is captured. Given this feature of MTMM models, the three trait factors in Figure 10.3 are not allowed to correlate with the three method factors. The traits themselves are allowed to intercorrelate, and, for this model, the method factors are also allowed to correlate with each other. The full MTMM model in Figure 10.3 can be empirically underidentified. Empirical underidentification occurs when a model is technically identified but two or more of the parameter estimates for the model are too highly correlated to allow an acceptable empirical solution. In such situations, limiting restrictions or alternative variants would need to be estimated. In the hypothetical example I am working with, the model is empirically identified.

The loadings of the indicators show patterns that would be expected given the pattern of correlations in the raw matrix. For example, the loadings for Methods 2 and 3 are much larger than for Method 1. The correlations in the heterotrait–monomethod triangles of Methods 2 and 3 are generally higher than for Method 1. The correlation pattern suggests greater method variance relative to the trait variance. In addition, Methods 2 and 3 correlate quite highly with each other. The validity diagonal between Methods 2 and 3 has higher correlations than the two validity diagonals with Method 1; the heterotrait–heteromethod triangles between Methods 2 and 3 have much larger correlations among the traits than do the heterotrait–heteromethod triangles involving Method 1. In fact, the overlap in method variance between Methods 2 and 3 (after controlling for any influence of the traits) is a correlation of .51. The method correlations in Campbell and Fiske's (1959) hypothetical example are similar to what one finds when teacher and peer reports are used along with either self- or parent reports of different characteristics. Also note that Method 1 has correlations that are essentially 0 with Methods 2 and 3.

In terms of the trait relationships, Figure 10.4 shows that Traits A and B are the most highly correlated of the traits. When the method variance associated with the measurement of Traits A and B is removed, however, the magnitude of this association is substantially reduced. In the input data, the observed correlations were .51, .68, and .67 for Methods 1, 2, and 3, respectively. Controlling for the shared sources of method variance, these two traits correlate only .39 (Figure 10.4). This degree of change in absolute magnitude of correlation for any two traits is not uncommon. In

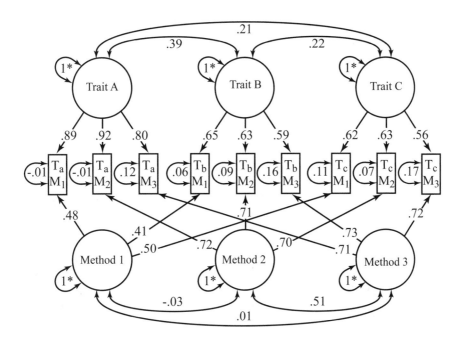

FIGURE 10.4. Results from estimating the correlated traits–correlated methods model to the Campbell and Fiske data. Model fit is essentially perfect: $\chi^2_{(12,\ n=100)} = 1.14$, $p = 1.0$. The reported estimates are from the completely standardized solution. See Campbell and Fiske (1959).

fact, the concerns about shared method variance in studies that rely on one reporter (e.g., self-report) are well founded. When method variance is shared, one cannot discuss absolute magnitudes with any certainty. Relative differences in magnitudes, on the other hand, are legitimate to test and discuss because the inflation of the magnitudes of correlations is generally uniform across the different traits.

Figures 10.5 and 10.6 show two alternative models that could be fit to MTMM data. In Figure 10.5, the method factors are not included, and the resulting model fit is terrible. In addition, the relations among the traits are biased. In Figure 10.6, the method variance is represented as correlated residuals among the corresponding indicators that use the same method. Although this method of modeling the MTMM data provides improved fit to the model, the correlated-methods approach is much better because Methods 2 and 3 are highly correlated. The correlated-residuals approach does not allow the methods to correlate. It only allows the corresponding method residuals to correlate.

PSEUDO-MTMM MODELS

Complex SEM decompositions such as the MTMM models just described have tremendous opportunity to unveil relationships among constructs that can't otherwise be established. The example that I walk through here comes from work that my colleagues and I have done examining the different forms and different functions of aggressive behavior. Our work began in the late 1990s, when we launched a set of cross-national comparisons to look at action-control beliefs and behaviors in the social domain (at the time, I was at the Max Planck Institute, which provided the support for the project). One key construct among many that we wanted to include

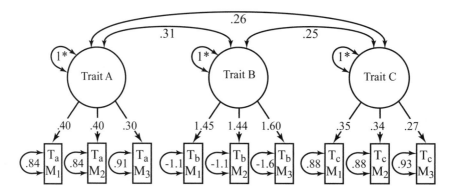

FIGURE 10.5. Results from estimating the MTMM data without accounting for the method variance. Model fit is very poor: $\chi^2_{(24,\ n=100)} = 422.23$; RMSEA = .33 (.29; .36), and the solution is severely nonadmissible. The estimates are from the completely standardized solution.

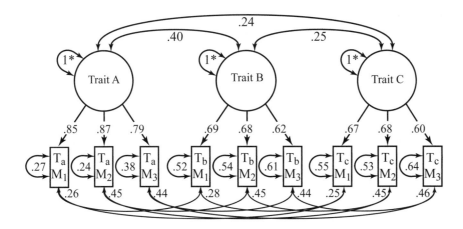

FIGURE 10.6. Results from estimating the correlated traits–correlated method residuals model to the Campbell and Fiske data. Model fit is quite good: $\chi^2_{(15, n=100)} = 21.61$, $p = .12$, RMSEA $= .071_{(.00; .13)}$. The correlated method model fit better because Methods 2 and 3 are highly correlated. Results are from the completely standardized solution. See Campbell and Fiske (1959).

was aggression. Before I can get into the details of our instrument and our modeling approach, which unveiled associations that heretofore had not been observed, I need to give a brief synopsis of two research traditions. A more detailed review of these traditions can be found in Little, Jones, Henrich, and Hawley (2003).

At the time we were planning our project, two dominant traditions existed in examining and understanding aggressive behavior. One tradition typified aggression in terms of the instrumental versus reactive functions of aggression. A second tradition typified aggression in terms of overt behavioral forms versus relational forms. The overt versus relational tradition focused on the forms of aggression, with behaviors such as hitting, kicking, punching, and saying mean or hurtful things being grouped as overt and direct perpetrations of aggression. Relational aggression consisted of behaviors such as social exclusion, gossiping behind another's back, rumor spreading, and the like, which relied on manipulating the relationships among groups of individuals to indirectly cause harm and hurt toward a victim. This tradition did not emphasize the reasons or functional purpose of the aggressive behavior but instead attempted to broaden our understanding about the kinds of behaviors that boys versus girls might employ in the conduct of aggressive actions. The instrumental versus reactive tradition, on the other hand, sought to understand aggression in terms of the underlying motives or attributions that may give rise to the perpetration of an aggressive act in the first place. This tradition emphasized the social information-processing aspects of aggression but relied almost solely on examining these reasons for aggression in the context of overt behavioral forms.

The tradition that was interested in examining the functional forms of aggression had strong theoretical reason to expect that two opposing mechanisms could give rise to aggression. Instrumental aggression involves using aggression as a means to gain some goal or reward. It is wielded deliberately and with a clear understanding of the likelihood that the aggressive act will yield a desired outcome. Reactive aggression, on the other hand, has a more disregulated nature to it and often may involve attributional biases that view socially ambiguous behaviors as signaling a hostile intent. This attribution bias, in turn, triggers a reactive aggressive behavioral response. Ample theoretical arguments kept pointing to the expected outcome that these two functions of aggression should be independent (i.e., uncorrelated) processes or mechanisms of aggression. Unfortunately, the ample literature examining this hypothesis kept finding strong positive correlations between the measures of instrumental and reactive aggression. This correlation was typically in the .7 range across numerous studies of youths from different ages and using different methods (Card, Stucky, Sawalani, & Little, 2008). This unexpectedly high positive correlation has even led some to conclude that the two functions of aggression are likely to co-occur in aggressive individuals.

When we examined the measures that had been developed for measuring instrumental versus reactive aggression, we noticed a fundamental flaw in the measurement process used to examine them. A prototypical question for assessing instrumental aggression is "I hit or punch others to get what I want." A prototypical question for assessing reactive aggression is "I hit or punch others when I have been hurt by them." The subordinate clause "to get what I want" reflects the instrumental reason for the aggressive behavior of the first question, and the clause "when I have been hurt by them" reflects the reactive reason for the aggressive behavior. Unfortunately, both questions share the same aggressive behavior "I hit or punch others." When a reporter responds to the first question, approximately 50% of the response is related to the form of the behavior, "I hit or punch others," and approximately 50% is due to the reason for the behavior, "to get what I want" or "when I have been hurt by them." These two items would have a tendency to correlate at least .714 if the only thing that was shared between the two items was the specific form. This type of double-barreled question is not uncommon in the social sciences. Left untreated, the responses to these kinds of questions are inherently confounded and cannot be disaggregated to examine which facet of the item response is responsible for the observed correlations with other variables.

The MTMM approach that I described previously provides the logic needed to create a measurement system that allows the statistical decomposition of the form of the aggressive act from the function or reason for the act. Specifically, we needed to develop measures that would use different forms to tap into the different functions. We also realized that we could measure the preferred form of aggression as a pure construct—that is, as a single-barreled item that measures the specific behavior used to aggress independent of the typical reasons for which one would aggress. In Table 10.1 I have listed the items that we created to assess six different aggression

TABLE 10.1. Items used in the Form–Function Aggression Measure

Pure Overt (Dispositional)

I'm the kind of person who often fights with others.
I'm the kind of person who pushes, kicks, or punches others.
I'm the kind of person who says mean things to others.
I'm the kind of person who puts others down.
I'm the kind of person who threatens others.
I'm the kind of person who takes things from others.

Overt Instrumental

I often start fights to get what I want.
I often threaten others to get what I want.
I often push, kick, or punch others to get what I want.
To get what I want, I often put others down.
To get what I want, I often say mean things to others.
To get what I want, I often hurt others.

Overt Reactive

When I'm hurt by someone, I often fight back.
When I'm threatened by someone, I often threaten back.
When I'm hurt by others, I often get back at them by saying mean things to them.
If others make me upset or hurt me, I often put them down.
If others have angered me, I often push, kick, or punch them.
If others make me mad or upset, I often hurt them.

Pure Relational (Dispositional)

I'm the kind of person who tells my friends to stop liking someone.
I'm the kind of person who tells others I won't be their friend anymore.
I'm the kind of person who keeps others from being in my group of friends.
I'm the kind of person who says mean things about others.
I'm the kind of person who ignores others or stops talking to them.
I'm the kind of person who gossips or spreads rumors.

Relational Instrumental

I often tell my friends to stop liking someone to get what I want.
I often say mean things about others to my friends to get what I want.
I often keep others from being in my group of friends to get what I want.
To get what I want, I often tell others I won't be their friend anymore.
To get what I want, I often ignore or stop talking to others.
To get what I want, I often gossip or spread rumors about others.

Relational Reactive

If others upset or hurt me, I often tell my friends to stop liking them.
If others have threatened me, I often say mean things about them.
If others have hurt me, I often keep them from being in my group of friends.
When I am angry at others, I often tell them I won't be their friend anymore.
When I am upset with others, I often ignore or stop talking to them.
When I am mad at others, I often gossip or spread rumors about them.

constructs: pure overt aggression, pure relational aggression, overt instrumental aggression, overt reactive aggression, relational instrumental aggression, and relational reactive aggression. Figure 10.7 shows the basic model of how the different functional reasons for aggression can be disentangled from the specific forms of the aggressive behaviors. The loading and residuals for each occasion are presented in Table 10.2.

In Figure 10.7, I have listed the two pure constructs at the top of the diagram, each represented by three measured indicators. A prototypical item for pure overt aggression is "I am the kind of person who . . . pushes, kicks, or punches others." A prototypical item for pure relational aggression is "I am the kind of person who . . . gossips or spreads rumors." Below these two pure constructs, I placed the four mixed-source or double-barreled constructs. These mixed constructs are predicted by their respective pure constructs. The two regressions of the mixed constructs onto pure overt aggression and onto pure relational aggression are freely estimated. Because the pure constructs have measured indicators, the regression estimates are easily identified.

To accomplish the pseudo-MTMM decomposition, I have also included two extra constructs. One aggression construct I have labeled "just instrumental," and the other I have labeled "just reactive." The two mixed constructs that share

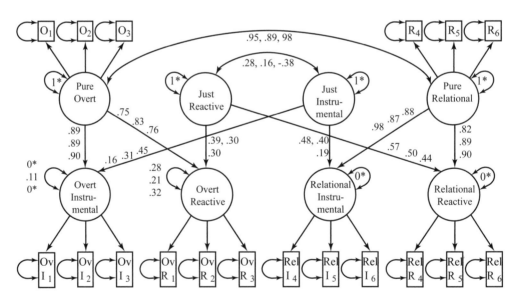

FIGURE 10.7. The form–function decomposition of aggression following a pseudo-MTMM logic. Model fit is acceptable: $\chi^2_{(359, n=422)} = 1670.37$, RMSEA $= .089_{(.085; .094)}$, CFI $= .931$, TLI/NNFI $= .905$. These estimates are from the completely standardized solution. The indicators with the same subscripted number are correlated with each other because they share the same set of item stems that are averaged to create the parceled indicators. These are original data that replicate the findings reported by Little, Jones, Henrich, and Hawley (2003). These values are from three times of measurement. Loadings and residuals for each occasion are presented in Table 10.2.

TABLE 10.2. Measurement model estimates from the form–function decomposition of aggression across three measurement occasions

Variable	λ^a	Time 1			Time 2			Time 3		
		λ^b	θ	h^2	λ^b	θ	h^2	λ^b	θ	h^2
OADisp1	1.0*	.31	.12	.46	.38	.09	.63	.22	.04	.53
OADisp2	1.08	.34	.09	.55	.41	.09	.64	.29	.03	.65
OADisp3	1.18	.37	.10	.59	.45	.07	.74	.26	.06	.54
OAInst1	1.0*	.34	.08	.60	.40	.03	.84	.23	.03	.66
OAInst2	0.87	.30	.07	.56	.35	.02	.83	.20	.02	.63
OAInst3	0.93	.32	.06	.64	.37	.04	.77	.21	.04	.53
OAReac1	1.0*	.47	.21	.51	.50	.15	.63	.32	.13	.45
OAReac2	1.04	.49	.17	.59	.52	.10	.73	.33	.05	.68
OAReac3	1.15	.54	.19	.60	.57	.13	.71	.37	.10	.57
RADisp4	1.0*	.29	.07	.54	.28	.08	.50	.21	.03	.63
RADisp5	1.08	.32	.11	.47	.30	.10	.47	.23	.05	.53
RADisp6	1.16	.34	.14	.45	.32	.08	.57	.25	.04	.59
RAInst4	1.0*	.32	.07	.59	.30	.05	.65	.22	.02	.68
RAInst5	0.99	.32	.10	.50	.30	.07	.55	.22	.04	.57
RAInst6	1.13	.37	.05	.73	.34	.03	.80	.25	.03	.67
RAReac4	1.0*	.37	.14	.50	.33	.08	.57	.24	.04	.58
RAReac5	0.99	.37	.22	.38	.33	.18	.37	.24	.08	.42
RAReac6	1.31	.49	.29	.45	.43	.25	.43	.32	.18	.36

Note. a = the unstandardized and factorially invariant estimated loading; b = the within-group standardized value of the loading at each time point; θ is the estimated (unstandardized) value of the residual at each time point; h^2 is the amount of variance explained in the indicator by the factor (i.e., the estimated communality); * = the fixed parameter that sets the scale of each construct's estimated parameters; OA = overt aggression, RA = relational aggression, Disp = dispositional, Inst = instrumental, Reac = reactive. Indicators with the same numeric suffix compose the same item stem and, therefore, share correlated residual estimates.

instrumental aggression information are regressed onto the instrumental aggression construct, and the two mixed constructs that share reactive aggression information are regressed onto the reactive aggression construct. To identify these parameter estimates, I placed equality constraints on the regression estimates within each measurement occasion. These equality constraints on the regressions are essential because the just instrumental and just reactive aggression constructs do not have measured indicators but instead are determined based on the common variance that is not explained by the pure construct regressions. The unstandardized values do come out to be equal, but after standardization, the values reported in Figure 10.7 come out to be different.

I set up this model in a nontraditional longitudinal framework. The key question for these data is whether the pseudo-MTMM decomposition of the different sources of variance works at each of the three measurement occasions. To address this question, therefore, I treated measurement occasions as a "group" and analyzed the three occasions as a three-group model. This setup eliminates the cross-time information from the sufficient statistics and eliminates the need to burden the model with all of the cross-time correlations among the constructs and the cross-time correlated residuals among the indicators. Simplifying the model in this way keeps the focus on the form–function decomposition and makes model estimation more efficient and more likely to converge.

The model in Figure 10.7 provides a number of pieces of validity evidence for the theoretical logic behind this type of measurement model for instrumental versus reactive aggression. First, the overall model is an acceptable approximation to the data. Of course, model fit is not the end-all and be-all of validity, but it is an important starting point. The parameter estimates of the model are a second source of validity evidence. Each of the parameters is reported for all three times of measurement. The order of reporting for the estimates of a given parameter for each time of measurement is left to right and then top to bottom, or just top to bottom.

At each measurement occasion, the variance in the mixed-content constructs (e.g., overt reactive) is fully disaggregated into (1) a part that is the pure form of aggression (pure overt vs. pure relational) and (2) a part that is the pure function of the aggressive act (just reactive vs. just instrumental). The only exception to this pattern was overt reactive aggression, which has a small amount of variance that is not related to the two forms or two functions of aggression as measured here. This consistent finding suggests that the nature of reactive aggression when wielded through relational means is a different flavor of reactive aggression than it is when wielded through overt means. The differences may have something to do with the emotional intensity of the reactive experience when expressed overtly versus relationally, or, perhaps, it is easier to express reactive aggression by overt means than it is when others are included in the reactive experience (i.e., including others may temper the expression of reactive aggression).

The most notable feature of the form–function decomposition in Figure 10.7 is the nature of the correlation between just reactive and just instrumental aggression. In these (as yet unpublished) data, the correlations between reactive and instrumental aggression are very small positive ones at Times 1 and 2 (fall and spring of these youths' sixth-grade year), and at Time 3 the correlation is a small negative one. All three correlations contraindicate the typical results of large positive correlations between the constructs of reactive and instrumental aggression. Here, separating out the variance that is due to the form of the aggressive behavior allows the functional nature to be represented in an unconfounded form. The model in Figure 10.7 provides the internal validity information of the foregoing conclusions. Further work would need to be done to examine the external validity of this decomposition. Some of this external validity information can be found in Little, Brauner, et al. (2003).

The key message here is that the logic of MTMM, coupled with a modified measurement tool, allowed us to conduct a study that disentangled the different sources of variance in aggression items. Many other constructs in the life sciences may similarly benefit from this approach. This project is an example of adapting a method to test the theory.

BIFACTOR AND HIGHER ORDER FACTOR MODELS

The bifactor model is another cousin of the MTMM logic. The distinction between a bifactor decomposition and an MTMM decomposition is mostly conceptual. Figure 10.8 is a simple bifactor model that decomposes self-reported perceptions of victimization and teacher-reported perceptions of victimization into three constructs. The primary construct is the perception of victimization that each reporter shares ("victimization" in Figure 10.8); the secondary constructs are (1) the unique child's self-perception of victimization and (2) the unique teacher report of victimization. With a bifactor representation, the primary construct or factor extracts all the common variance that is shared among the indicators. The secondary constructs extract the variance that remains and is unique to the specific vantage points (e.g., child report vs. teacher report) or types of measures (e.g., cortisol levels vs. a stress

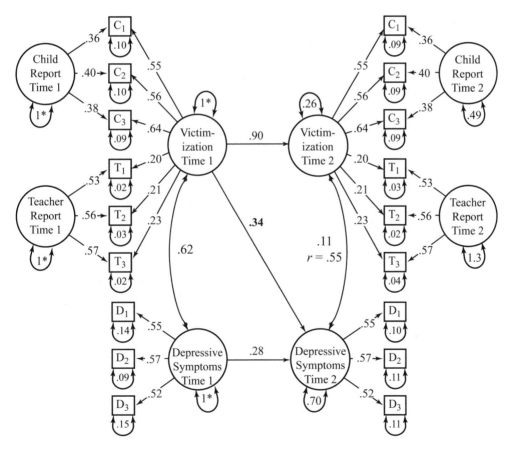

FIGURE 10.8. A longitudinal bifactor decomposition. Model fit is excellent: $\chi^2_{(n=376, 118)} = 153.70$, $p = .02$. The corresponding indicator's residuals are allowed to correlate across time. The child-report factor correlates with itself across time ($r = -.38$), as does the teacher-report factor ($r = .26$). The data for this example are compliments of Karen Rudolph. See Rudolph et al. (2011) for details.

inventory). By definition, the secondary constructs are independent of the primary factor. The secondary constructs may or may not be independent of each other, depending on the theoretical goals and statistical identification. In this example, with just two vantage points to represent the bifactor decomposition, the two secondary constructs are represented as independent of each other. If three or more vantage points are included in a bifactor decomposition, the secondary factors could potentially have some additional correlation. A very important concern in this regard is whether a specified correlation among the secondary factors is identified.

The model in Figure 10.8 is specified with factorial invariance of the loadings across time. The indicators of each construct are item parcels that I created using the balancing method. The original tool had 10 items assessing victimization. In addition, I selected Wave 2 and 3 of the multiwave data to illustrate longitudinal bifactor decomposition. The loadings of the parcel indicators are equated for both the specific factors and the common factors. For the test of strong invariance, the intercepts would be equated over time, but the constructs' means can be specified in a couple of different ways. For example, I could specify a mean for victimization and a 0 mean for the secondary factors. I could specify a mean for the secondary factors but no mean for the primary victimization construct. If I had strong theory to test some hypothesis that the mean of child report was greater than the mean of teacher report, for instance, I could specify a mean for victimization and a mean for the child-report construct. This specification would define victimization as the mean of teacher-reported victimization, and then the mean of the child-reported victimization would be interpreted as the mean difference. Because the means for this model are not of central concern, I have reported only the covariance structures model in Figure 10.8 with the factorial invariance of all loadings specified.

With the longitudinal bifactor decomposition depicted in Figure 10.8, I allowed the secondary factors to have cross-time stability correlations but no other correlations with the other factors either within a measurement occasion or between the two measurement occasions. As the figure caption indicates, the child-reported victimization construct has a stability correlation of −.38. This secondary factor represents the child's self-perception of victimization that is not shared with the teacher's reports of victimization. Because of the way that I specified this model, these perceptions, which are not shared with teachers' perceptions, show a small inverse relationship. The teachers' perceptions of victimization, on the other hand, show a small positive correlation of .26 over time. Because this correlation is rather small, it suggests that the stability in teacher's reports that is not shared with the child's perceptions is negligible. The construct labeled "victimization" contains the shared perspectives of victimization. This common variance is very stable across the 1-year interval for this particular longitudinal example. The loadings for the bifactor model indicate that a slightly higher proportion of the child-reported victimization is reflected in the primary victimization construct. Teacher-reported victimization shows an opposite pattern in that more variance is reflected in the reporter-specific factor for the teachers.

The longitudinal model for victimization clearly shows that earlier experiences of victimization are predictive of increases in depressive symptoms over a 1-year interval in this age cohort. These data also indicate that depressive symptoms are not very stable. Combined, the cross-lagged path and the autoregressive path account for a little over 30% of the variance in depressive symptoms, which suggests that other factors would also be key predictors of the changes in depressive symptoms. In peer-relations research, multiple reporters are not often examined in this manner. The bifactor model can be a very useful way to represent multiple reporters' perspectives on different social-behavioral characteristics.

CONTRASTING DIFFERENT VARIANCE DECOMPOSITIONS

To illustrate a number of different complex decompositions, I rely on data that I collected in the late 1990s. Here, I use the I FEEL scales to show various ways in which the sources of variance in measures with two or more veins of information can be extracted. The I FEEL has four subscales that measure positive dimensions of mood, and it has four subscales that measure negative dimensions of mood (it also has measures of anxiety, somatic complaints, and physiological disturbances—I focus here on just the positive and negative mood dimensions). Table 10.3 presents the results of a simple CFA analysis of the eight I FEEL subscales. Table 10.4 is a table of the model fit information for the various models that I fit to these data. The models that I have contrasted in Table 10.4 are not necessarily nested and aren't meant to be contrasted in terms of which model fits the data better. Instead,

TABLE 10.3. Correlations, means, and variances for the dimensions of positive and negative mood

| | Positive mood dimensions | | | | Negative mood dimensions | | | |
	Con	Eval	Nrg	Aff	Con	Eval	Nrg	Aff
pCon	1.00							
pEval	.82	1.00						
pNrg	.84	.87	1.00					
pAff	.84	.91	.90	1.00				
nCon	-.53	-.29	-.27	-.39	1.00			
nEval	-.47	-.38	-.33	-.46	.82	1.00		
nNrg	-.38	-.31	-.28	-.37	.88	.87	1.00	
nAff	-.42	-.31	-.29	-.43	.87	.90	.93	1.00
Mean	3.16	2.78	2.82	3.18	1.40	1.31	1.63	1.45
Var	.36	.29	.32	.44	.24	.18	.18	.29

Note. Con = connectedness, Eval = self-evaluation, Nrg = energy, Aff = affect, p = positive, n = negative.

TABLE 10.4. Fit information for the various decompositions of the I FEEL scales

Model tested	χ^2	df	AIC	BIC	RMSEA	RMSEA 90% CI	CFI	NNFI
Initial CFA	477.88	224	13.47	-866.2	.053	.046;.060	.988	.986
Bifactor	466.56	226	-7.58	-895.1	.051	.044;.058	.989	.987
Pseudo-bifactor	497.26	232	17.89	-893.2	.054	.047;.060	.987	.985
Mod pseudo-bifactor	505.61	235	16.06	-906.8	.053	.047;.060	.987	.985
Higher-order	522.98	242	18.59	-931.7	.054	.047;.060	.987	.985
Pseudo-higher-order	540.78	244	37.65	-920.5	.056	.049;.062	.986	.984

Note. These various models correspond with Table 10.3 and Figures 10.9–10.13. $N = 376$.

I just want to show the relative costs or benefits of the different models in terms of model fit information. As to which model one would fit, the primary determination should be based on theory.

In Table 10.3, the latent correlations among these eight constructs have a couple of distinctive features. First, the positive mood constructs have a strong positive correlational manifold, with no correlations below the .80 level. Similarly, the negative mood constructs have a strong positive correlational manifold with no correlations below the .80 level. In the four-by-four quadrant that contains the correlations between the positive mood constructs and the negative mood constructs, the correlations are all negative and generally in the .3 range. Negative self-evaluation has consistently higher correlations with the positive constructs, and the one correlation of −.53 stands out as being inconsistently higher than the other magnitudes of correlations. These subscales of the I FEEL battery have some similarity with the well-validated and well-established Positive and Negative Affect Scales (PANAS; Watson, Clark, & Tellegen, 1988). In particular, the Positive Affect subscale and the Negative Affect subscale of the I FEEL are most comparable to the two constructs of the PANAS. In this regard, the Positive Affect and Negative Affect subscales of the I FEEL can be viewed as the anchor constructs of positive and negative mood, whereas the other subscales are secondary facets of mood. As I show, this primary role for Positive and Negative Affect can lead to a couple of different, yet theoretically meaningful, models for these data.

The first decomposition model that I fit to these data is the bifactor decomposition of the positive mood indicators and of the negative mood indicators. This elaborate bifactor decomposition is presented in Figure 10.9. Like the simple bifactor model of victimization as rated by teachers versus the children themselves, the more elaborate decomposition has each indicator loading onto two independent constructs. In Figure 10.9, I have used the bifactor logic to decompose the information in each indicator into a primary construct of positive or negative mood. The four subscales from the positive battery and the four subscales from the negative battery are each represented as secondary factors for their respective domains. More specifically, in

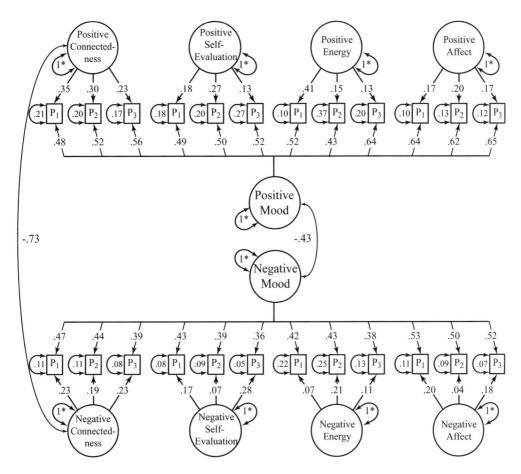

FIGURE 10.9. A bifactor model for the I FEEL scales of positive and negative affect. The fixed factor method of scaling and identification was used for this model because the effects coding method does not make sense for this kind of two-factor decomposition of the indicators' variances. The indicators are labeled P_1, P_2, and P_3 to denote that these indicators are parcels of the available items on the I FEEL.

the middle of Figure 10.9, I have listed two overarching constructs of positive mood and negative mood. All the indicators of the positive mood subscales load onto this overarching construct. Similarly, all of the indicators of the negative mood subscales load onto the overarching negative mood construct. The indicators also load onto their respective subscales. For this model, I used the fixed factor method of scale setting and construct identification. For the overarching constructs, the loadings are consistently larger than the corresponding loadings for the subscales. These differences in the magnitudes of the loadings are consistent with the high positive correlational manifold among the positive mood dimensions. Had the correlations among the subscales been at the .7 level, the loadings between the subscale construct and the overarching construct would have been about equal in magnitude. Correlations below .7 would make the subscale loadings larger than the corresponding loadings with the overarching construct.

The two overarching constructs are allowed to correlate in this decomposition, and the estimated correlation turns out to be –.43. In all bifactor models, the subordinate constructs are independent of the overarching construct. This independence is a necessary feature of the bifactor decomposition. If the subordinate constructs (in this case the four subscales of the I FEEL facets of mood) are allowed to correlate with the overarching construct, the solution is not identified, and a decomposition of the variance into the two component constructs is not possible. The model in Figure 10.9 is one that has two different bifactor models, one for positive mood and one for negative mood. In Figure 10.9, the two constructs that tap into the perceived quality of one's social relationships have an additional negative association of –.73 above and beyond the –.43 observed for the overarching mood constructs. The other three subscales did not show this pattern. The correlations in Table 10.3 suggested that an additional correlation for connectedness may have been needed. In particular, the CFA showed that these two constructs had a negative correlation that was clearly larger than the other correlations in the quadrant.

The correlation between positive connectedness and negative connectedness is reproduced using the correlation implied by the positive mood and negative mood correlation of –.43 plus the additional correlation of the connectedness subconstructs. The observed associations among the indicators are channeled through the magnitudes of the loadings on the constructs. For example, the model-implied covariance between the first indicator of positive connectedness and the first indicator of negative connectedness is reproduced by tracing the estimates in Figure 10.9: $(.35 \cdot -.73 \cdot .23) + (.48 \cdot -.43 \cdot .47) = -.157$. For the remaining constructs, there was no indication of a need for a correlation among the secondary constructs for the negative mood dimensions or the positive mood dimensions, and none of the other dimensions indicated a need for a cross-mood covariance of the secondary factors.

As shown in Table 10.4, the bifactor model in Figure 10.9 is clearly a good approximation of the data and indicates that positive and negative mood, as measured by the I FEEL in this age cohort, have a slight negative association (–.43) and that the social connection subscales have an additional correlation (–.73) above and beyond the overarching correlation. The other models that I fit to these data show a very similar pattern, even though the models are conceptually very different. The model fit information for each of the models to follow is presented in Table 10.4.

I mentioned earlier that the Positive Affect and Negative Affect subscales of the I FEEL can be viewed as the anchor constructs of positive and negative mood, while the other subscales are secondary facets of mood. Figure 10.10 is a pseudo-bifactor decomposition that uses the Positive and Negative Affect subscales as indicators of only the primary factor, whereas the other subscales have secondary constructs specified. A close look at Figure 10.10 shows that all indicators of positive mood load on the construct labeled positive affect. Similarly, all indicators of negative mood

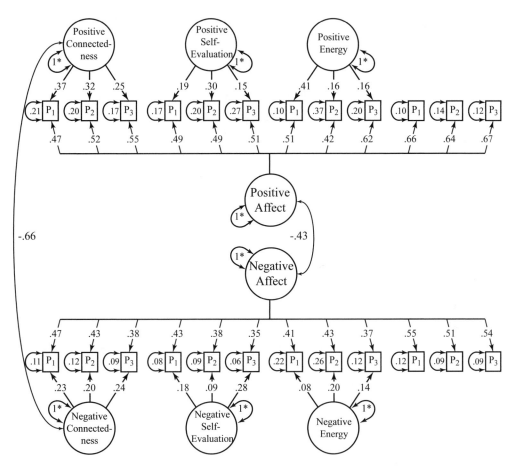

FIGURE 10.10. A pseudo-bifactor model for the I FEEL scales of positive and negative affect. The fixed factor method of scaling and identification was used for this model because the effects coding method does not make sense for this kind of two-factor decomposition of the indicator's variances. The indicators are labeled P_1, P_2, and P_3 to denote that these indicators are parcels of the available items on the I FEEL.

dimensions load on the construct labeled negative affect. The difference between the true bifactor model and the pseudo-bifactor is that the secondary factors for the indicators of positive and negative affect are not estimated. By not estimating these secondary factors, the overarching or primary factor takes on a different definition. In the true bifactor model, I labeled these constructs positive and negative mood because these primary factors extract common variance from each of the four subscales. In the pseudo-bifactor model, the primary factors are labeled positive and negative affect because the indicators of the respective affect subscales are the defining loadings. The other loadings on these constructs would be interpreted as the amount of variance explained by positive or negative affect in the indicators of the other subscales. For example, the first indicator of positive self-evaluation has a .49

loading on the positive affect construct, a .19 loading on the positive self-evaluation construct, and a .17 residual. In terms of the percentage variance that these estimates represent, the .49 loading is equal to 53% of the variance in the indicator that is associated with positive affect. The .19 secondary loading represents 8% of the variance related to self-evaluation only, and the .17 residual equals 39% of the variance in the indicator that is both unreliable and unique to the indicator.

Figure 10.11 is a modified version of the model presented in Figure 10.10. The key modification is that the secondary factor for negative energy has been removed. I removed this factor because the secondary loadings for this construct were all nonsignificant, indicating that negative energy and negative affect are indistinguishable

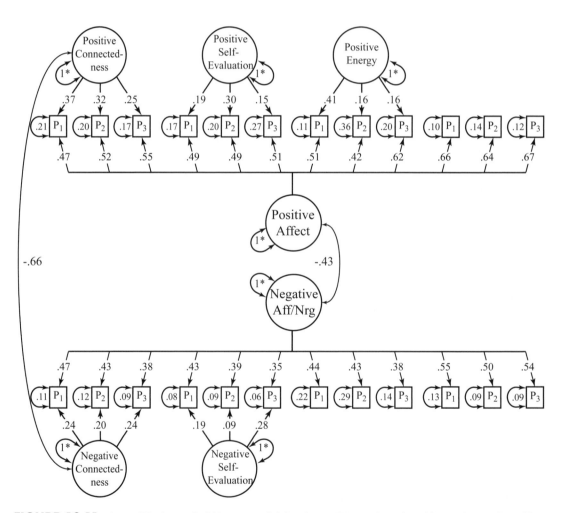

FIGURE 10.11. A modified pseudo-bifactor model for the I FEEL scales of positive and negative affect. The fixed factor method of scaling and identification was used for this model because the effects coding method does not make sense for this kind of two-factor decomposition of the indicators' variances. The indicators are labeled P_1, P_2, and P_3 to denote that these indicators are parcels of the available items on the I FEEL.

when assessed from the perspective of negative mood. The model in Figure 10.11 is nested within the model shown in Figure 10.10. The difference is that the three loadings for negative energy are fixed to 0. The difference in model fit is nonsignificant ($\Delta\chi^2_{(3, n=376)} = 8.35$, $p = .039$), indicating that of the two pseudo-bifactor models, the one in Figure 10.11 is a statistically better model. The key substantive relationships in Figure 10.11 are similar to those in Figure 10.10. Positive affect is correlated with the melded negative affect/energy construct at $-.43$, and the two connectedness constructs still have an additional negative correlation of $-.66$.

In Figure 10.12, I have fit a different type of model for the I FEEL data. Here, the model is a second-order or higher order factor model. These models are also referred to as hierarchical models, but this term has recently garnered disfavor and confusion

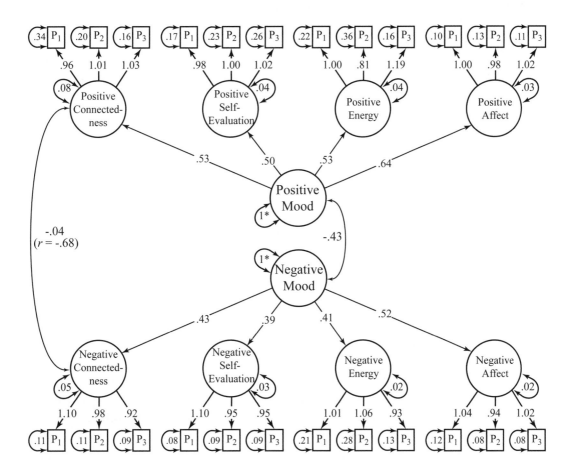

FIGURE 10.12. A second-order factor model for the I FEEL scales of positive and negative affect. I used the effects coding method of identification for the lower order constructs and the fixed factor method for the second-order constructs. The indicators are labeled P_1, P_2, and P_3 to denote that these indicators are parcels of the available items on the I FEEL.

when used to describe models such as the one in Figure 10.12. The term *hierarchical* is confusing because it is also used for models specifically designed to handle the nested data structures that I discussed in Chapter 8. Second-order factors do not account for nested data structures, but they do account for significant correlations among two or more lower order constructs. These models could also be described as factor-of-factors models, but I think the term *second order* captures the nature of these models quite well. Using *second order* as the term also opens the way to think about third-order and possibly even fourth-order factor models.

Unlike the bifactor model, where all indicators load onto the primary mood constructs, the model in Figure 10.12 has the lower order constructs regressed directly onto the second-order primary mood constructs. The lower order constructs were scaled using the effects coding method, whereas each of second-order primary constructs was scaled using the fixed factor method of scaling and identification. As with the bifactor model, the model fit is quite good, although the degrees of freedom are quite different. Again, these models are not nested, which makes determining which one is a better model a more difficult judgment, statistically speaking. Here, the conceptual/theoretical motivation for the model would likely trump a statistical rationale.

The model in Figure 10.12 reveals nearly identical substantive conclusions about the strength of the correlation between positive and negative mood ($r = -.43$) and the need for an additional correlation between the two connectedness constructs. Here, the correlation comes out to be $-.68$, which is essentially the same as the $-.73$ found from the bifactor model. The substantive conclusions about these associations would be identical between the two models. The key difference is that the second-order decomposition is more parsimonious than the bifactor model. The second-order model assumes that the common variance among the indicators associated with the primary, overarching mood factors can be adequately captured in the correlations among the lower order constructs. The bifactor model implies that some indicators may have more common variance than others, and the extraction of the common variance to create the primary, overarching mood constructs is best optimized by allowing each indicator to load onto its respective overarching mood construct.

When all the indicators of the correlated constructs are approximately equally good and factorially invariant, the two approaches will usually lead to the same associations among the constructs. As with the secondary factors of the bifactor model I fit earlier, the lower order constructs are not correlated with each other. The logic for these higher order factor models is that the covariances among the lower order constructs can be explained by a common higher order factor. Therefore, the covariances among the lower order constructs are not estimated. The covariances would be reproduced using simple tracing rules. I introduced tracing rules to show how to obtain the model-implied covariances among the indicators. This logic applies to the model-implied covariances among the lower order constructs when a higher order construct is included. For example, the model-implied covariance between negative self-evaluation and negative energy would be .39 · 1.0 · .41 = .16.

Figure 10.13 represents another hybrid model that relies on the theoretical supposition that the positive and negative affect constructs are each anchors or "pure" constructs of mood and the other constructs are secondary instantiations of mood. The model in Figure 10.13 is a pseudo-higher order model because the "higher order" constructs actually have measured indicators (the same reason the pseudo bifactor is classified as a pseudo variant). The lower order constructs are regressed onto the higher order construct, and the correlations among the lower order constructs are fixed at 0. The feature that makes the model in Figure 10.13 a pseudo–higher order model is the fact that the residual correlations among the lower order constructs are

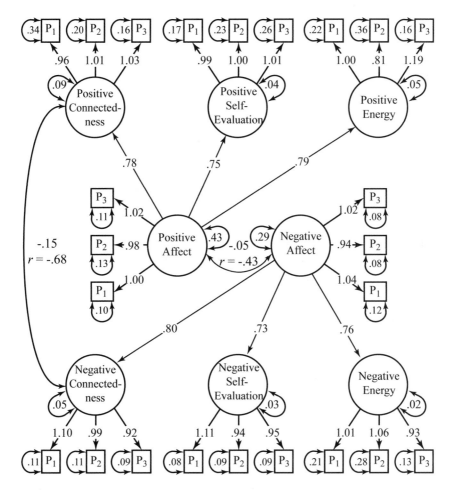

FIGURE 10.13. A pseudo-higher order model for the I FEEL scales of positive and negative affect. The effects coding method of identification was used for all constructs. The indicators are labeled P_1, P_2, and P_3 to denote that these indicators are parcels of the available items on the I FEEL.

fixed at 0. This fixing assumes that the residuals' covariances will be 0 after control-ling for the higher order construct. Because the higher order construct has measured indicators, this assumption could be tested by estimating the residual correlations to determine whether there are any significant correlations among the lower order constructs.

Like the bifactor decomposition of victimization in Figure 10.8, each of the various decompositions that I just presented can be fit longitudinally. For each of the models, longitudinal factorial invariance can be tested. For the higher order ver-sions, the longitudinal factorial invariance of the higher order factors can also be tested. With these models, the tests would typically be done in a two-stage process: first, I would establish the invariance of the measurement model for the lower order constructs, and then I would establish the invariance of the second-order constructs. With the bifactor variants, the factorial invariance of the primary and secondary constructs would be conducted at the same time.

DIGESTIF

The preceding jambalaya of models for multidimensional constructs generally will be appropriate when the subscales are sufficiently positively correlated. When the subscales are not very highly correlated, the amount of common variance is mini-mal. I've worked with many investigators who have ideas about how a set of con-structs should all be a reflection of an underlying process. In some cases, the set of constructs will be sufficiently correlated such that a higher order or bifactor rep-resentation can capture the commonality across the set of constructs to represent the unitary process. For example, positive mood is reflected in shared feelings of positive affect, positive energy, positive self-evaluation, and positive connectedness with others. In this situation, various models can be applied to gather the common variance into a single construct. And, generally speaking, the single common factor is the focal construct of interest. The subdimensions are generally considered nui-sance factors or minor factors that are extracted in order to remove the attenuation that can occur when the nuisance information commingles with common variance across the different subdimensions.

Sometimes the constructs are not sufficiently correlated to warrant a higher order structure. In this case, each construct has its unique predictive characteristic(s). Personal agency is an example. Agency is conceptualized as the degree to which one possesses or can utilize different means to attain one's goals (the concept of personal agency is very similar to self-efficacy). Different means can include effort, ability, teachers, and parents. These dimensions do not form a single higher order factor. Instead, they bifurcate into two higher order dimensions: intra-self agency (effort and ability) and extra-self agency (teachers and parents). Conceptually, to understand the role of agency in predicting performance, both higher order constructs need to be represented. Because the two higher order constructs are relatively uncorrelated, a predicted score can be obtained by summing the predictive influence of both higher order dimensions. Two persons can achieve the same predicted score through different avenues. One person may be higher on the intra-self agency dimension but not so high on the extra-self agency dimension, whereas the other person may be higher on the extra-self agency dimension than on the intra-self agency dimension. Both dimensions are needed to adequately predict performance and understand the role of agency in producing a given performance outcome. I emphasized this additive effects idea in the discussion of moderation (see Chapter 9). Intra-self agency and extra-self agency do not moderate one another. They each have a unique predictive influence that together define how agency predicts a given outcome variable.

Sometimes the commonality can be information that one wishes to control so that the unique predictive features of the subscales can emerge. For example, in a validity study of the Infant–Toddler Social and Emotional Assessment (ITSEA), we (Carter, Briggs-Gowan, Jones, & Little, 2003) used the bifactor model to extract a total-problems construct from 17 dimensions of child behavior. The 17 dimensions also had three secondary constructs—internalizing, externalizing, and dysregulation—that were of key interest in establishing the validity of the ITSEA. In this version of the bifactor model, the three secondary constructs were allowed to correlate with each other. One intent of the primary factor was to extract the overall problems construct so that the unique predictive associations of the three secondary constructs could be evaluated for validity. By extracting the total-problems construct as a source of variability, the unique predictive influence of the three secondary constructs was supported.

Each of the models that I outlined in this chapter can be fit longitudinally. Some of the models, such as the higher order models, are often difficult to estimate longitudinally because of the estimation demands. These models are notorious for making it hard for SEM software to converge. If the higher order structure can be verified in supplemental analyses, facet representative parcels of the lower order constructs can be used as direct indicators of the higher order factors of interest. This simplified approach would be easier to implement in a longitudinal study than attempting the full higher order decomposition longitudinally.

With complex indicators, carefully considering what the sources of variability are in a set of scores will always prove beneficial. Understanding how variance components can occur and how they can be successfully decomposed into their constituent parts is an essential skill for conducting successful research in the social and behavioral sciences. Just as understanding the sources of flavors and how they coalesce provides the basis for serving a satisfying meal, understanding the sources of variance and how they are interrelated provides the basis for published meaningful research. Enjoy!

KEY TERMS AND CONCEPTS INTRODUCED IN THIS CHAPTER

Bifactor. Bifactor means that two factors underlie the sources of variance in a given indicator. That is, part of the variance loads on one construct, and a second part of the variance loads on a second construct. The bifactor constructs must be independent sources of variance. Typically, the bifactor model has one factor that crosses over multiple sets of indicators of other factors. The one factor is usually the primary factor, and the sets of indicators for the other factors are usually considered secondary factors. The primary factor extracts all the variance that is common across the indicators, and the secondary construct extracts what remains among a subset of indicators conditioning on the common variance (i.e., after the common variance is extracted).

Decomposition. In the SEM world, something that decomposes is not dead. Instead, decomposition refers to separating the sources of information into a set of constituent parts (or sources of variance). Decomposition is typically accomplished by attributing the sources of variance in a given indicator to two or more orthogonal components. Traditional common factors separate the sources of variance in a given indicator into two orthogonal components: the common factor variance and the unique factor variance. MTMM frameworks separate the sources of variance into the unique factor and two orthogonal common factors.

Heterotrait–heteromethod. Different traits being assessed by different methods inform the discriminant validity of the traits. These associations are often attenuated by the degree of method variance that is present in the data. SEM decompositions will disattenuate the associations among the traits.

Heterotrait–monomethod. When different traits are assessed by the same method, it is a reflection of how much variance is due to the method of assessment. When method effects are strong, then different traits measured by the same method will correlate more highly than would be predicted by the trait characteristics alone.

Jambalaya. A tasty dish composed of a mixture of meats and seafood carried in a medium of vegetables, rice, and spices. When used metaphorically, it means a mixture of various and sometimes diverse elements—hence, the title of this chapter.

Lower order, higher order; first order, second order. Terms that describe fitting a factor model at different levels of data representation. First-order factors are extracted from the manifest variables or indicators, whereas second-order factors are extracted from the covariation among two or more first-order constructs. Lower and higher order are synonymous terms with first and second order. Third-order factors are also possible, as these would be factors that are extracted from two or more second-order factors.

Monotrait–heteromethod. The same trait being assessed by different methods forms the convergent validity information for a given trait in the MTMM framework. The fact that different methods correlate highly when measuring the same trait indicates that trait variance is strong and readily measured with different methods.

Monotrait–monomethod. The same trait being assessed by the same method forms the reliability diagonal of the traditional MTMM matrix. In an SEM model, it refers to the loadings of the indicators on a given construct, which adds a further degree of convergent and discriminant validity to the MTMM framework.

Pseudo. A modifier that means that something looks or behaves like something else. In some usages it can mean false, fake, or pretense. I don't use it in this extreme but rather in the sense that something appears to be like and is as valid as the core approach or model but contains one or more elements that make it different enough to modify it with *pseudo*.

RECOMMENDED READINGS

Multitrait Multimethod

Campbell, D. T., & Fiske, D. W. (1959). Convergent and discriminant validation by the multitrait–multimethod matrix. *Psychological Bulletin, 56*(2), 81–105.

> The classic on multitrait multimethod.

Grimm, K. J., Pianta, R. C., & Konold, T. (2009). Longitudinal multitrait–multimethod models for developmental research. *Multivariate Behavioral Research, 44*, 233–258.

> An outstanding application of an MTMM in the context of longitudinal data.

A Bifactor Application

Carter, A. S., Briggs-Gowan, M., Jones, S. M., & Little, T. D. (2003). The Infant–Toddler Social and Emotional Assessment: Factor structure, reliability, and validity. *Journal of Abnormal Child Psychology, 31*, 495–514.

> An application of the bifactor model for testing the validity of the ITSEA.

The Form–Function Decomposition

Little, T. D., Brauner, J., Jones, S. M., Nock, M. K., & Hawley, P. H. (2003). Rethinking aggression: A typological examination of the functions of aggression. *Merrill–Palmer Quarterly, 49*, 343–369.

Little, T. D., Jones, S. M., Henrich, C. C., & Hawley, P. H. (2003). Disentangling the "whys" from the "whats" of aggressive behavior. *International Journal of Behavioral Development, 27*, 122–133.

> These two articles give details of using the pseudo-MTMM approach to disentangling the functions and forms of aggression. The Little, Jones, et al. article shows the CFA validity of the decomposition in a sample of elementary-age children. The Little, Brauner, et al. article shows how the decomposition can be done using OLS regression analysis to address other questions related to the functions of aggression.

References

Anderson, J. G. (1987). Structural equation models in the social and behavioral sciences: Model building. *Child Development, 58*, 49–64.

Arthur, M. W., Hawkins, J. D., Pollard, J., Catalano, R. F., & Baglioni, A. J. (2002). Measuring risk and protective factors for substance use, delinquency, and other adolescent problem behaviors: The Communities that Care Youth Survey. *Evaluation Review, 26*, 575–601.

Baltes, P. B. (1968). Longitudinal and cross-sectional sequences in the study of age and generation effects. *Human Development, 11*, 145–171.

Baron, R. M., & Kenny, D. A. (1986). The moderator–mediator variable distinction in social psychological research: Conceptual, strategic and statistical considerations. *Journal of Personality and Social Psychology, 51*, 1173–1182.

Bauer, D. J. (2003). Estimating multilevel linear models as structural equation models. *Journal of Educational and Behavioral Statistics, 28*, 135–167.

Bauer, D. J., Preacher, K. J., & Gil, K. M. (2006). Conceptualizing and testing random indirect effects and moderated mediation in multilevel models: New procedures and recommendations. *Psychological Methods, 11*, 142–163.

Bauer, D. J., & Shanahan, M. J. (2007). Modeling complex interactions: Person-centered and variable-centered approaches. In T. D. Little, J. A. Bovaird, & N. A. Card (Eds.), *Modeling contextual effects in longitudinal studies* (pp. 255–284). Mahwah, NJ: Erlbaum.

Bell, R. Q. (1953). Convergence: An accelerated longitudinal approach. *Child Development, 24*, 145–152.

Bentler, P. M. (1990). Comparative fit indexes in structural models. *Psychological Bulletin, 107*, 238–246.

Bentler, P. M., & Bonett, D. G. (1980). Significance tests and goodness of fit in the analysis of covariance structures. *Psychological Bulletin, 88*, 588–606.

Bickel, R. (2007). *Multilevel analysis for applied research: It's just regression!* New York: Guilford Press.

Biesanz, J. C., Deeb-Sossa, N., Papadakis, A. A., Bollen, K. A., & Curran, P. J. (2004). The role of coding time in estimating and interpreting growth curve models. *Psychological Methods, 9*, 30–52.

Bijleveld, C. C. J. H., & van der Kamp, L. J. T. (1998). *Longitudinal data analysis: Designs, models and methods*. Thousand Oaks, CA: Sage.

Birnbaum, A. (1961). Confidence curves: An omnibus technique for estimation and testing statistical hypotheses. *Journal of the American Statistical Association, 56,* 246–259.

Blaga, O. M., Shaddy, D. J., Anderson, C. J., Kannass, K. N., Little, T. D., & Colombo, J. (2009). Structure and continuity of intellectual development in early childhood. *Intelligence, 37,* 106–113.

Blozis, S. A., Conger, K. J., & Harring, J. R. (2007). Nonlinear latent curve models for multivariate longitudinal data. *International Journal of Behavioral Development, 31,* 340–346.

Bollen, K. A. (1989). *Structural equations with latent variables.* New York: Wiley.

Bollen, K. A., & Curran, P. J. (2004). Autoregressive latent trajectory (ALT) models: A synthesis of two traditions. *Sociological Methods and Research, 32,* 336–383.

Bollen, K. A., & Curran, P. J. (2006). *Latent curve models: A structural equation perspective.* Hoboken, NJ: Wiley.

Bollen, K. A., & Stine, R. (1990). Direct and indirect effects: Classical and bootstrap estimates of variability. *Sociological Methodology, 20,* 115–140.

Bovaird, J. A. (2007). Multilevel structural equation models for contextual factors. In T. D. Little, J. A. Bovaird, & N. A. Card (Eds.), *Modeling contextual effects in longitudinal studies* (pp. 149–182). Mahwah, NJ: Erlbaum.

Box, G. E. P. (1979). Some problems of statistics and everyday life. *Journal of the American Statistical Association, 74,* 1–4.

Bronfenbrenner, U. (1975). The ecology of human development in retrospect and prospect. In H. McGurk (Ed.), *Ecological factors in human development* (pp. 275–286). Amsterdam: North-Holland.

Bronfenbrenner, U. (1977). *The ecology of human development: Experiments by nature and design.* Cambridge, MA: Harvard University Press.

Brown, T. A. (2006). *Confirmatory factor analysis for applied research.* New York: Guilford Press.

Browne, M. W., & Cudeck, R. (1992). Alternative ways of assessing model fit. *Sociological Methods and Research, 21*(2), 230–258.

Browne, M. W., & Cudeck, R. (1993). Alternative ways of assessing model fit. In K. A. Bollen & J. S. Long (Eds.), *Testing structural equation models* (pp. 136–162). Newbury Park, CA: Sage.

Burkholder, G. J., & Harlow, L. L. (2003). An illustration of a longitudinal cross-lagged design for larger structural equation models. *Structural Equation Modeling, 10,* 465–486.

Byrne, B. M., & Crombie, G. (2003). Modeling and testing change: An introduction to the latent growth curve model. *Understanding Statistics, 2,* 177–203.

Cairns, R. B., Bergman, L. R., & Kagan, J. (Eds.). (1998). *Methods and models for studying the individual.* Thousand Oaks, CA: Sage.

Campbell, D. T., & Fiske, D. W. (1959). Convergent and discriminant validation by the multitrait–multimethod matrix. *Psychological Bulletin, 56*(2), 81–105.

Campbell, D. T., Stanley, J. C., & Gage, N. L. (1963). *Experimental and quasi-experimental designs for research.* Boston, MA: Houghton, Mifflin and Company.

Card, N. A., & Little, T. D. (2005). On the use of the social relations and actor–partner interdependence models in developmental research. *International Journal of Behavioral Development, 29,* 173–179.

Card, N. A., & Little, T. D. (2006). Analytic considerations in cross-cultural research on peer relations. In X. Chen, D. C. French, & B. Schneider (Eds.), *Peer relations in cultural context* (pp. 75–95). New York: Cambridge University Press.

Card, N. A., & Little, T. D. (2007a). Longitudinal modeling of developmental processes. *International Journal of Behavioral Development, 31,* 297–302.

Card, N. A., & Little, T. D. (2007b). Studying aggression with structural equation modeling. In D. Flannery, A. Vazsonyi, & I. Waldman (Eds.), *Cambridge handbook of violent behavior* (pp. 727–739). New York: Cambridge University Press.

Card, N. A., Little, T. D., & Bovaird, J. A. (2007). Modeling ecological and contextual effects in longitudinal studies of human development. In T. D. Little, J. A. Bovaird, & N. A. Card (Eds.), *Modeling contextual effects in longitudinal studies* (pp. 1–11). Mahwah, NJ: Erlbaum.

Card, N. A., Selig, J. P., & Little, T. D. (Eds.). (2008). *Modeling dyadic and interdependent data in developmental research.* Mahwah, NJ: Erlbaum.

Card, N. A., Stucky, B. D., Sawalani, G. M., & Little, T. D. (2008). Direct and indirect aggression during childhood and adolescence: A meta-analytic review of gender differences, intercorrelations, and relations to maladjustment. *Child Development, 79,* 1185–1229.

Carter, A. S., Briggs-Gowan, M., Jones, S. M., & Little, T. D. (2003). The infant–toddler social and emotional assessment: Factor structure, reliability, and validity. *Journal of Abnormal Child Psychology, 31,* 495–514.

Cattell, R. B. (1952). The three basic factor-analytic research designs: Their interrelations and derivatives. *Psychological Bulletin, 49,* 499–551.

Cattell, R. B. (1963). The structuring of change by P- and incremental R- technique. In C. W. Harris (Ed.), *Problems in measuring change.* Madison: University of Wisconsin.

Cattell, R. B. (1988).The data box. In J. R. Nesselroade & R. B. Cattell (Eds.), *Handbook of multivariate experimental psychology.* New York: Plenum Press.

Chan, D. (1998). The conceptualization and analysis of change over time: An integrative approach incorporating longitudinal mean and covariance structures analysis (LMACS) and multiple indicator latent growth modeling (MLGM). *Organizational Research Methods, 1,* 421–483.

Cheung, G. W., & Rensvold, R. B. (1999). Testing factorial invariance across groups: A reconceptualization and proposed new method. *Journal of Management, 25,* 1–27.

Cheung, G. W., & Rensvold, R. B. (2002). Evaluating goodness-of-fit indexes for testing measurement invariance. *Structural Equation Modeling, 9,* 233–255.

Chou, C.-P., Bentler, P. M., & Pentz, M. A. (1998). Comparisons of two statistical approaches to study growth curves: The multilevel model and the latent curve analysis. *Structural Equation Modeling, 5,* 247–266.

Coie, J. D., & Dodge, K. A. (1983). Continuities and changes in children's social status: A five-year longitudinal study. *Merrill–Palmer Quarterly, 29*(3), 261–282.

Cole, D. A., & Maxwell, S. E. (2003). Testing mediational models with longitudinal data: Questions and tips in the use of structural equation modeling. *Journal of Abnormal Psychology, 112,* 558–577.

Collins, L. M. (2006). Analysis of longitudinal data: The integration of theoretical model, temporal design, and statistical model. *Annual Review of Psychology, 57,* 505–528.

Collins, L. M., & Horn, J. L. (Eds.). (1991). *Best methods for the analysis of change: Recent advances, unanswered questions, future directions.* Washington, DC: American Psychological Association.

Collins, L. M., & Sayer, A. G. (Eds.). (2001). *New methods for the analysis of change.* Washington, DC: American Psychological Association.

Collins, L. M., Schafer, J. L., & Kam, C. M. (2001). A comparison of inclusive and restrictive strategies in modern missing data procedures. *Psychological Methods, 6,* 330–351.

Coxe, S., West, S. G., & Aiken, L. S. (2012). Generalized linear models. In T. D. Little. (Ed.), *The Oxford Handbook of Quantitative Methods,* Vol. 2. (pp. 26–51). New York: Oxford University Press.

Cudeck, R., & Du Toit, S. H. C. (2003). A version of nonlinear multilevel models for repeated measures data. In N. Duan & S. R. Reise (Eds.), *Multilevel modeling: Methodological advances, issues and applications.* Mahwah, NJ: Erlbaum.

Cudeck, R., & MacCallum, R. C. (2007). *Factor analysis at 100: Historical developments and future directions.* Mahwah, NJ: Erlbaum.

Curran, P. J. (2003). Have multilevel models been structural equation models all along? *Multivariate Behavioral Research, 38*, 529–569.

Curran, P. J., & Bauer, D. J. (in press). *Applied Multilevel Modeling for the Behavioral and Social Sciences.* New York: Guilford Press.

Curran, P. J., & Bollen, K. A. (2001). The best of both worlds: Combining autoregressive and latent curve models. In L. M. Collins & A. G. Sayer (Eds.), *New methods for the analysis of change* (pp. 105–136). Washington, DC: American Psychological Association.

Deci, E. L., & Ryan, R. M. (1985). *Intrinsic motivation and self-determination in human behavior.* New York: Plenum Press.

Ding, C. (2007). Studying growth heterogeneity with multidimensional scaling profile analysis. *International Journal of Behavioral Development, 31*(4), 347–356.

Duncan, O. D. (1969). Some linear models for two-wave, two-variable panel analysis. *Psychological Bulletin, 72*, 177–182.

Duncan, T. E., Duncan, S. C., & Strycker, L. A. (2006). *An introduction to latent variable growth curve modeling: Concepts, issues, and applications* (2nd ed.). Mahwah, NJ: Erlbaum.

Efron, B. (1979). Bootstrap methods: Another look at the jackknife. *Annals of Statistics, 7*, 1–26.

Efron, B., & Tibshirani, R. J. (1993). *An introduction to the bootstrap.* New York: Chapman & Hall.

Enders, C. K. (2010). *Applied missing data analysis.* New York: Guilford Press.

Espelage, D. L., Bosworth, K., & Simon, T. R. (2000). Examining the social context of bullying behaviors in early adolescence. *Journal of Counseling and Development, 78*, 326–333.

Espelage, D. L., & Holt, M. L. (2001). Bullying and victimization during early adolescence: Peer influences and psychosocial correlates. *Journal of Emotional Abuse, 2*, 123–142.

Espelage, D. L., Holt, M. K., & Henkel, R. R. (2003). Examination of peer-group contextual effects on aggression during early adolescence. *Child Development, 74*, 205–220.

Farrell, A. D., Kung, E. M., White, K. S., & Valois, R. (2000). The structure of self- reported aggression, drug use, and delinquent behaviors during early adolescence. *Journal of Clinical Child Psychology, 29*, 282–292.

Gallagher, M. W., & Johnson, D. K. (2008, November). *Neuroticism partially mediates age related declines in negative affect.* Poster presented at the Gerontological Society of America Annual Convention, National Harbor, MD.

Geldhof, G. J., Pornprasertmanit, S., Schoemann, A. M., & Little, T. D. (2013). Orthogonalizing through residual centering: Extended applications and caveats. *Educational and Psychological Measurement, 73*, 27–46.

Gollob, H. F., & Reichardt, C. S. (1987). Taking account of time lags in causal models. *Child Development, 58*, 80–92.

Gollob, H. F., & Reichardt, C. S. (1991). Interpreting and estimating indirect effects assuming time lags really matter. In L. M. Collins & J. L. Horn (Eds.), *Best methods for the analysis of change: Recent advances, unanswered questions, future directions* (pp. 253–259). Washington, DC: American Psychological Association.

Gonzalez, R., & Griffin, D. (2001). Testing parameters in structural equation modeling: Every "one" matters. *Psychological Methods, 6*, 258–269.

Gottman, J. M. (Ed.). (1995). *The analysis of change.* Mahwah, NJ: Erlbaum.

Graham, J. W., Cumsille, P. E., & Elek-Fisk, E. (2003). Methods for handling missing data. In I. B. Weiner (Ed.-in-Chief), W. F. Velicer & J. A. Schinka (Vol. Eds.), *Handbook of psychology: Vol. 2. Research methods in psychology* (pp. 87–114). New York: Wiley.

Graham, J. W., Olchowski, A. E., & Gilreath, T. D. (2007). How many imputations are really needed? Some practical clarifications of multiple imputation theory. *Prevention Science, 8*, 206–213.

Graham, J. W., Taylor, B. J., Olchowski, A. E., & Cumsille, P. E. (2006). Planned missing data designs in psychological research. *Psychological Methods, 11*, 323–343.

Grimm, K. J. (2007). Multivariate longitudinal methods for studying developmental relationships between depression and academic achievement. *International Journal of Behavioral Development, 31*, 328–339.

Grimm, K. J., Pianta, R. C., & Konold, T. (2009). Longitudinal multitrait–multimethod models for developmental research. *Multivariate Behavioral Research, 44*, 233–258.

Grob, A., Little, T. D., Wanner, B., Wearing, A. J., & Euronet. (1996). Adolescents' well-being and perceived control across fourteen sociocultural contexts. *Journal of Personality and Social Psychology, 71*, 785–795.

Guttman, L. (1955). A generalized simplex for factor analysis. *Psychometrika, 20*, 173–192.

Hamaker, E. L. (2005). Conditions for the equivalence of the autoregressive latent trajectory model and a latent growth curve model with autoregressive disturbances. *Sociological Methods and Research, 33*(3), 404–418.

Hancock, G. R. (2006). Power analysis in covariance structure analysis. In G. R. Hancock & R. O. Mueller (Eds.), *Structural equation modeling: A second course* (pp. 69–115). Greenwich, CT: Information Age.

Hancock, G. R., & Choi, J. (2006). A vernacular for linear latent growth models. *Structural Equation Modeling, 13*, 352–377.

Hancock, G. R., & Lawrence, F. R. (2006). Using latent growth models to evaluate longitudinal change. In G. R. Hancock & R. O. Mueller (Eds.), *Structural equation modeling: A second course.* Greenwich, CT: Information Age.

Hawley, P. H., & Hensley, W. A. (2009). Social dominance and forceful submission fantasies: Feminine pathology or power? *Journal of Sex Research, 46*, 568–585.

Hawley, P. H., Johnson, S. E., Mize, J. A., & McNamara, K. A. (2007). Physical attractiveness in preschoolers: Relationships with power, status, aggression, and social skills. *Journal of School Psychology, 45*, 499–521.

Hawley, P. H., & Little, T. D. (2003). Modeling intraindividual variability and change in biobehavioral developmental processes. In B. Pugesek, A. Tomer, & A. von Eye (Eds.), *Structural equation modeling: Applications in ecological and evolutionary biology research* (pp. 143–170). Cambridge, UK: Cambridge University Press.

Hayes, A. F. (in press). *Introduction to Mediation, Moderation, and Conditional Process Analysis.* New York: Guilford Press.

Hedeker, D., & Gibbons, R. D. (2006). *Longitudinal data analysis.* Hoboken, NJ: Wiley.

Hershberger, S. L. (1998). Dynamic factor analysis. In G. A. Marcoulides (Ed.), *Modern methods for business research.* Mahwah, NJ: Erlbaum.

Horn, J. L., & McArdle, J. J. (1992). A practical and theoretical guide to measurement invariance in aging research. *Experimental Aging Research, 18*(3–4), 117–144.

Horn, J. L., McArdle, J. J., & Mason, R. (1983). When is invariance not invarient? A practical scientist's look at the ethereal concept of factor invariance. *Southern Psychologist, 1*(4), 179–188.

Howell, R. D., Breivik, E., & Wilcox, J. B. (2007). Reconsidering formative measurement. *Psychological Methods, 12*, 205–218.

Hox, J. (2002). *Multilevel analysis: Techniques and applications.* Mahwah, NJ: Erlbaum.

Humphreys, L. G., & Parsons, C. K. (1979). A simplex process model for describing differences between cross-lagged correlations. *Psychological Bulletin, 86,* 325–334.

Jaccard, J., & Jacoby, J. (2010). *Theory construction and model-building skills: A practical guide for social scientists.* New York: Guilford Press.

Jones, J. C., & Nesselroade, J. R. (1990). Multivariate, replicated, single-subject, repeated measures designs and P-technique factor analysis: A review of intraindividual change studies. *Experimental Aging Research, 16,* 171–183.

Jöreskog, K. G. (1970). Estimation and testing of simplex models. *British Journal of Mathematical and Statistical Psychology, 23,* 121–145.

Jöreskog, K. G., & Sörbom, D. (2001). Simplex models. In *LISREL 8 User's Reference Guide* (pp. 230–238). Lincolnwood, IL: Scientific Software International.

Jöreskog, K. G., & Sörbom, D. (2008). *LISREL 8.80 user's guide* [with software]. Lincolnwood, IL: Scientific Software International.

Jöreskog, K. G., Sörbom, D., Du Toit, S., & Du Toit, M. (2003). *LISREL 8: New statistical features* (3rd ed.). Lincolnwood, IL: Scientific Software International.

Kärnä, A., Voeten, M., Little, T. D., Poskiparta, E., Alanen, E., & Salmivalli, C. (2011). Going to scale: A nonrandomized nationwide trial of the KiVa antibullying program for grades 1–9. *Journal of Consulting and Clinical Psychology, 79,* 796–805.

Kärnä, A., Voeten, M., Little, T. D., Poskiparta, E., Kaljonen, A., & Salmivalli, C. (2011). A large-scale evaluation of the KiVa anti-bullying program. *Child Development, 82,* 311–330.

Kenny, D. A., Kashy, D. A., & Cook, W. L. (2006). *Dyadic data analysis.* New York: Guilford Press.

Kerr, N. L. (1998). HARKing: Hypothesizing after the results are known. *Personality and Social Psychology Review, 2,* 196–217.

Klein, A., & Moosbrugger, H. (2000). Maximum likelihood estimation of latent interaction effects with the LMS method. *Psychometrika, 65,* 457–474.

Kline, R. B. (2010). *Principles and practice of structural equation modeling* (3rd ed.). New York: Guilford Press.

Kreft, I. G. G., & de Leeuw, J. (1998). *Introducing multilevel modeling.* London: Sage.

Lee, I. A., & Little, T. D. (2012). P-technique factor analysis. In B. Laursen, T. D. Little, & N. A. Card (Eds.), *Handbook of developmental research methods* (pp. 350–363). New York: Guilford Press.

Lee, J. (2009). *Type I error and power for mean and covariance structure confirmatory factor analysis for differential item functioning detection: Methodological issues and resolutions* (University of Kansas). ProQuest Dissertations and Theses.

Lee, J., Little, T. D., & Preacher, K. J. (2011). Methodological issues in using structural equation models for testing differential item functioning. In E. Davidov, P. Schmidt, & J. Billiet (Eds.), *Cross-cultural data analysis: Methods and applications* (pp. 55–84). New York: Routledge.

Lerner, R. M., Schwartz, S. J., & Phelps, E. (2009). Problematics of time and timing in the longitudinal study of human development: Theoretical and methodological issues. *Human Development, 52,* 44–68.

Lin, G. C., Wen, Z., Marsh, H. W., & Lin, H. S. (2010). Structural equation models of latent interactions: Clarification of orthogonalizing and double-mean-centering strategies. *Structural Equation Modeling, 17,* 374–391.

Little, R. J. A., & Rubin, D. B. (2002). *Statistical analysis with missing data* (2nd ed.). Hoboken, NJ: Wiley.

Little, T. D. (1997). Mean and covariance structures (MACS) analyses of cross-cultural data: Practical and theoretical issues. *Multivariate Behavioral Research, 32*, 53–76.

Little, T. D. (1998). Sociocultural influences on the development of children's action-control beliefs. In J. Heckhausen & C. S. Dweck (Eds.), *Motivation and self-regulation across the life span* (pp. 281–315). New York: Cambridge University Press.

Little, T. D., Bovaird, J. A., & Card, N. A. (Eds.). (2007). *Modeling contextual effects in longitudinal studies.* Mahwah, NJ: Erlbaum.

Little, T. D., Bovaird, J. A., & Slegers, D. W. (2006). Methods for the analysis of change. In D. K. Mroczek & T. D. Little (Eds.), *Handbook of personality development* (pp. 181–211). Mahwah, NJ: Erlbaum.

Little, T. D., Bovaird, J. A., & Widaman, K. F. (2006). On the merits of orthogonalizing powered and product terms: Implications for modeling interactions among latent variables. *Structural Equation Modeling, 13*, 497–519.

Little, T. D., Brauner, J., Jones, S. M., Nock, M. K., & Hawley, P. H. (2003). Rethinking aggression: A typological examination of the functions of aggression. *Merrill–Palmer Quarterly, 49*, 343–369.

Little, T. D., Card, N. A., Bovaird, J. A., Preacher, K., & Crandall, C. S. (2007). Structural equation modeling of mediation and moderation with contextual factors. In T. D. Little, J. A., Bovaird, & N. A. Card (Eds.), *Modeling contextual effects in longitudinal studies* (pp. 207–230). Mahwah, NJ: Erlbaum.

Little, T. D., Card, N. A., Slegers, D. W., & Ledford, E. C. (2007). Representing contextual effects in multiple-group MACS models. In T. D. Little, J. A. Bovaird, & N. A. Card (Eds.), *Modeling contextual effects in longitudinal studies* (pp. 121–147). Mahwah, NJ: Erlbaum.

Little, T. D., Cunningham, W. A., Shahar, G., & Widaman, K. F. (2002). To parcel or not to parcel: Exploring the question, weighing the merits. *Structural Equation Modeling, 9*, 151–173.

Little, T. D., Jones, S. M., Henrich, C. C., & Hawley, P. H. (2003). Disentangling the "whys" from the "whats" of aggressive behavior. *International Journal of Behavioral Development, 27*, 122–133.

Little, T. D., Lindenberger, U., & Maier, H. (2000). Selectivity and generalizability in longitudinal research: On the effects of continuers and dropouts. In T. D. Little, K. U. Schnabel, & J. Baumert (Eds.), *Modeling longitudinal and multilevel data: Practical issues, applied approaches, and specific examples* (pp. 187–200). Mahwah, NJ: Erlbaum.

Little, T. D., Lindenberger, U., & Nesselroade, J. R. (1999). On selecting indicators for multivariate measurement and modeling with latent variables: When "good" indicators are bad and "bad" indicators are good. *Psychological Methods, 4*, 192–211.

Little, T. D., Preacher, K. J., Selig, J. P., & Card, N. A. (2007). New developments in latent variable panel analysis of longitudinal data. *International Journal of Behavioral Development, 31*, 357–365.

Little, T. D., Rhemtulla, M., Gibson, K., & Schoemann, A. M. (in press). Why the items versus parcels controversy needn't be one. *Psychological Methods.*

Little, T. D., Schnabel, K. U., & Baumert, J. (Eds.). (2000). *Modeling longitudinal and multilevel data: Practical issues, applied approaches, and specific examples.* Mahwah, NJ: Erlbaum.

Little, T. D., Slegers, D. W., & Card, N. A. (2006). A non-arbitrary method of identifying and scaling latent variables in SEM and MACS models. *Structural Equation Modeling, 13*, 59–72.

Little, T. D., Wanner, B., & Ryan, R. (1997). *Development and initial validation of the Inventory of Felt Emotion and Energy in Life (I FEEL)* (ACCD Technical Report No. 5). Berlin, Germany: Max Planck Institute for Human Development and Education.

Loehlin, J. C. (2004). *Latent variable models: An introduction to factor, path, and structural equation analysis* (4th ed.). Mahwah, NJ: Erlbaum.

Luke, D. A. (2004). *Multilevel modeling.* Thousand Oaks, CA: Sage.

MacCallum, R. C. (2003). Working with imperfect models. *Multivariate Behavioral Research, 38,* 113–139.

MacCallum, R. C., & Austin, W. T. (2000). Applications of structural equation modeling in psychological research. *Annual Review of Psychology, 51,* 201–226.

MacCallum, R. C., Browne, M. W., & Cai, L. (2006). Testing differences between nested covariance structure models: Power analysis and null hypotheses. *Psychological Methods, 11,* 19–35.

MacCallum, R. C., Browne, M. W., & Sugawara, H. M. (1996). Power analysis and determination of sample size for covariance structure modeling. *Psychological Methods, 1,* 130–149.

MacCallum, R. C., Kim, C., Malarkey, W. B., & Kiecolt-Glaser, J. K. (1997). Studying multivariate change using multilevel models and latent curve models. *Multivariate Behavioral Research, 32,* 215–253.

MacCallum, R. C., Widaman, K. F., Zhang, S., & Hong, S. (1999). Sample size in factor analysis. *Psychological Methods, 4*(1), 84–99.

MacCallum, R. C., Zhang, S., Preacher, K. J., & Rucker, D. D. (2002). On the practice of dichotomization of quantitative variables. *Psychological Methods, 7,* 19–40.

MacKinnon, D. P. (2008). *Introduction to statistical mediation analysis.* Mahwah, NJ: Erlbaum.

MacKinnon, D. P., Lockwood, C. M., Hoffman, J. M., West, S. G., & Sheets, V. (2002). A comparison of methods to test the significance of the mediated effect. *Psychological Methods, 7,* 83–104.

MacKinnon, D. P., Lockwood, C. M., & Williams, J. (2004). Confidence limits for the indirect effect: Distribution of the product and resampling methods. *Multivariate Behavioral Research, 39,* 99–128.

MacKinnon, D. P., Warsi, G., & Dwyer, J. H. (1995). A simulation study of mediated effect measures. *Multivariate Behavioral Research, 30,* 41–62.

Marsh, H. W., Wen, Z., & Hau, K. T. (2004). Structural equation models of latent interactions: Evaluation of alternative estimation strategies and indicator construction. *Psychological Methods, 9,* 275–300.

Marsh, H. W., Wen, Z., Hau, K.-T., Little, T. D., Bovaird, J. A., & Widaman, K. F. (2007). Unconstrained structural equation models of latent interactions: Contrasting residual- and mean-centered approaches. *Structural Equation Modeling, 14,* 570–580.

Maxwell, S. E., & Cole, D. A. (2007). Bias in cross sectional analysis of longitudinal mediation. *Psychological Methods, 12,* 23–44.

McArdle, J. J. (2009). Latent variable modeling of differences and changes with longitudinal data. *Annual Review of Psychology, 60,* 577–605.

McArdle, J. J., & Hamagami, F. (1991). Modeling incomplete longitudinal data using latent growth structural equation models. In L. Collins & J. L. Horn (Eds.), *Best methods for the analysis of change* (pp. 276–304). Washington, DC: American Psychological Association.

McArdle, J. J., & Wang, L. (2008). Modeling age-based turning points in longitudinal life-span growth curves of cognition. In P. Cohen (Ed.), *Applied data analytic techniques for turning points research* (pp. 105–128). Mahwah, NJ: Erlbaum.

McDonald, R. P. (1989). An index of goodness-of-fit based on noncentrality. *Journal of Classification, 6,* 97–103.

McDonald, R. P. (1999). *Test theory: A unified treatment.* Mahwah, NJ: Erlbaum.

McDowell, D., McCleary, R., Meidinger, E. E., & Hay, R. A. (1980). *Interrupted time series analysis.* Thousand Oaks, CA: Sage.

Meade, A. W., Johnson, E. C., & Braddy, P. W. (2008). Power and sensitivity of alternative fit indices in tests of measurement invariance. *Journal of Applied Psychology, 93*, 568–592.

Mehta, P. D., & West, S. G. (2000). Putting the individual back into individual growth curves. *Psychological Methods, 5*, 23–43.

Menard, S. W. (1991). *Longitudinal research*. Newbury Park, CA: Sage.

Meredith, W. (1964). Notes on factorial invariance. *Psychometrika, 29*, 177–186.

Meredith, W. (1993). Measurement invariance, factor analysis and factorial invariance. *Psychometrika, 58*, 525–543.

Meredith, W., & Tisak, J. (1990). Latent curve analysis. *Psychometrika, 55*, 107–122.

Millsap, R. E. (1997). Invariance in measurement and prediction: Their relationship in the single-factor case. *Psychological Methods, 2*(3), 248–260.

Mistler, S. A., & Enders, C. K. (2012). Planned missing data designs for longitudinal research. In B. Laursen, T. D. Little, & N. A. Card (Eds.), *Handbook of developmental research methods* (pp. 742–754). New York: Guilford Press.

Molenaar, P. C. M. (2004). A manifesto on psychology as idiographic science: Bringing the person back into scientific psychology, this time forever. *Measurement: Interdisciplinary Research and Perspectives, 2*, 201–218.

Moskowitz, D. S., & Hershberger, S. L. (Eds.). (2002). *Modeling intraindividual variability with repeated measures data: Methods and applications*. Mahwah, NJ: Erlbaum.

Muthén, B. O., & Asparouhov, T. (2003). *Modeling interactions between latent and observed continuous variables using maximum-likelihood estimation in Mplus*. Mplus Web Notes: No. 6.

Muthén, L. K., & Muthén, B. O. (2012). *Mplus 7.0 user's guide* (with software). Los Angeles, CA: Muthén & Muthén.

Nesselroade, J. R. (2007). Factoring at the individual level: Some matters for the second century of factor analysis. In R. Cudeck & R. C. MacCallum (Eds.), *Factor analysis at 100: Historical developments and future directions* (pp. 249–264). Mahwah, NJ: Erlbaum.

Nesselroade, J. R., & Baltes, P. B. (Eds.). (1979). *Longitudinal research in the study of behavior and development*. New York: Academic Press.

Nesselroade, J. R., McArdle, J. J., Aggen, S. H., & Meyers, J. (2001). Dynamic factor analysis models for representing process in multivariate time-series. In D. M. Moskowitz & S. L. Hershberger (Ed.), *Modeling intraindividual variability with repeated measures data: Methods and applications* (pp. 235–265). Mahwah, NJ: Erlbaum.

Nesselroade, J. R., & Molenaar, P. C. M. (1999). Pooling lagged covariance structures based on short, multivariate time series for dynamic factor analysis. In R. H. Hoyle (Ed.), *Statistical strategies for small sample research*. Thousand Oaks, CA: Sage.

Nunnally, J., & Bernstein, I. (1994). *Psychometric theory* (3rd ed.). New York: McGraw-Hill.

Poteat, V. P., & Espelage, D. L. (2005). Exploring the relation between bullying and homophobic verbal content: The Homophobic Content Agent Target (HCAT) Scale. *Violence and Victims, 20*, 513–528.

Preacher, K. J., Cai, L., & MacCallum, R. (2007). Alternatives to traditional model comparison strategies for covariance structure models. In T. D. Little, J. A. Bovaird, & N. A. Card (Eds.), *Modeling contextual effects in longitudinal studies* (pp. 33–62). Mahwah, NJ: Erlbaum.

Preacher, K. J., Curran, P. J., & Bauer, D. J. (2006). Computational tools for probing interaction effects in multiple linear regression, multilevel modeling, and latent curve analysis. *Journal of Educational and Behavioral Statistics, 31*, 437–448.

Preacher, K. J., & Hayes, A. F. (2008a). Asymptotic and resampling strategies for assessing and comparing indirect effects in multiple mediator models. *Behavior Research Methods, 40*, 879–891.

Preacher, K. J., & Hayes, A. F. (2008b). Contemporary approaches to assessing mediation in communication research. In A. F. Hayes, M. D. Slater, & L. B. Snyder (Eds.), *Sage sourcebook of advanced data analysis methods for communication research* (pp. 13–54). Thousand Oaks, CA: Sage.

Preacher, K. J., & Selig, J. P. (2012). Advantages of Monte Carlo confidence intervals for indirect effects. *Communication Methods and Measures, 6*, 77–98.

Preacher, K. J., Wichman, A. L., MacCallum, R. C., & Briggs, N. E. (2008). *Latent growth curve modeling*. Thousand Oaks, CA: Sage.

Ram, N., & Grimm, K. J. (2007). Using simple and complex growth models to articulate developmental change: Matching theory to method. *International Journal of Behavioral Development, 31*, 303–316.

Raudenbush, S. W., & Bryk, A. S. (2002). *Hierarchical linear models: Applications and data analysis methods* (2nd ed.). Thousand Oaks, CA: Sage.

Reise, S. P., Widaman, K. F., & Pugh, R. H. (1993). Confirmatory factor analysis and item response theory: Two approaches for exploring measurement invariance. *Psychological Bulletin, 114*, 552–566.

Rensvold, R. B., & Cheung, G. W. (1999). Identification of influential cases in structural equation models using the jackknife method. *Organizational Research Methods, 2*, 293–308.

Rindskopf, D. (1984). Using phantom and imaginary latent variables to parameterize constraints in linear structural models. *Psychometrika, 49*, 37–47.

Rosel, J., & Plewis, I. (2008). Longitudinal data analysis with structural equations. *Methodology, 4*, 37–50.

Rovine, M. J., & Molenaar, P. C. M. (2000). A structural modeling approach to a multilevel random coefficients model. *Multivariate Behavioral Research, 35*, 51–88.

Rudolph, K. D., Troop-Gordon, W., Hessel, E. T., & Schmidt, J. D. (2011). A latent growth curve analysis of early and increasing peer victimization as predictors of mental health across elementary school. *Journal of Clinical Child and Adolescent Psychology, 40*, 111–122.

Ryan, R. M., & Deci, E. L. (2000). Intrinsic and extrinsic motivations: Classic definitions and new directions. *Contemporary Educational Psychology, 25*, 54–67.

Ryu, E., & West, S. G. (2009). Level-specific evaluation of model fit in multilevel structural equation modeling. *Structural Equation Modeling, 16*, 583–601.

Saldaña, J. (2003). *Longitudinal qualitative research: Analyzing change through time*. Walnut Creek, CA: Alta Mira.

Satorra, A., & Bentler, P. M. (1994). Corrections to test statistics and standard errors in covariance structure analysis. In A. von Eye & C. C. Clogg (Eds.), *Latent variables analysis: Applications for developmental research* (pp. 399–419). Thousand Oaks, CA: Sage.

Savalei, V., & Rhemtulla, M. (2012). Teacher's Corner: On obtaining estimates of the fraction of missing information from FIML. *Structural Equation Modeling, 19*, 477–494.

Schafer, J. L. (1997). *Analysis of incomplete multivariate data*. London: Chapman & Hall.

Schafer, J. L., & Graham, J. W. (2002) Missing data: Our view of the state of the art. *Psychological Methods, 7*, 147–177.

Schaie, K. W. (1965). A general model for the study of developmental problems. *Psychological Bulletin, 64*, 92–107.

Schaie, K. W., & Hertzog, C. (1982). Longitudinal methods. In B. B. Wolman (Ed.), *Handbook of developmental psychology* (pp. 91–115). Englewood Cliffs, NJ: Prentice-Hall.

Selig, J. P., Card, N. A., & Little, T. D. (2008). Latent variable structural equation modeling in cross-cultural research: Multigroup and multilevel approaches. In F. J. R. van de Vijver, D. A. van Hemert, & Y. H. Poortinga (Eds.), *Individuals and cultures in multilevel analysis* (pp. 93–119). Mahwah, NJ: Erlbaum.

Selig, J. P., Preacher, K. J., & Little, T. D. (2012). Modeling time-dependent association in two-occasion longitudinal data: A lag as moderator approach. *Multivariate Behavioral Research, 47,* 697–716.

Shadish, W. R., Clark, M. H., & Steiner, P. M. (in press). Can nonrandomized experiments yield accurate answers? A randomized experiment comparing random to nonrandom assignment. *Journal of the American Statistical Association.*

Shrout, P. E., & Bolger, N. (2002). Mediation in experimental and nonexperimental studies: New procedures and recommendations. *Psychological Methods, 7*(4), 422–445.

Singer, J. D., & Willett, J. B. (2003). *Applied longitudinal data analysis: Modeling change and event occurrence.* New York: Oxford University Press.

Snijders, T., & Bosker, R. (1999). *Multilevel analysis: An introduction to basic and advanced multilevel modeling.* London: Sage.

Sobel, M. E. (1982). Asymptotic confidence intervals for indirect effects in structural equation models. In S. Leinhart (Ed.), *Sociological methodology 1982* (pp. 290–312). San Francisco, CA: Jossey-Bass.

Steenkamp, J. E. M., & Baumgartner, H. (1998). Assessing measurement invariance in cross-national consumer research. *Journal of Consumer Research, 25*(1), 78–90.

Steiger, J. H. (1998). A note on multiple sample extensions of the RMSEA fit index. *Structural Equation Modeling, 5,* 411–419.

Steiger, J. H., & Lind, J. M. (1980, June). *Statistically based tests for the number of common factors.* Paper presented at the annual meeting of the Psychometric Society, Iowa City, IA.

Tabachnick, B. G., & Fidell, L. S. (2007). *Using multivariate statistics* (5th ed.). Boston, MA: Pearson Education.

Tanaka, J. S. (1987). "How big is big enough?": Sample size and goodness of fit in structural equation models with latent variables. *Child Development, 58,* 134–146.

Thornberry, T. P., Krohn, M. D., Lizotte, A. J., Smith, C. A., & Tobin, K. (2003). *Gangs and delinquency in developmental perspective.* Cambridge, UK: Cambridge University Press.

Tofighi, D., & Enders, C. K. (2007). Identifying the correct number of classes in a growth mixture model. In G. R. Hancock & K. M. Samuelsen (Eds.), *Advances in latent variable mixture models* (pp. 317–341). Greenwich, CT: Information Age.

Tucker, L. R., & Lewis, C. (1973). A reliability coefficient for maximum likelihood factor analysis. *Psychometrika, 38,* 1–10.

van Buuren, S. (2012). *Flexible imputation of missing data.* Boca Raton, FL: CRC Press.

Vandenberg, R. J., & Lance, C. E. (2000). A review and synthesis of the measurement invariance literature: Suggestions, practices, and recommendations for organizational research. *Organizational Research Methods, 3,* 4–70.

Velicer, W. F., & Fava, J. L. (2003). Time series analysis. In W. F. Velicer & J. A. Schinka (Eds.), *Handbook of psychology: Research methods in psychology* (Vol. 2, pp. 581–606). New York: Wiley.

Voelkle, M. (2008). Reconsidering the use of autoregressive latent trajectory (ALT) models. *Multivariate Behavioral Research, 43,* 564–591.

Walls, T. A., & Little, T. D. (2005). Relations among personal agency, motivation, and school adjustment in early adolescence. *Journal of Educational Psychology, 97,* 23–31.

Walls, T. A., & Schafer, J. L. (Eds.). (2006). *Models for intensive longitudinal data.* New York: Oxford University Press.

Wang, L., & McArdle, J. J. (2008). A simulation study comparison of Bayesian estimation with conventional methods for estimating unknown change points. *Structural Equation Modeling, 15,* 52–74.

Watson, D., Clark, L. A., & Tellegen, A. (1988). Development and validation of brief measures of positive and negative affect: The PANAS Scales. *Journal of Personality and Social Psychology, 47,* 1063–1070.

Widaman, K. F. (2000). Testing cross-group and cross-time constraints on parameters using the general linear model. In T. D. Little, K. U. Schnabel, & J. Baumert (Eds.), *Modeling longitudinal and multilevel data: Practical issues, applied approaches, and specific examples* (pp. 163–186). Mahwah, NJ: Erlbaum.

Widaman, K. F. (2012, February). *Theoretical models, statistical models, and testing conjectures strongly.* Paper presented at the Developmental Methodology off-year conference presented by the Society for Research in Child Development, Orlando, FL.

Widaman, K. F., Little, T. D., Preacher, K. J., & Sawalani, G. (2011). On creating and using short forms of scales in secondary research. In B. Donnellen & K. Trzesniewski (Eds.), *Archival data analysis* (pp. 39–61). Washington, DC: American Psychological Association.

Widaman, K. F., & Reise, S. P. (1997). Exploring the measurement invariance of psychological instruments: Applications in the substance use domain. In K. J. Bryant, M. Windle, & S. G. West (Eds.), *The science of prevention: Methodological advances from alcohol and substance abuse research* (pp. 281–324). Washington, DC: American Psychological Association.

Widaman, K. F., & Thompson, J. S. (2003). On specifying the null model for incremental fit indices in structural equation modeling. *Psychological Methods, 8,* 16–37.

Willett, J. B., & Sayer, A. G. (1994). Using covariance structure analysis to detect correlates and predictors of individual change over time. *Psychological Bulletin, 116,* 363–381.

Wohlwill, J. F. (1973). *The study of behavioral development.* New York: Academic Press.

Wood, P., & Brown, D. (1994). The study of intraindividual differences by means of dynamic factor models: Rationale, implementation, and interpretation. *Psychological Bulletin, 116,* 166–186.

Wright, D. B. (2006). Comparing groups in a before–after design: When *t*-test and ANCOVA produce different results. *British Journal of Educational Psychology, 76,* 663–675.

Wu, A. D., & Zumbo, B. D. (2008). Understanding and using mediators and moderators. *Social Indicators Research, 87,* 367–392.

Wu, W., & Little, T. D. (2011). Quantitative research methods. In B. B. Brown, M. Prinstein (Eds.-in-Chief), & R. K. Silbereisen (Vol. Ed.). *Encyclopedia of Adolescence: Vol. 1: Normative Development* (pp. 287–297). Oxford, UK: Elsevier.

Wu, W., Selig, J. P., & Little, T. D. (2012). Longitudinal models. In T. D. Little (Ed.), *Oxford handbook of quantitative methods* (Vol. 2, pp. 718–758). New York: Oxford University Press.

Yuan, K.-H., & Bentler, P. M. (2007). Multilevel covariance structure analysis by fitting multiple single-level models. *Sociological Methodology, 37,* 53–82.

Author Index

Subject Index

About the Author

Todd D. Little, PhD, is Professor of Educational Psychology and Leadership at Texas Tech University and founding Director of the Texas Tech University Institute for Measurement, Methodology, Analysis, and Policy (*immap.educ.ttu.edu*). Dr. Little is a Fellow of the American Association for the Advancement of Science, the American Psychological Association (APA) Divisions 5, 7, and 15, and the Association for Psychological Science. He is editor of Guilford's Methodology in the Social Sciences series and past president of APA Division 5 (Evaluation, Measurement, and Statistics). Dr. Little organizes and teaches in his renowned "Stats Camp" each June. Partly because of the impact and importance of Stats Camp, Dr. Little was awarded the Cohen Award from APA Division 5 for Distinguished Contributions to Teaching and Mentoring.